TERRA VIRGINUM (?)
SINUS SEPTENTRIONALIS (?)
Caribdis & Scilla (?)
BIARMONIA
IAMTONIA
LUNDICUM
MARE
Insule
Solunde
Bergonia
NORWEGIA
Asloia
SWETHIA
SINUS
ORIENTALIS
GAUTONIA
Limafiorth
DACIA
Selandia
Insula Ewnorum
Insula Gottorum
BALTICUM MARE
EISTRIA
Holmgardia
Eisisla
(CURIA)
RUSCIA
FRISIA
OLLANDIA
(SAXONIA)
Iomne
SCLAVIA
IA

Historia Norwegie

Historia Norwegie

Edited by

Inger Ekrem † and

Lars Boje Mortensen

Translated by

Peter Fisher

Museum Tusculanum Press

University of Copenhagen

2003

Composed by Lars Boje Mortensen (Adobe Garamond)
Maps and cover design by Veronique van der Neut
Printed by Special-Trykkeriet Viborg on Book Design Smooth
ISBN 87-7289-813-5

The cover illustration is based on
the *Physiologus* manuscript (*c.* 1200),
Det Arnamagnæanske Institut (Copenhagen), AM 673a, 4°

Published with grants from
Norges Forskningsråd
Nordea Danmark Fonden

Museum Tusculanum Press
Njalsgade 92
DK-2300 København S
www.mtp.dk

Contents

Preface (LBM) ... 6

Introduction (LBM) ... 8

1 Contents and Structure ... 8
2 Date and Place ... 11
3 Style and Narrative ... 24
4 The Manuscripts (Michael Chesnutt & LBM) ... 28
5 Transmission of the Text ... 33
6 Conclusion ... 44
7 Editorial Principles ... 45

The Latin Text (IE, LBM) & English translation (PF) ... 49

Commentary (IE, LBM) ... 107

Essay on Date and Purpose (IE) ... 155

Bibliography ... 226
Index nominum ... 236

Preface

The foundations of the present critical edition of the twelfth-century *Historia Norwegie* — the first to appear since Gustav Storm's in 1880 — were laid by Inger Ekrem. When she died in early 2000, she left behind a manuscript which in some parts was near completion. She had produced a preliminary text, and the English translator, Peter Fisher, had had the opportunity to discuss a number of points with her. A long introduction and rich materials for a commentary were also at hand, together with drafts for a bibliography and index. When I took up the work of finishing the edition in late 2000, I realized, however, that not only were some updatings and adjustments called for as a result of other research going on simultaneously, but also that a rearrangement of her material would benefit the reader. Most importantly, her long introduction — which was a slightly edited English version of her 1998 book in Norwegian, *Nytt lys over Historia Norwegie. Mot en løsning i debatten om dens alder?* ("New Light on *Historia Norwegie*. Towards a Resolution in the Debate Concerning its Age?") — focused almost entirely on describing a possible political context for the work in connection with the establishment of the Norwegian archdiocese at Trondheim in 1152/1153. Though her theory certainly merits serious attention, she was herself well aware of its somewhat speculative nature. What her introduction offered by way of information neutral to any theory of date and place was difficult to find; some points needed further elaboration while others were lacking. On the other hand, her wealth of material and line of argument should definitely not be broken up; her introductory text also has great value as a supplement to our commentary which often refers to paragraphs in that text.

What I decided to do, then, was to write a new introduction and to print Inger Ekrem's old one as an Essay on Date and Purpose and place it as a postscript. This seemed the better solution because it would give an opportunity to present the text in a broader framework, including discussions of transmission, literary style and other matters on which she had barely touched. I now contacted Michael Chesnutt of the Arnamagnæan Institute at the University of Copenhagen, who was the only scholar to have scrutinized the privately-owned Dalhousie manuscript (the single witness to most of the text) since Storm in 1875 and had published a fundamental study of its contents and historical context in 1986. He directed my attention to the better photographs kept at the Institute and kindly agreed to write a summary description of the manuscript for the present volume.

By another stroke of good luck and kind service Brian Smith of the Shetland Archives and Virginia Russell of the Scottish National Archives informed me in autumn 2001 that the Earl of Dalhousie had recently deposited the manuscript in Edinburgh, thus making it possible for me to consult it in a public collection. Through the swift action of our administrative officer, Ane Landøy, and a generous grant from my own Institute (IKRR, Bergen) I managed to go there in time and look through a number of points in the *Historia Norwegie* text that were left undescribed by Storm or were hard to assess from his reporting and from the photographs. I am most grateful to all of the above.

For various advice, information and inspiration I am also indebted to Monika Asztalos, Sverre Bagge, Gunilla Björkvall, Barbara Crawford, Karsten Friis-Jensen, Tomas Hägg, Odd Einar Haugen, Christian Høgel, Patrick Kragelund, Else Mundal, Birger Munk Olsen, Carl Phelpstead, Håkan Rydving, Inge Skovgaard-Petersen and Peter Zeeberg.

On behalf of Inger Ekrem I would also like to thank Lars Ivar Hansen, Jon Gunnar Jørgensen, Bjørg Tosterud and Trygve Skomedal for their good advice.

Peter Fisher and Michael Chesnutt both offered welcome emendations of my English in various parts of the book; both have been very supportive in matters of content as well: it was always a pleasure to receive the precise notes and suggestions of the former and the philological and historical advice of the latter.

I owe a very special debt of gratitude to my two partners in editing medieval Latin Norwegian texts, my wife Karen Skovgaard-Petersen (Royal Library, Copenhagen) and Egil Kraggerud (University of Oslo), who read through the manuscript in various stages and not only saved me from more mistakes in text and commentary than are left now, but whose interest and support throughout have been crucial.

Finally my sincere thanks go to the present Earl of Dalhousie who put the manuscript in his possession in a public collection and allowed me to benefit from consulting it directly and to reproduce some pages from it here, and to Norges Forskningsråd which not only gave Inger Ekrem a grant for working with *HN* but also supported the publication and was patient with my prolongation of the process.

Lars Boje Mortensen — Bergen / Copenhagen 2002

Introduction

1 Contents and Structure

In its transmitted form the anonymous *Historia Norwegie* (*HN*)[1] from the second half of the twelfth century offers us little unique information on its professed subject: the series and deeds of Norwegian rulers. Little more than half the text (ch.s IX–XVIII) gives us an overview of the royal lineage, beginning with the mythical Yngling kings and breaking off suddenly in the middle of Olav Haraldsson's rise to power (1015). The narrative opens up in the later of these chapters (XII–XVIII), dealing mostly with the second half of the tenth century and casting Queen Gunnhild (and her sons) and Håkon Jarl (and his sons) as villains against the just and Christian heroes, Olav Tryggvason (995–1000) and Olav Haraldsson (1015–1030). Either we are simply sceptical of any stories of events purporting to have taken place before the turn of the millennium and transmitted centuries later, or, if we want to believe them or at least study their traditions, we usually turn to the scarce, but important, evidence of Adam of Bremen (*c.* 1070) or the fuller sources in Old Norse, written down mainly in the thirteenth century in Iceland or Norway. But together with Theodoricus Monachus's similar brief Latin *History of the Norwegian Kings* (*c.* 1180) the *HN* constitutes a primary source for our knowledge of the beginnings of Norwegian historiography and gives us a valuable, if somewhat elusive, glimpse of the rise of literate culture in Norway. In *HN* we are offered an early and unique geographical description of Norway and the North Sea realm (ch.s I–VIII) as well as some ethnographic details, the highlight of which is the detailed account of a shamanistic séance among the Sami. Furthermore the author draws on natural philosophy of the twelfth-century Renaissance when presenting the *mirabilia* of the North. Owing to these qualities the *HN* becomes important in terms of literary history, and it stands as a respectable pioneering effort from a European periphery in the process of identifying itself in relation to the centre — in the literary medium of the centre: a narrative in schooled Latin, drawing on foreign and ancient learning. If the majority of nineteenth- and twentieth-century scholars, including the present two editors, are right in assuming an early date of composition (*c.* 1150–1175), *HN* enjoys the fur-

[1] The original title, if there was one, is more likely to have been *Ystoria Norwagensium* (see commentary to the chapter heading of I). We have kept Storm's suggestion for reasons of tradition and bibliography.

ther attraction of being the earliest literary monument by a Norwegian in our possession — in fact it represents the beginning of Norwegian literature.

Better than much else, a comparison with Theodoricus Monachus reveals some basic facts about *HN* as well as the limits of our knowledge. Let us briefly note the similarities first: both works were written by Norwegians, clearly espousing a Norwegian point of view, geographically as well as politically. The christianization of Norway is central to the authors' narratives, who agree on the decisive role played by the two Olavs (Tryggvason and Haraldsson) around the turn of the millennium and on the importance of the subsequent cult of the latter Olav in establishing Trondheim as Norway's metropolis. They both insist on a royal lineage from Harald Fairhair, whom competing twelfth-century war-lords and their ecclesiastical ideologues agreed to credit with the first unification of Norway back in the ninth century. Both authors present their works as the first of their kind. The Latin learning and style bear the mark of a twelfth-century schooling acquired abroad. Both draw on foreign (and ancient) Latin sources (and to some degree utilize these for an *interpretatio Romana* of the Norwegian past) as well as on local (including Icelandic) historical traditions. In short, Theodoricus and the author of *HN* wrote in very similar circumstances and with very similar messages; strangely, there are no signs that the one knew of the other — a point to which we shall return.

There are dissimilarities too; the most important one concerns the scope. Theodoricus's *History* limits itself to the period from the alleged unification of Norway by Harald Fairhair (early tenth century?) to the death of Sigurd Jorsalfar (d. 1130). This scope was planned: He wants to leave out rulers before Harald Fairhair because nothing certain is known about them, and he stops in 1130 because he does not want to go into the sad period of civil war following. *HN*, on the contrary, was more comprehensive and probably longer. Unfortunately, it is not transmitted in its full length. We have, however, some good pointers to remind us that we are here dealing with a more ambitious work than that of Theodoricus.[2]

First of all, our text presents itself as 'Liber primus' and ends at a most significant moment some twenty-five pages later when Olav Haraldsson lands in Norway with four English bishops. That would be a very suitable end of Book One (which was originally longer as there are signs of a redactor's shortening at the penultimate paragraph, see note at XVIII 32). Book Two would then begin with Olav's mission, his wars and proceed to his martyrdom, indeed his history may have taken up much or the whole

[2] *Cf.* Phelpstead 2001, xvii-xviii.

of the book. Either Book Two was rather long, or the work comprised even more books, because it is clear from the Prologue that the author intended to cover the history of Norway up to his own times. First he writes that his subject is demanding, including as it does not only geography and the genealogy of rulers, but also an account of the conflict between Christianity and heathendom in Norway, "with the present situation of each" (Prologus 3: *aduentum Christianitatis simul et paganismi fugam ac utriusque statum exponere*). Next his sources are hinted at at the end of the Prologue (8–9): information about "earlier ages" (*de uetustatis serie*) derives from the elders, but events "of our own times" (*nostris temporibus*) he has added himself because he wants to save "many men's splendid feats, together with their performers" from oblivion (*multorum magnificencias cum suis auctoribus*). The only event of "our age" (*nostra etate*) we find in the transmitted text is an uncertain eruption of Mount Hekla (VIII 10–12). But it cannot be digressions on natural phenomena of this sort he had in mind with his phrase on men's splendid feats. He must have written about recent kings, wars, ecclesiastical developments etc., and it is natural to assume that he did so in a chronological framework. One hint of his interest in recent history is found in XV 8 when he praises the royal lineage: ... *de quo quasi quodam filo textus genealogie regum Norwegie hucusque protelatus gloriose descendit* ("and from him, as if along a thread, descended the glorious Norwegian royal line in its genealogical pattern up to the present").

Linguistic and literary considerations consolidate this impression of an ambitious undertaking. I shall return to a few specifics on style, structure, and learning below; here it suffices to say that the long geographical introduction concerning Norway and its North Sea realm — taking up almost half of the text as we know it — makes little sense except as the prelude to a narrative of considerable size. Consequently we must allow for at least a large Book Two or perhaps three or four books in all. A moderate estimate of the whole would put it at more than double the size of today's remnants, *e.g.* sixty to eighty pages, and a narrative of more than hundred pages is no less probable. The possibility of an unfinished work cannot, of course, be entirely ruled out, but the fact that the author did finish the Prologue and completed the first book, together with various circumstances of the textual transmission (for which see below), in my mind marginalizes such a position. And even in that case we should judge our present torso from the author's plans of telling the history of Norway up to his own times.

2 Date and Place

When were "his own times"? This is a complex issue mainly because it is bound up with a variety of scholarly opinions on *HN*'s sources, the identity of the dedicatee and the author, the place where he wrote, the possible political or ideological message in his work, and his primary intellectual milieu and audience. The guessing game involved in identifying the dedicatee and the author has especially marred the discussion, each scholar wanting to contribute a fresh name and in the process lowering his own critical standards. Such riddle-solving based on very thin evidence has overshadowed the fact that almost all scholars who have done independent work on *HN* agree on a date in the second half of the twelfth century, leaning towards the earlier part of the period, though with various degrees of certainty and precision.[3] One should start by listing the textual features that any dating attempt must take into account, irrespective of any other convictions one might hold.

(1) *King Henry I of England.* The most recent person to be mentioned in *HN* (apart from the unidentified dedicatee, Agnellus) is King Henry I of England (1100–1135). He figures in his capacity as Duke of Normandy (VI 19 where the dukes are briefly listed because of their Norwegian ancestry). Ekrem makes a point of the author's failing to include the successors Stephen (1135–1154) and especially Henry II (1154–1189), likewise dukes of Normandy (below Essay § 3), but her argument is not decisive as the author of *HN* may not have been particularly interested in this point and just followed an older source. The passage on Henry, however, not only gives a certain *terminus post quem* of 1100, but actually extends it to around 1140 by saying (VI 19) "... Henry, who in the prophecy of royal Merlin was named 'the Lion of Justice'". The prophecies of Merlin were composed by Geoffrey of Monmouth *c.* 1134; they spread rapidly in various forms through Western Europe and were quoted by Orderic Vitalis around 1135 who is the first known author to add the historical identification of the lion (*cf.* commentary on VI 19).

(2) *The eruption of Hekla* mentioned in VIII 10-12 (see above) cannot and need not be dated. The eruption mentioned by Icelandic annals in 1211 has been promoted as a strong candidate.[4] But this event is also described as an earthquake; therefore earthquakes of 1164 and 1182 should also be considered — in addition to those we have no sources for. Storm and

[3] *E.g.* Storm 1880, Koht 1919–20, Steinnes 1946–48, Hanssen 1949, Ellehøj 1965, Krag 1991, Ekrem 1998, Phelpstead 2001 (less committed); for a survey of opinions see Ekrem 1998, 88 and Phelpstead 2001, xvi.

[4] Esp. by Bugge 1873.

all major scholars of the twentieth century have therefore, reasonably, let this matter rest.[5] And if it is necessary to eliminate it in a new way, one should add the *mirabilia* context of the statement: the author wants to illustrate the strange natural phenomena on the island. The term *nostra etate* is vague and should be taken as a confidence builder: recent reports tell us what an eruption is like.

(3) *The status of the Scottish islands.* The key passage on the Hebrides, Orkneys and Shetlands for the dating of *HN* is V 3: *Que quidem diuersis incolis acculte nunc in duo regna sunt diuise: Sunt enim Merediane Insule regulis sublimate, Brumales uero comitum presidio decorate, qui utrique regibus Norwegie non modica persoluunt tributa* ("They are populated by different peoples and now split into two domains; the southern isles have been elevated by petty kings, the northern graced by the protection of earls, both of whom pay no mean tribute to the kings of Norway."). The southern isles are the Hebrides whereas the northern ones must comprise both Orkney and Shetland (*cf.* commentary *ad locum*).

(a) The author is little interested in Shetland and mentions it explicitly only once (XVII 31). The joint rule — by one or more earls — over a sort of client chiefdom of Orkney and Shetland as presupposed by *HN* had been exercised by predominantly Norwegian families for a long time.[6] The first time we hear about formal submission to the crown including payment is when Earl Harald Maddadsson paid homage to King Inge Krokrygg (1136–61) in 1148 and to his co-ruling brother Øystein Haraldsson (1142–57) in 1151. Whether this involved regular tribute is uncertain.[7] The author of *HN* may also be thinking about the formal submission of the Orkney bishopric to Trondheim when the archdiocese was established in 1152/1153.

The final years of the long rule of Earl Harald Maddadsson (1138–1206, sole ruler from 1158) saw a major change in the status of the islands: a rising against King Sverre (1177–1202) ended in defeat in 1194; in 1195 the earldom was punished by the separation of Shetland, which was put directly under Norwegian rule. This rearrangement was, in the words of a recent authority, "the single most important event which shaped Orkney in the later Middle Ages".[8] Halvdan Koht was the first to argue that *HN* must have been written before that date — otherwise the author would not have included Shetland (implicitly) in this passage.[9] Had he known that some

[5] Storm 1880, 94; Koht 1919–20, 104; Steinnes 1946–1948, 33; Hanssen 1949, 10–11.

[6] Thomson 2001, 113.

[7] *Ibid.* 115–116.

[8] *Ibid.* 121.

[9] Koht 1919–20, 108 & 1950, 21.

of the islands were ruled directly from Norway, he would not have failed to make this point in a text that clearly seeks to accentuate Norwegian influence in the entire North Sea realm. This argument has been accepted by subsequent commentators.[10] Both the *termini* provided by this passage, *i.e. post quem c.* 1150 and *ante quem* 1195, can of course be questioned by appealing to the author's ignorance. He may have been late in learning about Sverre's reorganization, but if we want to have him writing this after *c.* 1200, he must have been very out of date and much less interested in Orkney and in Norwegian power overseas than his text otherwise leads us to assume.

(b) Finally it must be added that the passage provides us with a certain *terminus ante quem* of 1266 because the Hebrides then passed from Norway to Scotland.[11]

(4) *The status of Jämtland.* In the geographical description *HN* situates the province of Jämtland (in present-day Sweden) outside Norway (I 5). It did not belong to the archdiocese of Nidaros before 1570, but King Sverre claimed it as part of his kingdom in 1177; he may have had Magnus Erlingsson or Øystein Haraldsson as predecessors in this ambition already in the 1150s and 1160s.[12] According to Halvdan Koht — who has paid most attention to this question — a conscious effort to subject the province to Norwegian rule took place in the 1160s and 1170s.[13] Dating the *HN* after *c.* 1170 or 1177 would again entail significant ignorance on the part of an author displaying much interest in mapping out Norway. Our sources for the annexation of Jämtland seem to imply that the process was long; hence a *terminus ante quem* of 1177 or *c.* 1170 cannot be insisted upon. Contemporaries may have differed for decades in their views on the status of Jämtland (*cf.* Essay § 6.1.1.). However, our author would hardly have hesitated to include this province if he had had that possibility — and allowing him some leeway in this question would still not lead us beyond *c.* 1200.

(5) *The status of Iceland and Greenland.* Iceland is described under the general heading of tributary islands, but, as noted by Storm,[14] the author does not say that the Icelanders actually paid tribute to Norway as he does in the cases of the Scottish islands and the Faroes. Its inclusion in the Norwegian realm is no doubt, for the author, connected to the establish-

[10] Steinnes 1946–48, 47 (with a small reservation), Salvesen 1969, 41, Phelpstead 2001, 83.

[11] Storm 1880, xxiv.

[12] For references to sources (*e.g. Sverris saga*, 26) see Phelpstead 2001, 77; for the discussion see furthermore Hanssen 1949 8–9.

[13] Koht 1949–51, 51–52.

[14] Storm 1880, xxv.

ment of the archdiocese in 1152/1153 when the Icelandic bishops had to answer to Trondheim. But secular dependence including payment of tribute was only introduced when Norway took over government of the island in 1262. The small Icelandic colonies in Greenland were also part of the Trondheim diocese and are mentioned briefly in *HN* (I 10–14), but not as part of Norway. They accepted Norwegian rule in 1261.[15] This gives a certain *terminus ante quem* of, at the very latest, *c.* 1265.

(6) *The geographical division of Norway*. The division of Norway into three zones, of which the two 'civilized' and christianized ones each consist of four *patriae* (law provinces) and twenty-two and twelve counties respectively, is unique to *HN*. It has given rise to various speculations since Munch and Storm (and is treated in Ekrem's Essay § 6 and *passim*), and I shall not go into any details here. Suffice it to say that Storm's contention that we are dealing with an early attempt to divide the country — rather than *e.g.* a late distorted version of the one found in Magnus Lagabøter's *Landslov* of 1274 — has not met with any serious criticism, and it has been supported by the comments of Robberstad, Koht and Ekrem. Due to the lack of comparable texts before the *Landslov* no hard dates can be drawn from *HN*'s division, but on the authority of Storm, Koht, and Ekrem we can take it for granted that it makes good sense for their respective pre-1200 datings of *HN*, *i.e. c.* 1180–1190, before 1170, and about 1150.

(7) *"Olauus perpetuus rex Norwegie"*. This phrase about the royal saint is used in *HN* XV 5. The underlying idea is expressed more fully in King Magnus Erlingsson's (1164–81) *Letter of Privilege*, probably drawn up by Archbishop Øystein Erlendsson (1161–88) around 1163/64: Norwegian kings take the country as a fief from the eternal royal saint, in whose possession it remains.[16] The *Letter* forms part of a cluster of important documents surrounding the crowning of the child King Magnus in 1163/64, including the *Canones Nidrosienses* and Magnus's *Coronation oath*.[17] The idea may have circulated widely — just like the consensus among pretenders to the throne that one should ultimately be descended from Harald Fairhair — and there is no need to claim any direct connection between the two texts. But just as in the King Magnus documents in general and the *Passio Olaui* from the same period, the idea of a perpetual saintly kingship centred in Trondheim does seem to actualize the potential of the new

[15] On the status of Iceland and Greenland see *e.g.* Helle 1974, 119-22 & Phelpstead 2001, 78.

[16] The passage of the *Letter* is quoted and discussed in Essay § 8.13.

[17] For these documents see the survey by Helle 1974, 57-68. They are conveniently gathered in Vandvik 1959. *Cf.* the recent discussion by Bagge 2001, 309–21.

archdiocese as a centralizing factor in the recognition of Norwegian kings and their recent insistence on the ideal of a *rex justus*; hence, the use of the phrase in *HN* is, in my view, a strong indicator of a *terminus post quem* of 1152/1153.

The above is the closest we get to hard evidence on dating in the text itself. It emerges that a completely certain interval for the composition of *HN* lies between *c.* 1140 (1) and 1265 (3b & 5). However, very strong evidence favours an interval between 1150 and 1200. As for the *terminus post quem* (3a), (5), and (7) mention a taxation or express an attitude that makes much better sense around or after the establishment of the archdiocese in 1152/1153. Ekrem 1998 & 1999, and her present Essay, advocate a reading of *HN* as a sort of foundation document for the archdiocese, and it must, consequently, have been written around 1150. For reasons set out below I do not agree with her, but many of her arguments still work well within a broader framework of ideology connected to the new situation; whichever one chooses, one accepts a *terminus post quem* of *c.* 1150. As regards the *ante quem*, (3a) and (4) both bring us to a time before 1200. A number of softer arguments for this — concerning literature, learning, language, and transmission — will appear below. No reasonable doubts can be raised against a rough dating in the second half of the twelfth century, and, as already mentioned, this is indeed the interval almost all scholars since Storm have proposed. The question of an early or a late date for *HN* should no longer be seen as a choice between the twelfth and the thirteenth centuries;[18] we should rather think of 'early' or 'late' as signifying the third or the fourth quarter of the twelfth century.

Before trying to balance the arguments in favour of an early (*c.* 1150–1175) or a late (*c.* 1175–1200) date, one is bound to take up the complex of problems related to place of composition, or, rather, primary intellectual milieu. First it must be stressed that an enterprise such as this in twelfth-century Europe is directly linked to power and privilege. A text written in ambitious Latin prose defining the geography, wars, and rulers of Norway by an author who had studied abroad, and copied on to precious parchment by professional scribes, is a product of an elite milieu. It demands resources before and after composition and the plan of such a work only emerges in proximity to power. All talk of a school exercise or an isolated monastic product must be dismissed.[19] Historians in general were trusted

[18] As is still done in handbooks, *e.g.* Marold 1999.

[19] See Ekrem, Essay § 2 below for references. For the elite character of twelfth-century Latin historiography see Werner 1987 & Mortensen 1999 & 2000a. A monastic setting for *HN* in

to speak of rulers from a vantage-point of government, episcopal or secular. A few Nordic parallels will suffice here: Saxo and Sven Aggesen were both canons at Lund and close to archiepiscopal and royal power; Theodoricus Monachus was connected to Archbishop Øystein and the Trondheim milieu of the 1170s–1180s.[20]

Many attempts at locating our author (including that of the sober Storm)[21] have fallen into the trap of making a tentative identification of the dedicatee Agnellus or of the author an important factor in their equation. We will rest on much firmer ground if instead we depart exclusively from the texts used by *HN* and the *Nachleben* of *HN*. What textual horizon did the author have and what intellectual milieu(s) did *HN* become part of?

The discussion about the sources has been dominated by assessments of the complex textual relations obtaining between the 'Norwegian synoptics', *i.e.* Theodoricus Monachus, *HN*, and the incompletely transmitted Old Norse chronicle *Ágrip* from the Trondheim area *c.* 1190. Despite impressive research a consensus has failed to emerge, but for the present purpose we can confine ourselves to noting that there is general agreement that Theodoricus and *HN* are not related and that the occasional close verbal parallels between *HN* and *Ágrip* — from chapter XI (Harald Fairhair) on — are best explained by a common source, possibly one (or both) of the pioneering Icelandic works of historiography from around 1130 that included Norwegian rulers and events: the lost Latin history by Sæmund Sigfusson (1056–1133) or the Old Norse *Konunga ævi* by Ari Thorgilsson (1067/68–1148), also lost and known solely through hints in later Old Norse chroniclers and in his own surviving *Íslendingabók*.[22] The latter text (*c.* 1125) also plays a key role for evaluating the list of mythical kings in *HN*, the genealogy of Yngling kings presented in chapters IX–X. This series forms a subset of *Quellenforschung* problems because it involves a number

Norway has never been vigorously proposed. Our knowledge of intellectual milieus and libraries in the few Benedictine (founded around 1100) or Cistercian (founded 1146 & 1147) monasteries is almost non-existent (for a recent survey of Nordic monasticism see Nyberg 2000). They cannot be ruled entirely out, but there is nothing particularly monastic about our author, *cf.* commentary to VIII 19-20.

[20] *Cf.* the forthcoming edition by Kraggerud, and Mortensen 2000b+c+d.

[21] Storm 1880, XXIII.

[22] The best surveys of the source discussions are Ellehøj 1965 and Andersson 1985. The parallels between *HN* and *Ágrip* are juxtaposed and discussed by Ulset 1983; he is alone in concluding that *HN* was used by *Ágrip*, but as far as I can see his arguments might as well apply to a common Latin source which was occasionally followed closely by both texts.

of other Old Norse texts, some of them poetic — all written down after 1200, but of debatable age and transmission. The two major studies of this tradition, Ellehøj 1965 and Krag 1991, agree that *HN*'s list is without doubt the text closest to Ari's summary list in *Islendingabók* and consequently must be related to the fuller list in the lost work. Krag, especially, insists that the similarities must be explained exclusively in terms of textual relations.[23]

The tangled web of Old Norse source relations has drawn attention away from the two foreign Latin texts we know positively that our author took as models — both of them German: Adam of Bremen's *Gesta Hammaburgensis ecclesiae pontificum* (written in Hamburg *c.* 1065–1070) and Honorius of Autun's *Imago mundi* (written in various versions between 1110 and 1139, very probably in Regensburg).[24]

Adam's work not only provided phrases and pieces of information (for which see the commentary), but defined the entire undertaking of our anonymous author. The geographical introduction of *HN* is a correction and an extension of Adam's missionary map of the North; the praise of Olav Tryggvason is likewise an *Auseinandersetzung* with Adam's more ambiguous picture of the king. The author's ambition to show the present state of Christianity and paganism in the Norwegian realm forms a clear parallel between the contemporary concerns of the missionary mandate of the archdiocese of Trondheim and the former one of Hamburg-Bremen as described by Adam.

Despite his traditional name, Honorius of Autun (Augustodunensis) had nothing to do with France. He was perhaps German by birth, spent some time in England, but the major part of his working life (*c.* 1098–1140) was passed in Regensburg in southern Germany. His succinct encyclopedia *Imago mundi* was the first to surpass Isidore's in popularity. In *HN* we find a number of phrases and explanations from *Imago mundi* (see commentary), but it also served as a general inspiration for Latin style (see below), and for our author's interest in *mirabilia* and natural phenomena.

Before reviewing what the pervasive influence of Adam and Honorius on *HN* can tell us about its intellectual surroundings, we may pause for a moment to summarize the chronological implications of *HN*'s world of learning. The literature known to have been studied by the author is: Adam's *Gesta* from *c.* 1070, *Imago mundi* which occupied Honorius from 1110 to 1139 (earlier versions of the work spread before 1139),[25] a work of Ari, before 1148, perhaps as early as the 1120s, and a piece of interpretation

[23] Ellehøj 1965, 117 and Krag 1991, 146. [24] Flint 1983, 8 & 35–42. [25] *Ibid.*

of Geoffrey of Monmouth's prophecies of Merlin (*c.* 1134) that circulated from the late 1130s or the 1140s. A horizon of learning on which we can only spot works available in the 1140s or 1150s would be very strange if *HN* was a product of the thirteenth century. As a parallel one can quote Theodoricus (*c.* 1180) and Saxo (*c.* 1200) by whom we find borrowings from recent foreign works (respectively of Richard of St. Victor, *c.* 1160, and Gauthier of Chatillon, *c.* 1180). And not only would our author have ignored more than 50 years of foreign learning, he must also have been in the dark as to the important historical literature composed in Iceland and Norway before or just around the turn of the century, *e.g.* Theodoricus, *Passio Olaui*, *Ágrip*, *Sverris saga*, and Oddr Munk's biography of Olav Tryggvason. To my mind, this presents in itself an insurmountable body of evidence against a thirteenth-century date for *HN*, and furthermore gives a pointer in the direction of an early timeframe, *c.* 1150–1175.

Let us return to the question of primary intellectual milieu and *HN*'s German models, Adam and Honorius. Adam's work is only known through German and Danish medieval manuscripts.[26] Nor is his work quoted or used directly in the twelfth century outside northern Germany or Denmark.[27] Some early users outside Hamburg-Bremen itself are the *Roskilde Chronicle* (Roskilde, 1137/1138), Helmold of Bosau (Bosau, Holstein, *c.* 1170), and Saxo (Lund, *c.* 1200). In its knowledge of Adam, *HN* stands alone in Norwegian literature of the twelfth century.

By its very nature Honorius's encyclopedia was able to create interest beyond its region of production. Like other of Honorius's works (e.g. the theological primer *Elucidarius*), *Imago mundi*, as noted, became a remarkable, instant success; twelfth-century manuscripts and users are known mainly in Germany, but also in England and France.[28]

In a substantial contribution of 1946–48 Asgaut Steinnes attempted to locate this literary background, not in Germany, but in Denmark. His main argument was the so-called Sorø manuscript, lost in 1728, but known to have existed in Denmark in the twelfth century. This manuscript was important in the Danish transmission of Adam of Bremen (the B branch) and also contained Solinus's *Mirabilia* and Honorius's *Imago mundi* — in other words a geographical miscellany of both local interest and encyclo-

[26] For a survey of the transmission see Nyberg 1984, 302–307.

[27] It is possible, however, that Ari's *Íslendingabók* is imitating aspects of Adam's work, as suggested by Mundal 1994 (and previously in 1975 by Aksel E. Christensen); the Icelandic bishops Ísleifr and Gizurr are known to have studied in Saxony in the second half of the eleventh century; *cf.* Ellehøj 1965, 66–67.

[28] Flint 1983, 8.

pedic ambitions. Steinnes supported this theory with bits of information in *HN* that seem to derive from Danish sources.[29] Furthermore he pointed to a likely occasion for the writing of a Norwegian history in a Danish intellectual milieu: the exile of the Norwegian archbishop, Eirik Ivarsson, in Lund in the 1190s. When Eirik succeeded Øystein Erlendsson (1188) he soon reverted to conflict with King Sverre (1177–1202). Øystein had been in English exile for a brief period for the same reason, 1180–1183, but had returned to Trondheim and found a *modus vivendi* with Sverre. Eirik, on the contrary, stayed in Denmark with much of his entourage until Sverre's death.[30] Sandaaker 1985, who wants a slightly earlier dating of *HN*, favours a Danish sojourn of Eirik's around 1180 — when he was still bishop of Stavanger. He and others have taken Steinnes's suggestion of *HN*'s direct dependence on the Sorø manuscript as proof that *HN* was composed in Denmark. However likely the connection between the two, some reservations must be expressed. There were many manuscripts of *Imago mundi* circulating at this time — other extant ones from the twelfth century are similarly paired with texts relevant for *HN*.[31] Adam of Bremen may have been consulted in Denmark, but equally well in Saxony. The Sorø manuscript does not prove a Danish setting for *HN*, but it does allow for the possibility that the author of *HN* could have found his literature in Denmark. A strong Danish candidate is the archiepiscopal (and in effect, royal) library of Lund, no doubt a leading centre of learning in the Nordic countries during this period, probably equipped with the best library for historical research. Lund was also visited by learned Icelanders and it is possible that Ari's texts were to be found there in the twelfth century.

But there are other possibilities when we want to locate *HN*'s access to Latin sources. First of all our knowledge of Icelandic, Norwegian, Danish,

[29] For instance that the evil Gunnhild was the daughter of King Gorm of Denmark (XII 1). Such information peculiar to *HN* can be compared to the statement that Olav Tryggvason was born on the Orkneys (XV 14). Bits and pieces like this are hard to evaluate as they could be traces of a great many lost sources, oral and written. They may certainly reflect interviews with Danish or Orkney informants, but they do not come in such significant clusters that they can locate the composition of *HN*. Nor do I see, as Ekrem does (Essay § 8.9 & 9.3), any sustained anti-Danish attitude in *HN*.

[30] For Eirik's exile and his Danish connections see Helle 1974, 85–90 & Boserup 2000.

[31] Solinus and Honorius are combined in a manuscript from the second half of the twelfth century, probably of German origin (Bruxelles, Bibliothèque royale, 10862–10865, *cf.* Munk Olsen 1982–89 (vol. II), 490). Honorius is combined with Orosius (for his possible significance for *HN*, see below p. 28) in another late twelfth century German manuscript, Uppsala, Universitetsbiblioteket, C 699 (*cf.* Mortensen 2000e, 149).

and Saxon libraries before 1200 is very restricted — we must simply admit that our chances of pinpointing the exact matches for *HN*'s learned background are virtually non-existent. On general grounds we should also look to the rich literary world of Henry the Lion's Saxony: his court at Braunschweig flourished in the second half of the twelfth century; the nearby archbishopric of Hildesheim took pride in its famous school, attended in the early twelfth century by Danes, and it was still an important seat of learning and historiography later in the century; the cities of Hamburg and Lübeck had good episcopal libraries as well.[32] Henry was also duke of Bavaria from 1154, and it was in the decades around the mid-century that *Imago mundi* spread from Bavarian Regensburg towards the north and west. He is known to have taken an active interest in Honorius's work and encouraged a German adaptation of the theological primer *Elucidarius* and of the *Imago mundi*.[33]

Secondly we need not presume that the author of *HN* composed his work in the same place(s) he had visited abroad as a student or as an envoy in a royal or episcopal entourage. It is equally probable that he — like Theodoricus and Saxo — visited a foreign centre for some years and then brought home materials in the form of excerpts or copies of entire texts for work at home.

To sum up so far: from his German reading we take it for granted that the Norwegian author must have been south at some point for purposes of study; his inspiration most probably came from a Danish or Saxon centre of learning — perhaps both. But there are two more clusters of indirect evidence that to some degree can help us narrow down the place and period of his activity.

The first is our knowledge of the Trondheim milieu in the period of Archbishop Øystein Erlendsson (1161–1188). As already noted by Koht and others,[34] it is significant that the Trondheim-based historian Theodoricus (*c.* 1180) and the author *HN* show no signs of knowing each other. This lack of cross-reference implies another place of composition for *HN*; such an impression is strengthened when we consider that the French learning of Theodoricus and the German of *HN* seem to be worlds apart. The foreign authorities that Theodoricus draws on are all French or Roman (he would almost certainly have used Adam of Bremen had he known

[32] For cultural life during the reign of Henry the Lion (1142–95) see Luckhardt & Nierhoff 1995.

[33] Only the former materialized, *cf.* Flint 1983, 11.

[34] Koht 1919–20, 112 & Sandaaker 1985.

of him[35]). Nor are there any positive signs that Theodoricus used written Icelandic sources.[36] The axis of learning between Trondheim and northern France is completely ignored by the author of *HN*: not only is Theodoricus unknown, but also *Passio Olaui* is undetectable; in particular the debate about the place of Olav's baptism could have left traces in *HN* — had it been known by the author. We find it in Theodoricus, *Passio Olaui*, an exchange between Øystein and the Pope, and in a northern French manuscript of *Passio Olaui* copied in the last quarter of the twelfth century from a Norwegian exemplar.[37] The books used by *HN* were not, it seems, present in Trondheim in its twelfth-century renaissance during the time of Øystein, and the books studied and produced there were unknown to the author of *HN*.

The other cluster concerns the transmission. The single manuscript witness to most of our text has led scholars to see *HN* as a very isolated work, even as a work left unfinished or disregarded by its own author. Against this weighs the above argument that *HN*, when compared to similar contemporary historiography, has all the hallmarks of being a 'collective' elite endeavour, and the fact that it has been transmitted by two entirely different routes. This is discussed below (Transmission), but we can anticipate the conclusion that at least two or three medieval manuscripts of the entire text are likely to have existed, one or two of which were in Norway before *c.* 1300. The implication is important, namely that the text lived on in one or more Norwegian libraries and was recognized institutionally — it was not a text left to the care of a single person. Its reception was still narrow — something like the modest spread of similar cases of official Latin historiography in the North (Theodoricus, Saxo). But if one or more institutions in Norway did take care of the text before *c.* 1300, the probability of a primary Norwegian intellectual environment — other than a purely exile one — for *HN* increases significantly.

It is fraught with difficulty, then, to place the composition of *HN* in Trondheim, especially during or immediately after the flourishing of Latin letters in the reign of Archbishop Øystein. This is why the Danish exile environment has been an attractive possibility. But if we accept the more

[35] The distinctive French learning in Theodoricus was established by Johnsen 1939; additional evidence in Mortensen 2000a.

[36] *Pace* Lange 1989, *cf.* Mortensen 2000b.

[37] Mortensen 2000d with further references. The missing text at the end of our extract of *HN* (between XVIII 32 & 33 — see commentary) could have been so large that it might have included a discussion of Olav's baptism along the lines we see in the Trondheim sources.

modern view that historiography of this sort is an institutional undertaking of some importance for others apart from the author and the dedicatee alone, it becomes equally difficult to see how the text was produced during Archbishop Eirik Ivarsson's exile in Lund in the 1190s: someone in his entourage must have known about Theodoricus's work (and the other relevant writings, *e.g. Passio Olaui* which seems to have been known in Lund by Saxo during the same period).[38] For this very reason Sandaaker 1986 proposed an earlier Danish occasion around 1180 — *i.e.* exactly contemporary with Theodoricus but outside the immediate reach of Trondheim scholars. A third possibility was developed by Ekrem (1998 and Essay below): *HN* is an archiepiscopal product of the time before Øystein, though not necessarily produced in Trondheim. Again it is problematic to presume that such an endeavour could have been forgotten within a decade in the same intellectual milieu. If really sponsored directly by the archbishopric the text of *HN* would not just have been a book on the archiepiscopal shelves; rather some kind of collective elite memory would have registered the composition and physical existence of the text — as they would indeed have become aware of the utmost importance of its major model, Adam of Bremen. A similar argument would apply against placing *HN* in the Trondheim dominated by King Sverre in the 1180s and 1190s (never suggested by anyone, probably because scholars would have expected clear signals of this already in the Prologue).

If Trondheim is problematic and we do seem to have a Norwegian transmission of the text, one must look for other centres of power having connections with ecclesiastical institutions or at least a clerical / scribal entourage. As stated, our knowledge of personnel and libraries of this period is extremely deficient; either of the other bishoprics on the west coast, Bergen and Stavanger, or in the east, Oslo and Hamar, could qualify. Ekrem (Essay § 10) gave a certain priority to Bergen and the circle around King Inge Haraldsson ('Krokrygg', 1136–1161). Of the many rulers and pretenders to the throne in the decades after 1150, Inge, indeed, seems a probable figure around whom a project of *HN*'s character might have been planned and carried out: Inge was central, it seems, in the establishment of the Trondheim see; he had a reputation of being bookish and the Icelandic historian Eirik Oddsson (author of a Norwegian kings' chronicle or biography now lost) was probably in close contact with Inge's men around

[38] Friis-Jensen 2000.

1150.[39] During the civil wars and his joint kingship Inge often stayed in the Viken area (the Oslo Fjord) — which would be a strong rival to Bergen in our quest; here Oslo, or the thriving port of Tønsberg, are possibilities that come to mind. Against Inge, however, a strong argument can be mustered: the later archbishop Øystein had been Inge's chaplain. Thus he would have known about *HN* if it had been written in Inge's entourage, and it is difficult to see how Øystein would not have established some connection between *HN* and the Trondheim texts about to be produced.[40] But even without or after King Inge, Viken has some points in its favour: the author pays somewhat more attention to the east than the west in his description and narrative. The connections with Denmark and Germany were direct and this was the well-trodden path of cultural exchange between Viken and the Continent, in contrast to the west coast's traditional connections with England and France. A composition of *HN* in the east during the third quarter of the twelfth century would also account better for the mutual isolation of *HN* and the Trondheim texts than, for instance, in Stavanger or Bergen. Perhaps the best timeframe for an eastern location would be the poorly documented political turmoil of the 1160s and early 1170s (including the Danish King Valdemar's claim on Viken).[41] Finally, one should not totally dismiss other locations outside Norway proper. It is possible that a well-connected learned Norwegian might not (only) have been inspired by Danish contacts or libraries, but perhaps spent time in Iceland or the Orkneys. That would explain his access to sources (Iceland), his interest in both insular societies, and his lack of direct contact with Trondheim. However, the Norwegian viewpoint in the text as well as its Norwegian transmission (*cf.* below) cannot be questioned; therefore Norway remains the obvious suggestion as the base of the author, with good pointers away from Trondheim and towards eastern Norway.

The location must remain a hypothesis, but as regards the dating, an early one, *i.e. c.* 1150–1175, is most attractive. For one thing, as mentioned above, the most recent layer of learning in *HN* is texts from the 1130s and 1140s. Irrespective of location, the apparent ignorance of the Trondheim texts produced in the 1170s and 1180s is easiest to explain if *HN* had been written shortly before or contemporary with the first Trondheim efforts. The main message in the text as we have it — as Ekrem was the first

[39] See Ekrem, Essay § 5.2 below.

[40] I am grateful to Sverre Bagge for advice on this point. *Cf.* Essay § 11.2.1.

[41] *Cf.* Helle 1974.

to draw attention to — is, through geographical and genealogical definition, to demonstrate the ability of the Norwegian kingdom to control its area for missionary and 'civilizing' purposes. Such a statement makes more sense in the first decades after its inheriting the missionary mandate from Lund.[42] It is not clearly made in *Passio Olaui* and in Theodoricus's *History* (both after *c.* 1175), texts more focused on the sanctity of Olav Haraldsson. On the other hand I think that *HN* presupposes the establishment of the archdiocese rather than the other way round. That brings us to the following result: *HN* must have been conceived in government circles, episcopal, royal, or both, in Norway in the second half of the twelfth century. I would furthermore favour a date in the third quarter, and this could perhaps be narrowed down to *c.* 1160–1175, thus giving the author of *HN* a little time to reflect on the ecclesiastical reorganization but not so much that we should expect more recent impulses of foreign and Trondheim learning.

3 Style and Narrative

The only investigation into *HN*'s language was done by Skard 1930. Though of course very dated in its knowledge of Medieval Latin, it is still a useful collection of material with basically sound judgements. For more examples and detailed analysis I refer the reader to Skard and to various linguistic and stylistic points discussed in the commentary.

Among Skard's findings the following deserve mention.

– *HN* is rich in vocabulary and the author set high goals for synonymic variation and poetic expressions in his prose. A few examples will illustrate this. Synonyms for 'tell' are: *astruere, affirmare, dicere, ferre, intimare, meminisse, memorare, narrare*; 'famous': *celeber, inclitus, opinatus*; *preclarus*; 'viking': *pirata, predo, tirannus.*[43]

– The syntax is predominantly paratactic, even the longer periods. There is a predilection for adding new nexuses by accumulating present participles, gerunds in the ablative (functioning as present participles in the nominative), and relative clauses rather than other subordinate clauses or absolute ablative. Ellipsis of *esse* is widespread, not only as an auxiliary verb.

[42] The author's unique Latin naming in several instances can also be taken as an argument for an early date, inasmuch as no Latin nomenclature had yet been established, *e.g. Rodulfus* for *Rollo* (VI 10), *Bergonia* for *Bergae* (XIV 3), *Solundicum Mare* for *Mare Occidentale* (V 1), *Roda* for *Rothomagus* (VI 10), *Sinus Orientalis* for *Wic.*

[43] For these and numerous other examples: Skard 1930, 49–52.

– There seems to be no consistent prose rhythm,[44] but rhyme and alliteration are two embellishments often put to use.

– Major inspirations for the style and phraseology are the *Vulgate*, especially the Old Testament. Classical Roman authors are only present through poetic expressions they helped to make popular in twelfth-century schools (*e.g. brumali frigore* (II 11), *celsa stantem in puppi* (XVII 50)), not through quotations or obvious allusions (with two exceptions — see below). Apart from stressing the borrowings from Adam and Honorius, Skard does not single out any medieval model of style but hints that *HN* belongs to one of the two international currents of the time, Theodoricus to the other (perhaps meaning what later has become known as mannerist versus classicist styles).[45]

A few examples will show some of the characteristics. First a brief period (IX 24): *Sed paulo post ipsum regem truculentus taurus confodiens trucidauit* ("Shortly afterwards however the monarch was gored and slaughtered by a ferocious bull"). Here as often elsewhere two acts are expressed by adding a present participle rather than an ablative absolute or another verb, juxtaposed or subordinated. The alliterative (here violent) sound of the clause is typical of *HN*.

A longer period can be exemplified by XVII 11: *Factus adolescens piraticam excercens Baltica littora perlustrando, cunctis gentilibus id locorum formidabilis existendo, inscius deuiatur a deo ille magnificus predo* ("Grown to early manhood, he pursued viking expeditions right along the Baltic coasts, a terror to all the heathens who inhabited those regions; yet this splendid sea rover was unconsciously directing his steps away from God"). Such periods may not be particularly long, but at times they come across as heavy, because of the author's preference for participles and gerunds in the ablative used in apposition or even, in some instances, in place of finite verbs. The choice of such an accumulative parataxis also makes for a rhyming effect (*adolescens ... excercens*; *perlustrando ... existendo*). Alliteration is aimed for again by choosing *predo* for 'viking' to connect with the sound of *deuiatur a deo*.

Another example with some subordination is XVII 15: *Verum enimuero curam gerens Conditor creature sue, hunc tirannum tam remotum tamque indomitum per uiscera misericordie sue mirabiliter uisitauit, uisitando illumi-*

[44] No investigation with modern methods has so far been carried out, but prose rhythm certainly seems to be desired by the author, especially *cursus planus* and *cursus tardus*. This would put him in the German tradition of which Adam is an exponent, *cf.* Janson 1975, 54–55 and Ekrem 1998, 65. There is room for a thorough study in this area.

[45] Skard 1930, 85.

nauit, ut quos eo tenus umbra mortis operuerat, stola claritatis eterne indueret ("But the Creator, bestowing concern on His creature, through the bowels of His compassion miraculously came to this viking, so alienated from Him and so untamed, and in his visitation enlightened him in such a way that those whom He had hitherto shrouded beneath the shadow of death He might now garb with the robe of eternal brightness"). Again there is a preference for participles and gerunds in the ablative, but the rhetorical crescendo is arrived at by the subordination and the additional effects of repetition and ellipsis (*uisitauit, uisitando illuminauit*) and the Biblical phrasing mingling no less than three scriptural passages (see commentary).

A final example from a descriptive rather than a narrative part of the text shows how the author achieves a demanding style mostly by way of remote vocabulary and *exaggeratio* (accumulation) (II 14–15): *Ibi equini ceti monoculi iubis diffusis profunda pelagi sulcantes ferocissimi reperiuntur. Illic pistrix, illic hafstrambus, maxima bellua, sed sine cauda et capite solum susum et iusum dissiliendo ueluti truncus, non nisi nautarum pericula prefiguret, apparet* ("One-eyed, very ferocious walruses are to be found here, cutting furrows through the ocean depths, with manes fanning out. There, also, are the whale and the havstramb, a gigantic creature but without tail or head, which merely springs upwards and downwards like a tree-trunk, and only appears in order to predict perils for sailors"). The exotic vocabulary is highlighted by three recurring trademarks: ellipsis, rhyme, and alliteration.

In general the style of *HN* can be said to represent one of several ways in which eleventh- and especially twelfth-century historians strive to construct a high-level discourse that goes beyond the mere biblical and Sallustian imitation of *e.g.* Adam of Bremen. The twelfth-century Renaissance and its increasing use of Roman authors in the schools has left its stamp on *HN* as well. In this case it has not led to a classicist imitation but rather to one of various possible mannerisms which draws on biblical and patristic language as well as on the fashion of inserting many poetic expressions in the prose. On one scale *HN* places itself between the transparent and less ambitious medievalizing style of Theodoricus and the heavy, hypotactic and classicizing one of Saxo Grammaticus. Among the mannerists, however, *HN* is less extreme in its parataxis and verbosity than Dudo of St. Quentin (*c.* 1000) or the sometimes very recherché language of the Polish national historian, Vincent Kadlubek (*c.* 1200). The rich vocabulary and the paratactic tendency is somewhat similar to the Danish historian Sven

Aggesen's (*c.* 1190) and the elliptic style owes much to Honorius of Autun (*c.* 1130). Stylistic definitions and trends in the twelfth century are still largely uncharted territory, but it is at least safe to say both that *HN* is a typical twelfth-century product and that it displays a certain individuality that must have been the result of serious study at a foreign centre, perhaps in Saxony.

The authorial voice in *HN* is projected more with Saxo's secretive monumentality than with Adam's or Theodoricus's explicit transparency. The 'I' is expressed mostly in exordial conventions, but also in a few other authorial deliberations (*e.g.* IV 25, XVII 54). As in Saxo the narrator appropriates authoritative language rather than quotes it (see the biblical allusions above). He names only two authors, both of them Roman authorities (Tullius, Solinus). The desire to express — on the level of language and style — a local re-enactment of holy and Roman history is similar to that of many other historians, but the technique is more monumental and unified than that of *e.g.* Theodoricus, who often yields the floor to ancient or medieval authorities.

No research has been undertaken into *HN*'s narrative technique and literary models. Such a study would probably be rewarding as the author seems to find himself somewhere between the brief and 'exemplary' narrative with learned digressions we find in Theodoricus,[46] and the much broader visual narrative with interest in military matters as known from the kings' sagas. It would be difficult to reach a definite assessment of *HN* in these terms because an investigation would be hampered by the fact that we mostly possess the atypical parts of the text: Prologue, geographical description, the brief lineage of Yngling kings; only the beginning of a broader narrative is preserved in Olav Tryggvason's history and the opening paragraphs of Olav Haraldsson's. The account of Olav Tryggvason is very different in *HN* and Theodoricus. Their sources were obviously not the same, but their dissimilarity can hardly be put down to that alone. For one thing Theodoricus splits up the narrative with digressions on Roman history, Iceland, and the baptism of Olav Haraldsson, whereas the author of *HN* presents his history as one unit. Furthermore Theodoricus focalizes the history through its characters by stating their thoughts and knowledge — it becomes a history of individuals and moral choice with little interest in politics and military affairs. It is significant for instance that there is no explanation of the background for Olav's fatal battle at Svold (1000),

[46] *Cf.* Bagge 1989 & Mortensen 1993.

perhaps the most famous battle in viking history.[47] In *HN*, however, the narration is more 'objective' and distant. A mixture of cosmic powers and military necessities governs the events: there is a balance between Olav as a tool of heaven and as the great warrior, all expressed in a more 'authoritative' discourse.

The author must have had some other reading in his baggage than the Bible and the German and Icelandic texts that can be demonstrated through borrowings of phrases or names. There must be other inspirations behind the literary structure — the mastery of exordial topics displayed in the Prologue presupposes more reading. Also the placing and the scope of the geographical introduction may have been inspired by other texts than Adam alone. A strong candidate is Orosius's popular *Historiae adversus paganos* (finished 417) which opens with a large geographical canvas of the Roman Mediterranean world. Structural borrowings, however, are difficult to prove, especially in the case of *HN*, where we only know the first part of the text.

4 The Manuscripts

A **Edinburgh, National Archives of Scotland, Dalhousie Muniments, GD 45/31/1 – II** (by *Michael Chesnutt*)

Paper, 35ff., 27 x 18.5 cm, copied in Scotland *c.* 1500. It contains: *HN* (ff. 1r–12r), *Genealogy of the Orkney earls* ('Diploma Orcadense') (ff. 12v–17v), List of the kings of Norway reaching Erik of Pomerania (reigned 1396–1439) (f. 18r–18v), various Scottish chronicles and documents in Scots and Latin, some of them postdating *c.* 1490 (ff. 18v–35v).

This manuscript, the only source to have preserved a considerable bulk of the text of *HN*, is not Norwegian but Scottish. The property of the Earl of Dalhousie, it is now deposited in the National Archives of Scotland, Edinburgh. Until 1998 it was kept at the Earl's ancestral home at Brechin Castle, located north of the city of Dundee in eastern Scotland.

The binding of the manuscript, also enclosing a late fifteenth-century printed book of continental provenance (part I of the bibliographical entity, hence the 'II' in the signature for the manuscript), was made *c.* 1700 or later. It is of brown leather with the title "Orcades" stamped on the spine. The volume was examined by me in 1974 at The Arnamagnæan Institute, University of Copenhagen, and exhaustively described and ana-

[47] For other aspects of Theodoricus's narrative of Olav Tryggvason see Bagge 1989.

lysed in my article "The Dalhousie Manuscript of the *Historia Norvegiae*" (Chesnutt 1986).[48]

The manuscript now contains 35 paper leaves, with a lacuna of uncertain extent between ff. 23/24. *HN* is written at the beginning; it ends on f. 12r with the rubric "Explicit" followed by a few blank lines at the bottom of the page (see ill.), and the next article begins at the top of f. 12v. There are therefore no grounds for thinking that the text of the chronicle was not already defective in the exemplar from which the Dalhousie manuscript was copied. From the position of the catchwords, watermarks and binding threads it can be determined that *HN* fills the whole of a first quire of 10 leaves plus the first three pages of a second quire of 12 leaves. The second quire continues with a *Genealogy of the Orkney earls* and a list of the kings of Norway, both in Latin. In the middle of f. 18v there is an abrupt transition to Scottish subject-matter and the Scots vernacular. The rest of the manuscript is of exclusively Scottish interest, though the language reverts to Latin from the beginning of the third quire.

The discovery of the manuscript of *HN* is usually attributed to the Norwegian historian P. A. Munch, but his attention was in fact drawn to it by the Scotsman David Laing during Munch's visit to Edinburgh in 1849. Laing was at that time preparing an edition of selections from the Scottish material in the manuscript; this edition eventually appeared in 1855, while Munch's edition of the Norwegian and Orcadian material had been published already in 1850 (Chesnutt 1986, 61 & 63). On the other hand, the *Genealogy of the Orkney earls* had been edited long before by James Wallace, Jr. in his *Account of the Islands of Orkney* (London 1700), where it is stated that the manuscript belonged at that date to a Scottish Nonjurant clergyman, the Rev. Robert Norie of Dundee, whose signature indeed appears twice in the printed book with which the *HN* manuscript is bound, and once at the end of the manuscript itself. On the back page of the printed book there is also an inscription recounting how that book was presented by Bishop Robert Reid of Orkney to his chamberlain Thomas Tulloch[49] in the year 1554. But this is not, as Munch incorrectly asserted, evidence that the manuscript was written in the Orkneys; on the contrary,

[48] In Norwegian historical literature the manuscript of *HN* is sometimes referred to as the "Panmure" manuscript, reflecting the fact that it first came into public view 10 years before the owner's family name was changed from Panmure to Dalhousie (Chesnutt 1986, 55 & 64). – A complete photographic record of the manuscript is available for study at The Arnamagnæan Institute and is the source of the illustrations included in the present edition.

[49] Not to be confused with the fifteenth-century bishop of that name. Bishop Tulloch seems, however, to have been the compiler of the historical dossier whose remnants make

the recurrence of its scribe's hand as identified by me in two important Scottish literary manuscripts would indicate that it was produced at a cultural centre in the Scottish Lowlands.[50]

One of the two manuscripts in question is Oxford, Bodleian Library MS Arch. Selden B. 24, containing among other items Chaucer's *Troilus and Criseyde* in Scots dialect transcription and the unique extant copy of the Scottish Chaucerian *Kingis Quair*. Here the Dalhousie scribe is one of two hands responsible for the original portion of the book, which was owned by — and doubtless written for — the Scottish nobleman Henry Lord Sinclair of Dysart (d. 1513). This owner was head of the senior branch of a family descended from William Sinclair, Lord Chancellor of Scotland in the mid-fifteenth century, who had been Earl of Orkney until 1470, the year in which he gave up his northern earldom to the Scottish crown. In 1456 Chancellor Sinclair had commissioned a set of translations of French courtly texts into Scots prose, and a copy of these is to be found in Edinburgh, National Library of Scotland MS T.D. 209, the second literary manuscript in which the hand of the Dalhousie scribe can be recognised. It belonged throughout the sixteenth century to the lairds of Rosslyn (Roslin) near Edinburgh, who were the junior branch of the Sinclair family. Later it was in the library of Sir Walter Scott at Abbotsford.

In my study published 16 years ago I drew the conclusion that the Dalhousie scribe was a professional copyist employed by the Sinclairs, and I gave reasons why he was probably retained by the senior branch of the family. Internal evidence fixes the scribe's career in the reign of King James IV of Scotland; the three identified examples of his work belong to the period *c.* 1490–1510, with the manuscript of *HN* at the end of that period rather than the beginning. My proposed dating is supported by the style of writing, a so-called "pre-Secretary" hand that was popular in Scotland in the late fifteenth century but went out of fashion after 1500 (Chesnutt 1986, 88–89).

An idiosyncracy of *HN* as compared with other articles copied in the Dalhousie manuscript is the regular use of coloured chapter initials and of display script for proper names. Display script is also used in the second

up the first three articles in the Dalhousie manuscript (see below Transmission).

[50] For Robert Norie see further Chesnutt 1986, 58–60. The proximity of Norie's home to Brechin probably explains how the volume comprising both printed book and manuscript came to be in the ownership of the Panmure-Dalhousie family nearly a century and a half later; whether the manuscript as such was ever in the Orkneys must remain a matter of speculation, *cf.* Chesnutt 1986, 89–90.

article (the *Genealogy of the Orkney earls*) to mark the beginning of important subdivisions in the text. Here the Dalhousie scribe was possibly imitating the layout of the exemplars from which he copied these documents of northern interest.[51] It is likely that the exemplars were Sinclair family heirlooms brought to the mainland when William Sinclair relinquished the earldom of Orkney (see below Transmission). It was, however, a mistake on the part of Munch (and all subsequent Scandinavian historians who have accepted his authority) to think that Orkney around the middle of the fifteenth century was the actual environment in which the surviving copy of the chronicle was produced.

I consulted the manuscript at length in 1974 for codicological, palaeographical, and contextual analysis and Lars Boje Mortensen consulted it briefly in 2002 in Edinburgh for a renewed scrutiny of the *HN* text. In addition both of us used the photographs made in 1974 kept in the Arnamagnæan Institute in Copenhagen. Inger Ekrem had previously been working from the older reproductions kept in Riksarkivet in Oslo.

Stockholm, Kungliga Biblioteket, B 17 – II *B*

Paper (except 12, 14, 16, 18 of parchment), 161 ff., quarto, 20 x 14 cm. B 17 is a composite manuscript of which ff. 12-119 is the oldest element (II), consisting of several fascicles written in the first half of the fifteenth century in Sweden.

The main contents of the manuscript are Swedish Laws: Sodermannalagens Kyrkobalk, Magnus Erikssons Landslag (main text, promulgated 1347). Many scribes and layouts. Ff. 31v–32v (originally blank pages at the end of a fascicle) contain a Latin list of Swedish kings, of which the first half (f. 31v) is an excerpt from *HN*'s lineage of Yngling kings up to Halfdan Whiteleg, who left Sweden for Norway, *i.e.* *HN* IX 2–X 2. The text is written in one column in the space of *c.* 15.5 x 10.5 cm. This part is reproduced diplomatically by Storm, pp. 225–26. The list continues (31v–32v), without graphic break, with Swedish kings up to 1333. On f. 112r–112v (also on a blank space at the end of a fascicle) the same hand gives a Swedish translation of the list. The lower half of the leaf has now been lost but Storm's assessment that the space allowed only a listing of heathen kings seems probable. Thus the text would have comprised exactly the excerpt from *HN* as above, without any continuation. The surviving Swedish text is

[51] The scribe was also sometimes at pains to have a new chapter begin at the top of a page, hence the slight cramming and additions at the bottom of f. 1r and f. 4v.

reproduced diplomatically by Storm on pp. 226–28. It covers *HN* IX 2–6 & 15–26.

The last fascicle in the element, ff. 113–119 contains Latin annals copied in a hand similar to the excerpts from *HN*. They end with a long entry for the year 1412 and made ready for 1413 which, however, was corrected to 1430 by another hand which wrote a few additional lines.

It would seem, then, that between 1412 and 1430 one or more scribes added some historical material to a recently-produced law collection. He or they copied the post-1333 list of kings (in Latin and Swedish) into the blank spaces available between the fascicles of the law collection (itself containing texts mainly from the mid-fourteenth century), and an updating of annalistic notes up to 1412 at the end of the volume.

There is an old and brief description of the manuscript by C.J. Schlyter in his edition of *Konung Magnus Erikssons Landslag* (Lund 1862) [Samling af Sweriges gamla lagar, vol. X], pp. xxxv-xxxvi.

I consulted the manuscript in 2001.

C **Stockholm, Riksarkivet, A 8** ('Registrum ecclesie Upsalensis')
Parchment, 182 ff., 32.5 x 18.5 cm. The main part of the codex was written in Sweden (Uppsala) in 1344, probably on the initiative of Archbishop Heming and the cathedral chapter. Additions were made, especially from f. 173v on, in the fifteenth century. The main contents of the manuscript are (1) register of land, (2) archiepiscopal correspondence, (3) miracles of the martyr king, Erik, and (4) various liturgical and administrative documents pertaining to Uppsala cathedral. To the latter section, though still in the fourteenth-century part, belongs f. 163 where we find a very brief excerpt from *HN*'s line of kings (*HN* IX 2–11) on 163ra–163rb. It may have been added somewhat later in the fourteenth century. Storm gives a diplomatic reproduction of the text on p. 225. There is a facsimile and an edition in *Scriptores rerum Suecicarum* vol. I, 14–15 by Fant (Uppsala 1818) — who was unaware, of course, that the text derived from *HN*. After the excerpt the lineage continues with Swedish pagan and Christian kings in another hand as an addition (edited *ibid.*).

I have seen a photocopy of this page. There is a description of the manuscript and its contents in *Diplomatarium Suecanum* vol. V: 12 (349–50) and in Göran Dahlbäck, *Uppsala domkyrkas godsinnehav med särskild hänsyn till perioden 1344–1547* (Stockholm 1977), 6-11. Further information was kindly provided by Gunilla Björkvall from Riksarkivet.

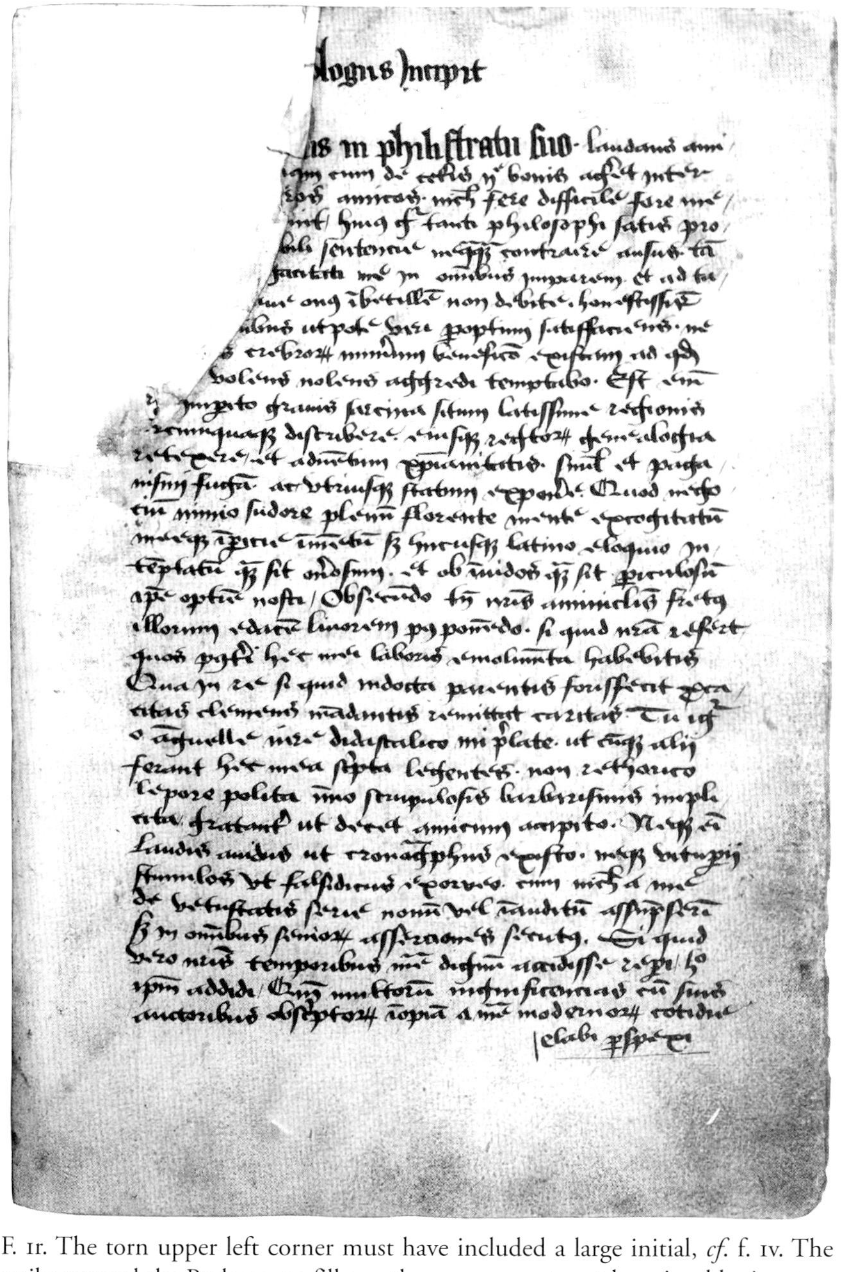

F. 1r. The torn upper left corner must have included a large initial, *cf.* f. 1v. The scribe wanted the Prologue to fill exactly one page, a target he missed by just two words added at the bottom right 'elabi perspexi'.

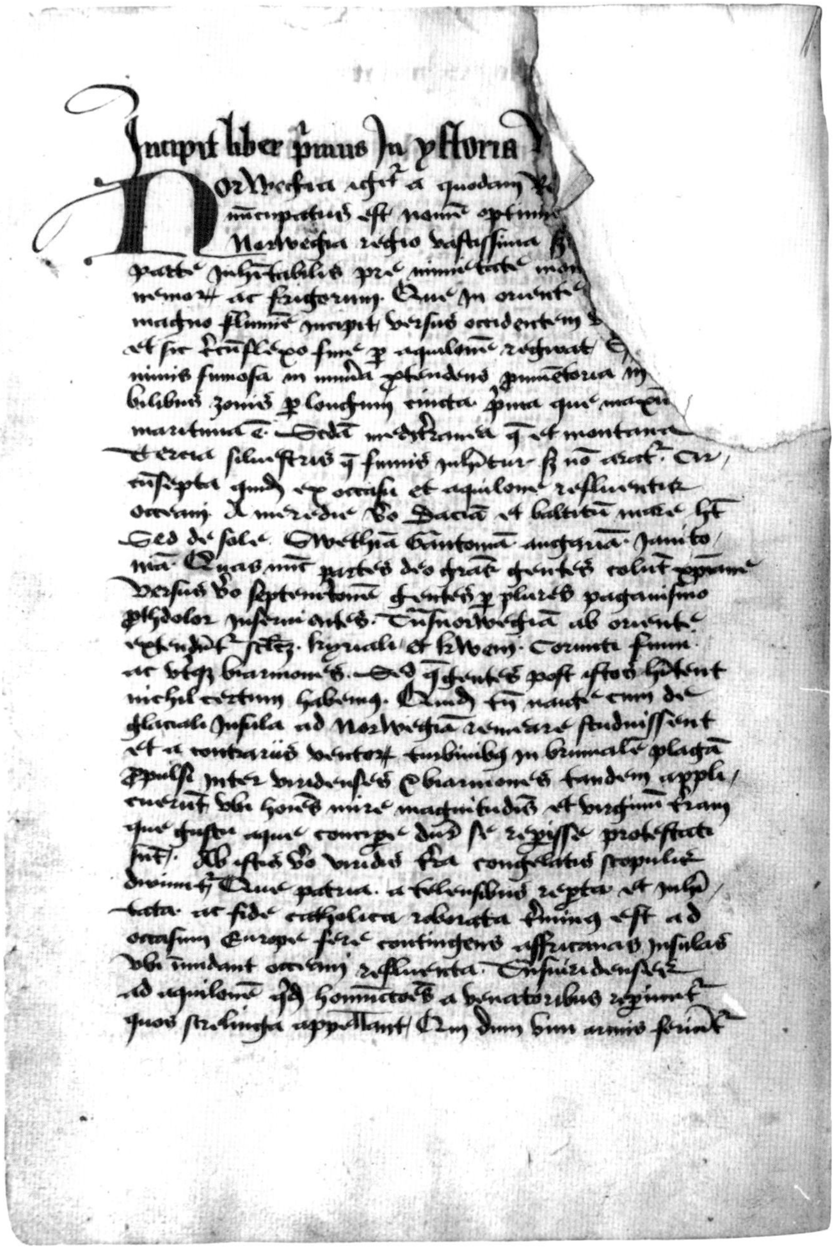

F. 1v. Notice the display script and the initial *(cf.* f. 1r).

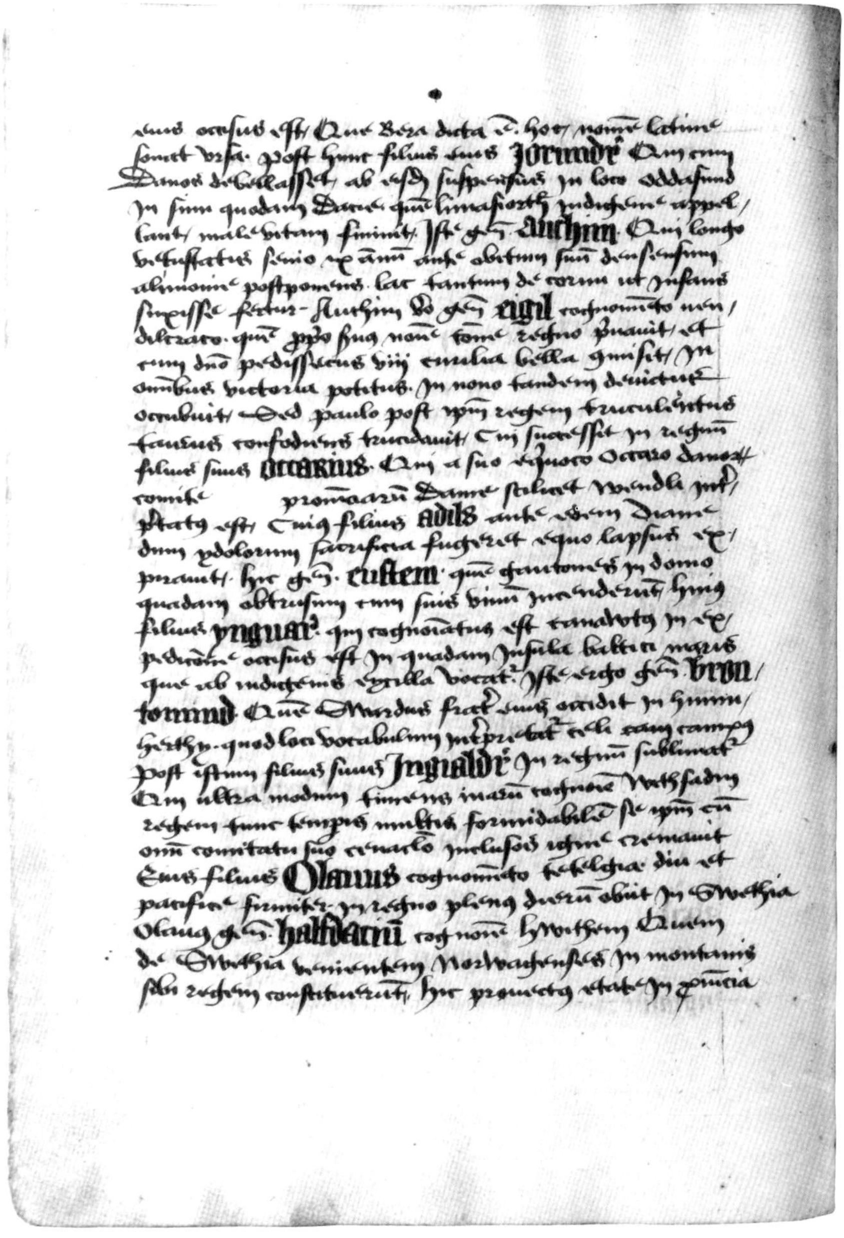

F. 6v. Notice the display script used for names in the Yngling genealogy and the space left in line 15 (*cf.* *HN* IX 25). Notice also the misunderstood Old Norse abbreviational curl on top of 'r' occuring *e.g.* in line 2 'Iorundr" and in line 9 from bottom 'Ingialdr" (*cf.* Introduction p. 33).

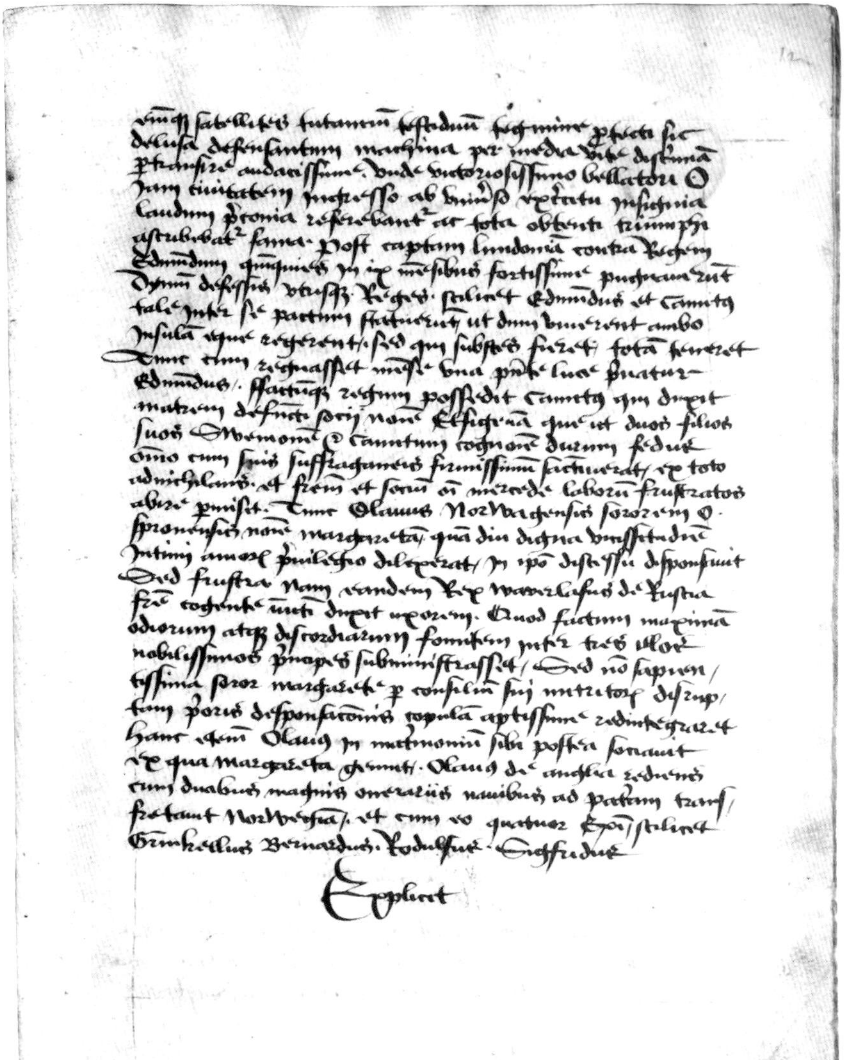

F. 12r. The orderly explicit of the text indicates that the exemplar ended in a similar fashion (*cf.* Introduction p. 29).

5 *Transmission of the Text*

It would be very helpful if we could establish knowledge of *HN* by other medieval authors. It is for instance of importance that scholars generally agree that the Old Norse chronicle *Ágrip* (*c.* 1190) used Theodoricus — thus we have a confirmation of an immediate Trondheim *Nachleben* for him and a corroboration of the passages in his text which indicate that Trondheim was the horizon within which he oriented himself.[52] As mentioned above, the similarities between *Ágrip* and *HN* are such that a common Latin source can explain them well. The only certain traces of the *Nachleben* of *HN* are the above three manuscripts that transmit excerpts of the text.[53] But their evidence has not been exploited systematically in previous scholarship — they can in fact tell us more about the copying of the text in the Middle Ages.

Scribal errors in A

First we can group the scribal errors that have accumulated in *A*.

1) Troubles in recognising or reproducing Old Norse graphemes: the superfluous abbrevational curl (in various executions) after names ending in the nom. m. sing., as in *Dagr'* (e.g. IX 13, 18, 20 ,28, 30, XI 8, XIII 8). The abbreviation itself indicates the ending -r and all these instances must go back to a resolution of the abbrevation and its simultaneous retention by someone unaccustomed to Old Norse language or script. Another telling instance is that noted by Storm (1880, xvii–xviii): *Spronensis* for *Sueonensis* reflecting a misreading of the insular 'v' (with a long left descender and an almost closed bow) regularly in use in Old Norse up to *c.* 1300.

2) 'i' for 'a': *id* for *ad* (VI 6); *inuitim* for *inuitam* (XVIII 30); *hollindia* for *hollandia* (VI 20); *in fractibus* for *anfractibus* (VIII 9); *stipitus* for *stipatus* (XVIII 3). A reverse form of this may be found in XVIII 23: *subematus* for *subeuntes* (misunderstanding of minims and reading one of them as 'a'). This is not a typical confusion and all these five (or six) instances are likely to reflect the same copying process. In a Protogothic Caroling-

[52] *Cf.* Mortensen 2000a.

[53] One possible user of *HN* deserves to be mentioned: Saxo Grammaticus. His information about Olav and Knud accords better with *HN* than any other known sources — *cf.* Moberg 1941, 62–63 and Friis-Jensen 2000, 251. The latter suggests that *HN* may have been the key source for Saxo's Norwegian chapters in his later books, *i.e.* Saxo may be our only source for forming an opinion about some of the lost parts of *HN*. This suggestion, which deserves to be explored further, gives another hypothetical pointer in the direction of a Lund connection of our author — see below.

ian Minuscule (in Scandinavia in use perhaps as late as mid-thirteenth century, otherwise up to the beginning of the thirteenth century) and in some Gothic Textura hands the vertical stroke of the 'a' is not treated like a minim, but is curved in one stroke. The mistake is more likely to happen when copying from a strict Textura where the stroke is exactly like a minim and the connecting horizontal strokes can be hair thin. Even more likely is the case of a Gothic Cursive (some sort of Bastard or pre-Secretary) where the stroke in 'a' is similar to the 'i' and the bow is sometimes detached and can connect more with the previous letter (as in *A* itself).

3) Misreading of abbreviations: *C' ete, i.e. et ete* for *cete* (I 14); *etenim* probably for *etiam* (II 7, II 13), *nec* for *ut* (VI 7), *si* for *sibi* (IV 7); *protendere* for *portendere* (VIII 12); *cretante* for *-certante* (VIII 17). Most of these are trivial and can happen at any stage from Carolingian minuscule to Gothic Cursive. The first, however, is probably significant and indicates that the scribe of *A* was working from a late exemplar written in a similar Gothic Cursive: the true reading is *cete*; when working from a Carolingian or an early Gothic Textura one hardly confuses the 'c' with a standard abbreviation for 'et' as the ampersand and the tironian signs have little in common with the 'c'; when copying a text written in *e.g.* a pre-Secretary hand similar to that of *A* there is little difference between a large 'c' and the abbreviation 'C'' for 'et'.

4) Confusion of 'h' and 'b': *brorleifr* for *hiorleifr* (VIII 2); *hwithein* for *hwitbein* (X 1); *haltica* for *baltica* (XVII 11). This confusion points to an early stage, before *c.* 1300, because the similarity between the two letters is very great in the Carolingian minuscule where both curves are of x-height and the opening in the 'h' is often very small. In Gothic scripts the difference increases with time and in fourteenth- and fifteenth-century hands the right stroke of the 'h' will go well below the line and is often not attached to the left ascender.[54]

5) *-um* for *-unt*: *uerum* for *ierunt* (VI 9); *petum* for *petunt* (XVIII 18). These can be put down to misreadings of a horizontal stroke for *-(r)unt* or to confusions of minims (with 't' taken as one minim).

6) 'cl' for 'd': *claniam* for *daniam* (XVII 29). Although singular, this mistake is significant because it reflects a Carolingian or Protogothic stage. This misreading is unlikely from a Gothic Textura or Cursive where the ascender of the 'd' is no longer straight, but always heavily curved or broken towards the left.

[54] *Cf.* Hægstad 1919–20, 121.

7) Confusion or omission of minims: *non* for *noui* (prol. 2); *fumosa* for *sinuosa* (I 4); *holingard* for *holmgard* (XVII 9). A common mistake (in all relevant scripts) of which there are many more examples in *A*. Their frequency points to a Gothic stage dominated by minims and with no or few bows.

8) Confusion of long 's' and 'f': *fumosa* for *sinuosa* (I 4), *fusum* for *susum* (II 15) etc. A common problem in all relevant scripts.

At least two layers of antecedents are needed to explain the errors in the *A*-text. Those reflecting a late stage, *i.e.* either a strict Gothic Textura after *c.* 1250 or a Gothic Cursive from the fourteenth or fifteenth century are (2) and the first instance of (3) (*cete*). A Carolingian or Protogothic stage (before *c.* 1250, probably somewhat earlier) is apparent in (4) and (6). To this layer one could add the mistake (1) arising from the insular 'v'. It is hardly possible to stretch the evidence towards a single exemplar of around 1300 — (4) and (6) point strongly to an earlier script whereas (2) and (3) (*cete*) point to a later one. The evidence also makes possible a three-layer explanation: a Carolingian or Protogothic (before *c.* 1250), a Gothic Textura (*c.* 1250–1400), and a Gothic Cursive (*c.* 1350–1500).

The relationship between A, B, and C

Next we must review the relationship between the Swedish excerpts (*B* & *C*) and the Scottish-Orkney transmission (*A* and its antecedent(s)). Storm simply stated that the textual witnesses only had a distant relationship and 'should be used alongside each other' (probably intending that their readings have equal stemmatic value).

For the brief passage where all textual witnesses are available (IX 2–11) *A* on the one hand and *BC* on the other display a number of significant variants. The text of *B* cannot have been copied from *C* or vice versa, *B* being longer and later. They must share at least one common ancestor different from the exemplar of *A* (*A* itself is excluded because it is younger than both *B* and *C*). (In the listing below I disregard spellings of names because they so easily change from one copy to the next and because they are susceptible to much more wilful emendation and guessing):

IX 3 uero *A* : *om. BC* **4** per longa secula *A* : *om. BC* **5** medonis *BC* : medionis *A* **6** nanum in petram persequitur nec redisse dicitur *A* : manum in petram proiciens non retraxisse dicitur *BC* : de quo arguitur fortis *add. C* **8** demoniorum *A* : *om. BC* **8** Norwaico *A* : sweco *BC* **8** uocatur *A* : dicitur *BC* **9** hereditarentur *A* : hereditaretur *BC* **10** filium *BC* : filius *A*.

The preferred reading is quoted first, and, as will be seen, both *A* and *BC* contain obvious errors against the other. Particularly telling are the readings in IX 6 (*nanum* / *manum*) and IX 8 (*norwaico* / *sweco*): the strange story of King Sveigde who pursued a dwarf into a stone and never returned (similarly told in Old Norse sources) has been transformed into a story of putting his hand into a stone and not being able to withdraw it. This is likely to have happened in two stages: first a simple copyist's error by which *nanum* becomes *manum*; next a plausible reinterpretation of *persequitur* into *proiciens* and of *redisse* into *retraxisse* to make some sense of it. The *C* text moreover wants to drive home a point of the new story by saying: *de quo arguitur fortis* ('which shows how strong he was'). The other alteration where a 'Swedish' word is explained (instead of *A*'s 'Norwegian') points to Sweden as the origin of the common ancestor of *C* and *B* (confirmed by other features, see below).

Other groupings of the three manuscripts are unlikely. There are two insignificant private readings of *B*, both errors:

IX 2 primum *AC* : primam *B* 3 genuit *AC* : genus *B*.

Of the four private readings of *C* against *AB* one is insignificant:

IX 2 itaque *AB* : *om. C.*

But the others demand some attention:

IX 9 incenderunt *AB* : incenderunt ac familiam *C* 10 Cereri *AB* : dee Cereri *C* 11 obiit *AB* : obiit morbo *C*.

All these make sense but both *ac familiam* and *morbo* break the style of the genealogy by not having a verb last (see commentary). They could be explained as clarifications on the part of the *C*-redactor just like the addition of 'goddess' to explain Ceres and the above-mentioned addition to the story of Sveigde. If one tries to give these private readings of *C* independent value — *i.e.* to place *C* with *A* or by itself in a separate branch in the stemma and not with *B* — one is at a loss to explain the highly significant common readings of *B* and *C*, no doubt reflecting a common Swedish ancestor of the genealogy. Consequently the private readings of *C* have little stemmatic weight and can in fact, as mentioned, all be accounted for as deliberate clarifications.

With one exception all the examples of tripartite variation concern the spelling of names. The exception is

IX 10 Sweones suspendentes *A* : sweui omnes *B* : sweci *C*.

Here *C*'s omission of the nonsensical *omnes* (probably arising from the latter part of *Sweones*) can also be seen as a redactor's attempt to save the sentence.

For the rest of the genealogy (IX 12–X 2) we can only compare *A* to *B*. Again we find significant errors in both transmissions. In the following instances *A* preserves a better reading than *B*:

IX 12 uite metam inuenit *A* : uitam finiuit *B* 18 eius *A* : *om.* *B* 19 ursa *A* : *om.* *B* 17 Agnafit : agnasit *A* : Agnasit qui nunc Stokholmr dicitur *B* 20 indigene *A* : indigne *B* 29 Himinherthy *A* : næricia *B* 31 timens *A* : *om.* *B* 31 inclusos *A* : inclusus *B* X 1 constituerunt *A* : constituunt *B*.

Two of these deviations in *B* reflect a deliberate Swedish alteration: the addition of 'Stockholm' and the choice of *næricia* (Närke, a small Swedish province north of Lake Vättern). The rest testify to the independent value of the *A*-tradition.

The reverse is true for:

IX 13 passeris *B* : pasceris *A* 18 ob infamiam *B* : ab infamia *A* 25 interemptus *B* : interpretatus *A* 32 functus *B* : firmiter in *A*.

The two first readings may be seen as minor variations, but the latter two make no sense in *A* and perfect sense in *B*; moreover, *A*'s mistakes can be well accounted for palaeographically. Therefore the *B*-version has a similar independent value.

Next we have a fuller text in some instances in *B*, where the shorter version in *A* makes good sense on its own; whether these instances reflect readings of the archetype or are additions in the hyparchetype of *BC* cannot be decided with certainty (see commentary):

IX 13 scrotā uath *A* : stotamuadh uel wapnawadh *B* 17 interfecit *A* : interfecit suspendendo ad arborem cum catena aurea *B*.

The net result of the textual comparison is that we must stipulate a hyparchetype for *BC* (γ) different from the exemplar of *A* (δ). Due to significant errors in both groups neither γ nor δ can be identical to the archetype (ω).

The contexts of A, B, C and their exemplars

Since Storm important advances have been made in understanding both the Scottish and the Orkney circumstances of *HN*'s transmission (Crawford 1977, Chesnutt 1986) and those of the Swedish genealogical excerpts, *B*, *C*, and γ (Bolin 1931). Let us begin by reviewing the historical context of *A* and its exemplar.[55]

As has been set out above by Michael Chesnutt, and in great detail in Chesnutt 1986, *A* in its entirety reflects Scottish historical interests during the reign of James IV (1488–1513) and in particular those of the Sinclair family and Lord Henry Sinclair (1489–1513). Only the latter items in the manuscript deal directly with Scottish history, but the Orkney-related texts in the first part also mattered to the Sinclairs, the former Earls of Orkney. This group of texts, *i.e. HN*, The *Orkney Genealogy* and a list of

[55] I am also drawing on Thomson 2001.

Norwegian kings, no doubt mirror an editorial effort of the mid-fifteenth century; they misled Munch and Storm into promulgating a date for *A* around 1450. We know now that we possess only a copy of those efforts, but, importantly, a copy that hardly tampers with the textual selection already made of Orkney-related material. First of all, the excerpt of *HN* was found as such in the exemplar (see description of *A* above and of δ below). Why, when and how was this (partial) excerpt of Book One of *HN* made?

Henry Sinclair's grandfather, William Sinclair, had been the last Earl of Orkney (1434–1470) when the islands were still subject to the Danish-Norwegian crown. (They were pawned by Christian I in 1468 and the transfer became complete when they became subject to the Scottish crown and the bishopric shifted allegiance from Trondheim to St. Andrews in 1472.) William's inheritance of the Orkneys from his father (d. *c.* 1420) was a troubled and long-drawn-out process of legitimacy claims, mainly in conflict with his guardian David Menzies. The historical dossier of which we have the copy in the first part of *A* seems to have been put together by the learned Orkney bishop Thomas Tulloch (1418–*c.* 1461) between *c.* 1420 and 1434; in the latter year William's position was finally acknowledged by the Danish-Norwegian King Erik of Pomerania (1400–1439). Bishop Tulloch certainly was principal signatory to the *Orkney Genealogy*, which provides the background for the selection of texts:[56] King Erik had asked Sinclair for documents on his lineage, but due to lack of family records the quest was continued for "authentic and approved" chronicles and documents in the bishopric. The *Genealogy* itself is probably dated 1443[57] (mistakenly interpreted by Storm as the *post quem* date for *A*), but as Barbara Crawford has shown it must have been drawn up already in the 1420s and then re-used. There is no reason to doubt the intense search for historical material of every kind. In Crawford's words: "There is certainly a professional air about the 1443/6 Genealogy which gives the impression that a remarkable amount of research and historical zeal was put into it".[58] The two main sources for the *Genealogy* were *HN* and Snorri's *Heimskringla*, both, it is reasonably presumed, found in the cathedral library in Kirkwall.[59] In fact *Heimskringla* provided almost the entire material for the Orkney lineage, *HN* only being quoted for its unique information on the Norse ousting of the previous population of the islands in the time of

[56] The Genealogy has been edited many times, see Chesnutt 1986, 67 and note 42 — *e.g.* in *Diplomatarium Norvegicum* XX,1 (1915, 120–28).

[57] The date has been corrected in *A*.

[58] Crawford 1977, 174.

[59] *Ibid.* 175.

Harald Fairhair (the *Peti* and *Pape*, a summary of *HN* VI 1-8) and the statement that the Orkney earls enjoyed free dominion over the Islands except for a tribute to the Norwegian kings (direct quotation from *HN* VI 21 — *A1* in the stemma below). *A1*

The motive for unearthing and excerpting an old text like *HN* is thus quite clear: it was an old 'authentic and approved' Norwegian Latin chronicle with relevant information on the first chapter of Norse Orkney history — not directly useful for William's lineage, but venerable and a good confidence builder for local historical material. The mechanisms of excerpting are unfortunately less clear. The use of *HN* does not exceed the excerpt we possess in *A*; the Orkney Genealogist therefore presumably already had the excerpt ready-made and worked from it. There is one variant reading in the direct quotation: the *Genealogy* has the correct genitive *posteritatis* whereas A has *posteritates*. That led Storm to assume that the Genealogist used the exemplar (of *A* in Storm's opinion, in reality of δ) rather than the excerpt itself. But the error (or spelling variant) is hardly significant — it is something one can corrupt or correct *in scribendo*.

A possible scenario emerges if we assume that Bishop Thomas Tulloch or one of his assistants came across a complete *HN* in Kirkwall in the primary search for documents. By leafing through it they saw the Orkneys mentioned quite often in Book One, in headings as well as in the narrative; references to the Orkneys after Book One did not leap to the eye; they decided to have a copy of the first book made for their dossier (an unkown amount of text on St. Olav towards the end of the book was perhaps also omitted — see commentary). As noted by Chesnutt, the use of display script in *A* for headings and kings' names may reflect a similar usage in the exemplar. The question arises whether Tulloch's excerpt itself reflected the use of display script in the older complete copy. For the chapter headings that is a reasonable assumption, but doubts can be raised about the kings' names: was this not the kind of genealogical information that the dossier was supposed to highlight? However that may be, the (incomplete) use of coloured initials in *A* is likely to reflect, through its exemplar, a rather stately volume of official Norwegian historiography in the cathedral library of Kirkwall.

This is, to me, a likely account of the circumstances of the excerpt made in Orkney in the 1420s. It is not contradicted by textual, palaeographical, codicological or historical evidence. It explains those errors in *A* stemming from a later, probably cursive Gothic script like that of *A* itself. Furthermore, if one considers the practical circumstances of document hunting, it makes better sense to have Tulloch and his team decide to copy the excerpt for the dossier and subsequently quote from their own copy in the *Genealogy* rather than recur to the old volume. This scenario, in turn, also provides a good explanation of why we only possess the first book. The details are, admittedly, a matter of conjecture, but the approximate date, the motive, and the perpetrators can be established beyond reasonable doubt.

The circumstances behind the brief Swedish excerpts *B* and *C*, or rather their exemplar, have been explained well by Bolin 1931, 192–200. The list of the heathen Yngling kings from *HN* is incorporated in *B* into a genealogy of Swedish kings going up to 1333, ending with Magnus Eriksson (reigned 1319–64); the shorter related extract in *C* is used in another royal genealogy. As *B* and *C* cannot have been dependent one on the other, they must both descend from the excerpt made originally for the genealogy reaching 1333. (These observations concur with the purely textual analysis made above). Magnus Eriksson inherited Norway in 1319 and acquired Skåne in 1332. The genealogy up to 1333 is a product of this new situation (e.g. it focuses out of proportion on the single previous episode where a Swedish king is connected with Skåne). It must have been made shortly afterwards, *c.* 1340, and represents a serious effort to collect historical arguments for Magnus's rule. It uses a source derived from Saxo (probably the *Compendium Saxonis* or perhaps Saxo himself) and it draws on Icelandic material that had already begun to spread in Sweden around 1300.[60] And finally the Swedish Genealogist excerpted from *HN*. In Bolin's words, the Genealogy expresses the self-consciousness brought about by the union of Sweden, Norway, and Skåne. It is not just symbolic that it draws on the literatures of all three countries.[61]

Where did the Swedish Genealogist of *c.* 1340 find a copy of *HN*? Bolin did not speculate about this, but his explanation of the motives behind the excerpt makes it clear — as in the case of the *Orkney Genealogy* — that we are dealing with excerpts fitting that particular occasion; the chances that they were copied from exemplars of exactly the same extent would necessitate a superfluous reduplication of the same historical interests lying behind their exemplars as well. In other words, the chances are that both the Orkney and the Swedish Genealogist originally consulted a full text of *HN*.[62] As mentioned, one such exemplar could have been present in

[60] Bolin 1931, 192. [61] *Ibid.* 199.

[62] Storm thought that the *HN* Yngling list circulated in Sweden separately before the Gene-

Kirkwall (as implied by the *Orkney Genealogy*), whereas we are left with more possibilities in the Swedish case. It is obvious to think of the cathedral library at Lund in newly annexed Skåne, especially if the Genealogist also borrowed from Saxo. But eastern Norway, perhaps Oslo, Hamar or Tønsberg, would be in frequent communication with Sweden. Even western Norway and Iceland ought to be mentioned, because there were other imports of Old Norse literature in this period. The most important issue in this context, however, would be the conclusion that the Swedish transmission depends on a thirteenth/fourteenth-century branch of transmission separate from the Orkney copies. That both branches are at least two copies removed from the archetype is indeed what the palaeographical, textual and historical evidence would suggest, but we must first discuss two possibilities which would both make the Orkney transmission a unique link back to the original.

1) The Yngling kings' lineage in the Swedish excerpts could derive not from *HN* but from a common Latin source (ultimately Ari / Sæmund). Since Munch first directed attention to the Swedish excerpts no scholars have doubted that they are indeed copies from the *HN* text. The present editors are equally convinced, but one should mention that the genealogy sets itself somewhat apart from the narrative and style of the remainder of our *HN* text. The possibility exists that *HN* here copied an existing Latin genealogy *verbatim* and that the Swedish Genealogist had access to the same source. An argument against this is that an *interpretatio Romana* of the goddesses (Diana, Ceres, IX 10 & 26) is much more likely to have been made in an ambitious work of Latin historiography than in a translation of a brief list from Old Norse into Latin. Furthermore we may be dealing with an inspiration from Adam of Bremen, consistent with the rest of *HN* as we know it. The Latin explanation of names in IX 19 and IX 29 illustrates the same tendency. It cannot, however, be completely ruled out that such an *interpretatio Romana* could have been present in a source like Sæmund. The access to such a text by the Swedish Genealogist would, however, not make the the textual landscape any easier to understand than his access to *HN*.

2) The Swedish excerpts may descend directly from the exemplar of *A*. This was argued by Steinnes 1946–48 who referred to Bolin's findings and to the marriage of two Swedish noblemen to two daughters of the Orkney Earl around 1350. These would supposedly have brought back copies or

alogist of *c.* 1340 (of whom he did not know); Steinnes 1946–48, 9 rightly says that this is an unnecessary assumption.

excerpts of both Old Norse literature and of *HN* to Sweden to be perused by the Genealogist. From the discussion of textual relationships above it emerged that the exemplar of *A* (δ) must be different from the exemplar of *BC* (γ). But Steinnes did not know that *A* was a later Scottish copy of a similar excerpt made in Orkney in the 1420s (δ), hence *we* are dealing with one more layer of tradition than he was: therefore it cannot be proved from the variants that γ did not descend from an Orkney original, namely the exemplar of δ (α). But in itself Steinnes's historical case is thin. Swedish noblemen married in the Nordic countries as well as further abroad by the hundreds in the fourteenth century. This does not make them historians. Seen from the point of view of the Genealogist of *c.* 1340, Orkney would not be an obvious place to look, considering the proximity of sees in Lund and Oslo, and of Norwegian monasteries in Tønsberg, Konghelle, etc.[63]

What lies behind Steinnes's suggestion is a misplaced trust in *A*'s representativity. What we now know of medieval copies of other Nordic Latin historical works which have barely survived (and only in foreign collections or copies) tells us otherwise. *Passio Olaui*, *Historia De profectione Danorum in Hierosolymam*, the works of Theodoricus and Saxo are such cases, all written before or around 1200 and all known to have existed in at least two to three pre-1300 manuscripts.[64] In all likelihood the centres that produced these texts, *e.g.* Trondheim and Lund, also saw to their survival by having more than one copy made — for their own and perhaps for other institutions. Once the impetus behind the production of the texts had petered out, for instance in the fourteenth century, copies were still kept in various episcopal and monastic libraries but were no longer reproduced *in toto*. If they still received any attention it was for purposes of excerpting or abbreviating. But during and after the Reformation they disappeared almost entirely, only to leave chance foreign copies to us.

This outline is somewhat hypothetical, but I am convinced that *HN* went through the same phases. As stated, Steiness's theory cannot be discarded on hard evidence, but from the point of view of general textual and library history it is improbable. The resources going into an ambitious Latin history of Norway by a Norwegian would *a priori* also be spent on copying the work at least once or twice in Norway — especially when we do have late-medieval foreign reflections of such a transmission. An elabo-

[63] Already Aðalbjarnarson 1937, 7 observed that the Swedish excerpts point to a Norwegian exemplar.

[64] *Profectio* & Theodoricus: Skovgaard-Petersen 2002; Saxo: Boserup 1981; *Passio Olaui*: Mortensen 2000a+d.

rate Latin depiction of a Norwegian North Sea realm would have commanded interest in the century or so after the writing of *HN*. Such general considerations, together with the evidence of palaeography and of textual history, lead me to presume at least two late-twelfth- or thirteenth-century full copies of *HN* (α and β), in addition to the archetype (ω):

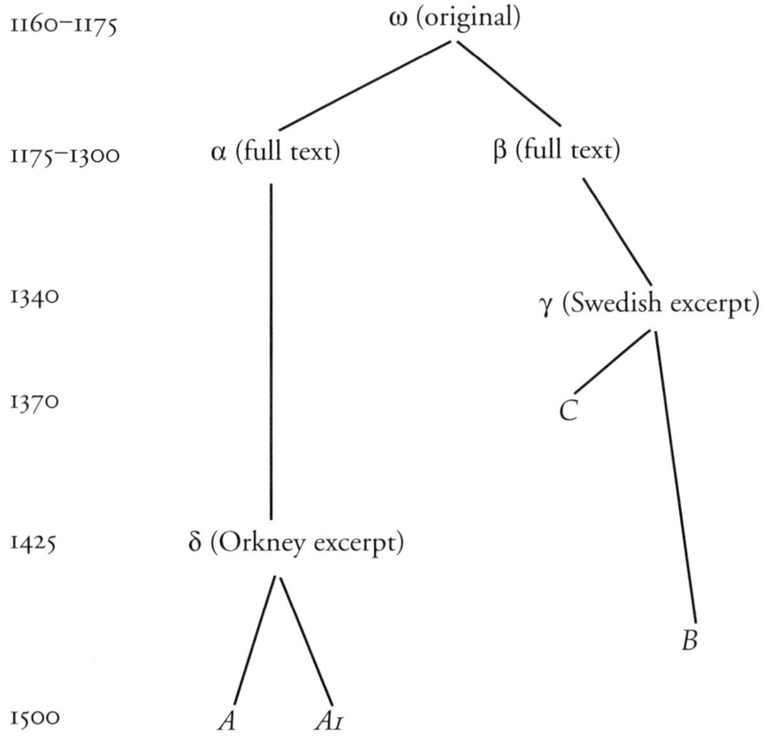

6 Conclusion

Only a small introductory part of *Historia Norwegie* has been transmitted to us — in its original form it may have run to a hundred pages or more, covering Norwegian history from mythical beginnings to the author's time in the second half of the twelfth century. As far as we can judge from the extant opening it was a codification of a nascent sense of nationhood intimately connected to the centralizing efforts of twelfth-century Norway that begin to appear in the sources in the decades after the establishment of the archdiocese in Trondheim. A central part of the surviving text, a unique geographical survey of Norway, espouses a missionary view of the territory: the far North is included in the realm, but it has not yet been christianized. As an ideological document *HN* is especially interesting because it almost certainly emerged from a centre outside Trondheim, perhaps in Viken in eastern Norway — thus giving us a glimpse of a richer Latin culture than we might have expected. In literary terms *HN* followed a main trend for a new nation raising Latin monuments about its past and its new status as a Christian commonwealth: some sort of Roman pedigree was implied in the medium — in the case of *HN* there is a good deal of *interpretatio Romana christiana* in the geography and a general striving for a difficult mannerist style that signals a high level of recent learning imbibed at a foreign centre. The author was probably, like other comparable historians, a high-ranking member of an episcopal or royal retinue and had studied abroad, perhaps in Saxony or Denmark. It is likely that he had stayed in Denmark at some point to gather texts (Lund is the obvious candidate) and that he finished his work in Norway for the same exclusive peer group with whom he had planned it. His efforts were crowned with little success, to judge from our evidence. Like other Latin historians, he was not used by the writers of Kings' sagas in the thirteenth century. However, we have no means of knowing what happened to the lost later books of the work, but his manner of presenting Olav Tryggvason at least shows an author who shared some of the sagas' concern for visual writing and military reasoning. The only certain echo of *HN* is found in the late medieval excerpts made from it in Orkney and in Sweden, but they do testify that at least two or three earlier medieval copies of the full text had existed, some of them no doubt in Norway.

7 Editorial Principles

The Text

Like Storm's edition the constitution of the text is 'synthetical', *i.e.* we have not done a 'best-manuscript' edition of *A* (as did Munch), but rather attempted to reconstruct the readings of the archetype ω. In contrast to Storm we follow the spelling of *A*, including inconsistencies, in so far as they fall within the normal variations of medieval morphology and orthography. A few examples will illustrate the difference: Storm corrected *stipendarius* to *stipendiarius*, but the first form is well documented in Medieval Latin. He classicized *excercitus* into *exercitus*, again the former is well attested. We also allow the author a few more elliptic periods — one of the characteristics of his style. *Dignus* takes the genitive in *A* as it often does in Medieval Latin, whereas Storm classicized to the ablative. In this sense we restore the medievalisms present in *A*. Apart from the spelling of names, *A* reflects medieval usage very well, and we have found it useless to normalize *-ci*/*-ti* etc. when medieval manuscripts are not consistent. A note in the apparatus or the commentary helps those unaccustomed to medieval practices. We mostly differ from *A*'s spellings in names which are often corrupt (and we follow twelfth-century practice in writing 'u' (capital form 'V') and 'i', never 'v' or 'j'). Furthermore we have not reproduced the display script in the series of kings as this may not have been present in the high medieval exemplar (α) of the Orkney excerpt. The numbering of chapters and paragraphs as well as the punctuation is new.

Apart from entertaining a more medievalizing attitude to the received text in terms of orthography and morphology (including a recognition of the high qualities of *A*) we also differ from Storm on a number of points that have a bearing on the sense. These differences are mainly due to 1) a new restitution of the lost text on f. 1 of *A*; 2) a stemmatic assessment of the variants between *A* and *BC* (for the brief passage available in all three manuscripts); 3) various restitutions of Medieval Latin syntax; 4) re-evalution of the line of thought in various periods that has been elucidated by more recent historical or philological scholarship on *HN* and its related texts; 5) a renewed scrutiny of the entire text of the Dalhousie manuscript. Storm's edition cannot be reconstructed from our text and apparatus. However, as his edition has been very influential, not least as the basis of the three existing translations of the text (Koht 1950, Salvesen 1969, and Kunin (in Phelpstead 2001)), it may be useful to list the major differences in the readings between our and Storm's edition, *i.e.* those cases where the sense or the style is affected. Our text is quoted first, Storm's after the colon:

Prologus 1 Tullius : .....tus | philosophie tractatu : Philostrato | eius : vitæ | caros : veros | **2** tametsi tali : tantæ enim | imbecillem : me imbecillem | beneficio : beneficiis | **4** immensum : injunctum | **9** memorie : memoria | ipse : ipsum | **I** Norwagensium : Norwegie **1** optinuisse dicitur : obtinuerat | **2** Tota : Est autem | moncium, nemorum : montium et nemorum | **3** ab Albia : a ...... | **9** propulsi : propulsi essent | **IV 2** solummodo : solitudo | **3** corticea : coriacea | **7** aduentantibus : addentantibus | **18** sub : super | prepararet : præparat | **19** totus : totusque | **21** implens : implevit | **24** † Item – impleuerunt † : Item – impleuerunt | **VI 2** in structuris : instructuris | **3** per ledonem : quas per ledonem | **18** Ricardus habuit filium Robertum, qui : Ricardus | **VII 1** propria : patria | **VIII 2** Ingwar : Ingulfr | Oddo : anbă | **3** ubique inhabitata : est ubique inhabitata | **8** conuertentur : conuertuntur | **12** monstris : monstri | sua sponte : suapte sponte | **19** quidem : quidam | **IX 10** Cereri : deæ Cereri | **11** obiit : obiit morbo | **13** Sciotanuath : Sciotanuath vel Wapnawath | **17** Agnafit : Agnafit, qui nunc Stockholmr dicitur, | **26** Adils : Adils vel Athisl | faceret : fugeret | **30** regnum : regem | **XI** 7 a quadam : qui a quadam | **8** XI^{us} : XI | optinuit Ericus Sanguinea Securis, qui sibi : Ericus sanguinea securis acquisivit | **XII 3** et : sed | **XIII 2** deseruiret : serviret | **XV 12** Denique : namque | **XVI 2** nobilissima Morensium : Morensium | **XVII 1** Sed : Sed cum | **3** Quem cum : Qui eum cum | **7** Olauo : Olavus | **13** Flandream : in Flandream | **14** perperam : perquam | **22** uixque : vixque vivus | **25** et eciam : etiam | **26** inde : inibi | **27** inde executurum : executurum | **33** quidam : quidem | **44** XX : XXX | **49** quippe : suis | **56** Sweinone, scilicet Tiuguskeg : Sweinone tiuguskeg | **XVIII 23** subeuntes : supervectus | ipse eiusque : ipsi namque | **31** maximum : maximam | postea sociauit : sociauit | **32** qua Margareta : qua

Apparatus

The critical apparatus is positive and documents all the rejected readings of the primary textual witnesses (*ABC*). We have taken pains to register all corrections by the scribe of *A* as well. The received text should hence be reconstructable on the basis of the edition. The apparatus does not note the numerous deviations from the editions of Munch and Storm. First of all, many are mere orthographical or morphological variants; others are typographical or reading errors on the part of Munch and Storm that need no further record.[65] Of the many felicitous and obvious emendations and conjectures made by Munch and Storm (and by Bugge, Gjessing, and Skard), we only register when a reading was first suggested. Only in controversial cases are various suggestions quoted: it is valuable to consider the thoughts of men so learned in *HN* and contemporary texts whenever there is doubt.

[65] Both conscientiously recorded the use of 'ff' instead of 'f', but they were not aware that this was a common Gothic cursive usage for capital F (*cf.* L. C. Hector, *The Handwriting of English Documents*, London 1958 (2nd ed. 1966), 56–57); it is not noted here.

The Translation (by *Peter Fisher*)
The translation adheres closely to the Latin text, though there must naturally be a continual tension between the need for a fairly literal rendering for those who wish for assistance in reading the Latin text, and the desire to provide a readable, non-Latinate piece of English. This has sometimes understandably occasioned the breaking up of some of the longer sentences in the original.

As so often in medieval prefaces, the author here tries for a more elevated, formal style, which is reflected in the translation. In the body of his text he writes in a simpler style, but from time to time employs special effects, as in the word-play at VIII 19 or XVII 44, or the sporadic use of biblical vocabulary, as at XVII 15 (*cf. Col* 3.12, "bowels of mercies"), and where possible some analogy in English has been found. Latinized names have normally been given an English translation although Norwegian names are generally kept in a Scandinavian form.

The translator owes a firm debt to the guidance of the editors, who have tactfully helped where necessary in the interpretation of the Latin text.

The Commentary
The commentary has its focus on the Latin text, but it attempts to give all-round guidance in literary and historical matters as well. The reader of the Latin text will find discussions of linguistic and textual problems. We have aimed at giving a full account of our decisions in controversial cases. Those unaccustomed to medieval usage and vocabulary will find a number of medievalisms explained. ML is used as an abbreviation for 'Medieval Latin'. Only occasionally do we supply references for common ML expressions; in general we draw on the specialized dictionaries and on handbooks, *e.g.* Blaise 1994 and Stotz 1996–2000.

The Latin sources (and other background texts in Latin) are documented in full; we also refer to parallels from Old Norse texts, but the student of Old Norse literature should supplement our commentary with the parallels quoted and explored more fully by (especially) Ellehøj 1965, Ulset 1983, Krag 1991, and Phelpstead 2001.

Inger Ekrem's Essay
See the preface above for more information on the Essay. With very few exceptions I have let her text stand as she left it and have consequently made no adjustments or updatings to her manuscript in the light of my work. This means that her references are sometimes to other editions and translations than those in the Introduction and the Commentary.

Sigla

Codices

A Edinburgh, National Archives of Scotland, Dalhousie Muniments, GD45/31/1 – II

A1 Eiusdem codicis *Genealogia* citans *Historiam Norwegie* (cf. supra pp. 38–39)

B Stockholm, Kungliga Biblioteket, B 17 – II

C Stockholm, Riksarkivet, A 8

Commentatores et editores veteres

Bugge in Storm 1880

Bugge 1873

Gjessing in Storm 1880

Laing 1855, 33–34

Munch 1850, 1–18

Skard 1930

Storm 1880, 69–124

Huius editionis

Ekrem Inger Ekrem, editrix

Fisher Peter Fisher, interpres Anglicus

Kraggerud Egil Kraggerud, editor Theodorici Monachi

Mortensen Lars Boje Mortensen, editor

Alia

| initium paginae novae codicis *A* (beginning of a new page in *A*)

[...] lacuna propter chartam mutilatam codicis *A* (lacuna caused by physical damage of *A*)

⟨...⟩ voces desunt sine mutilatione (lacuna without physical damage)

Historia Norwegie

1r

[Pr]ologus incipit

[1][Tull]ius in philosophie tractatu suo laudans ami[cit]iam, cum de ceteris eius bonis ageret, inter [ca]ros amicos nichil fere difficile fore me[m]init. [2]Huius igitur tanti philosophi satis pro[ba]bili sentencie nequaquam contraire ausus, tam[etsi tali sa]gacitati me in omnibus imparem et ad ta[le et tam gr]aue onus imbecillem noui, debite honestissimis [adhortaci]onibus utpote uiri peroptimi satisfaciens, ne [ingratu]s crebrorum munerum beneficio existam, ad quod [posco]r, uolens nolens aggredi temptabo. [3]Est enim [mihi] imperito grauis sarcina situm latissime regionis [ci]rcumquaque discribere eiusque rectorum genealogiam retexere et aduentum christianitatis simul et paganismi fugam ac utriusque statum exponere.

[4]Quod negotium nimio sudore plenum, florente mente excogitatum meeque imperitie immensum, sed hucusque Latino eloquio intemptatum, quam sit onerosum et ob inuidos quam sit periculosum, ipse optime nosti. [5]Obsecundo tamen nostris aminiculis fretus, illorum edacem liuorem postponendo (si quid nostra refert), quod uos posteri hec mei laboris emolumenta habebitis. [6]Qua in re si quid indocta parentis forisfecit procacitas, clemens mandantis remittat caritas. [7]Tu igitur, o Agnelle, iure didascalico mi prelate, utcumque alii ferant hec mea scripta legentes non rhetorico lepore polita, immo scrupulosis barbarismis implicita, gratanter, ut decet amicum, accipito. [8]Neque enim laudis auidus ut cronographus existo, neque

Prologus *Munch* | 1 Tullius *Mortensen* : Solinus *aut fortasse* Honorius *Ekrem* : *Storm legendum putauit* .....tus | philosophie tractatu *Fisher* : philistratu *A* : Philistrato *Munch* : Philostrato *Storm* | amicitiam *Storm* | eius *Mortensen* : n^e *aut* u^e *A* : nature *Ekrem* (*fortasse* nobis) : uitae *Munch et Storm* | caros *Ekrem* : ueros *Storm* | meminit *Storm* | 2 probabili *Munch* | tametsi tali sagacitati *Kraggerud* : tā [......]gacitati *A* : tam .... sagacitati *Munch* : tam preclare sagacitati *Bugge 1873* : tantae enim sagacitati *Storm* | tale et tam graue *Storm* : tam graue *Munch* | noui *Storm* : non *A* | adhortacionibus *Storm* : precibus *Munch* | ingratus *Bugge* | beneficio *A* : beneficiis *Storm* | poscor *Storm* : prouocor *Bugge* | 3 mihi *Gjessing* | circumquaque *Munch* | rectorum *Munch* : regtorum *A* | genealogiam *Munch* : genealogia *A* | 4 immensum *Munch* : ı̂mētū *A* : iniunctum *Bugge et Storm* : commendatum *Bugge 1873* : immeritum *Ekrem* | 5 quod uos *Gjessing* : quos *A* : quod *Munch in app.* | 7 Agnelle *Munch et Storm* : āguelle *uel* āgnelle *A* : *fortasse ut* Augustinelle *soluendum Ekrem* |

Here begins the Prologue

[1]Cicero in his philosophical treatise, while praising friendship and dealing with all its other benefits, mentions that almost no difficulties will exist between loving friends. [2]I have not in any way dared to contradict this very convincing opinion from this great philosopher, and though I am aware of my total inferiority in comparison with such perspicuity and of my weakness in shouldering so weighty a burden of this kind, whether I wish to or no I shall try to address what is demanded of me and duly satisfy the noble exhortations of an excellent man, in order not to show myself ungrateful for all those many kind favours I have received. [3]It is a serious imposition on one as unpractised as myself to be obliged to describe the full extent of this wide-flung region, to recreate the genealogy of its rulers and to reveal both the arrival of Christianity and the expulsion of heathendom, with the present situation of each.

[4]You yourself know all too well how oppressive this task is and how hazardous on account of jealous critics — full of excessive toil, devised by a distinguished intellect and prodigious considering my lack of experience, yet hitherto unattempted in the Latin tongue. [5]Even so, I shall comply, trusting to such resources as I have, and disregarding the biting malice of those persons, if they are at all capable of doing me harm, since you, my successors, will possess these fruits of my labours. [6]If, though obedient, my untutored presumption has transgressed at all in this undertaking, may my kind and affectionate director be lenient. [7]However much, then, others who read this document of mine may say it is unpolished and lacks the charm of eloquence, or indeed accuse it of being tangled up in jagged, barbaric expressions, you, Agnellus, who have been set over me with a teacher's authority, receive it graciously as befits a friend. [8]I do not thirst for fame as a historian, nor do

uituperii stimulos ut falsidicus exorreo, cum nichil a me de uetustatis serie nouum uel inauditum assumpserim, sed in omnibus seniorum asserciones secutus. [9]Si quid uero nostris temporibus memorie dignum accidisse repperi, hoc ipse addidi, quoniam multorum magnificencias cum suis auctoribus ob scriptorum inopiam a memoria modernorum cotidie elabi per-
IV spexi. |

I Incipit liber primus in ystoria N[orwagensium]

[1]Norwegia igitur a quodam re[ge, qui Nor] nuncupatus est, nomen optinu[isse dicitur]. [2][Tota] Norwegia regio uastissima, sed [maxima ex] parte inhabitabilis pre nimietate mon[cium], nemorum ac frigorum. [3]Que in oriente [ab Albia], magno flumine, incipit, uersus occidentem u[ero uergit] et sic circumflexo fine per aquilonem regirat. [4]Es[t terra] nimis sinuosa, innumera protendens promunctoria, III [habita]bilibus zonis per longum cincta: prima, que maxima [et] maritima est, secunda mediterranea, que et montana [dicitur], tertia siluestris, que Finnis inhabitatur, sed non aratur. [5]Circumsepta quidem ex occasu et aquilone refluentis Occeani, a meredie uero Daciam et Balticum Mare habet, sed de sole Swethiam, Gautoniam, Angariam, Iamtoniam. [6]Quas nunc partes — Deo gratias — gentes colunt christiane. [7]Versus uero septemtrionem gentes perplures paganismo — proh dolor — inseruientes trans Nor-

9 memorie *A* : memoria *Storm* | ipse *Bugge* : ipsum *A* | magnificencias *Munch* : mgnificencias *A* | I Norwagensium *Mortensen* : Norwegie *Munch* | 1 rege, qui Nor *Storm* : rege nomen traxit, qui Nor *Munch* | optinuisse dicitur : obtinuisse dicitur *Storm in app.* : optinuerat *Storm in textu* : optimum *Munch* : optinuit *Bugge 1873* : obtinuit *Storm in apparatu* | 2 Tota *Mortensen* : Est autem *Storm* | maxima ex *Storm* : magna ex *Bugge 1873* | moncium, *Mortensen* : moncium et asperitate *Bugge 1873* : montium et *Storm* : moncium ... *Munch* | 3 ab Albia *Storm in notis, cf. III 3* : a Gothelba *Ekrem, cf. Adam IV 21 schol. 131* : ex *Bugge 1873* : a ... *Storm in textu* : ab Albia *uel* Albiae *uel* a Gautorum *uel* a Gautelf *Storm in notis* | regirat *i.e.* regyrat | uero uergit *Storm* | 4 Est terra *Bugge 1873 et Storm* : est ... *Munch* | sinuosa *Bugge 1873 et Storm* : fumosa *A* | innumera : in numera *A* | promunctoria *Ekrem* (*cf. infra II 11 & XIII 6*) : promontoria *Munch in notis et Storm* : promuētoria *A* | habitabilibus *Storm* | maxima et *Storm* : maxima *cum spatiolo uacante in lacuna ut uidetur A* : maxime *Munch* | dicitur *Storm* | 5 Balticum *Munch* : baltitum *A* | Iamtoniam *Munch* : Ianitoniam *A* |

I shudder at the smarts inflicted by those who might brand me a liar, since I have incorporated on my own account nothing new or unheard of from earlier ages, but have followed the statements of my elders in every respect. [9]If I have discovered any happening of our own times worth remembering, I have inserted that fact myself, since I have observed that many men's splendid feats, together with their performers, sink daily into oblivion among our contemporaries owing to the shortage of written records.

I Here begins the first book of the History of the Norwegians

[1]Norway is said to have taken its name from a king called Nor. [2]As a whole its territory is immense but for the most part uninhabitable, due to the huge number of its mountains, forests and cold temperatures. [3]It starts in the east from the Great River, but bends towards the west and so turns back as its edge circles round northwards. [4]Full of fjords and creeks, it is a country that pushes out countless headlands, and along its length encompasses three habitable zones: the first and largest is the seaboard; the second is the inland area, also known as the mountain region; the third is wooded and populated by the Finns, but there is no agriculture there. [5]To the west and north, Norway is enclosed by the Ocean tides, to the south lie Denmark and the Baltic Sea, while to the east are Sweden, Götaland, Ångermanland and Jämtland. [6]The peoples who live in these regions, thanks be to God, are now Christians. [7]However, towards the north there are, alas, a great many tribes who have spread across Norway from the east and who are in thrall to

wegiam ab oriente extenduntur, scilicet Kyriali et Kweni, Cornuti Finni ac utrique Biarmones. [8]Sed que gentes post istos habitent, nichil certum habemus. [9]Quidam tamen naute cum de Glaciali Insula ad Norwegiam remeare studuissent et a contrariis uentorum turbinibus in brumalem plagam propulsi, inter Viridenses et Biarmones tandem applicuerunt, ubi homines mire magnitudinis et Virginum Terram (que gustu aque concipere dicuntur) se reperisse protestati sunt.

[10]Ab istis uero Viridis Terra congelatis scopulis dirimitur. [11]Que patria a Telensibus reperta et inhabitata ac fide catholica roborata terminus est ad occasum Europe, fere contingens Africanas insulas, ubi inundant occeani refluenta. [12]Trans Viridenses ad aquilonem quidam homunciones a uenatoribus reperiuntur, quos Screlinga appellant. [13]Qui dum uiui armis
2r feriuntur, | uulnera eorum absque cruore albescunt, mortuis uero uix cessat sanguis manare. [14]Sed ferri metallo penitus carent; dentibus cetinis pro missilibus, saxis acutis pro cultris utuntur.

[15]Hucusque situm et circumstancias Norwegie ostendimus. [16]Nunc autem trifariam eius habitacionem exequamur.

II De tripartito incolatu Norwegie

[1]Zona itaque maritima Decapolis dici potest, nam X ciuitatibus inclita est, IIII patrias complectens XXII prouinciarum capaces. [2]Prima patria Sinus Orientalis dicitur, a terminis Dacie oriens, et usque ad locum, qui Rygiarbit appellatur, extenditur IIII prouincias continens. [3]Secunda Gulacia ad insulam, que Media nuncupatur, usque protelatur VI complectens prouincias. [4]Quarum ultima nomine Mor uillam quandam habet nature mirabilis. [5]Omnes enim stipites arborumque abcisi ra-

9 propulsi *A et Skard* : propulsi essent *Storm* | 14 cetinis *Bugge 1873 et Storm* : C' (*i.e.* et) etinis *A* : ecinis *Munch in textu* : echinis *Munch in app.* | II 1 XXII *Storm* : XXX *A* | 2 Rygiarbit *Munch* : rygiarbitot *A* | extenditur *Storm* : extendit *A* | 3 complectens *Bugge et Storm* (*cf. infra* III 2) : ĩplectens *A* | 5 stipites *Bugge 1873 et Storm* : stipentes *A* | abcisi *i.e.* abscisi |

paganism, that is, the Kirjalers and Kvens, the Horned Finns and the two kinds of Bjarms. [8]Yet we know nothing for sure about the races living beyond these. [9]Nevertheless, after some sailors had tried hard to voyage back from Iceland to Norway but had been buffeted by adverse gales into the Arctic sphere, they finally put in among Greenlanders and Bjarms, where, they claimed, they came upon people of extraordinary size, and a land of maidens, who are reputed to conceive when they have sipped water.

[10]Greenland however is separated from these areas by rocks covered with ice. [11]This country, discovered, settled and confirmed in the Catholic faith by Icelanders, marks the western boundary of Europe, and almost touches the islands off Africa, where the Ocean tides surge in. [12]Farther north beyond the Greenlanders, hunters have come across dwarves whom they call Skrælings. [13]If these creatures are struck with weapons and survive, their wounds grow white without bleeding, but if the blows are fatal the blood scarcely stops flowing. [14]They are totally without iron and employ walrus teeth as missiles, sharp stones as knives.

[15]So far I have shown the position and surroundings of Norway. [16]And now I want to describe its three populated areas.

II On the three inhabited zones of Norway

[1]The seaboard tract may be termed Decapolis, because it is renowned for its ten townships, and embraces four law provinces, which contain twenty-two counties. [2]The first law province in the east is called Viken and extends from the bounds of Denmark right to the place known as Rygjarbit; it contains four counties. [3]The second, Gulatingslag, brings us as far as the island of Mia, and comprises six counties, [4]of which the farthest, named Møre, includes a farm with astonishing properties: [5]all boughs and twigs that are cut from trees turn to stone,

musculi, si per unius anni spacium terre inhereant, in lapides conuertuntur. [6]Tercia patria Trondemia uocitatur. [7]Et est sinus ostio angustissimo, octo capiens prouincias in sua latissima receptacula, III etiam extra sumens, et fiunt XI. [8]Quarta Halogia, cuius incole multum Finnis cohabitant, et inter se commercia frequentant. [9]Que patria in aquilonem terminat Norwegiam iuxta locum Wegestaf, qui Biarmoniam ab ea dirimit.

[10]Ibi ille profundissimus Septemtrionalis Sinus, qui Caribdim, Scillam et ineuitabiles uoragines in se continet. [11]Ibi et promunctoria congelata, que immensas glacies fluctiuomis inundacionibus augmentatas brumalique frigore concretas in maria precipitant. [12]Quibus crebro institores Viridam Terram petentes inuiti applicant sicque naufragium passi periclitantur. [13]Ibi etiam cete grandia diuersi generis fortissimas naues confringentia, nautas diglutiunt, quosdam submergunt. [14]Ibi equini ceti monoculi iubis diffusis profunda pelagi sulcantes ferocissimi reperiuntur. [15]Illic pistrix, illic hafstrambus, maxima bellua, sed sine cauda et capite solum susum et iusum dissil-
2v iendo ueluti | truncus, non nisi nautarum pericula prefiguret, apparet. [16]Illic hafguua et haffkitta, pre cunctis marinis monstris maxima, et cetera huiuscemodi infinita reperiuntur.

[17]Reuertentes a maritimis transferamur ad montana.

III De montanis Norwegie

[1]Mediterranea zona a metis Gautonie excipitur. [2]Que item IIII patrias et XII prouincias complectens usque Trondemiam porrigitur. [3]Huius prima patria Regnum Raumorum ac Ringorum cum continuis prouinciis, secunda Thelamarchia cum remotis

7 etiam *Munch in app., Bugge 1873 et Storm* : etenim *A* | **9** Biarmoniam *Munch et Storm* : Bearmoniam *A* | **11** promunctoria *i.e.* promontoria *(cf. I 4 & XIII 6)* | **12** Viridam *A* : Viridem *Munch et Storm* | **13** etiam *Munch in app. et Storm* : etenim *A* | nautas *Munch et Storm* : nautos *A* | **15** hafstrambus *Munch et Storm* : hafftrābus *A* | bellua *i.e.* belua | susum et iusum *i.e.* sursum et deorsum | susum *Bugge 1873* : fusū *A* | **16** haffkitta *A* : hafkitta *Storm* | **III 3** Thelamarchia *Storm* : thelamathia *A* : Thelemarchia *Munch* |

if they happen to lie in contact with the ground for as much as a year. [6]The third law province is called Trøndelag; [7]here there is a fjord which has a very narrow entrance and envelops eight counties within its extensive arms, with another three outside its reach, making eleven in all. [8]The fourth is Hålogaland, whose inhabitants dwell a good deal with the Finns, so that there are frequent transactions between them; [9]this law province forms the northern boundary of Norway next to Vegestav, which separates it from Bjarmaland.

[10]Here to the north lies the very deep fjord which encloses within itself Charybdis, Scylla and inescapable whirlpools. [11]Here too are solid-frozen capes and these hurl into the seas gigantic blocks of ice, whose size is increased when they are deluged by the gushing waves, since they freeze together in the cold of winter. [12]Here traders making for Greenland often put in against their wishes and consequently undergo great danger after they suffer shipwreck. [13]For here live huge sea-beasts of various species, that will smash the stoutest vessels to smithereens and gulp down the crews; some of these they will drown. [14]One-eyed, very ferocious walruses are to be found here, cutting furrows through the ocean depths, with manes fanning out. [15]There, also, are the whale and the hafstramb, a gigantic creature but without tail or head, which merely springs upwards and downwards like a tree-trunk, and only appears in order to predict perils for sailors. [16]There, too, one may discover the hafguva and the hafkitta, the very largest of marine monsters, and all the countless others of their kind.

[17]Now let us return from the seaboard and cross over to the mountains.

III On the mountain region of Norway

[1]The inland area begins at the frontiers of Götaland; [2]it likewise incorporates four law provinces and twelve counties, and extends as far as Trøndelag. [3]Its first law province comprises Romerike, Ringerike and the adjoining counties; the second

ruribus, tercia Heidmarchia cum Conuallibus Albie, quarta Valles Gudbrandi cum Loariis et finitimis prouinciis. [4]Illam terminat magnus Mons Doffrarum. [5]Sunt preterea perplures incolatus inter maritima et montana, ut Waldresia et Vallis Haddingorum ac ceteri, qui Gulaticis subiacent legibus. [6]Est fluuius in montanis aureis rubens arenis, qui de illo magno stagno Miorso surgens mare Orientalis Sinus intrat. [7]Nam quondam Saxones illo aduentantes et per ungulas boum eundem amnem transnatancium auri metallum inesse deprehendentes furtim conflatum infinitum detulerunt aurum. [8]Est item iuxta ciuitatem Asloiam magna copia argenti metalli, que nunc nimia aquarum fluencia hominibus uetita sub petrina mole latet absconsa.

[9]Peragratis montanis siluas Finnorum ingrediamur perscrutatum.

IV De Finnis

[1]Est igitur uastissima solitudo affinis Norwegie diuidens eam per longum a paganis gentibus. [2]Que solummodo Finnis et bestiis incolitur, quarum carnibus semicrudis uescuntur et pellibus induuntur. [3]Sunt equidem uenatores peritissimi, soliuagi et instabiles, tugurea corticea pro domibus insidentes, que humeris inponentes leuigatis asseribus pedibus subfixis, quod instrumentum 'ondros' appellant, et per condensa niuium ac
3r deuexa | moncium agitantibus ceruis cum coniugibus et paruulis aue uelocius transferuntur. [4]Est enim illorum incerta mansio, prout copia ferarum tempore instante eis dictauerit uenationis loca.

[5]Ibi infinita numerositas bestiarum, scilicet ursorum, luporum, lyncorum, uulpium, sabelorum, lutrearum, taxonum,

ruribus : ru ruribus *A* | Heidmarchia *Munch et Storm* : herdmarthia *A* | 4 Doffrarum *A* : Dofrarum *Storm* | 7 perplures : per plures *A* | 8 Asloiam *Munch in app. et Storm* : Elsioiam *A* | **IV** 3 corticea *A* : coriacea *Bugge* | ceruis *Munch in app.* : teruis *uel* ternis *A* | 5 lyncorum *A* : lyncum *Storm* | sabelorum *Storm* : Sabulorum *A* | lutrearum *A* : lutrarum *Ekrem* |

Telemark and the far-flung country parishes; the third Hedmark with Alvdalene; the fourth Gudbrandsdalen with Lom and its neighbouring counties. [4]It is bounded by the great Dovrefjell range. [5]Apart from those there are a large number of inhabited parts between the seaboard and the mountains, such as Valdres, Hallingdal and the other settlements which are subject to Gulatingslag. [6]There is a river in the mountains which bears a reddish tinge on account of its gold-bearing sands; it rises from the great lake, Mjøsa, and flows into the sea at Viken. [7]On one occasion Saxons arrived there, and realizing that it contained gold ore because this stuck in the hooves of their cattle as they swam across its stream, they stealthily melted down an immense quantity of the metal and carried it off. [8]Moreover, not far from the city of Oslo there lies an abundance of silver ore, which lurks hidden beneath a mass of rock, but at present men are barred from obtaining it owing to the water's violent current.

[9]Having wandered across the mountains, let us enter and explore Finnmarken.

IV On the Finns

[1]On the borders of Norway is an immense wilderness, which divides the country along all its length and separates the Norwegians from the heathens. [2]Only Finns dwell here and wild animals whose flesh they eat half-raw and whose skins they clothe themselves with. [3]They are truly the most skilful of huntsmen, patrolling alone and always on the move; for homes they occupy leather tents, which they carry on their shoulders; with smooth planks fastened beneath their feet, implements which they call 'ondrar', swifter than birds they are conveyed with their wives and little ones, swept forward by their reindeer across the packed snow and down the mountain slopes. [4]For they have no fixed abode, inasmuch as the supply of wild beasts dictates their hunting-grounds at any one time.

[5]In that region there live vast numbers of animals, including bears, wolves, lynxes, foxes, sables, otters, badgers and bea-

castorum. [6]Que bestia mirabiliter cauta: dum sepius a ueltribus uenatorum petatur, tres subterraneas ad aquas sibi foueas concauat. [7]Succrescente limpha mediam siue supremam tenet, decrescente uero canibusque aduentantibus, seruulo catellis obiecto secus fenestram relicto, se quasi domum cum coniuge et catulis in infimum confert latibulum, unde sibi ad aquas liberior pateat aditus. [8]Plus enim in lymphaticis quam in terrestribus confidit meatibus. [9]Dum uero pro hiemalibus alimoniis congregandis plus insudauerint ulmos pregrandes dentibus circumcidentes, cuius arboris subere libentissime uescuntur, seruulo suo suppino anterioribus pedibus fustem tenenti superponunt, sicque illo pro uectigale utentes magnam copiam domum contrahunt, ipsi fustem rectibus capientes utrimque baiulum trahendo amminiculantur. [10]Est enim quoddam castorum genus seruile minimi pretii et ob frequentem laboris usum haut pilosum, immo leue.

[11]Sunt eciam apud Finnos scuriones quam plures ac mustele. [12]De quarum omnium bestiarum pellibus regibus Norwegie, quibus et subiecti sunt, maxima tributa omni anno persoluunt.

[13]Horum itaque intollerabilis perfidia uix cuiquam credibilis uidebitur, quantumue diabolice supersticionis in magica arte excerceant. [14]Sunt namque quidam ex ipsis, qui quasi prophete a stolido uulgo uenerantur, quoniam per immundum spiritum, quem 'gandum' uocitant, multis multa presagia, ut eueniunt, quandoque percunctati predicent. [15]Et de longinquis prouinciis res concupiscibiles miro modo sibi alliciunt, nec non absconditos thesauros longe remoti mirifice produnt.

7 tenet *Storm* : teneat *A* | aduentantibus *Bugge 1873 et Storm in notis* : addentatibus *A* | catellis *ex* c catellis *corr. A* | in infimum *Munch in app. et Storm* : inî simũ *A* | sibi *Munch* : si *A* | **8** lymphaticis *Bugge* : lymphatis *A* | **9** suppino *i.e.* supino | superponunt *Munch* : supponunt *A* | illo *Munch* : illi *A* | rectibus *i.e.* rictibus | **10** quoddam *supra lineam addidit A* | castorum *Munch* : castrorum *A* | minimi *Storm* : nimii *A* | **13** Horum *Munch* : harum *A* | quantumue *Bugge* : quantam ue/ne *A* : quantam ui *Munch* | **14** gandum *Storm* : gandium *Munch* : gaudiũ *uel* gandiũ *A* | **15** produnt *Bugge 1873 et Storm* : prodeunt *A* |

vers. [6]This last creature is astonishingly wary and because it is often pursued by hunters with their hounds, it digs itself three undergound tunnels leading to the water. [7]As the water rises it keeps to the middle or the upper one, but as the level subsides and the dogs get near, it sets a slave at one entrance, leaving it to confront the pack, while it seeks the lowest lurking-place with its female and pups as if this were its home, since from that point there lies easier access to the water. [8]It puts more trust in paths through the water than through the earth. [9]When the beavers have sweated a good deal gathering their winter provisions, they saw round lofty elms with their teeth (they are particularly fond of chewing the bark of this tree), and load the wood on to one of their slaves, who lies on his back holding a log between his forepaws; in this way, using him as a cart, they drag home a large stack of timber, for by gripping the log with their jaws on each side, they help to drag their porter along. [10]You see, there is a certain menial type of beaver, very poorly valued, whose fur is worn quite threadbare through the incessant repetition of this drudgery.

[11]In Finnmarken there are also very large numbers of squirrels and ermines. [12]From all these animals' pelts the people pay a large tribute every year to the Norwegian kings, who are their overlords.

[13]A person will scarcely believe their unendurable impiety and the extent to which they practise heathen devilry in their magic arts. [14]There are some who are worshipped by the ignorant masses as though they were prophets, since, whenever questioned, they will give many predictions to many folk through the medium of a foul spirit which they call gand, and these auguries come true. [15]Furthermore they attract to themselves desirable objects from distant parts in an astounding fashion and miraculously reveal hidden treasures, even though they are situated a vast distance away.

[16]Quadam uero uice dum christiani causa commercii apud Finnos ad mensam sedissent, illorum hospita subito inclinata
3v expirauit. [17]Vnde christianis multum | dolentibus non mortuam, sed a gandis emulorum esse depredatam, sese illam cito adepturos ipsi Finni nichil contristati respondent. [18]Tunc quidam magus extenso panno, sub quo se ad profanas ueneficas incantaciones prepararet, quoddam uasculum ad modum taratantarorum sursum erectis manibus extulit, cetinis atque ceruinis formulis cum loris et ondriolis nauicula eciam cum remis occupatum, quibus uehiculis per alta niuium et deuexa moncium uel profunda stagnorum ille diabolicus gandus uteretur. [19]Cumque diutissime incantando tali apparatu ibi saltasset, humo tandem prostratus totus niger ut ethiops, spumans ora ut puta freneticus, preruptus uentrem uix aliquando cum maximo ⟨fremore⟩ emisit spiritum. [20]Tum alterum in magica arte peritissimum consuluerunt, quid de utrisque actum sit. [21]Qui simili modo, sed non eodem euentu suum implens officium — namque hospita sana surrexit — et defunctum magum tali euentu interisse eis intimauit: [22]Gandum uidelicet eius in cetinam effigiem inmaginatum ostico gando in preacutas sudes transformato, dum per quoddam stagnum uelocissime prosiliret, malo omine obuiasse, quia in stagni eiusdem profundo sudes latitantes exacti uentrem perforabant. [23]Quod et in mago domi mortuo apparuit.

[24]† Item dum Finni unacum christianis gregem squamigeram hamo carpere attemptassent, quos in casis fidelium pagani perspexerant, sacculis fere plenis unco suo de abysso attractis scapham cum piscibus impleuerunt. †

16 inclinata *Munch et Storm* : inclita *A* | **18** sub *A et Tolley 1994 136 & 141* : super *Storm* | profanas *Storm* : profundas *A* | prepararet *Bugge 1873 et Skard* : preparet *A et Ekrem* : praeparat *Storm* | taratantarorum *Storm* : caratantatorum *A* | **19** fremore *Storm et Skard* : clamore *Munch in app.* | **20** alterum *Munch* : altrū *A* | **21** implens *A et Skard* : impleuit *Munch et Storm* | **22** gandum *Storm* : gandium *Munch* : gaudiū *uel* gandiū *A* | ostico (*i.e.* hostico) *Bugge 1873 et Storm* : ostio *A* : *forte corrigendum in* hostili *Munch in app.* | homine *in* omine *corr. A* | stagni *Bugge 1873* : stagno *A* | **24** Item – impleuerunt *cruces posuit Mortensen* | unacum *i.e.* una cum | fere *Bugge* : ferre *A* : ferro *Munch* |

[16]Once, when Christians who had come to trade had sat down at table with some Finns, their hostess fell forward all of a sudden and expired. [17]While the Christians felt serious grief at this calamity, the Finns were not in the least saddened, but told them that the woman was not dead, merely pillaged by the gands of her adversaries, and that they could quickly restore her. [18]Then a magician, spreading out a cloth under which he might prepare himself for intoning unholy sorcerer's spells, raised aloft in his outstretched hands a small vessel similar to a riddle, decorated with tiny figures of whales, harnessed reindeer, skis, and even a miniature boat with oars; using these means of transport the demonic spirit was able to travel across tall snowdrifts, mountain-sides and deep lakes. [19]After chanting incantations for a very long time and leaping about there with this paraphernalia, he finally threw himself to the ground, black all over like a negro and foaming at the mouth as if he were mad; ripped across his stomach, with a mighty roar he eventually relinquished his life. [20]Next they consulted another specialist in the magic arts as to what had happened in each case. [21]This individual went through all his practices in similar fashion, though with a different outcome: the hostess arose in sound health and then he revealed to them that the sorcerer had died in the following way: [22]his gand, having taken on the likeness of a whale, was shooting rapidly through a lake when it had the misfortune to encounter a hostile gand, which had transformed itself into sharply pointed stakes; these stakes, hidden in the depths of the lake, penetrated the repulsed creature's belly, [23]and this was also manifested by the death of the magician in the house.

[24]Again, when the Finns, together with the Christians, had gone about catching by hook a flock of fish such as these heathens had seen in Christian dwellings, they drew almost full traps out of the deeps with their wand, and so loaded the boats to capacity.

[25]Hec de Finnorum innumeris prestigiis carptim excerpsi et quasi quasdam notulas tam prophane secte plus remotis proposui.

[26]Circumscriptis utcunque Norwegie finibus tendamus ad tributarias insulas, nam insulas, que adiacent Norwegie, pre multitudine nemo numerare potest.

V De tributariis insulis

4r [1]⟨S⟩unt ergo quedam insule preiacentes Gulacie, que ab | incolis Solunde nominantur, unde Solundicum Mare dictum, quod inter Norwegiam et Iberniam fluit. [2]In quo sunt Orchades insule numero plusquam XXX, a quodam comite Orchano nomine uocate. [3]Que quidem diuersis incolis accułte nunc in duo regna sunt diuise: Sunt enim Merediane Insule regulis sublimate, Brumales uero comitum presidio decorate, qui utrique regibus Norwegie non modica persoluunt tributa.

VI De Orcadibus Insulis

[1]Istas insulas primitus Peti et Pape inhabitabant. [2]Horum alteri, scilicet Peti, paruo superantes pigmeos statura in structuris urbium uespere et mane mira operantes, meredie uero cunctis uiribus prosus destituti in subterraneis domunculis pre timore latuerunt. [3]Sed eo tempore non Orchades, ymmo Terra Petorum dicebantur, unde adhuc Petlandicum Mare ab incolis appellatur, quod seiungit insulas a Scotia, ubi omnium maxima uorago, que fortissimas naues per ledonem attrahendo deglutit, earundem fragmenta per malenam eructando euomit. [4]Qui populus unde illuc aduentasset, penitus ignoramus. [5]Pape uero propter albas, quibus ut clerici induebantur, uocati sunt, unde in Theutonica lingua omnes clerici 'pape' dicuntur. [6]Adhuc

V 1 Sunt *rubrica* S *non impleta* | 3 sublimate : sublimatae *Munch in notis* : sullimate *A* | in structuris *Munch et Laing.* : instructuris *A* | VI 1 prosus *i.e.* prorsus | 3 adhuc *Munch* : id huc *A* | seiungit : se iungit *A* | per ledonem attrahendo diglutit *Kraggerud* : quas per ledonem attrahendo diglutit *A et Storm* : aquas per ledonem attrahendo diglutit *Ekrem* | 5 albas *A* : albas ⟨uestes⟩ *Munch et Laing* |

[25]I have selected these random samples from the Finns' countless illusions and put down, as it were, brief notes concerning this unholy band for the benefit of those who live farther away.

[26]Now that I have defined the frontiers of Norway in one way or another, let me pass over to the islands that are subject to tribute, for those islands which lie in the vicinity of Norway cannot be counted because of their vast number.

V On the tributary islands

[1]Certain islands lying close to Gulatingslag are called by their inhabitants the Solund Islands, from which the sea that flows between Norway and Ireland is known as the Solund Sea. [2]In these waters are situated the Orkney Islands, totalling over thirty and named after a particular Earl Orkan. [3]They are populated by different peoples and now split into two domains; the southern isles have been elevated by petty kings, the northern graced by the protection of earls, both of whom pay no mean tribute to the kings of Norway.

VI On the Orkney Islands

[1]Originally those islands were inhabited by Pents and Papes. [2]One of these races, the Pents, only a little taller than pygmies, accomplished miraculous achievements by building towns, morning and evening, but at midday every ounce of strength deserted them and they hid for fear in underground chambers. [3]At that period these islands were not called the Orkneys but rather Pentland, so that the sea which separates the islands from Scotland is still known by the natives as the Pentland Firth; here is the most gigantic of all whirlpools, which draws in and swallows the stoutest vessels at ebb-tide, and at high-tide spews up and disgorges their wreckage. [4]Of the place where these Pents came from, we know nothing at all. [5]The Papes were so called on account of the vestments in which they clothed themselves like priests, and for this reason all priests are

quedam insula Papey ab illis denominatur. [7]Sed ut per habitum et apices librorum eorum ibidem derelictorum notatur, Affricani fuerunt iudaismo adherentes.

[8]Istas itaque naciones in diebus Haraldi Comati, regis uidelicet Norwegie, quidam pirate, prosapia robustissimi principis Rogwaldi progressi, cum magna classe Solundicum Mare transfretantes de diuturnis sedibus exutas ex toto deleuerunt ac insulas sibi subdiderunt. [9]Vbi securius hiemalibus sedibus
4v muniti, estiuo tempore tum in Anglos, tum in Scotos, | quandoque in Hibernios suam excercentes tyrannidem ierunt, ut de Anglia Northimbriam, de Scotia Kathanasiam, de Hybernia Diflinniam ceterasque maritimas urbes suo imperio subiugarent. [10]De quorum collegio quidam Rodulfus — a sociis Gongurolfr cognominatus quia ob enormem corporis quantitatem equitare nequiens semper incessit — Rodam ciuitatem Normandie cum paucis mirabili ingenio deuicit. [11]Namque in quodam flumine cum XV nauibus latitantes singuli quique naute singulas precauantes fossas, tenuis glebis campi spissitudinis identitatem simulantibus, ordinata acie ultra loci concaua parati ad pugnam progressi sunt. [12]Quo comperto ciues directis ordinibus hostes insecuntur. [13]At illi ficta fuga quasi ad naues festinantes, equites cunctis uelocius se subsequentes ac cateruatim in latencia precipicia cum loricatis sonipedibus proruentes, illi, inquam, Norwagenses tyranni funesta manu eos trucidabant. [14]Itaque fugatis ciuibus urbem libere intrabant simulque cum ea omnem illam regionem obtinebant. [15]A quibus Normandie nomen adepta est.

[16]Ast idem Rodulfus regni primatu potitus defuncti comitis uxorem duxit. [17]Ex qua genuit Willelmum cognomento Lon-

7 ut *Bugge 1873 et Storm* : nec *A* | **8** Rogwaldi *A et Munch* : Rognwaldi *Laing et Storm* | **9** ierunt *Bugge* : uerum *A* : iuerunt *Bugge 1873* | **11** tenuis *A* : tenuibus *Bugge 1873 et Storm* | ordinata *Munch* : ordina *A* | **13** Norwagenses *A* : Norwegenses *Storm* | **17** Willelmum *Munch* : Wilelmum *Storm* : Willm̄ *A* |

known as papen in the German tongue. [6]One of the islands is still named Papey from them. [7]However, as the appearance and letter-forms of the books they left there behind them testify, they were from Africa and clove to the Jewish faith.

[8]In the days of Harald Fairhair, king of Norway, certain vikings, descended from the stock of that sturdiest of men, Ragnvald jarl, crossing the Solund Sea with a large fleet, totally destroyed these peoples after stripping them of their long-established dwellings and made the islands subject to themselves. [9]When they had gained safety and security by building winter residences, they went off in summer on pirating expeditions against the English and the Scots, and occasionally on the Irish; the result was that in England they brought Northumbria, in Scotland Caithness, and in Ireland Dublin and all the other coastal towns under their domination. [10]One of this band, Rolf — known to his comrades as Gongu-Rolf, because he was unable to ride on horseback owing to his enormous physical size and therefore always walked — captured the city of Rouen in Normandy, aided by a few followers, with a wonderful device. [11]While their fifteen ships lurked on a river, each individual sailor dug out a ditch in advance and with a thin layer of turves made it look exactly level with the plain; afterwards they prepared for battle by drawing up their line beyond the hollowed-out strips and then marched forward. [12]As soon as they perceived this, the inhabitants pressed upon their enemy in ordered ranks. [13]But the latter, feigning flight, pretended to rush back to the ships; the horsemen, pursuing them more rapidly than the rest, crashed in droves with their armoured steeds down into the concealed drops, and these men, I mean the Norwegian vikings, butchered them with deadly hands. [14]And so, once the townsfolk had been routed, their foes entered the city without resistance and along with it gained that entire region, [15]which took from them its name of Normandy.

[16]Now this Rolf, after acquiring control of that domain, married the widow of its deceased count. [17]By her he sired

gosped, patrem Ricardi, qui item filium genuit sibi equiuocum. [18]Iunior uero Ricardus ⟨habuit filium Robertum, qui⟩ pater erat Wilelmi Bastardi, qui Anglos deuicit. [19]Iste genuit Willelmum Rufum et Henricum fratrem eius, qui in prophetia Merlini regis 'leo iusticie' prenominatus est. [20]Radulfus uero comes Normandie effectus hostili manu Fresones inuasit, uictoriam optinuit, sed paruo interuallo a priuigno suo in Hollandia dolo interemptus est. [21]Interim socii eius in Orchadibus suum regnum firmiter stabilierunt, reuera enim usque hodie illorum posteritatis dominio subiacent, excepto quod iure tri-
5r butario regibus Norwegie deseruiunt. |

VII De Insulis Ouium

[1]Sunt item in refluentis occeani Insule Ouium numero ⟨XVIII⟩, quas propria lingua Fereyiar incole appellant. [2]Ibi enim ruricolis opimus grex affluit; sunt quibusdam inde milia ouium. [3]Qui item insulani regibus nostris certis temporibus tributa persoluunt.

VIII De Glaciali Insula

[1]Deinde uersus occasum illa magna insula, que ab Italis 'ultima Tile' dicta est, nunc quam magna frequencia colonum culta, quondam uasta solitudo et usque ad tempus Haraldi Comati hominibus incognita. [2]Tunc quidam Norwagenses Ingwar et Hiorleifr ob reatus homicidiorum patriam fugentes cum con-

18 Iunior uero Ricardus habuit filium Robertum, qui *uel sim. proposuit Storm* : Iunior uero Ricardus *A* | **19** Willelmum *Munch* : Wilelmum *Storm* : Willm̄ *A* | **20** Radulfus *A* : Rodulfus *Munch, Laing et Storm* | optinuit *fortasse* impetrauit *Bugge 1873* : ı͛ᷤptinuit *A* (*i.e.* 'impretinuit') : impertiuit *Laing* | Hollandia *Munch* : hollindia *A* | **21** posteritatis *A1 et Munch* : posteritates *A* | dominio *A* : dominio nullo *add. Laing* (!) | regibus Norwegie *A* : Norwegie regibus *A1* | **VII 1** Sunt *rubrica* S *non impleta, sed in margine indicata* | XVIII *add. Munch in notis et Storm* | propria *Bugge 1873* : prima *A* : patria *Munch in app. et Storm* | Fereyiar *Ekrem* : farcar' *A* : Fareyiar *Munch* : Faereyar *Storm* | **VIII 1** Deinde *rubrica* D *non impleta, sed in margine indicata* | Italis *Storm* : Ital' *A* : Italicis *Munch* | ultima *Storm* : ultimum *A* | **2** Ingwar *A* : Ingulfr *Storm* : Ingólfr *Munch in notis* | Hiorleifr *Munch et Storm* : brorleifr *A* | fugentes *A* : fugientes *Munch* |

William Longsword, father of Richard, who in turn produced a son of the same name. [18]This younger Richard had a son, Robert, who was father to William the Bastard, conqueror of England. [19]From him were born William Rufus and his brother Henry, who in the prophecy of royal Merlin was named 'the Lion of Justice'. [20]Rolf, once he had been created count of Normandy, made a hostile attack on the Frisians and won victory over them, but shortly afterwards was treacherously murdered by his step-son in Holland. [21]Meanwhile his associates firmly established their realm in the Orkneys, which in fact remain up to this moment under the lordship of their descendants, with the proviso that they are bound to pay tribute to the Norwegian kings.

VII On the Islands of Sheep

[1]Again, amid the surging ocean there lie the Islands of Sheep, eighteen of them, which in their mother tongue the inhabitants call Færeyjar (the Faeroes), [2]for the peasants there have a rich, abundant flock, and some of them own thousands of sheep. [3]As before, these islanders pay tribute to our kings at set times.

VIII On the Island of Ice

[1]Still farther west is situated that large island called by the Romans Ultima Thule, which today is inhabited by a great host of settlers, but which was once a vast wilderness and unknown to mankind right up to the days of Harald Fairhair. [2]Then two Norwegians, Yngvar and Hjorleiv, fleeing their homeland because they had been accused of murders, took ship with their

iugibus et pueris naues ingredientes insulam, prius inuentam a Gardaro post ab Oddo, inquirendo per pendulas pelagi undas tandem reperierunt. [3]Et in quinquaginta fere annis ubique inhabitata, ut nunc est distributa. [4]Que a Norwagensibus igitur Islandia, quod interpretatur 'glaciei terra', nuncupatur. [5]Habet namque eadem insula innumerabiles montes, uerum continua glacie contectos, unde illis resplendentibus naute longe a terra in salo positi portum sibi oportunum per hos denotare solent. [6]Inter quos Mons Casule ad instar Ethne totus pruriens terrebili tremefactus terre motu sulphureas eructat faces. [7]Proinde in diuersis locis feruidi fonticuli ebulliunt, qui tectis operti ac frigidarum exhibicione aquarum temperati, balnealia accolis prebent lauacra. [8]Sunt item quidam putei eiusdem insule, in quis si lana aut pannus unius noctis spacio inmersi iaceant, in lapides conuertentur. [9]Est preterea ibidem fons quidam in arenatis cuiusdam fluuii anfractibus scaturiens saporem colo-
5v remque tenens ceruisie, qui potantem reficere, uix adimplere | dicitur.

[10]Nec pretereundum puto, quod nostra etate inibi accidisse ferunt. [11]Nam tria miliaria totum mare more euripi inestuare ac quasi cacabus feruere cepit, dum terra adhiscens ab imo igniuomos uapores montem⟨que⟩ magnum undis emergentem ex se produxit. [12]Quod multis monstris simile uidetur, mundumue mira portendere uel sui interitum in talibus prefigurare con-

Gardaro *Munch in notis et Storm* : giardàro (*i.e. fortasse* giardraro) *A* | ab Oddo *Storm in notis* : ab anbă *uel* aubă *A* : ab anbă *Storm in textu* : *fortasse* ab Auda *uel* ambo *Storm in notis* : a Flokone *Munch in notis* : ambo *Bugge* : *fortasse* ab altero | undas *Munch* : undis *A* | **3** ubique *Ekrem* : utrobique *A* : est ubique *Storm* | distributa *A* : ista insula *Bugge* | **4** Norwagensibus *Munch* : Norwegensibus *Storm* : Norwagensis *A* | igitur *Bugge 1873 et Storm* : dicitur *A* | **5** positi *Munch et Storm* : posite *A* | oportunum *i.e.* opportunum | **6** terre motu : terrae motu *Storm* : terremotu *A* | **7** operti *Bugge 1873 et Storm* : aperti *A* | **8** conuertentur *A* : conuertuntur *Storm* | **9** anfractibus *Munch in app. et Storm* : in fractibus *A* | **11** Eurippi *i.e.* Euripi | montemque *Storm* : montem *A* | **12** monstris *A* : monstrum *Bugge 1873* : monstri *Storm* | simile *Storm* : silē *A* : silere *Munch* : scilicet *Bugge 1873* | mundumue *Storm* : mundum ue *uel* ne *A* : mundum ne *Munch* : mundumque *Bugge 1873* | portendere *Munch* : protendere *A* |

wives and children and through pitching ocean waves sought the island, earlier discovered by Gardar and afterwards by Odd, till at long last they found it. [3]Within about fifty years every district was populated, in accordance with the present distribution. [4]So, it was given the name Iceland by the Norwegians, which means the Land of Ice. [5]For the island contains innumerable mountains overlaid with unmelting glaciers, so that mariners at sea, far distant from land, can perceive them glittering, and customarily take note of a convenient harbour, using them as seamarks. [6]Among these fells rises Mount Hekla, whose whole surface twitches like Etna and when it has shaken with a horrifying earth tremor, it belches up sulphurous fireballs. [7]Hence, at various points hot springs gush out, which, after being covered with roofs and tempered by supplies of cold water, provide the inhabitants with facilities for bathing. [8]Again, if wool or cloth should lie steeped in certain wells on this island for a single night, they will turn to stone. [9]There also spouts up there from the sands of a winding river a fountain with the taste and colour of beer, which is reckoned to reinvigorate the drinker, even if he does not take his complete fill of it.

[10]Furthermore I think it wrong to omit mention of an event which they say happened there in our own time: [11]for an extent of three miles the whole sea began to churn like rapids and boil as if it were a cauldron, while the ground at the bottom yawned, emitting fire and fumes, till a huge mountain rose up out of the waves. [12]Many liken this to portents and guess that the world is either predicting marvels to come or by such signs

iectant, cum elementa ineuitabiles accessus et naturales sua sponte excercent motus. [13]Dixit namque Solinus in libro suo, quem de mundi mirabilibus scripsit, abyssum profundissimam in ipsa terra existere (unde scriptum est: "Rupti sunt fontes abyssi magne"); iuxta quam speluncas propatulas uentos aquatica spiracione conceptos in se continere, qui sunt spiritus procellarum. [14]Hii uero uenti sua spiracione per occultos terre meatus aquas maris ad se contrahunt et in thesauros abissi recondunt, quas iterum eadem ui a se repellunt, unde estus et torrentes uoraginumque uertigines excitantur. [15]Inde eciam terre motus et uarie uaporum exustionumque emissiones contingunt. [16]Quidam uentorum enim flatus terrenis buccis inclusi dum erumpere gliscunt, terre molem horribili fremore conquassant eamque trepidare cogunt. [17]Sic nimirum spiritu uentorum introrsum cum ⟨igne⟩ concertante et eciam in medio pelago prerupto profundo fumigeri uapores sulphureique ignes emergi cernuntur. [18]Simili modo quod in terra tremor, in nube tonitruum, hic hiatus, ibi fulgur creditur.

[19]Ista quidem et maiora mundi mirabilia licet minime perspicaciter intelligamus, tamen nec eo magis monstra credenda sunt nec portenta mundialis cataclismi presaga reputanda, ymmo omnium incognitorum Cognitori, immutabili mutabilium Conditori quodam mirabili processu preclare famulancia in cunctis naturam obseruant. [20]Verum quoniam corpulente ca-
6r liginis obliuione nostri ingenioli igniculus | undique circumfusus ad inuestiganda altissima profunda haut satis efficax deprehenditur, ipsum, qui illuminat abscondita tenebrarum spiritu intelligencie, nos ut inflammet, inuocemus.

sua sponte *Ekrem* : suapte *A* : suopte *Munch in app. et Bugge 1873* : suapte sponte *Storm* | motus *A* : motu *Munch in app. et Bugge 1873* | **13** existere *ex* existere exist *corr. A* | **17** cum igne concertante *Storm* : cum cretante *A* : concretante *Bugge 1873* | **19** mirabilia *Bugge 1873 et Storm* : mutabilia *A* | portenta *Munch et Storm* : portanda *A* | quodam *Munch* : quoddam *A* | **20** corpulente : corpulentae *Munch et Storm* : copulente *A* | ingenioli *Munch* : ingeluoli *A* | haut : hauc *A* |

foreshowing its own destruction, though cosmic forces cause unavoidable rifts and natural upheavals of their own volition. [13]For in his book on the wonders of the universe Solinus has said that there is a vast, yawning pit in the earth itself (whence it is written: "the fountains of the great deep were broken up"); that by the side of this, unobstructed hollows contain winds engendered by watery exhalations, and these form the breath of storms. [14]Such winds, blowing through the hidden corridors of the earth, draw the sea's waters to them and bury them in the storehouses of the abyss; by the same energy the winds drive the waters back again, and from these are born tidal waves, floods and spinning whirlpools. [15]Thence too earthquakes occur and the discharge of vapours and flames of various kinds. [16]For when certain gusts of wind, trapped inside the earth's maw, are eager to burst out, with a hideous roar they severely shake its great structure and cause it to tremble. [17]Without doubt when these internal gales blow like this and contend with fire, and when the depths are torn up in mid-ocean, one sees smoky emanations and sulphurous blazes emerge. [18]In the same way as a tremor takes place in the earth, so does thunder in the clouds; a chasm in the one is thought to correspond to a flash of lightning in the other.

[19]Though we people have little close understanding of these and greater marvels in the universe, that is no more reason to think them omens, nor to regard them as warnings which presage a world cataclysm; indeed in their amazing progress they are clearly subservient to the Comprehender of all things incomprehensible, the unchanging Creator of all things changeful, and comply with Nature in all respects. [20]Yet since the spark of our small intellect is enveloped on every side by the oblivion of corporeal darkness and so does not find itself sufficiently capable of penetrating the deepest regions, let us call upon Him who lights the shadowy recesses with the spirit of reason, to kindle it into a flame.

[21]Hactenus tributarias insulas carptim descripsimus. [22]Nunc uero, qui reges Norwegiam rexerunt uel unde processerunt, ad exponendum stilum uertamus.

IX De ortu regum

[1]Vetus prosapia regum Norwegie a Swethia sumpsit exordium, unde eciam inhabitata est Trondemia, que patria principalis est in Norwegia. [2]Rex itaque Ingui, quem primum Swethie monarchiam rexisse plurimi astruunt, genuit Neorth. [3]Qui uero genuit Froy. [4]Hos ambos tota illorum posteritas per longa secula ut deos uenerati sunt. [5]Froyr uero genuit Fiolni, qui in dolio medonis dimersus est. [6]Cuius filius Swegthir nanum in petram persequitur nec redisse dicitur, quod pro certo fabulosum creditur. [7]Iste genuit Wanlanda, qui in sompno a demone suffocatus interiit. [8]Quod genus demoniorum Norwaico sermone 'mara' uocatur. [9]Hic genuit Wisbur, quem filii sui cum omni curia sua, ut cicius hereditarentur, uiuum incenderunt. [10]Cuius filium Domald Sweones suspendentes pro fertilitate frugum Cereri hostiam obtulerunt. [11]Iste genuit Domar, qui in Swecia obiit. [12]Huius filius Dyggui item in eadem regione uite metam inuenit. [13]Cui successit in regnum filius eius Dagr, quem Dani in quodam uado, quod Sciotanuath dicitur, dum

21 Hactenus *rubrica* H *non impleta, sed in margine indicata* | **IX** De *rubrica* D *non impleta, sed in margine indicata* | **2** *Hic BC ineunt* | itaque *AB* : *om. C* | Ingui *A* : Ingo *B* : Inge *C* | primum *AC* : primam *B* | Neorth *A* : Neork *B* : Neroth *C* | **3** uero *A* : *om. BC* | genuit *AC* : genus *B* | Froy *AC* : stroy *B* | **4** per longa secula *A* : *om. BC* | **5** Froyr *C et Storm* : Froy *A* : stroyer *B* | medonis *BC, Munch et Storm* : medionis *A* | dimersus est *AC* : est dimersus *B* | **6** Swegthir *A et Storm* : swerchir *B* : swærkir *C* | nanum in petram persequitur nec redisse dicitur *A* : manum in petram proiciens non retraxisse dicitur *BC* : de quo arguitur fortis *add. C* | **7** Wanlanda *A* : Valanda *BC* | **8** demoniorum *A* : *om. BC* | Norwaico *A* : sweco *BC (!)* : Norwegico *Storm* | uocatur *A* : dicitur *BC* | **9** Wisbur *A* : uysbur *B* : uiisbyr *C* | hereditarentur *A* : hereditaretur *BC* | incenderunt *AB* : incenderunt ac familiam *C* | **10** filium *BC* : filius *A* | Domald *BC* : dōnald *A* | Sweones suspendentes *A* : sweui omnes *B* : sweci *C* | Cereri *AB* : dee Cereri *C* | **11** obiit *AB* : obiit morbo *C (hic C Latine finit) et Storm* | **12** Dyggui *Storm* : Dyggur *A* : Dyggr *Munch* : Digguir *B* | item *A* : *om. B* | uite metam inuenit *A* : uitam finiuit *B* | **13** in regnum filius eius *A* : filius eius in regem *B* | Dagr' *A* : Daghr *B* | Sciotanuath : scrotā uath *A* : stotamuadh uel wapnawadh *B* : Sciotanuath uel Wapnauath *Storm* |

[21]So far we have described the separate tributary islands. [22]Now we should certainly turn our pen to a representation of the monarchs who have ruled Norway and where they originated.

IX On the lineage of the kings.

[1]The ancient family of Norwegian kings traced its beginnings from Sweden, from which Trøndelag, the chief law province of Norway, was also settled. [2]King Yngve, who according to a great many was the first ruler of the Swedish realm, became the father of Njord, [3]whose son was Frøy. [4]For centuries on end all their descendants worshipped these last two as gods. [5]Frøy engendered Fjolne, who was drowned in a tun of mead. [6]His son, Sveigde, is supposed to have pursued a dwarf into a stone and never to have returned, but this is plainly to be taken as a fairy-tale. [7]He sired Vanlande, who died in his sleep, suffocated by a goblin, [8]one of the demonic species known in Norwegian as 'mare'. [9]He was the father of Visbur, whose sons burnt him alive with all his hirdsmen, so that they might attain their inheritance more swiftly. [10]His son Domalde was hanged by the Swedes as a sacrificial offering to Ceres to ensure the fruitfulness of the crops. [11]Domalde begot Domar, who died in Sweden. [12]Likewise Dyggve, his son, reached the limit of his life in that same region. [13]His son Dag succeeded to his throne; he was killed by the Danes in a royal battle at a ford named Skjotansvad, while he was trying to avenge the violence done

passeris iniurias uindicare conaretur, publico bello occiderunt. [14]Qui genuit Alrik. [15]Hunc frater suus Erikr freno percussit ad mortem. [16]Alricr autem genuit Agna. [17]Istum uxor sua iuxta locum Agnafit propriis manibus interfecit suspendendo ad arborem cum catena aurea. [18]Cuius filius Ingialdr in Swecia a fratre
6v suo ob infamiam uxoris | eius occisus est. [19]Que Bera dicta est (hoc nomen Latine sonat 'ursa'). [20]Post hunc filius eius Iorundr qui, cum Danos debellasset, ab eisdem suspensus in loco Oddasund in sinu quodam Dacie, quem Limafiorth indigene appellant, male uitam finiuit.

[21]Iste genuit Auchun, qui longo uetustatis senio IX annis ante obitum suum dense usum alimonie postponens lac tantum de cornu ut infans suxisse fertur. [22]Auchun uero genuit Eigil cognomento Vendilcraco. [23]Quem proprius seruus nomine Tonne regno priuauit, et cum domino pedissecus VIII ciuilia bella commisit, in omnibus uictoria potitus, in nono tandem deuictus occubuit. [24]Sed paulo post ipsum regem truculentus taurus confodiens trucidauit.

[25]Cui successit in regnum filius suus Ottarus, qui a suo equiuoco Ottaro, Danorum comite, et fratre eius Fasta ⟨in una⟩ prouinciarum Danie, scilicet Wendli, interemptus est. [26]Cuius filius Adils ante edem Diane, dum ydolorum sacrificia faceret,

passeris *B* : pasceris *A* | **15** Erikr *Storm* : Emkr̄ *A* : Erich *B* : Eriker *Munch* | **16** Alricr *Storm* : Alricr̄ *A* : Alrich *B* : Alrikr *Munch* | Agna *Storm in notis* : hogana (an *ligatae*) *A* : Ingimar *B* : Hogaia *Munch* : Hogna *Storm in textu* | **17** Agnafit *Munch* : agnasit *A* : Agnasit qui nunc Stokholmr dicitur *B* : Agnafit qui nunc Stokholmr dicitur *Storm* | interfecit suspendendo ad arborem cum catena aurea *B et Storm* : interfecit *A* | **18** Ingialdr : ingialdr' *A* : ingialdir *B* | ob infamiam *B* : ab infamia *A* | eius *A* : *om. B* | **19** latine *A* : lat' *B* | ursa *A* : *om. B* | **20** Iorundr : iorundr' *A* : iorundir *B* | cum *A* : dum *B* | suspensus *A* : suspensus est *B* | Limafiorth *A* : Limofiordh *B* | indigene *A* : indigne *B* | **21** Auchun *Munch et Storm* : auchim *A*: haqon *B* | **22** Auchun *Munch et Storm* : Auchim *A* : aukun *B* | Eigil *A* : Eghil *B* | **23** pedissecus *i.e.* pedissequus | nono *A* : ix *B* | **24** Sed *A* : et *B* | **25** Ottarus *Storm* : occarius *A* : Ottarius *Munch in app.* : otharus *B* | Ottaro *Storm* : Occaro *A* : Otharo *B* | comite et fratre eius Fasta *B, Munch in app. et Storm* : comite *vac. spat. 4–8 litt. A* | in una *Storm* | interemptus *B, Munch et Storm* : int̓p̓tatus *i.e.* interpretatus *A* | **26** Cuius *A* : eius *B* | Adils *A* : Adhils uel Adhisl *B* : Adils uel Athisl *Storm* | faceret *Kraggerud* : fugeret *A* : fugat *B* : fungeretur, *fortasse* fungeret *Ekrem* |

to a sparrow. [14]This man engendered Alrek, [15]who was beaten to death with a bridle by his brother, Eirik. [16]Alrek was father to Agne, [17]whose wife dispatched him with her own hands by hanging him on a tree with a golden chain near a place called Agnafit. [18]His son, Ingjald, was murdered in Sweden by his own brother because he had brought discredit on the latter's wife, [19]whose name was Bera (Ursa in Latin). [20]After him his son Jorund ruled, who ended his days unhappily once he had fought a war against the Danes, who hanged him at Oddesund, on an arm of the sea in Denmark which the natives call Limfjorden.

[21]He became the father of Aukun, who, in the feebleness of a protracted old age, during the nine years before his death is said to have abandoned the consumption of solid food and only sucked milk from a horn, like a babe-in-arms. [22]Aukun's son was Egil Vendelkråke, [23]whose own bondman, Tunne, drove him from his kingdom; and though a mere servant he joined in eight civil combats with his master and won supremacy in all of them, but in a ninth he was finally defeated and killed. [24]Shortly afterwards however the monarch was gored and slaughtered by a ferocious bull.

[25]The successor to the throne was his son Ottar, who was assassinated in Vendel, a law province of Denmark, by his namesake, a Danish jarl, and this man's brother, Fasta. [26]His son Adils gave up the ghost after falling from his horse before the temple of Diana, while he was performing the sacrifices

equo lapsus expirauit. [27]Hic genuit Eustein, quem Gautones in domo quadam obtrusum cum suis uiuum incenderunt. [28]Huius filius Ynguar, qui cognominatus est Canutus, in expedicione occisus est in quadam insula Baltici Maris, que ab indigenis Eycisla uocatur. [29]Iste ergo genuit Broutonund, quem Siwardus frater eius occidit in Himinheithy, quod loci uocabulum interpretatur 'celi campus'. [30]Post istum filius suus Ingialdr in regnum sublimatur. [31]Qui ultra modum timens Iuarum cognomine Withfadm, regem tunc temporis multis formidabilem, se ipsum cum omni comitatu suo cenaculo inclusos igne cremauit. [32]Eius filius Olauus cognomento Tretelgia diu et pacifice functus regno plenus dierum obiit in Swethia.

X [1]Olauus genuit Halfdanum cognomine Hwitbein, quem de
Swethia uenientem Norwagenses in montanis sibi regem con-
7r stituerunt. [2]Hic prouectus etate in prouincia | Tothne reddidit
spiritum. [3]Huius filius Eustein cognomento Bumbus, dum inter duas insulas strictim in pluribus nauibus uelificassent, trabe alterius nauis e puppi percussus undisque submersus disparuit. [4]Huic successit in regnum filius suus Halfdan Auri Prodigus Cibique Tenacissimus: stipendarios namque suos auro donauit eosdemque fame macerauit. [5]Hic genuit Guthrodum Regem

27 Eustein *A* : Eysten *B* | Gautones *A* : goutones *B* | obtrusum *A* : obstrusum *B* | uiuum incenderunt *A* : incenderunt uiuum *B* | **28** Ynguar : Ynguar' *A* | Canutus *Bugge 1873 et Gjessing* : canawtus *A* : kanutus *B* | cogmonimatus est canawtus *A* : kanutus cognominatus est *B* | Eycisla : Eysisla *Munch in notis et Storm* : eycilla *A* : Øsyliae *B* | **29** Broutonund *Munch et Storm* : broutonnud *A* : brætomūd *B* | Siwardus : Sigwardus *B et Storm* : Swardus *A* | eius *A* : suus *B et Storm* | Himinheithy *Munch* : Himinherthy *A* : Himinheithi *Storm* : næricia *B* | campus *ex* cam campus *corr. A* | **30** Ingialdr *Storm* : Ingialdr' *A* : Ingiaeldir *B* : Ingialder *Munch* | regnum *A* : regem *B et Storm* | **31** timens *A* : *om. B* | cognomine *A* : cognomento *B* | withfadm *A* : Vithfadhin *B* | inclusos *A* : inclusus *B* | **32** Tretelgia *Munch et Storm* : tetelgia *A* : trætælghiæ *B* | functus *B, Munch et Storm* : firmiter in *A* | **X 1** Halfdanum *A* : Haldauum *B* | Hwitbein *Munch et Storm* : huitben *B* : hwithein *uel* hwithem *A* | Norwagenses *A* : Norwegenses *Storm* : Noruegenses *B* | constituerunt *A* : constituunt *B* | **2** Tothne *A* : Thothne *B* : Thotne *Storm* | *Hic B finit* | **3** Eustein *Storm* : eusten *A* | undisque *Munch et Storm* : undique *A* | **4** tenacissimus *Bugge 1873 et Storm* : tentissimus *A* | stipendarios *A* : stipendiarios *Munch* | **5** Guthrodum *Storm* : Gunthrodum *A* |

made to idols. [27]He became sire to Øystein, whom the Götar thrust into a house and incinerated alive there with his men. [28]His son Yngvar, nicknamed the Hoary, was killed by the inhabitants while campaigning on an island in the Baltic called Ösel. [29]Yngvar bred Braut-Ånund, whose brother, Sigurd, laid him low in Himinheid, a place-name which means 'field of heaven'. [30]After him his son Ingjald ascended the throne. [31]Being abnormally terrified of King Ivar Vidfadme, at that time an object of dread to many, he shut himself up in a dining-hall with his whole retinue and burnt all its inmates to death. [32]His son, Olav, known as Tretelgje, accomplished a long and peaceful reign, and died in Sweden, replete in years.

X [1]Olav sired Halvdan Hvitbein, whom the Norwegians in the mountains appointed as their king as he was returning from Sweden. [2]Here in the county of Toten he gave up the ghost at an advanced age. [3]While his son, Øystein, nicknamed Fart, was making a voyage between two islands with several ships sailing close to each other, he was knocked from the poop by the yardarm of another vessel, sank below the waves and vanished. [4]Succession to the crown fell to his son, Halvdan Gold-Lavisher and Food-Niggard, since, whereas he bestowed gold on his retainers, he weakened them with hunger at the same time. [5]He became father of Gudrød the Hunter King, who was

Venatorem, qui a sua propria uxore seductus est: ipsa enim quendam tironum precio corrupit, qui regis latus lancia perforauit. [6]Huius filius Halfdanus cognomento Niger regnum post patrem item in montanis optinuit. [7]Qui dum noctu per cuiusdam stagni glaciem, quod Rond nominatur, iter ageret, cum curribus et equitatu magno a cena rediens, in quandam scissuram, ubi pastores gregem suum adaquare solebant, improuide aduectus sub glacie deperiit.

XI [1]Post istum filius suus Haraldus Comatus, ob decoram cesariem sic cognominatus, totius maritime zone regnum nactus est primus; mediterranee quidem zone adhuc reguli presidebant, sic tamen quasi sub eius dominio. [2]De hoc memorantur multa et mirabilia, que nunc longum est narrare per singula. [3]Hic regnabat LXXIII annos et genuit XVI filios. [4]Primogenitus Ericus, qui cognominatus est Blothex, id est Sanguinea Securis. [5]Secundus Hacon, quem Adalstanus rex Anglorum sibi in filium adoptauit. Tercius Olauus. Quartus Berno, quod interpretatur 'ursus'. [6]Quintus Siwardus cognomento Gigas. Sextus Gunrodus. Septimus Guthrodus. Octauus Halfdanus Hafoeta. [7]Nonus Rogualdus Recilbein a quadam fetonissa in prouincia Hatlandia nutritus est et in eadem arte mira ut nutrix operatus est. [8]Decimus Eusteinus. XI^us Iorundus. Duodecimus Sigtrygr. XIII^us Ynguar. XIIII^us Truggui. XV^us Ringr. XVI^us Rolfr.

XII [1]Quorum etate primus regnum post patrem ⟨optinuit⟩ Ericus Sanguinea Securis, qui sibi ducens de Dania uxorem

lancia *i.e.* lancea | **6** Niger *Munch* : ingar *A* | **XI 4** Blothex *A* : blothoex *Storm* | **5** Adalstanus *ex* Ald Adalstanus *corr. A* | **6** Siwardus : Sigwardus *Storm* : Swardus *A* | 7 Rogualdus *uel* Rognaldus *A* : Rognualdus *Storm* | Recilbein *A* : retilbein *Munch* : retilbein qui *Storm* | fetonissa *A* : fitonissa *Storm* | Hatlandia *A* : Hadalandia *Munch in app.* : Hathalandia *Storm* | **8** XI^us : XI *A* | Sigtrygr *Storm* : Sygtygr' *A* : Sigtryggr *Munch in app.* | Ynguar *Munch* : Ynguar' *A* | Truggui *Munch in app.* : Truggin *A* | Ringr *Storm* : Ringr' *A* : Ringer *Munch* | Rolfr *Storm* : Rolfr' *A* : Rolfer *Munch* | **XII 1** Sanguinea Securis : sanguinea securis *Storm* : sanguine securis *A* : sanguinesecuris *Munch* | optinuit *add. Munch* | qui sibi *A et Skard* : acquisiuit *Bugge 1873 et Storm* |

betrayed by his own wife, for she bribed one of the squires to pierce the king's side with a spear. [6]His son, Halvdan the Black, acquired the realm after his parent, once again in the mountain region. [7]While he was pursuing a journey by night across a frozen lake called Rand, returning from a feast with a large company of sleighs and horsemen, he unsuspectingly encountered a fissure where the shepherds used to water their flocks, and perished there beneath the ice.

XI [1]After him came his son, Harald Fairhair, so named because of his handsome locks, and he was the first to gain control of the whole seaboard; the mountain region was still ruled by petty kings, seemingly governing under his lordship. [2]There are many marvellous recollections of him, which would take too long now to relate individually. [3]He reigned for seventy-three years and had sixteen sons. [4]The first-born was Eirik, who was given the name Blodøks, that is, Bloodaxe. [5]The second was Håkon, whom King Æthelstan of England adopted as his son; third was Olav; fourth Bjørn, meaning bear; [6]the fifth was Sigurd the Giant, sixth Gunnrød, seventh Gudrød, eighth Halvdan Håføtt; [7]the ninth, Ragnvald Rettilbeine, was reared by a sorceress in Hadeland county and wrought miraculous achievements in the same art as his foster-mother; [8]the tenth was Øystein, eleventh Jorund, twelfth Sigtrygg, thirteenth Yngvar, fourteenth Tryggve, fifteenth Ring and the sixteenth Rolf.

XII [1]The eldest of these, Eirik Bloodaxe, obtained the kingdom after his father and took a wife from Denmark, Gunnhild,

7v nomine Gunnildam quandam malificam | et iniquissimam, Gorms Stultissimi Danorum regis filiam ac Thyri mulieris prudentissime. [2]Ex qua, scilicet Gunnilda, genuit sex filios, scilicet Haraldum cognomine Grafeld, secundum Gamla, tercium Siwardum Lioma, quartum Gunrodum, quintum Erlingum, sextum Gorm. [3]Hic cum annum regnasset, ⟨et⟩ ob nimiam insolenciam uxoris nemini placuisset, a fratre suo Hacone, alumpno Adalstani regis Anglie, idem consiliantibus Norwegie primatibus, regno priuatus in Angliam profugus secessit. [4]Ibi a pedagogo fratris sui bene susceptus fonteque baptismatis lotus toti Northimbrie comes preficitur, eratque omnibus gratissimus, quousque improba uxor eius, scilicet Gunnilda, illo aduentasset. [5]Cuius pestiferam rabiem non ferentes Northimbri iugum illorum intollerabile statim a se discusserunt. [6]At ille in Hispanie finibus, cum piraticam excerceret, bello temptatus occubuit, ipsa uero cum filiis ad fratrem suum Haraldum, regem Danorum, reuersa est.

XIII [1]Hacon a maritimis Norwegie gentibus rex assumitur. [2]Hic a christianissimo rege in Anglia officiosissime educatus in tantum errorem incurrit, ut miserrima commutacione eterno transitorium preponeret regnum ac detinende dignitatis cura — proh dolor — appostata factus, ydolorum seruituti subactus, diis et non Deo deseruiret. [3]Qui quamuis labilis regni ceca ambicione a durabili dignitate eternaliter labefactus, cunctis tamen in paganismo degentibus diligencius leges patrias et scita plebis obseruabat regibus. [4]Ob hoc quidem principibus carus, uulgo deuotus, XXVII annis suam hereditariam strenuissime defensabat patriam.

Gorms *Munch* : Gorins *A* | **2** Siwardum : Sigwardum *Storm* : Swardum *A* | **3** et *add. Ekrem* : sed *add. Bugge 1873 et Storm* | Adalstani regis *Munch et Storm* : ad Alstani regem *A* | **4** sui *Munch et Storm* : suis *A* | toti *Storm* : totus *A* : tocius *Munch* | Gunnilda, illo *Storm* : *fortasse* Gunnilla : Gūn̄ illo *A* : Gunilla *Munch* | **5** discusserunt *Munch et Storm* : discusserit *A* | **6** piraticam *Munch* : paraticā *A* | **XIII 2** detinende : detinendae *Bugge 1873 et Storm* : deinde *A et Munch* | deseruiret *A* : seruiret *Storm* | **3** plebis *Munch et Storm* : plebem *A* | **4** annis *Munch* : ānū *A* |

cruel and double-dyed in wickedness, daughter of the Danish king, Gorm the Stupid, and his very clever wife, Tyra. [2]By this Gunnhild he got six sons, namely Harald Gråfell, next Gamle, third Sigurd Ljome, fourth Gunnrød, fifth Erling and sixth Gorm. [3]When Eirik had reigned for a year and had suited no one owing to his wife's overweening arrogance, on the advice of the Norwegian magnates he was divested of the realm by his brother Håkon, the foster-son of the English king, Æthelstan, and departed as a refugee to England. [4]There he was well received by his brother's foster-father and was cleansed at the baptismal font; he was appointed earl, commanding the whole of Northumbria, and was most acceptable to all, that is until his villainous wife, Gunnhild, appeared on the scene. [5]As the Northumbrians could not brook her pernicious fury, they straight away flung off the intolerable yoke imposed by this pair. [6]And while Eirik was pursuing a viking expedition in Spanish territory, he suffered an armed attack and met his end; Gunnhild however returned with her sons to her brother Harald, the Danish king.

XIII [1]Håkon was accepted as their ruler by the coastal dwellers of Norway. [2]He had been brought up in the most dutiful manner by that peerless Christian, the sovereign of England, but fell into such serious delusion that he underwent a wretched change and valued his temporal monarchy before the eternal kingdom; and in his concern to hold on to royal grandeur, sad to say, he turned apostate and submitted himself to the bondage of idolatry, serving gods instead of God. [3]Yet though in his blind ambition for a perishable kingdom he was swayed forever from lasting merit, he heeded the laws of his forefathers and the decrees of the populace more carefully than all the kings who lived in heathen times. [4] Loved by his noblemen for this reason and devoted to his people, for twenty-seven years he defended with all his might the fatherland he had inherited.

[5]Cui contra nepotes suos ex fratre matremque eorum Gunnildam in ultimis annis uite sue ferme continuum bellum fuit. [6]E quibus publica et precipua duo fuerunt: Aliud in prouincia
8r Northmore in quadam insula Frethi, | loco Rastarcalf, ubi Gamle filius Gunnilde et maxima pars excercitus illorum de quodam promunctorio in maria precipitati sunt. [7]Aliud in Gulacie finibus in quodam oppido nomine Fittium maximum commiserunt bellum, in quo congressu plurimi ceciderunt de utralibet parte. [8]Ceciderunt eciam duo filii Gunnilde, scilicet Gormr et Erlingr, reliqui uero fratres eorum fugerunt. [9]At in ipsa fuga puer quidam de cohorte illorum hastam dirigens in aciem hostium, qua ipsum regem Haconem in dextro lacerto letali plaga uulnerauit. [10]Quod factum diuina ulcione tali euentu accidisse lippis et tunsoribus liquido apparet, ubi puerum Christum denegare ausus hic deuictis hostibus ab ignobili puero deuinceretur. [11]Sed dum ad uillam suam Alrecstathi redire disponeret, in quodam portu, ubi genitus, eciam mortuus est, unde idem locus perpetuum sortitus est uocabulum 'Haconar hella', id est 'Haconis petra'.

XIV [1]Post hec tota maritima zona Gunnilde filiisque eius, Haraldo, Siwardo et Gunrodo, XIIII annis subdita erat. [2]Sub istorum imperio exigente nequicia prelatorum maxime oppressa est Norwegia fame ac qualibet iniuria. [3]Sed Siwardus a plebeis Vorsorum principante Wemundo Volubriot in consilio cum multis occisus est, Gunrodum uero in uillula Alrecstadum, iux-

5 annis *Munch* : ānū *A* | **6** Northmore *Ekrem* : Northimore *A* : Northmoere *Storm* | Rastarcalf *Storm* : Restarcalf *A* | promunctorio *i.e.* promontorio (*cf. I.4 & II.11*) | 7 Fittium *Storm* : ficicum *A* : Fitium *Munch* | **8** Gormr *Storm* : bornir' *A* : Gormer *Munch* | Erlingr *Storm* : Erlingr' *A* : Erlinger *Munch*| **10** ubi *A et Storm* : uti *Ekrem* | **11** Alrecstathi *Storm* : Alretstrathr *A* : Alrecstather *Munch* | genitus *Storm, fortasse* natus : genitus natus *A* : genitrice natus *Bugge 1873* | Haconar *Munch* : haconarer *A* | **XIV 1** Haraldo *Munch et Storm* : harald' Sig̃ et bũrodo (et bũrodo *expunctum*) *A* | **3** Vorsorum *Munch* : Vrsorum *A* : Worsorum *Storm* | principante *Munch* : principate *A* | Volubriot : uolubriot *Storm* : uolobrut *Munch* : uolubiut *A* | consilio *A* : concilio *Storm* | Gunrodum *Munch* : Gunrodus *A* | Alrecstadum *Munch et Storm* : Alretstadum *A* |

[5]During the last period of his life there was almost continual warfare between him and his brother's sons along with their mother Gunnhild. [6]Two of these royal encounters were of outstanding significance: one was in the county of Nordmøre at a place called Rastarkalv on the island of Frei, where Gunnhild's son Gamle and the majority of their army were hurled from a promontory headlong into the seas. [7]They joined in another huge battle on the confines of Gulatingslag at a town named Fitjar, a clash in which large numbers fell on either side. [8]The casualties included two of Gunnhild's sons, Gorm and Erling, but the remaining brothers made their escape. [9]Nevertheless in that very flight a boy from their troop, hurling his spear at the enemy front, dealt a mortal wound to King Håkon himself, in his right arm. [10]It is as clear as daylight to every bleary-eyed man and barber that such an outcome was brought about through divine vengeance, since this man, who had dared to renounce the Christ-child, after the defeat of his foes was himself vanquished by a humble child. [11]When he decided to return to his manor at Alrekstad, he died at the particular harbour where he had been born, so that the locality gained an abiding name, Håkonshella, in other words, Håkon's rock.

XIV [1]Afterwards the entire seaboard was subservient to Gunnhild and her sons, Harald, Sigurd and Gunnrød, for fourteen years. [2]Under their dominion Norway suffered hardship from hunger and all kinds of injustice, which resulted from the sinfulness of these overlords. [3]Sigurd, however, was assassinated at an assembly with many others by the peasants of Voss led by Vemund Volubrjot, while Gunnrød's life was taken when a certain Torkell Klypp stabbed him with a sword at the manor of ta quam nunc sita est Bergonia ciuitas opinatissima, quidam Torkellus Clyppr cognominatus, cuius uxorem inuitam stuprauerat, gladio perfossum uita priuauit. [4]Quem unus de stipendariis suis nomine Erlingus Senex uiriliter uindicauit. ⟨...⟩

XV [1]Ast e magna numerositate filiorum Haraldi Comati illi duo, scilicet Ericus et Hacon, loco patris maritimis imperasse memorantur, ceterique in montanis regnabant, quidam autem ex ipsis ante regnandi tempora uitam finierunt: [2]Halfdan uero Hafota ab Orchadensibus interfectus est, sed Regualdus Retil-
8v bein ob usitatam | inertissime artis ignominiam infamatus iussu patris in Hatlandia fertur ingurgitatus.

[3]At Berno et Olauus, fratres illorum, admodum utilem suis posteris reliquerunt sobolem, quippe cum de illorum progenie sint progressi illi salutares equiuoci duo Olaui, qui quasi clara celi luminaria suam sacre luce fidei illustrabant patriam. [4]Berno etenim, filius Haraldi Comati, nutritus in Grenlandia, ubi eciam regnasse dicitur, genuit Gudrodum, item Gudrodus genuit Haroldum Grensca, qui in Grenlandia educatus ibique regnauit. [5]Iste duxit uxorem ualde elegantem nomine Asta, filiam Gudbrandi Culu, que sibi peperit Olauum perpetuum regem Norwegie. [6]Istam Astam post mortem mariti sui in matrimonium sibi copulauit Siwardus Scroffa rex montanus. [7]Siwardus Risi (id est Gigas), filius Haraldi Comati, genuit Halfdanum, patrem istius Siwardi. [8]Hic uero genuit Haroldum ex eadem Asta, uirum sagacissimum et in bellica arte peritissimum, de quo quasi quodam filo textus genealogie regum Norwegie hucusque protelatus gloriose descendit.

opinatissima *Bugge* : opp̄matissima *uel* oppīnatissima *A* : opulentissima *Munch* | **4** stipendariis *A* : stipendiariis *Munch (cf. X 4)* | *lacunam posuit Storm* | **XV 1** ceterique *Ekrem* : ceteri qui *A* : ceteri *Storm* | **2** Halfdan *Munch* : halfdam *A* | uero *A et Skard* : enim *Storm* | Hafota *A* : hafoeta *Storm* | Regualdus *Ekrem* : Rognualdus *Storm* : Regnaldus *A* | Hatlandia *A* : Hadalandia *Munch in app.* : Hathalandia *Storm* | **4** Haroldum *Munch* : harold' *A* : Haraldum *Storm* | ibique *A et Skard* : ibidem *Storm* | **5** Culu *Storm* : culii *A* | **6** Siwardus : Suardus *A* (*cf. infra*) | **8** Haroldum *Munch* : har' *A* : Haraldum *Storm* | regum *Munch et Storm* : regnū *uel* reguū *A* |

Alrekstad, close to the present site of the famous city of Bergen, for raping Torkell's wife when she resisted his advances. 4This murder was manfully avenged by one of Gudrød's retainers, Erling the Old. ⟨...⟩

XV 1Of Harald Fairhair's very many sons, those two, Eirik and Håkon, are said to have governed the seaboard in their father's stead, whereas the others held authority in the mountain region, although some met their end before they came to rule: 2Halvdan Håføtt was slaughtered by the men of Orkney, but Ragnvald Rettilbeine, who was branded with the dishonour which usually comes to those who dabble in the idle arts of magic, is reported to have been drowned in Hadeland on the orders of his father.

3Even so, Bjørn and Olav, their brothers, left progeny who were very advantageous to the generations following them, since from their stock arose those two benefactors of the same name, Olav, who like bright celestial stars illuminated their country with the light of the Holy Faith. 4Bjørn, Harald Fairhair's son, was reared in Grenland, where he is also said to have reigned; he became father to Gudrød, who in his turn begot Harald Grenske, for he too was brought up in Grenland and held dominion there. 5He married a superlative wife called Åsta, daughter of Gudbrand Kula, who bore Olav, everlasting king of Norway. 6After the death of her husband this Åsta was joined in marriage to Sigurd Sow, a king from the mountain region. 7Sigurd Rise (the Giant), Harald Fairhair's son, had sired Halvdan, the father of Sigurd Sow. 8Åsta bore him Harald, a man of deep perspicacity, a great expert in the science of warfare, and from him, as if along a thread, descended the glorious Norwegian royal line in its genealogical pattern up to the present.

[9]At Olauus, filius Haraldi Comati, genuit Turgonem. Iste Turgo nutritus in prouincia Roumorum, ubi primitus regnasse dicitur, quandam Astridam uirginem decoram de montanis duxit uxorem. [10]Hic postea Orientali Sinu sibi subiugato a patruelibus suis, uidelicet filiis Erici, callide seductus in quadam insula parua penes prouinciam Renorum, dum inter se pacem firmare deberent, dolo occisus est, unde usque hodie locus ille Trugguaroyr, id est 'tumulus Turgonis', uocitatur. [11]Huius dolosam necem multi aliter accidisse astruunt: [12]Denique cum ipsi prouinciales, scilicet Reni, eius imperialem rigorem minime ferre ualerent, indicto consilio quasi pro communi utilitate regni, in quo ipsum regem per manus quorundam tironum, Saxa, Scorra ac Screyiu, precio corruptorum fraudulenter
9r necatum fecerunt. [13]Sed siue ab istis | siue ab illis, in eadem insula loci uocabulum ipsum demonstrat occisum.

[14]Interea ipsa Astrida iam grauida in tribus nauibus cum decenti comitatu Orchades petiit, ibique fidissime concesso asylo felix puerpera regem futurum, quem nominauit Olauum, est enixa, per quem Christi monita tandem Norwegia cepit saluberima.

XVI [1]Post mortem uero filiorum Gunnilde quidam Hacon, ob intemperatam animi crudelitatem Nequam cognominatus, cunctis exterminatis regulis perditisque tributiferis Sweonum, totius Norwegie monarchiam sub comitali dignitate sibi usurpauit maluitque comes quam rex secundum suos seniores uocari. [2]Hic namque patre Siwardo, matre uero Bergliota, filia

10 Renorum *A* : Ranorum *Munch in app.* | Trugguaroyr *Storm* : Trygguaroyr *Munch* : Turgguuaroyrer *A* | **12** Denique *A et Skard* : namque *Storm* | Reni *A* : Rani *Munch in app.* | eius *Munch et Storm* : cuius *A* | minime *Munch* : miime *A* | indicto consilio : indicto concilio *Storm in textu et Skard* : in dicto consilio *A* : indicto consilio conuenerunt *Storm in notis* | tironum *Munch et Storm* : tirannorum *A* | Screyiu *Bugge* : streȳm *A* : Sueynn *Munch in app.* | **14** enixa : enexa *A* | **XVI 1** tributiferis : tributariis (*expunctum*) tributiferis *A* | **2** Bergliota *Munch* : beglioca *A* |

[9]Harald Fairhair's son Olav was the father of Tryggve. This boy was fostered in the county of Romerike, where he is stated to have been its ruler to begin with, and married Astrid, a good-looking girl from the mountains. [10]Later, after he had brought Viken under his sway, on a small island near Ranrike he was cunningly drawn away by his cousins, Eirik's sons, when they were about to establish a pact between them, and treacherously put to death; therefore to this very day that spot is spoken of as Tryggvarøyr, that is, 'Tryggve's mound'. [11]Many people however affirm that his insidious murder took place in a different manner: [12]that because in the end the natives, that is the countrymen of Ranrike, could barely stand his harsh dictatorial rule, they called an assembly, ostensibly for the public benefit in that domain, where their king was deceitfully dispatched at the hands of some squires who had been bribed, namely Sakse, Skorre and Skrøya. [13]Whether Tryggve was removed by the former or the latter, the name of the locality on that island signifies that he was cut down there.

[14]Meanwhile Astrid, now pregnant, made her way to the Orkneys with a fit escort in three ships and, having been loyally granted a refuge in those parts, had a successful confinement in which she gave birth to the future king, whom she called Olav; it was through him that Norway eventually received the wholesome teachings of Christ.

XVI [1]After the deaths of Gunnhild's sons, one Håkon, styled the Wicked owing to his unbridled cruelty of temperament, first eliminated every chieftain and destroyed those who paid taxes to the Swedes; he appropriated the crown of all Norway by his authority as jarl, but preferred that title to being known as king, in the same way as his predecessors. [2]He took his origin from his father, Sigurd, and his mother, Bergljot, daughter of

Thoris Tacentis, ex nobilissima ⟨Morensium⟩ ac Halogensium comitum prosapia extitit oriundus. [3]Iste in armis potens, sed ydolatrie obnixe deseruiens, plerasque patrias circumcirca debellans suum longe lateque perampliauit imperium.

XVII [1]Sed in Orchadibus pupillum puerum didicit natum; protinus illi parat insidias, quem se suspicatur regno priuaturum. [2]Mater uero, quamquam filium utpote unicum tenerrime diligeret, postquam comitis consilia comperuit maliuola, ipsum cum Dei — credo — prouidente clemencia a se sequestrando cuidam ⟨Thorolfo⟩ cognomento Lusaskeg in Swethiam deferendum dedit alumpnum. [3]Quem cum omni diligencia enutriendum suscipiens ac proprio sinu imponens per maxima pericula Throndemie transiuit confinia. [4]Post hec uenit in Swethiam, ubi moram gessit per horam, inde tendit in Rusciam, sed deuenit in Eistriam. [5]Denique dum ante Eisislam uela tenderet, a piratis preuenti partim predantur, partim necantur. [6]Inter quos pueri nutritor eciam capite plectitur, ipseque puer Olauus Eistriis in seruum uenumdatur. [7]Inde a quodam Olauo suo cognato redimitur, qui tunc forte a rege Ruscie causa colligendi tributa eo legatus fuit. [8]Cum quo aliquot annis latenter mansit in Ruscia.

[9]Hic cum esset circiter XII annorum, in medio foro Holm-
9v gardie pedagogum suum uiriliter | uindicauit. [10]Et inaudita ulcio uix duodennis pueri ilico auribus regiis intonuit, unde regi presentatur, a quo demum filius adoptatur. [11]Factus adolescens

nobilissima Morensium ac Halogensium *Ekrem* : nobilissiū ac halogensuū *A* : nobilissima Moerensium ac Halogensium *Bugge* : nobilissima halogensium *Munch et Bugge 1873* : Moerensium ac Halogensium *Storm* | 3 potens *Storm* : inpotens *A* | **XVII** 1 Sed *A* : Sed cum *add. Storm* | 2 prouidente *A* : prouidenti *Storm* | Thorolfo *add. Storm* | lusaskeg *Munch et Storm* : lusaskeo *A* | 3 quem cum *A et Skard* : qui eum cum *Storm* | sinu *A* : sinui *Munch* | 4 Eistriam *Munch et Storm* : Sistriam *A* | 5 Eisislam *Storm* : Eisisla *A* | 6 ipseque *Storm* : ipse autem *Munch* : ipē quē *A* | Eistriis *Storm* : Eistris *Munch* : cistriis *A* | uenundatur *Munch* : uenudatur *A* | 7 Olauo *A et Munch* : Olauus *Storm* | legatus : ligatus *A* | 9 Holmgardie : Holmgardiae *Munch et Storm* : holingardiar *A* | duodennis pueri ilico *Storm* : duodennis puerilico *A* : duodenarii pueri illico *Munch in app.* : duodenarii eius pueri *Bugge 1873* |

Tore the Silent, and so came from the noble family of jarls in Møre and Hålogaland. [3] He was mighty in war, but obstinately paid homage to idols, and he vanquished many surrounding areas, extending his power far and wide.

XVII [1]However, he learnt that this fatherless boy had been born in the Orkneys and prepared to mount a surprise attack on him, supposing that the lad was going to wrest away his crown. [2]Even though his mother held him in the most tender affection since he was her only boy, when she learnt about the jarl's evil-minded plots, helped by God's merciful foresight, as I believe, she surrendered him to the safekeeping of Torolv Luseskjegg, to be brought to Sweden as his foster-son. [3]Torolv undertook to rear him with all due care and, cradling the child in his bosom, crossed over the borders of Trøndelag through utmost perils. [4]Afterwards he came to Sweden, but when he had lingered there for a while, he set sail for Russia, though in fact he went off course towards Estland. [5]Subsequently, while Torolv was spreading his sails off Ösel, his crew were intercepted by vikings, who captured some of them as booty and slew others. [6]Among these the boy's foster-father was also put to death, but young Olav was sold as a slave to the Estonians. [7]He was ransomed from there by one of his kinsmen, also named Olav, who, as luck would have it, had been sent as ambassador by the Russian king in order to gather taxes there, [8]so that the boy Olav spent some years in hiding with him in Russia.

[9]When he was about twelve years old he courageously avenged his upbringer in the middle of Holmgard market-place. [10]This unheard-of act of retribution by a boy of scarcely a dozen years promptly came to the ears of the king, with the result that Olav was presented to him and afterwards adopted as his son. [11]Grown to early manhood, he pursued viking expe-

piraticam excercens Baltica littora perlustrando, cunctis gentibus id locorum formidabilis existendo, inscius deuiatur a Deo ille magnificus predo. [12]Augmentabant enim eius classem Norwegenses ac Dani, Gautones et Sclaui, qui cum illo ciuitate Iomne, que est firmissima inter Sclauie urbes, hyemales frequentabant sedes. [13]Hinc tetendit in Frisiam, post hanc uenit Flandream, inde pergit in Angliam. [14]Quas depredans perperam, mira gessit in Scotia, nulli parcens in Hybernia.

[15]Verum enimuero curam gerens Conditor creature sue, hunc tirannum tam remotum tamque indomitum per uiscera misericordie sue mirabiliter uisitauit, uisitando illuminauit, ut quos eo tenus umbra mortis operuerat, stola claritatis eterne indueret. [16]Nam cum idem Olauus in prefatos populos nimis debacharet, quendam anachoritam penes Britanniam in parua insula Deo famulantem inuenit, quem per armigerum suum ueste mutata temptauit. [17]Sed hunc regis uernaculum statim agnouit ac domino suo fideliter seruire ammonuit. [18]Exinde ad eum ipse predonum princeps properauit, quem iam Dei prophetam non dubitauit; tum et ab eo multa futura audiuit, que paulo post in re comperuit:

[19]"Rex eris," inquit, "inclitus, in fide Christi deuotissimus tueque genti utilissimus. [20]Per te enim christianissimus populus fiet innumerus. [21]Et si uera sunt, que predico, istud habeto pro signo: perendie cum naues excesseris, ad litus armenta conspexeris idque dolo actum agnoueris, quia ab inimicis insidiaberis. [22]Sed dum tuos perdideris, fere ad mortem ipse plaga-

11 Baltica *Munch* : haltica *A* | deuiatur : deviatur *Munch* : deniatĩ *uel* deuiatĩ *A* | **12** ciuitate *A* : in ciuitate *Storm* | Iomne *A* : Iome *Storm* | **13** Hinc *Munch et Storm* : Hic *A* | post hanc *A et Skard* : posthac *Storm* | Flandream *A et Skard* : in Flandriam *Storm* | **14** perperam *A et Skard* : perquam *Bugge 1873 et Storm* | **15** uisitando *Munch* : uisitand *A* | **16** hunc *A et Storm* : hic *Munch* | **18** properauit : properavit *Munch* : proparauit *A* | dubitauit; tum et *Storm* : dubitatum, et *A et Skard* : dubitatum est *Ekrem* | audiuit, que : audivit, quae *Storm* : audiendum que *A* : audit, eademque *Ekrem* : audit inter colloquendum, que *Bugge 1873* | **21** perendie *Munch* : perendic *A* | ad *Storm* : nisi ad *A* : missa ad *Ekrem* : iuxta *uel* iusum ad *uel* tuas, ad *Bugge 1873* |

ditions right along the Baltic coasts, a terror to all the heathens who inhabited those regions; yet this splendid sea-rover was unconsciously directing his steps away from God. [12]His fleet was swelled by an influx of Norwegians, Danes, Götar and Wends, who flocked to join him at his winter quarters in Jomsborg, that strongest of Wendish towns. [13]He sailed to Friesland, from there to Flanders, then proceeded to England. [14]During these misguided plunderings he performed incredible feats in Scotland and spared no one in Ireland.

[15]But the Creator, bestowing concern on His creature, through the bowels of His compassion miraculously came to this viking, so alienated from Him and so untamed, and in his visitation enlightened him in such a way that those whom He had hitherto shrouded beneath the shadow of death He might now garb with the robe of eternal brightness. [16]As this man was rampaging mightily against the peoples I have mentioned, at the edge of Britain he came upon a hermit serving God on a small island and put him to the test by exchanging clothes with his armour-bearer. [17]The recluse however at once recognized the servant of the king-to-be and urged him to minister loyally to his lord. [18]The viking leader immediately hastened to the anchorite, whom he no longer doubted was God's prophet. From his lips he heard many future events, which he shortly found to be true.

[19]"You shall be a famous king," proclaimed the other, "a fervently devout follower of Christ and a large benefit to your race. [20]Through you countless people will become pious Christians. [21]And if my predictions are correct, you will receive this sign: on the day after tomorrow, when you have disembarked, you will spy herds brought to the shore, which you will realize was done out of guile, since foes will ambush you. [22]But when you have lost your followers, you yourself will be wounded

beris uixque ad naues scuto portaberis, post septimanam celitus sanaberis, ac cum inde redieris, fonte uite lauaberis."

[23]Ista omnia, ita ut predixit, exitus rei comprobauit. [24]Postquam uero beatus Olauus per salutarem dextre excelsi muta-
101r cionem gratiam baptismi | cum maxima parte excercitus sui
assecutus est, ad Norwegiam transfretauit, habens secum Iohannem episcopum et Tangbrandum presbyterum, quem ad Glaciales misit predicare. [25]Habuit et eciam alios plures Dei ministros, qui omnes unanimes uno ore ewangelizare Christum gentilibus cepere. [26]Norwagenses uero inestimabili magni Dei clemencia ad fidem conuersi Olauum sibi regem constituunt, comitemque Haconem, cum inde regnasset XXXIII annos, a regno expulerunt. [27]Quem seruus suus nomine Carcus in una prouinciarum Throndemie, scilicet Gauladale, nequiter noctu necauit, caput quoque eius abscisum regi obtulit sperans se magnas largiciones inde executurum, quod sibi in contrarium accidit. [28]Nam communi iudicio dampnatus homicida pessimus ut latro suspensus est. [29]Sed filii comitis Haconis, Sweino et Ericus, in Daniam fugerunt; qui a rege Sweinone pacifice recepti sunt.

[30]Interim Olauus Regi regum reconsilians omnes compatriotos suos in maritimis, et si quos ipse episcopus spirituali gladio nequiuit, rex adhibito materiali nobilem cum ignobili, lactentem cum homine sene Christi subiugauit imperio. [31]Sicque factum est, ut infra quinquennium omnes tributarios, id est Hatlendenses, Orchadenses, Fereyingenses ac Tilenses, fide preclaros, spe gaudentes, caritate feruentes redderet Christo. [32]Vnde

22 uixque *A et Skard* : uixque uiuus *Bugge et Storm* | assecutus *Bugge 1873 et Storm* : secutus *A* | **23** predixit : prædixit *Storm* : predixi *A* | **25** et eciam *A* : etiam *Storm* | **26** comitemque *Storm* : comitem quē *A* : comitem autem *Munch* | Haconem *Munch* : hacone *A* | inde *A et Skard* : inibi *Storm* | **29** Haconis, Sweino et *Storm* : Swethino hacon *A* : Haconis Sweino *Munch* | Daniam *Munch* : claniam *A* | Sweinone *Storm* : Swenone *A* | **30** regi *Bugge 1873 et Storm* : rex *A* | reconsilians *A* : reconcilians *Munch, Bugge 1873 et Skard* : reconciliat *Storm* | compatriotos *A* : compatriotas *Munch* | lactentem *A* : lactantem *Munch in app.* | **31** Hatlendenses *A* : Hiatlendenses *Munch* : Hialtlendenses *Storm* | Fereyingenses : Faereyingenses *Storm* : Freyngenses *A* : Ffereyngenses *Munch* |

almost to the point of death and by the skin of your teeth carried to the ships on your shield; after a week Heaven will heal you and when you return from there you will be bathed in the font of life."

[23]The outcome confirmed every detail, exactly as he predicted. [24]Once the blessed Olav along with the majority of his soldiers had achieved the grace of baptism owing to the healthful change wrought in him by the right hand of the Most High, he crossed the seas to Norway, taking with him Bishop Johannes and the priest, Tangbrand, whom he sent to preach to the Icelanders. [25]He also had with him several other servants of the Lord, who all together with one voice began to proclaim Christ to the heathen. [26]By the inestimable mercy of the great God the Norwegians were converted to the Faith and elected Olav their king, while Håkon jarl, after having ruled there for thirty-three years, was driven out of the realm. [27]His slave, Kark, brutally murdered him one night in Gauldalen, one of the counties of Trøndelag, and even carried his severed head to King Olav, hoping it would win from him a handsome remuneration, but he found it went just the opposite way; [28]for this despicable killer was condemned at a public trial and hanged in brigand fashion. [29]But the sons of Håkon jarl, Svein and Eirik, fled to Denmark, where they were received in friendly manner by King Svend.

[30]In the meantime Olav brought all those of his compatriots who lived along the seaboard into union with the King of Kings, and if the bishop was unable to achieve this with his spiritual sword, the king, applying his earthly weapon, led captive into Christ's empire the noble and ignoble, the babe at the breast and the greybeard. [31]This was effected in such a way that within five years he made all the tributary territories, that is, Shetland, the Orkneys, the Faeroes and Iceland, remarkable in their devotion, joyous in their expectations and glowing in their affection for Christ. [32]Hence God's triumphal car,

currus Dei decem milibus multiplicatus ac quadriga Christi gratuita eiusdem saluacione referta per hunc mirificum regem ueluti ualidissimo equo usque in fines orbis terre circumducti retrogrado cursu ad patriam Paradisum reuehuntur.

[33]Hic autem Olauus de Dania duxit uxorem, sororem Swei-
nonis regis nomine Tyri, quam prius dux quidam de Sclauia
desponsauerat inuitam. [34]Sed quoniam rex Sweino integram
Selandiam, quam sorori in sponsalia concesserat, omnino re-
tentare decreuerat, hanc ob causam rex Olauus contra Danos
bellum instituit copiosamque classem de Throndemia ac Gu-
10v lacia per manus | principum ordinari iussit. [35]Ipse namque ex-
peditis Orientalibus in confinio Danie et Norwegie ceteros ex-
pectabat. [36]Venientibus ergo quibusdam Gulacensibus rex cum
paucis premeditatum iter arripuit sperans reliquum excercitum
se subsequi. [37]At ille metas patrias transire nolens, presertim
cum princeps ipse abisset, domum reuersus est. [38]Rex itaque
cum se cerneret illusum ab eis, ad Sclauos ire disposuit et ab
eis petere suffraganeum excercitum, quos in piratica fidissimos
habuerat socios. [39]Sed dum iuxta Selandiam iter ageret, ut ouis
a lupis, ita iste ab inimicis insidiatus preuenitur. [40]Cum uero
rex Sweyno hunc in manu forciorum aduenturum audierat et
ideo regem Sweonum Olauum suum priuignum ac Ericum fi-
lium Haconis comitis accersierat, hii tres circa unum tali or-
dine nauale instituunt bellum:

[41]Primus Sweino ⟨XXX⟩ nauibus Olauum inpugnabat, ipseque non nisi XI repugnauit. [42]Sed regia nauis LXXX spaciolis intus munita erat; hec, que instar serpentini capitis puppi prora

32 reuehuntur *Munch* : reuehiuntur *A* | **33** Sweinonis *Mortensen* : Swein *A et Storm* | Tyri *Munch* : Cyri *A* : Thyri *Storm* | dux *Storm* : duxit *A* | quidam *A* : quidem *Storm* | **34** Sweino *Skard* : S. *A* : Sweno *Munch* : Swein *Storm* | **36** Venientibus *Munch et Storm* : ueentibus *A* : aduehentibus *Bugge 1873* | premeditatum : praemeditatum *Munch* : premeditantū *A* | **40** Sweyno : Sweino *Storm* : G (*expunctum*) Swyeno *A* | Sweonum *Munch* : Sweyonū *A* | hii : hi *Storm* : et hii *A* | **41** XXX *add. Storm* | ipseque *Storm* : ipē quē *A* : ipse autem *Munch* | **42** hec, que : haec, quae *Bugge 1873 et Storm* : hecque *A* | serpentini *Storm* : serpentum *A* |

increased by ten thousand souls, and Christ's chariot, filled with His freely-granted deliverance, were drawn by this wonder-working monarch as if by a powerful steed right to the ends of the earth till they turned around in their course and drove back to our homeland, which is Paradise.

33 Now Olav married the Danish sister of King Svend, Tyra, who had earlier been betrothed to a Wendish leader against her will. 34 However, because King Svend was absolutely determined to hold on to Sjælland in its entirety, even though he had yielded it to his sister as a dowry, King Olav consequently opened hostilities against the Danes and ordered a substantial fleet to be assembled from Trøndelag and Gulatingslag by the efforts of his magnates. 35 He himself, after fetching troops from Viken, waited for the others on the borders of Denmark and Norway. 36 When certain of them arrived from Gulatingslag, with this slender force the king started out on his intended journey, hoping that the remainder of the army would follow hard on his heels. 37 But unwilling to cross the frontiers of their land, especially when their leader was not accompanying them, they turned back home again. 38 Once their sovereign realized they had made him look ridiculous, he resolved to approach the Wends and ask them for a body of warriors to support him, since he had found them exceedingly loyal associates in his viking ventures. 39 Nevertheless, while he was pursuing his voyage close to Sjælland, his enemies forestalled him and he was waylaid as a sheep is by wolves. 40 Indeed, as soon as King Svend had learnt that he was coming with a band of strong men and had therefore summoned his step-son, King Olof of Sweden, and Eirik, son of Håkon jarl, with the three of them encircling the one they initiated a naval encounter in the following manner.

41 Svend was the first to attack Olav, with thirty vessels, while the latter could only retaliate with eleven. 42 But the Norwegian royal ship was furnished inside with eighty sections; this craft,

gestabat, Serpens Longus dictus est. [43]Et in remigando per om-
nes insimul mansiunculas CLX remiges capiebat, qui uniuersi
in pugna, unde nunc sermo est, loricati fuisse feruntur. [44]Cleri-
cos eciam XL in XX spaciolis puppi proximis continebat; qui in-
docti ad pugnam plus in deprecando quam debellando labora-
bant. [45]Sed post longum conflictum depopulatis singulis naui-
bus Sweinonis ipse magno dedecore rediit ad socios. [46]Tunc
priuignus eius Olauus cum totidem ⟨nauibus⟩ suo equiuoco
applicuit. [47]Sed priore peiorem passus est perdicionem et cum
magna ⟨ignominia⟩ conuersus est. [48]Ericus ordine ultimus, nec
non uictoria primus cum undenis nauibus acerime hostes in-
uasit; patrie necis ac proprie fuge haud immemor uulnera uul-
neribus addidit ipsis. [49]At Olauus eosdem proteruos fortissime
11r rebellantes resistendo, | quippe pro uiribus quasi ex nouo in-
cipiens, saxa, hastas ceteraque missilia in aduersarios reicere
conabatur. [50]Tandem destituti uiribus nauesque intrantibus in-
imicis, nemine tum dante dextras, omnes, quos tum uitalis
calor uegetabat, ore gladii consumpti sunt excepto ipso rege,
quem celsa stantem in puppi postremo uiderunt.

[51]Sed bello finito ⟨nec uiuum⟩ nec mortuum reperierunt illum, unde nonnulli ipsum loricatum undis submersum affirmant. [52]Quidam eciam longo interuallo in quodam cenobio se illum uidisse protestati sunt. [53]Sed qualiter per equoris discrimina littoris soliditati aduectus sit (siue proprio natatu, seu scaphe uehiculo, seu famulantibus angelicis spiritibus), seu ibidem mersus, a cunctis, credo, nostris coequeuis ignoratur. [54]Quare honestius hoc parum determinatum omittendo quam de re incerta falsa diffiniendo pretereamus.

[55]Ast coniux intemperanter uiri mortem ferens dolore deperiit. [56]Post hec filiis Haconis comitis regnum totius Norwegie

44 XL in XX *Storm in notis* : XL in XXX *A* | deprecando *Storm* : defensando *A* | **46** nauibus *add. Storm* | **47** magna *Storm* : magnam *A* | ignominia *add. Munch et Storm* | **48** patrie necis : patriae necis *Munch et Storm* : prīenenses *A* | ac *supra lineam additum A* | **49** quippe *Mortensen* : quibus *A* : suis *Bugge 1873 et Storm* | **51** nec uiuum *add. Storm* | **54** parum determinatum *Storm* : piū uid'et (*i.e.* uideret) minatum *A* : dubium indeterminatum *Bugge 1873* | **55** coniux *Munch* : oncius *A* | **56** regnum *Munch* : regum *A* |

which bore the carving of a serpent's head at stern and prow, was called The Long Serpent. [43]When all its seats were used at once it housed a hundred and sixty oarsmen, who, in the conflict I am speaking of, had all, it is said, been fitted with armour. [44]It also held forty priests in twenty sections next to the stern, but these were untrained in fighting and expended their energies more in prayers than pugnacity. [45]None the less, after a long contest, when his ships had been ravaged one by one, Svend made his way back to his comrades in considerable disgrace. [46]Then his step-son Olof set upon his own namesake with the same number of vessels [47]but suffered even worse losses than his forerunner and turned tail, to his great shame. [48]The last in line, Eirik, assaulted his foe hotly with eleven ships and was the first to win victory; not forgetting his father's death and his own flight, he inflicted wound upon wound. [49]Olav however resisted these brazen opponents, who fought against him with the utmost vigour; for, battling with all his might, he began afresh, as it were, and endeavoured to retaliate against his adversaries with rocks, spears and every other kind of missile. [50]Nevertheless, in the end their strength was exhausted so that, as the foe entered their ships, none raised a hand to oppose them and all whose bodies still had warm blood left in their veins were put to death at the edge of the sword; all, that is, with the exception of King Olav, who could be seen at the last, standing high up in the stern.

[51]When the battle was over he could not be traced, dead or alive, from which some maintain that he sank in his armour beneath the waves. [52]But certain folk also claimed to have seen him after a long lapse of time in a particular monastery. [53]How he reached firm soil through the hazards of the seas (whether it were by swimming on his own or being transported in a small boat or by the attendance of angelic spirits), or whether indeed he was drowned then and there is unknown, I believe, to all our contemporaries. [54]For this reason it would be more creditable to omit something so unsettled than give a false explanation of such a doubtful matter, and I shall pass over it.

a ⟨Sweinone⟩, scilicet Tiuguskeg, conceditur. [57]Qui XIIII annis eidem regno comites presidebant. [58]Et sanctam Dei ecclesiam, quam beatus Olauus egregie plantauerat, Iohannes rigauerat, isti fere eradicauerunt.

XVIII [1]Istis temporibus Olauus, filius Haraldi Grenscensis, in Ruscia clarus habetur. [2]Hic, quia herili solo priuatus erat, pyraticam excercere necesse habebat. [3]In ea poli, quam nos Holmgardiam appellamus, haut minuta classe stipatus hyemare solebat. [4]Qui estiuo tempore cunctos gentiles per ambitum Baltici Maris depredando lacessendo non desistebat urgere. [5]Insulam quoque Eysislam ualde spaciosam ac populosam ex toto uastauit. [6]Sed et alias duas colonum frequencia et magnitudine huic equales, scilicet Gottorum Insulam et Eynorum, adeo demolitus est, ut illarum incole, quamdiu in Ruscia morabatur, immania redderent tributa. [7]Item in finibus Curorum non minimas de ipsis dans strages celeberimo exaltabatur trihumpho.

11v [8]Post | diuturnam tirannidis seuiciam princeps gloriosus reuerti parat ad patriam. [9]At cum peruenisset ad Daniam, rogatus a Sweinone Danorum rege transfretauit cum eo ad Angliam comitante Canuto patrem ipsum, uidelicet Sweinonem. [10]Qui in cunctis congressibus illius beatissimi tiranni Olaui belligera astucia uictoriam adepti sunt. [11]Demum depulso Adelredo totam insulam breui tamen tempore detinuit Sweino, nam post tres menses ex hac luce subtrahitur ipse. [12]Cum Canutus repatriauit, a Danis rex patris loco constituitur.

[13]Olauus interim Britones debellat et usque Hispanie partes profectus ibique clarissimos sue uictorie titulos relinquens re-

a Sweinone scilicet Tiuguskeg *add. Skard* : a scilicet tiuguskek *A* : a Sweinone tiuguskeg *Storm* | **58** isti *ex* iste *correctum A* | eradicauerunt : eradicaverunt *Bugge 1873 et Storm* : eradicauerant *A* | **XVIII 1** filius : Filius *A* | Haraldi *Munch* : haroridi *A* | Grenscensis *Storm* : grenoscensis *A* | **2** pyraticam : piraticam *Munch* : parylicam *A* | **3** ea *Munch in notis, Bugge 1873 et Storm* : eo *A* | Holmgardiam *Munch* : holingardiā *A* | stipatus *Munch* : stipitus *A* | **4** lacessendo *Storm* : lascessando *A* | **5** Eysislam : Eysyslam *Munch in notis et Storm* : eysillam *A* | illarum *Munch* : illariū *A* | **9** Sweinone *Munch et Storm* : Swemone *A* | rege : tr (*expunctum*) rege *A* | Sweinonem *Munch et Storm* : S. *A* | **10** Olaui : Olavi *Munch et Storm* : O *A* | **11** hac luce *Munch* : haclude *A* |

[55]His wife however reacted so acutely to her husband's death that she perished from her grief. [56]Afterwards the rule of all Norway was consigned by Svend Tveskæg to the sons of Håkon jarl. [57]For fourteen years they governed this same realm as jarls, [58]and God's holy Church, which the blessed Olav had planted so painstakingly and Johannes had watered, was almost uprooted by these two.

XVIII [1]During that period Olav, son of Harald Grenske, achieved renown in Russia. [2]As he had been deprived of hereditary land, he found it necessary to go on viking expeditions. [3]Surrounded by a sizable fleet, he would spend winter in the city known to us as Holmgard, [4]and in summertime he never ceased to bear hard on all the heathens who dwelt in the environs of the Baltic Sea, plundering and harrying everywhere. [5]He completely devastated the extensive, well-populated island of Ösel, [6]and then went on to wreak such thorough destruction on two others as well, similar in the number of their inhabitants and in area, namely Gotland and Öland, that their peoples paid him enormous tribute as long as he lived in Russia. [7]Again after spreading huge slaughter among the Kurlanders inside their territories he was honoured for his notable triumph over them.

[8]Following this prolonged bout of viking ferocity the famous leader prepared to return to his homeland. [9]Yet when he arrived in Denmark, at the invitation of the Danish king, Svend, they both sailed across to England with Knud, Svend's son, also in their company. [10]In every clash encountered by this most holy viking, Olav, they won victory through his martial dexterity. [11]At length Æthelred was driven from the realm and Svend held the whole island, though merely for a short time; only three months later he was removed from this life. [12]When Knud returned to his own land, the Danes made him their king in place of his father.

[13]Meanwhile Olav defeated the Bretons and, pushing right on to localities in Spain, left behind a celebrated name for his

diit in Daniam et a socio suo tum Danorum rege multum honorifice susceptus est. [14]Qui inter se adoptiue fraternitatis fedus pepigerunt. [15]Sed quoniam ipse Canutus parente orbatus de Anglia inhoneste aufugerat, cum ingenti excercitu iterum illuc redire disposuit. [16]Socium suum Olauum et eiusdem uocabuli consortem fratrem suum se illo comitari maxime concitauit pollicendo dimidiam, si totam illorum amminiculis lucrari posset insulam. [17]Pergunt itaque alacres simul millenis nauibus constipati, plenis uelis prosperis uentis portum Iarmuthiam post triduum tenuerunt. [18]Inde conciti petunt Londonias, ubi forte rex Edmundus tunc temporis morabatur patre Etelredo iam orbatus.

[19]Rex igitur cognito hostium aduentu ciues conuocat, amnis Tamisie pontem munire iussit, ne inimicis liber pateret aditus. [20]Nec mora dicta factis impleuerunt, ipseque in finitimis prouinciis excercitum congregauit. [21]Interim Dani cum ingenti clamore ponti appropiantes municiones eorum omni conamine repugnare ceperunt; illi ex aduerso se suaque defensare summa ope nitebantur. [22]Cumque Canutus casso labore per totam diem sic concertasset ac plurimos de suis male perdidisset, Olauus noster pro capessenda uictoria seque suosque maximo dedit periculo. [23]Quippe cum undecim nauibus fortissime re-
12r migando pontis propugnacula subeuntes ipse | eiusque satellites tutancium testudinum tegmine protecti sic delusa defensantum machina per media uite discrimina pertransiere audacissime. [24]Vnde uictoriosissimo bellatori Olauo iam ciuitatem ingresso ab uniuerso excercitu insignia laudum preconia referebantur, ac tota obtenti triumphi ascribebatur fama.

15 cum : d (*expunctum*) cum *A* | excercitu : exercitu *Munch* : excertu *A* | **16** concitauit *Bugge 1873 et Storm* : cogitauit *A* : rogitauit *Skard* | posset *Storm* : possit *A et Skard* | **18** petunt *Munch* : petum *A* | Etelredo *Ekrem* : Eteldredo *A* : Adelredo *Storm* | **19** Tamisie : Tamisiae *Storm* : temiste *A* : temisce *Munch* | **20** impleuerunt : impleverunt *Bugge 1873 et Storm* : impleuit *A* | ipseque *Storm* : ipē quē *A* : ipse autem *Munch* | **22** perdidisset *Storm* : perdisset CCCC (*ornatus ut uidetur*) *A* | uictoria : uictoria uictoria *A* | **23** subeuntes *Bugge 1873* : subematus *A* : superuectus *Storm* | ipse eiusque *Bugge 1873* : ipsi enimque *A* : ipsi namque *Storm* : ipsi denique *Skard* | testudinum *Munch et Storm* : testiduū *A* | pertransiere *Storm* : pertransire *A* | **24** Olauo : Olavo *Munch* : O *A* |

conquests; then he sailed back to Denmark and was welcomed with great respect by his associate, now monarch of that country. [14]Between them these two forged a pact of sworn brotherhood. [15]However, because Knud had shamefully fled from England when he was bereaved of his father, he once more decided to return there with a large army. [16]He strongly urged Olof, his ally, and his foster-brother of the same name to accompany him, promising that if he could gain the entire island with their support, he would let them have half of it. [17]So they proceeded briskly together in the midst of a swarming fleet of ships and with favourable winds filling their sails after three days attained the port of Yarmouth. [18]Speedily they made for London, where King Edmund chanced to be staying at that time, now that his father Æthelred had been taken from him.

[19]As soon as he knew that the enemy had arrived, the king called the burghers together and commanded them to make the bridge over the Thames secure, so as not to allow his foes free passage up the river. [20]Without delay they put his words into practice, while Edmund gathered an army in the adjacent areas. [21]In the meantime, approaching the bridge with loud war-cries, the Danes started to use every effort to counteract the barricades, whereas for their part the other side struggled with all their might to protect themselves and their possessions. [22]When Knud found that, after contending the whole day, his labour was wasted and he had unhappily lost the majority of his soldiers, our countryman Olav exposed himself and his followers to dire hazard in the hope of gaining victory. [23]For, taking eleven vessels and rowing fearlessly, he and his followers attacked the bridge's fortifications; screened by a roof of sheltering shields, they foiled the mechanisms of the defenders and with supreme valour eventually passed through the midst of these mortal dangers. [24]The whole army repaid this most triumphant of warriors, Olav, who had now penetrated the city, with acclamations of high praise and all the credit for the victory they had won was ascribed to him.

[25]Post captam Lundoniam contra regem Edmundum quinquies in IX mensibus fortissime pugnauerunt. [26]Demum defessis utrisque reges, scilicet Edmundus et Canutus, tale inter se pactum statuerunt, ut, dum uiuerent ambo, insulam eque regerent, sed qui superstes fieret, totam teneret. [27]Tunc cum regnasset mense uno, presente luce priuatur Edmundus, totumque regnum possedit Canutus, qui duxit matrem defuncti socii nomine Elfigeuam, que ut ⟨...⟩ duos filios suos Sweinonem et Canutum cognomine Durum; [28]fedus omnino, ⟨quod⟩ cum suis suffraganeis firmissimum sanciuerat, ex toto adnichilans, et fratrem et socium omni mercede laborum frustratos abire permisit.

[29]Tunc Olauus Norwagensis sororem Olaui Sueonensis nomine Margaretam, quam diu digna uicissitudine intimi amoris priuilegio dilexerat, in ipso discessu disponsauit. [30]Sed frustra, nam eandem rex Iarezlafus de Ruscia fratre cogente inuitam duxit uxorem. [31]Quod factum maximum odiorum atque discordiarum fomitem inter tres illos nobilissimos principes subministrasset, si non sapientissima soror Margarete per consilium sui nutritoris disruptam prioris desponsacionis copulam aptissime redintegraret; hanc etenim Olauus in matrimonium sibi postea sociauit. [32]Ex qua Margareta genuit ⟨...⟩

[33]Olauus de Anglia rediens cum duabus magnis onerariis nauibus ad patriam transfretauit Norwegiam et cum eo quatuor episcopi, scilicet Grimkellus, Bernardus, Rodulfus, Sigfridus.

Explicit

26 superstes *Munch* : substes *A* | **27** uno *Storm* : una *A* | totumque *Bugge 1873 et Storm* : Factūque *A* | regnum *Bugge 1873 et Storm* : regum *A* : regni *Munch* | duxit *Munch et Storm* : dixit *uel* duxit *A* | *lacunam unius lineae posuit Storm* | **28** quod *add. Munch et Storm* | sanciuerat : sanciverat *Storm* : sanctiuerat *A* | **29** Olaui : Olavi *Storm* : O. *A* | Sueonensis *Storm* : spronensis *A* : Suionensis *Munch* | **30** Iarezlafus *Storm* : Warerlafus *A* : Iarislafus *Munch in app.* | inuitam : invitam *Munch* : ĩuitĩ *A* | **31** maximum *Ekrem* : maximam *A* | si *Munch et Storm* : Sed *A* | redintegraret *A* : redintegrasset *Storm* | **32** *lacunam posuit Storm* | **33** Grimkellus *Munch* : Grīmkellus *A* |

[25]After the capture of London they waged five courageous battles against King Edmund within nine months. [26]In the end when both rulers, Edmund and Knud, were worn out, they came to this mutual agreement: that as long as they both lived they would govern the island jointly, but whichever survived the other should retain all of it. [27]But then after one month's reign, Edmund was robbed of this world's light, with the result that Knud became master of the whole kingdom; he married the mother of his dead associate, Ælfgifu, who ⟨...⟩ his two sons, Svend and Harde-Knud; [28]the agreement which he had most strongly ratified with his supporters he now annulled utterly and totally and let his brother and his ally depart, disappointed of any reward for their exertions.

[29]At the time of his leaving, Olav of Norway was betrothed to Margareta, Olof of Sweden's sister, whom he had long had the joy of loving deeply and being deservedly loved in return. [30]But it came to nothing, since at her brother's instigation she reluctantly married the Russian king, Jarislav. [31]This act would have supplied abundant tinder for hatred and dissension between these three illustrious sovereigns, had not Margareta's prudent sister on the advice of her foster-father most appropriately restored the link that had been severed with the cancellation of his previous engagement; for Olav later joined with her in matrimony [32]and she bore him ⟨...⟩

[33]Returning from England with two large merchant vessels, Olav voyaged back to his homeland of Norway, bringing with him four bishops, Grimkel, Bernard, Rodolv and Sigfrid.

The End

Commentary

The Prologue

Prologus incipit The Dalhousie manuscript (*A*) begins with a large lacuna in the upper left-hand corner of the first leaf, extending over 12 lines. This lacuna is broadest at the top, and narrows gradually further and further towards the bottom. The torn-off part included the large initial capital letter (which probably took up 5 lines) of the first word of the first line, along with a number of letters and words of the first and subsequent lines (see ill.). It seems that ever since the identification of *HN* the lacuna has been filled in with a piece of white paper to protect the edge of the lacuna. Whether it has been re-repaired since the nineteenth century is unclear, but when I (LBM) consulted the original in 2002 I could not entirely agree with Storm as to what was visible (see below). This may be because the strip of paper has been fastened in a new way since he handled it.

1 Tullius in philosophie tractatu suo In *A* we read ......*ius in philistratu suo*. Munch printed ....*us*, but Storm read ...*tus*. The paper strip is loose at this point and by lifting it one can surely make out an 'i' or perhaps the last minim of another letter (the 'i's are not dotted in the display script used here). There is no trace of a long ascender or a cross-bar.

A work under the name of Philistratus or similar is not known by the Latin west and has been sought after in vain by Storm, Lehmann, and others. Therefore Fisher's suggestion of reading *philosophie tractatu* makes very good sense and is palaeographically explainable from two abbreviations (philē trātu) (another possibility is *philosophico tractatu* (Kraggerud), but that would be slightly more removed from the transmitted reading). This convincing emendation opens the possibilities of supplying a name at the beginning of the phrase. Ekrem favoured Solinus (third cent.), or perhaps Honorius (twelfth cent.), *cf.* her arguments in the Essay § 5.1.2-3; the two main arguments for choosing Cicero instead are: 1) Cicero was the author of a fairly well known treatise on friendship — Solinus or Honorius were not; although a suitable passage is not found in Cicero's *De amicitia*, the phrase from Cicero's *Orator* 10,33 (spoken to Brutus): *Sed nihil difficile amanti puto* ('But I think that nothing is difficult for a friend') circulated as a proverb in the Middle Ages (PL 144:665, 178:659; 112:1471 & Walter 1963–67 no. 16630a); perhaps Cicero's name was attached to the saying; if not, his authorship of *De amicitia* and other well-known treatises of moral philosophy could at least easily lead to that assumption. (Tullius was vaguely suggested by Koht 1919–1920, 115, but rejected because he had not found the saying in Cicero). 2) It is far more effective to begin with an ethical maxim if the quoted author is a well-known sage (*tantus philosophus* below); 'Tullius' qualifies better than 'Solinus' for this; 'Honorius' was not a household name in the twelfth century (and in some twelfth-century manuscripts his writings were anonymous or attributed to 'Henricus', *cf.* Flint 1983), and one would expect some kind of specification ('monachus illustris nostre etatis' or the like) if the author of *HN* really wanted to quote a near contemporary by name. (*Cf.* the prologue of Theodoricus Monachus where other twelfth-century authors are mentioned with some such explanation: *Hugo bone memorie canonicus Sancti Victoris Parisiis, uir undecunque doctissimus [...] Sigibertis quoque Gyemblacensis monachus*; the Roman authority, Boethius, on the other hand is taken for granted). Note also that although Honorius certainly gave inspiration for the prologue (see below), he did not provide the author of *HN* with the proverb itself. Whether or not we accept *philosophie tractatu*, we are in any case dealing with a wise author who pronounced an important sentence on friendship. That in itself points to Cicero. 'Tullius' was at least as common in ML as 'Cicero' for the Roman orator and philosopher, *cf. e.g.* the prologue of Adam of Bremen (see below for other, certain verbal parallels between *HN* & Adam): ... *qui dicant haec ficta et falsa veluti somnia Scipionis a Tullio meditata* (ed. Schmeidler, praefatio p. 3). For a contemporary and similar prefatory use of a Roman philosopher's proverb, see Otto of Freising, *Chronica* (prefatory letter to Rainald of Dassel, ed. Hofmeister, p. 4): *Cum iuxta Boetium in omnibus philosophiae disciplinis ediscendis atque tractandis summum vitae positum solamen existimem* ... **Tullius in philosophie tractatu suo laudans amicitiam, cum de ceteris eius bonis ageret, inter caros amicos nichil fere difficile fore meminit.** The author of *HN* drew inspiration from the prologue of Honorius's *Imago mundi*; for direct verbal parallels see below. Here he inherits a figure of thought: Having been asked by Christianus to provide an account of the world order, Honorius fears criticism from possible detractors. Nevertheless he will comply because, as he writes, brotherly love conquers all. (prol. ed. Flint, pp. 48–49): *Laboriosum (sc. negotium) quidem mihi in aliis occupato et multis ut scis animi molestiis pergravato, periculosum autem propter invidos qui cuncta quae nequeunt imitari, non cessant calumpniari. et quae assequi non poterunt, venenoso dente ut setiger hircus lacerare non omittunt* [...] *Enim vero cum non solum laborem meum, sed et meipsum tibi debeam praesertim cum me non mihi soli sed toti mundo genitum intelligam, omittens invidos tabescentes, non me sed seipsos livido corde corrodentes, ardua aggredior molimina, quia inprobus labor immo karitas vincit omnia.* This is no argument for reading *Honorius* instead of *Tullius* because Honorius does not praise friendship other than by saying *karitas vincit omnia.* **eius** The word abbreviated in *A* is an 'n' or 'u' (the two are usually not distinguishable in this hand) with a superscript 'e' (see ill.); Storm preferred *uite* and Ekrem *nature* (*cf.* Cappelli 1929, *e.g.* p. 230). If we look at the context *eius* (or *illius*) recommends itself: whoever the author referred to might be, we are certainly presented with a specification. A wise man, probably Cicero, wrote philosophy, more specifically on friendship; one statement about friendship was that there are no difficulties between true friends. The series of specifications is spoiled if we take *uite* or *nature*, two concepts belonging to other departments of philosophy. A typical *eius* abbreviation like ei⁹ could have been misunderstood at some point in the transmission. **caros amicos** On account of the above-quoted *caritas* in Honorius and the same below in *HN*, it is likely that *caros amicos* was the reading in *A* rather than Storm's *ueros amicos*. **nichil** *Nihil* is often written with 'ch' in ML; it indicates two syllables, since 'h' by itself is silent, *cf.* Blaise 1994, 132 and Elliot 1997, 5. **meminit** with the sense of *memorat*. It also occurs in this sense in, *e.g.*, Svenonis Aggonis Filii *Lex Castrensis* (ed. Gertz 1917–22, vol. I, 84, l. 23) and in the Prologue to Theodoricus Monachus.

2 philosophi For *philosophus*, *cf.* Essay § 5.1.2. In the *epistolae* which introduce Honorius's work we find *philosophia, scientia* and *sapientia.* **satis probabili** Storm claims to have read the 'a' as well (*pro[b]abili*), whereas Munch printed *pro(ba)bili*. Today the 'a' is not visible. Storm may have removed the strip here or he may have reported the reading inaccurately. The positive form of adjectives is often used in *HN* with an intensifying adverb of degree, such as *satis* here. This corresponds to I 4 (*nimis*), XV 3 *admodum* and 5 (*valde*), XVIII 5 (*valde*) and 13 (*multum*). The positive was sometimes felt to be too weak in the Middle Ages. Thus we often find an intensifying adverb together with the positive, *cf.* Elliot 1997, 9: *satis i.e.* 'very'. **satis probabili sentencie [...] contraire** *Cf. Est* 13,5: *nostrisque iussionibus contraire.* The use of a compound verb that governs the dative is frequent in *HN*. *Cf.* I 7 (*inseruientes*), II 5 (*inhereant*), 12 (*applicant*), III 5 (*subiacent*), IV 3 (*inponentes* and *subfixis*), 9 (*superponunt*), 12 (*subiecti sunt*), 22 (*obuiasse*), 26 (*adiacent*), V 1 (*preiacentes*), VI 7 (*adherentes*), 9 (*subiugarent*), 21 (*subiacent* and *deseruiunt*), X 3 (*submersus*), XVI 3 (*deseruiens*), XVII 46 (*applicuit*), 51 (*submersum*), 53 (*aduectus sit*), 57 (*presidebant*) and XVIII 21 (*appropiantes*). This often appears to reflect the influence of poetry and the Vulgate. **ausus** The use of the past participle instead of a dependent clause or as a main verb with an ellipsis of *esse* is frequent in *HN*. **tametsi tali sagacitati me in omnibus imparem et ad tale et tam graue onus imbecillem noui** *Tametsi tali sagacitati* is Egil Kraggerud's suggestion.

Bugge 1873 suggests *tam preclare sagacitati*, Storm *tantae enim sagacitati*, and Munch *tam ... sagacitati*. *A* has *tā [...] gacitati*. (Storms claims to have read the 'a' as well (*[s]agacitati*), whereas Munch printed *(sa)gacitati*. Today the 'a' is not visible. Storm may have removed the strip here or he may have reported the reading inaccurately). It is very likely that what we have here is not a parenthetical (Bugge, Storm, Munch), but a concessive clause (Kraggerud). The retention of the indicative *noui* is due to the fact that *A* has *non*, which is more likely to be a false reading of *noui* than, say, *norim*. Moreover, the indicative is customary in connection with *tametsi*. *Cf.* Adam's prologue (p. 2), which might have inspired the passage in its entirety: *Ad quod nimirum valde arduum et viribus meis impar onus*. For the use of Adam and various *topoi* in the Prologue, *cf.* Essay § 5.2. **ad tale et tam graue onus imbecillem** *Imbecillis* is a rarely used form of *imbecillus*. Here *imbecillis* occurs with *ad* + the accusative, instead of an objective genitive. This is consistent with an increasing use of prepositions in the Middle Ages. *Cf.* also *Hbr* 5,11. **honestissimis** The superlative is frequently employed in *HN*. It often stands just for the positive, or as a 'very high' degree. In certain places it is also used to denote the highest degree. It can be difficult to know exactly how to translate it. Here it is used as *superlativus elativus*. **ne ingratus crebrorum munerum beneficio existam** *Cf.* Adam's prologue (p. 1): *ne proselitus et advena tanti muneris beneficio ingratus existerem*. *Ingratus* + the dative are common in ML. *Cf.* also Blaise 1994 § 104 for adjective + dative. In classical Latin and post-classical Latin, *ingratus*, 'ungrateful', seems to appear mostly with *in*, *adversus* or *contra* + the accusative or with a pure genitive. **poscor** This verb suggested by Storm (1880, 71) is probably correct, since Honorius also uses this verb about the commissioner in his dedication: *Cum* [...] *poscis a me amicissime, ut* [...].

3 mihi The personal pronoun suggested here by Gjessing should be inserted because it accords with Honorius (*cf.* the quotation above under 1). **sarcina** f., 'a burden', is usually employed in the plural in classical Latin and in the Vulgate. **discribere** The prefixes *di* and *de* are used in some places interchangeably in *HN*, *cf.* II 13 (*diglutiunt*), VI 3 (*diglutit*), VIII 21 (*descripsimus*), XIII 10 (*diuictis* and *deuinceretur*), XVII 33 (*desponsauerat*), XVII 54 (*diffiniendo*) and XVIII 29 (*disponsauit*). **utriusque** This is the only place in *HN* in which *uterque* is used in the singular, *cf.* I 7, IV 20, V 3 and XVIII 26.

4 Quod negotium nimio sudore plenum [...] quam sit onerosum et ob inuidos quam sit pericolosum, ipse optime nosti *Cf.* Honorius's epistle dedicatory (ed. Flint 1983, 48): *Quod negotium sudore plenum ipse melius nosti, quam sit laboriosum, quamque periculosum*. **Nimio sudore plenum** *Plenum* takes the ablative here, but *cf.* IX 32. **Latino eloquio intemptatum** The author complains about the special problems involved in a pioneering project. So do Adam of Bremen, Theodoricus Monachus and Saxo Grammaticus in their prologues. This obviously forms part of a modesty topos, but there is no reason to doubt the sincerity of *HN*'s author here; there is no evidence that he used Theodoricus and it seems we have to accept that they worked about the same time without knowing of each other. For this, *cf.* also Introduction pp. 20–21 and Essay § 5.2. and 12. **ob** The author prefers *ob* to *propter*, which is used only in VI 5. *Cf.* Löfstedt 1936, 219–20.

5 nostris aminiculis It is debatable whether *nostris* means 'our' or 'my' here, *cf.* Essay § 5.2. The word *adminiculum* derives from the language of gardening, and denotes a support for the vine. It is also used in classical Latin in the sense of 'tool' or 'aid', or 'instrument', *cf.* also *Est* 16,20 and Svenonis Aggonis Filii *Lex Castrensis* (ed. Gertz 1917-22, vol. I, 74, l. 10). **edacem liuorem** The envy of possible critics is an exordial commonplace; *cf.* Honorius below and *e.g.* Adam, Praefatio: *Difficillimum est enim invidis placere etc*, and Saxo, Præfatio 2: *obtrectationis livorem etc.* **postponendo** The ablative of the gerund used in place of the present participle in order to designate the present is common in *HN*. This same use also occurs in Livy, and particularly in the Vulgate, *cf. e.g. Act* 10,38. *Cf.* also Kaulen 1904, 279-80, Löfstedt 1936, 159-60 and Elliot 1997, 43. **si quid nostra refert** *Cf.* Honorius in his epistle dedicatory: *Etenim vero cum non solum laborem meum, sed et meipsum tibi debeam (praesertim cum me non mihi soli, sed toti mundo genitum intelligam) omittens invidos tabescentes, non me, sed seipsos livido corde corrodentes, ardua aggredior molimina.* In other words, envious people harm only themselves, not others such as Honorius or the author of *HN*. The ablative *nostra* may also be translated by 'us'.

6 forisfecit *Forisfacere* is a common ML legal verb: 'offend', 'trangress'.

7 o Agnelle Despite numerous attempts, the dedicatee has not been identified; see Introduction p. 16; for various candidates see Ekrem 1998, 88 and Essay § 11.1. **iure didascalico mi prelate** The superiority of the dedicatee (*prelatus*) is commonplace in dedications; this turn of phrase, however, points more specifically to a teacher (*didascalicus* from *didascalus*, ML version of the Greek word for 'teacher'). *Prelatus* means superior of any kind, but it would be natural to take it here in the ordinary sense of bishop, or perhaps archdean in charge of an episcopal school. *Cf.* also Essay § 11.1. **hec mea scripta** Poetical use of the plural. We find this use in many places in *HN*, *cf. e.g.* the chs. II 11, III 8, IV 2 and 6, VIII 7, 9 and 17, XIII 6 and XVII 3 and 12. **polita** Ellipsis of *esse* is quite common in *HN*. **scrupulosis** An adjective formed by the diminutive of *scrupus*, 'filled with small, sharp stones', here 'uneven'. **implicita** From *implico*, 1st, 'infold', 'involve'. Here perhaps used instead of *impleta* or *plena* for the sake of rhyme: *polita – implicita.* It has the connotation of 'hampered', 'confused'. **gratanter** A common ML adverb, 'graciously'. **accipito** From *accipio*, 3rd. Here in the future imperative, which is employed in poetry, legal texts and general regulations.

8 cronographus [...] falsidicus An obvious borrowing from Adam's prologue (p. 3): *In quo opere talibus ausis sciant omnes, quod nec laudari cupio ut historicus nec improbari metuo ut falsidicus.* It has been noted that *HN* here relied on the B1 branch of Adam manuscripts because of *falsidicus*, which in B2 reads *falsiloquus* (Ellehøj 1965, 159). The variation, however, could have been made by the author of *HN*, even if he read *falsiloquus* in Adam. In his borrowings from Honorius' *Imago mundi* we see his way of handling a source with variation at work — see commentary at VIII 13–18. **exorreo** This is the reading of *A* It has not been changed in the present edition. *Exorreo* could well have been the original spelling, since ML spelling allowed suppression of the 'h', *cf.* Prologue 1 (*nichil*). **seniorum asserciones secutus** *Cf.* Theodoricus, who in his prologue and in the last chapter (34) refers to his sources, likewise oral testimonies of trustworthy men: *Veritatis uero sinceritas in hac nostra narratione ad illos omnimodo referenda est, quorum relatione hec annotauimus, quia nos non uisa sed audita conscripsimus. Cf.* also Essay § 5.2. For *assertio* and *senior*, *cf.* Adam (II 35 and his prologue p. 3, respectively). **secutus** Ellipsis of *sim.*

9 nostris temporibus This is the strongest evidence that *HN* originally covered Norwegian history up to the time of the author; *cf.* Introduction pp. 9–10. **memorie dignum** Storm classicized the phrase by changing *memorie* to *memoria*. But in ML *dignus* is as frequent with genitive or *ad*, *e.g.* Honorius's *Summa totius de omnimoda historia* (PL 172 col. 195): *Sed nihil dignum memoriae ibi geritur*; *dignus* is only used here in *HN*. **ipse** Bugge's suggestion was rejected by Storm but seems fair. The reading of *A*, *ipsum*, would be superfluous; furthermore the contrast prepared by 'distant past – testimonies of old men' / 'nowadays – my own findings' calls for *ipse*. **magnificencias** Rare in the present sense of 'great deeds'. The corresponding adjective, *magnificus*, is used about Olav Tryggvason in *HN* XVII 11; about the Russian, and Christian, King Jarislav in *Passio Olaui* (ed. Metcalfe 1881, 71), and in Theodoricus (ch. 16) as an adverb in connection with Olav Tryggvason. For these *magnificencias*, *cf.* also Essay § 9.3. **scriptorum** Translated here by 'writings' (from *scriptum* n.), *cf.* Honorius's epistle dedicatory: [...] *ad instructionem itaque multorum, quibus deest copia librorum, hic libellus edatur,* [...]; *cf.* also Theodoricus, prologue: ... *quos nimirum, ut ait Boetius, clarissimos suis temporibus uiros scriptorum inops deleuit opinio* with Kraggerud's commentary (forthcoming). It could also be taken in the sense of authors (from *scriptor* m.) as in Adam (prologue p. 2) *scriptorum, qui hoc posteris traderent, diligentia caruisse.* **modernorum** From *modernus*, a common expression in ML for 'contemporary'.

I. The location of Norway

The beginning of the first book in *A* is written on the *verso*-side of the Prologue; the same tear extends over the first 11 lines where textual elements have consequently disappeared (including the heading).

The pioneering account of Norwegian geography beginning here is structured in this way: (I) the situation and delimitation of Norway; (II–IV) the division of Norway proper into three zones; (V–VIII) the islands under Norwegian influence. The only earlier geographical description we know of is the brief, and entirely different, treatment by Orderic Vitalis (X.iv.27–29) from *c.* 1130; he probably drew on a written source, *cf.* Chibnall's commentary vol. V, 220.

Liber primus in ystoria Norwagensium Here the genitive, or *de* + ablative, is preferable to *in* + ablative in classical Latin. The spelling *ystoria* for *historia* is typical of the ML, since 'y' was interchangeable with 'i', *cf.* Elliot 1997, 3. For the missing 'h', *cf.* commentary on Prologue 8 (*exorreo*). The traditional title of the work, *Historia Norwegie*, was derived from Munch's filling of this lacuna as *N[orwegie]*. He talked himself of *Chronicon Norwegie*, but since Storm the title, *Historia Norwegie*, has been canonized and is retained in the present edition for practical and bibliographical purposes. But serious doubts can be raised against this form as no good parallels in contemporary literature can be found. The usual formulae are: *Historia regum Britannie, Gesta Danorum, Historia Ecclesiastica Anglorum, Chronica Boemorum, Historia Francorum, Historia Anglorum, Gesta ducum Normannorum* etc. Even if *Norwegia* is frequently mentioned in the text as a geographical concept, the author's promise in the prologue (above, 3) to treat the deeds of kings etc would tally better with *Historia Norwagensium* — and be in much better keeping with contemporary usage. *Norwagenses* is common in *HN* as well (used as a substantive in VIII 4, X 1, and XVII 26). The concept of a territory automatically comprising the state, people and rulers as historical agents, is modern. The title of the work was, probably, *Ystoria Norwagensium.*

1 igitur A filler which, like *itaque* (*cf.* II 1) and *ergo* (*cf.* V 1), in a number of places introduces a new sentence, a new paragraph, or a new chapter. Apart from *itaque*, 'and so', VI 14, they all appear as the second word in the sentence, *cf.*, however, commentary on VIII 4 for *igitur*. **quodam** The indefinite pronoun *quidam* is often used as an indefinite article in *HN*, *cf. e.g.* IX 13, X 5 and 7, XI 7 and XII 1. **Nor** Munch filled the lacuna with *Nor*, but with a different construction than Storm (see apparatus). Storm's shorter phrase (accepted here), however, works well only on the condition that *Nor* was written in the display script, otherwise there is too much space in *A*. This is very plausible because of the wide use of display script for kings' names from chapter IX on. *Cf. Flateyjarbók* (I 21-22), in which Nor comes from Kvenland via Västerbotten and Jämtland to Trondheim. In the paragraph on *Hversu Noregr bygðisk* the story is told of Nor, who founded the lineage of the petty kings Trond and Agde, after whom a law province (Trøndelag) and a county (Agder) were later named. *Cf.* also Oddr, *Saga Óláfs Tryggvasonar*, 22, where Nor is briefly mentioned. In Honorius, too, we find a number of similar etymologies, *cf.* Skard 1930, 80. *HN* is in line with other twelfth-century national histories in promoting eponymous heroes, *e.g.* Cosmas of Prague's Bohemus, Geoffrey of Monmouth's Brutus, and Saxo's Dan. Adam (IV 31) derives 'Nortmannia' / 'Norwegia' from its location to the north. For the account of Nor, *cf.* also Essay § 8.1. **optinuisse dicitur** From *obtineo* 2nd; for the spelling variants *ob / op*, *cf.* Elliot 1997, 36. The letter after *optinu* looks more like an 'i' or a minim than the first stroke of an 'e' (*pace* Storm, note *ad locum*). If 'i' is correct, then we should fill out with *optinuisse dicitur* or *optinuit* both suggested by Storm in the note. If one settles for a brief beginning of the next sentence, there is too much space for *optinuit* only.

2 Tota Storm filled in the opening as *Est autem*; Something must be supplied because we cannot have two sentences beginning with *Norwegia*. Especially at this monumental opening section of the geographical description our author would have striven for variation. Therefore Storm's suggestion is also problematical as sentence 4 just below begins with *Est* as well. A better contrast to *sed maxima ex parte [...]* would be obtained by saying 'The whole of Norway is immense, but for the most part uninhabitable'. One could thus consider *Omnis* or *Tota*; the latter is clearly preferred by the author when describing geography, *cf.* VIII 11, XIV 1, XVI 1, XVII 56, XVIII 11, XVIII 26 as against one instance of *omnis* in VI 14 (*omnem illam*). A short word like *tota* also goes well with a long filling as suggested for the end of the previous period. The lack of a verb is more a part of the author's style than was appreciated in the nineteenth century (*cf.* Skard 1930, 8–10). **pre** The causal sense is common in ML, *cf.* also IV 26 and VI 2. In II 16, *pre* is used in a comparison. **nimietate** From *nimietas* f., in ML usually 'a great amount'. **nimietate moncium, nemorum ac frigorum** Bugge suggested filling the lacuna with (1873, 43): *nimietate mon[cium et asperitate] nemorum ac frigorum*; this reads very well and it echoes Adam (IV 31): *Nortmannia propter asperitatem montium sive propter frigus intemperatum sterilissima est omnium regionum, solis apta pecoribus.* However, there is not space enough for *asperitate* which is probably why Storm chose the clumsy *moncium et nemorum ac frigorum.* By leaving out the *et* one gets a more presentable ending of the clause. Alternatively one could choose Bugge's reading, but as a conjecture against the transmission, not as a filling of the physical lacuna. **frigorum** Poet. plural, here for the sake of rhyme: *nemorum – frigorum.* In classical Latin, **nemus** n. is often poetical for *silua.*

3 ab Albia One of Storm's numerous suggestions for the filling of this space, relying on the parallel with III 3. It is in keeping with the author's tendency of *interpretatio Romana.* Another good possibility, favoured by Ekrem, is *Gothelba* which has strong support in Adam (IV 21 schol. 131): *Gothelba fluvius a Nordmannis Gothiam separat, magnitudine non impar isti Albiae Saxonum, unde ille nomen sortitur.* But after consulting *A*, I have difficulty seeing how *a Gothelba* would not exceed the margin very considerably (and it can hardly have been abbreviated). *Albia* could be a Latinization simply of Old Norse 'elfr', modern Norwegian and Swedish, 'elv', *i.e.* 'river', meaning perhaps Götaelven. **incipit** etc. The passage is inspired by Adam's description (IV 31): *Incipit autem ex prominentibus scopulis huius freti, quod Balticum appellari solet; deinde reflexo in aquilonem dorso, postquam frementis occeani marginem suo circuit ambitu, tandem in Ripheis montibus limitem facit, ubi et lassus deficit orbis.* **regirat** From *regyro* 1st, 'to return as if in a cycle', 'to come round'. It also occurs, *e.g.*, in *Historia de profectione Danorum*, ch. V.

4 nimis sinuosa *Nimis*, as 'very' is common in ML. **promunctoria** is also written as *promuntoria* and *promontoria*. In ML texts, 'u' and 'o' are often interchangeable, *cf.* Elliot 1997, 3. For the spelling *promunctoria*, *cf.* also Adam (IV 5 and 11). **per longum** The author here puzzles modern readers by maintaining that the three inhabited areas of Norway divide the country *per longum*, *i.e.* into three parallel zones in a north-south direction. In III 4 we read that the Uplands end at Dovre, south of Trøndelag, *i.e.* the Uplands cut Norway across, so to speak. So we have the coastland to the west, east of it the mountains stretching to Trøndelag, and east of Trøndelag Finnmarken (*cf.* also Essay § 6.1.6. and commentary on IV 1 where the same expression is used). A similar conception of the Scandinavian peninsula stretching towards the east rather than the north is found in Adam IV 25; as illustrated in Nyberg 1984, 318–19, Adam, and thus *HN*, are exaggerating the eastward turn, but many modern Scandinavian projections of the peninsula are in fact twisting it too much towards the north. **Finnis** *i.e. a Finnis.* The preposition *a/ab* is missing in a number of places in *HN* in connection with a personal agent in the passive, whereas in other places it occurs in connection with an impersonal agent, *cf.* I 9, III 1, IV 2 and 6, V 3 and XVII 39. This manner of presentation is often poetical in classical Latin but more common in Christian Latin, *cf.* Blaise 1994 § 111. For the translation of *Finni* by 'Finns', *i.e.* the Lapps (or Sami), *cf.* Essay § 6.1.6. with note. **inhabitatur [...] aratur** Rhyme.

5 Circumsepta Ellipsis of *est.* **refluentis Occeani** That is, the Great Ocean that surrounds and breaks against the land and subsides, returning to the source of its true origin. *Cf.* Adam (IV 40), Honorius (I 47) and Theodoricus (ch. 17) who illustrate the same view. The description of the Ocean as *refluens* (used again in I 11 and VII 1) is not traceable elsewhere, whereas we do find *fluenta* (from *fluentum*) in Honorius (I 45), and also *refluat* (I 47). *Occeani* is a variant spelling for *Oceani.* **ex occasu [...] a meredie [...] de sole** The prepositions *ex, a* and *de* are used interchangeably in *HN* in a local sense. This is characteristic of ML, *cf.* Elliot 1997, 26. **meredie** *i.e. meridie.* For the vacillation between 'e' and 'i', *cf.* Blaise 1994 pp. 129–30 and Elliot 1997, 3. **Dacia [...] Swethia** For the general background behind the use of *interpretatio Romana* in naming Denmark and Sweden in this way, see Hemmingsen 2000. **Swethiam, Gautoniam, Angariam, Iamtoniam** *Swethia* (in IX 11 and 18 also spelled *Swecia*) has in the present edition been translated by 'Sweden', which here primarily seems to correspond to the eastern part of modern Svealand, *i.e.* middle Sweden (the area around Uppsala and Mälaren), where the ancient Yngling monarchs are supposed to have resided. Like Adam, the author seems to believe that Sweden extended from west to east (*cf.* Nyberg 1984, 319ff.), and not towards the northeast; he mentions first Svealand (present-day Uppland, Södermanland, Västmanland, Närke, Dalarna, Värmland and Dalsland), *i.e.* the area where Sweden is broadest, which according to his view thus extends farthest south. After that, Götaland is mentioned, *i.e.* the land of the Götar or the Goths (the westernmost area that seems to include what we presently regard as southern Sweden (Öster- and Västergötland, Gotland and Småland, but not Bohuslän (which belonged to Norway), nor Halland, Skåne or Blekinge (which belonged to Denmark). Then comes Ångermanland, which in *HN* might seem to be on a line with Götaland, but located east of Svealand; and finally, Jämtland, which then becomes the northernmost area, bordering Norway. 'East' of Ångermanland (for a contemporary reader, northeast and southeast of Ångermanland), the peoples mentioned below, the Kirjalers, Kvens etc. seem to have resided, *cf.* Nyberg 1984, 312–23 and Hansen 1996. In the Middle Ages the Goths were believed by many also to have conquered Scythia, an area of undefined size that stretched between the Caspian Sea and the Baltic Sea. Adam also calls the Baltic (or the eastern part of it) 'the Scythian sea', *cf.* II 18, 21 and 22 and IV 10 and 20, and he makes a distinction between *Gothi* and *Sueones*, *cf.* IV 14. For Jämtland and its connection with Norway, *cf.* Essay § 6.1.1 and 7 and Phelpstead 2001, 77. For the Goths, *cf.* Essay § 8.1 with note.

6 quas partes probably refers to all of the above, but mainly to Norway; the Baltic area as such was certainly not christianized. The Finns are pagans, but live on Christian Norwegian soil, *cf.* IV 1.

7 paganismo inseruientes For these pagan peoples, *cf.* also Adam IV 32. **Kyriali** *I.e.* Karelians from eastern Finland. For these and the following non-Norwegian peoples, *cf.* Essay § 6.1.2 & 6.1.6 and Hansen 2000, 76–77. **Kweni** The author does not seem to believe that they are the same as women, *cf. Virginum Terra* below. The Kvens in *HN*, together with the Kirjalers, the Horned Finns and the two kinds of Bjarms, are real, whereas the virgins (or Amazons) are reported with some doubt. Thus he corrects Adam (III 16, IV 19 (with schol. 123) and 25) (*cf.* also Nyberg 1984, 311 and Hallencreutz 1984a, 365), who seems to understand Kvenland as 'Kvinneland' (*i.e.* Land of Women). This could be due to the fact that the Old Norse word for a woman (modern Norwegian: 'kvinne') was 'kvæn'. According to *HN* the Kvens came to Norway from the east (perhaps from the area of the Gulf of Bothnia, *cf.* Hansen 1996, 36), while the Land of Women, or rather of Maidens, seems to lie northwest of Bjarmeland and is mentioned a few lines further down in *HN*. If the author reckons Kvenland to be the same as the Land of Maidens, this would mean a futile repetition. *Cf.* Hansen 2000, 73–76. **Cornuti Finni** It is unclear why these Finns are called *Cornuti*. The Horned Finns are also mentioned in Hauk Erlendsson's book (from the beginning of the 1300s), in which it is said of them that they had horns that curved into their foreheads, and that they were cannibals (Fritzner 1886–96). They resemble Isidore's description of satyrs. In earlier research on *HN* they have been taken to be inhabitants of Finland. But according to *HN* some of them crossed over into Norway. Whether the nickname *Cornuti* is used traditionally, or whether it derives from their special caps, from their having used tools made of horn, their having been adorned with horn figures or jewellery, or their having been drawn by reindeer with horns when they went hunting, remains a matter of conjecture. *Cf.* Hansen 2000, 78–79. **utrique Biarmones** *Cf.* Saxo *Gesta Danorum* VIII.xiv.6 for the two kinds of Bjarms (although he only mentions *Biarmia ulterior*). In *HN* these seem to be the inhabitants of both sides of *Sinus Septentrionalis* (see below). For the Bjarms, *cf.* Hansen 1996, 45–52 & 2000, 80–82.

8 istos In *HN*, as in other medieval texts, *is, ille, ipse, iste, idem* and *hic* are often used interchangeably as simple demonstratives, *cf.* Elliot 1997, 33–34, Kaulen 1904, 165 and 169 and Löfstedt 1936, 64-66 and 123–24.

9 naute For the account of them and their journey, *cf.* Adam (IV 40) and Essay § 6.1.2. **Cum [...] studuissent** The temporal conjunction *cum* occurs in *HN* both with the indicative (XVII 21, 22 and 40 and XVIII 12) and the subjunctive (I 9, IV 19, IX 20, XII 3 and 6, XV 12, XVII 9, 16, 26 and 38, XVIII 9, 22 and 27). This is common in ML. As a causal conjunction it occurs only with the subjunctive (Prologue 8, XV 3 and XVII 37). **a contrariis** *Cf.* commentary on I 4 (*Finnis*) concerning the use of *a / ab* in connection with an impersonal agent. **Viridenses** The inhabitants of Greenland, a continent that was widely held to be connected to Europe in the north, and one that stretched nearly all the way to the islands off Africa. According to *HN* Greenland lies to the north and is separated from the Land of Maidens and the Land of Giants by *congelatis scopulis*, *cf.* commentary on I 10. The author translates the Norwegian term 'Grønlendere', *i.e.* Greenlanders, into Latin in contrast to Adam (IV 36), who Latinizes the Norwegian name and calls them *Gronlandi*. For the description of Greenland at this point in *HN*, *cf.* Essay § 6.1.1. **mire magnitudinis** The descriptive genitive (*cf.* also II 4), is more common in *HN* than the descriptive ablative, which is found only in II 7. For this, *cf.* Löfstedt 1936, 160 and Elliot 1997, 17. Adam writes that the Giants (IV 41) were *mirae altitudinis*, and that theirs was a land that lay far to the north, near the frozen Great Ocean, wrapped in a blanket of thick fog. In *HN* the Land of Giants is placed along with the Land of Maidens between Greenland and Bjarmeland. **Virginum Terra** The Land of Maidens, which in *HN* is located between Greenland and Bjarmeland. *Cf.* also Adam (IV 19), who believes that it is a stretch of coastline along the Baltic

Sea. For these legends, *cf.* Essay § 6.1.7. **que gustu aque concipere dicuntur** *Cf.* Adam, who writes about the Amazons (*ibidem*): *eas aquae gustu dicunt aliqui concipere.* **reperisse** Here, as in VIII 2 and XVII 51, written with a single 'p', but *cf.* Prologue 9, where we find *repperi.*

10 Viridis terra The author translates the Norwegian name 'Grønland' (*i.e.* Greenland) into Latin, *cf.* I 9 (*Viridenses*). Adam (IV 37) uses the Latinized Norwegian name *Gronlandia*, and he imagines it to be an island. **congelatis scopulis** From *scopulus* m., in classical Latin only in the sense of a rock in or by the sea. It might seem questionable whether this expression signifies 'icebergs' or 'ice-covered mountains' here, but *cf. promunctoria congelata* II 11, which means 'ice-covered promontories'. If the former is the case, then in the author's view Greenland seems to be an island; but with 'ice-covered mountains' Greenland seems to be a continent attached to Europe. In *HN* it lies to the north and one had to undertake a voyage in order to get there (*cf.* II 12), but that does not necessarily mean that it is thought to be an island (*cf.* commentary on II 10 *profundissimus*). Adam also uses the term *scopulus* in the sense of a rock by the coast or promontory (IV 31) as the starting point of the Norwegian land. For the mention made of Greenland at this point in *HN*, *cf.* Essay § 6.1.1.

11 patria Here used in the sense of *terra* or *regio*, 'a larger area of land', but *cf.* also commentary on II 1. *Patria* in the sense of *terra* is common in ML. **Telensibus** Or *Tilensibus*, *cf.* XVII 31. Concerning the confusion of 'e' and 'i' *cf.* commentary on I 5 (*meredie*). Here *Telensibus* means the Icelanders from Thule (or *Tile*, as Iceland is also called in *HN*). *Cf.* also Saxo *Gesta Danorum* Prol. I.4 who calls the Icelanders *Tylenses.* **reperta et inhabitata ac fide catholica roborata** This and the following statement concerning the Skrælings give the impression that in the author's time Greenland was inhabited solely by Icelandic Norwegians. For criteria that speak for Norwegian possession, *cf.* Essay § 7. **Affricanas insulas** This is the first time one encounters the notion of a curving landbridge connection from the Bjarms in the north through Greenland in the west to the African Islands in the south. Such an inclusion of the northern lands and north-western islands into the *orbis terrarum* resulted from a compromise between a northern viewpoint and the model inherited from Roman geography. *Cf.* Storm 1890, 345–47, Bjørnbo 1909, 228–33 (with ill.) & Benediktsson 1960, 267.

12 reperiuntur The historic present is used here for the perfect *reperti sunt.* **Screlinga** *Cf.* Ari (*Íslendingabók*, ch. 6) concerning the inhabitants of Vinland, *i.e.* the Eskimos. The form is accusative plural in Old Norse — thus congruent with *quos.*

13 absque A common preposition with abl. in ML, 'without', *cf.* Elliot 1997, 27. *Absque* is only used here in *HN. Sine* occurs only in II 15.

14 Sed Used here in a weakened adversative sense, *cf.* also VI 3 and 7 and XIII 11 **cetinis** Adj. *cetinus* from *cetus* 'sea monster', 'whale', *cf. e.g.* DN vol. 2, 206 (1342 A.D.). For the forms of *cetus* see below at III 13 & 14.

15 circumstancias From *circumstantia* f., 'circumstance', 'condition', 'surroundings', common in ML.

15–16 ostendimus [...] exequamur This form of chapter ending could have been influenced by Honorius: *Europam perambulavimus. Ad Africam transmigremus* (I 33), *Ignea inferni loca inspeximus, ad refrigerium aquarum confugiamus* (I 37) or *Post decursam Asiam, transeamus ad Europam* (I 21).

16 trifariam From *trifarius*, 'threefold'; it occurs in *e.g.* Solinus 27, and the prefatory letter to Honorius' *Imago Mundi* about philosophy: *trifaria philosophia* (ed. Flint 1983 p. 48).

II. The three inhabited zones of Norway

incolatu From *incolatus* m., 'residence' or 'settlement'.

1 itaque *Itaque* corresponds here to *igitur* and *ergo*, *cf.* commentary on I 1. **Decapolis** The name is an echo of *Mt* 4,25 or *Mc* 5,20, where the expression is used about a part of Palestine. According to Storm the ten cities are Konghelle, Sarpsborg, Oslo, Tønsberg, Skien, Stavanger, Bergen, Kaupang in Sogn or Steinkjer, Veøy and Nidaros. *Cf.* also Honorius, who uses the expressions *Pentapolis* and *Centapolis* (in I 17 and 34), and his note about the island of Taprobane which is *decem ciuitatibus inclyta* (I 11). For Stavanger's role in *HN*, *cf.* also Essay § 8.6. **patrias** Here 'law province' (Norwegian: 'lagdømme'), *cf.* Essay § 6.1.3. For a broader sense, *cf.* commentary on I 11. **prouinciarum** Here 'county' (Norwegian: 'fylke'), *cf.* Essay § 6.1.3. This term is used in a broader sense in IV 15 and XVIII 20 (as also in *Passio Olaui* and in Theodoricus, *cf.* Essay § 6.1.3.) as *regio, fines*, 'area'. Honorius also speaks of *prouinciae* in a broader sense (*e.g.* I 30 and 32). *Prouincia* used as *terra* is common in ML.

2 Sinus Orientalis 'The Eastern Bay' is a Latin rendering for the fjord of Oslo, Viken (and its adjacent land), *i.e.* the law province of Borgarting. For its extent, *cf.* Essay § 6.1.3. On the use of *sinus, cf.* commentary below on II 10. **oriens** Here used as a finite verb. **Rygiarbit** *I.e.* Jernestangen, the dividing line between Aust-Agder and Bamble.

3 Media *I.e.* the Island of Midøya, Mien, or Mia, that lies in present Romsdalen. The latinization evokes the sense of a location in the 'middle' of Norway. **VI complectens prouincias** These provinces are Agder, Rogaland, Hordaland, Sogn, Fjordane and Sunnmøre.

4 quarum This can be understood both as a regular relative pronoun, and as a transitional relative. The use of the latter is frequent in *HN*. **uillam quandam** *Cf.* the account of Bjørkedalsmyra (moor) in the Old Norse *Konungs Skuggsiá* (*King's Mirror*, *c.* 1250), ch. 32 (ed. Holm-Olsen 1945, 14), where wood which is thrown into the swamp and remains there for three successive winters turns to stone. *Cf.* also Essay § 6.1.7. **terre inhereant** Here the present subjunctive is used in a conditional clause, while the main clause is in the present indicative, *cf.* Blaise 1994 § 304–5. *Cf.* also commentary on VIII 8 (*si lana* ...). Concerning the use of the present tense to denote future time, *cf.* Löfstedt 1936, 212–13.

6 Trondemia This name stands for 'Trøndelag' everywhere in *HN*, *cf.* III 2, IX 1, XVII 3, 27 and 34. The city of Trondheim (or Nidaros) is not mentioned. For this, *cf.* Essay § 8.6. **uocitatur** Frequentative of *uoco* 1st. Frequentatives in *HN*, as often in ML, do not have an intensifying function, *cf. e.g.* IV 14 (*uocitant*), IX 28 (*uocatur*) and XV 10 (*uocitatur*). *Cf.* also commentary on XIII 4 (*defensabat*). For the use of frequentatives, *cf.* Elliot 1997, 12–13.

7 ostio angustissimo For the descriptive ablative *cf.* commentary on I 9 (*mire magnitudinis*). **octo** *I.e.* Orkdalen, Gauldalen, Strinda, Stjørdalen, Skaun, Verdalen, Sparbuen and Innerøya. **capiens [...] in sua latissima receptacula** Here one would expect the ablative, and not the accusative. This could be due to the influence of a similar expression in the Vulgate, *cf. e.g. Tb* 12,8. Also in *DN* vol. 5, 39 (1299 A.D.) we find a corresponding expression: *cepit eum quidam bonus homo* [...] *in domum suam*. According to Blaise 1994 § 76, a distinction in late Latin was often not made between the place 'where' and the place 'whither'. **III etiam extra sumens** These are Romsdalen, Nordmøre and Namdalen. **etiam** Munch's emendation here of *etenim* to *etiam* recommends itself. *Etenim* also occurs in *Brev. Nidrosiense* (Storm 1880, 233 l. 34) and in a considerable number of places in *Passio Olaui*, but only as an explanation of (or a justification for) a previous statement, 'for'. The intention of the author must be to give an addition, not an explanation here. The same applies in *HN* XV 4 and XVIII 31. **fiunt** Shift of the subject from *sinus* in the foregoing sentence to *prouincie*.

8 Halogia The term 'Hålogaland' nowadays covers the counties of Nordland, Troms and Finnmark. In the Middle Ages it comprised only the area roughly corresponding to Nordland and Troms. In *HN* Hålogaland denotes the coastland all the way from Trøndelag to Wegestaf on the Murman coast, but probably not the inland zone where the Finns lived, *cf.* Essay § 6.1.6. and commentary on III 9. For the northern geography in *HN* in general see Hansen 2000. **Finnis cohabitant** *Finnis* is probably dative. *Cf.* Honorius concerning the Amazons: *His cohabitant Massagetae* (I 19). The Finns, *i.e.* the Lapps, here mentioned must be the coastal Finns. *Cf.* also commentary on III 9. **commercia frequentant** Trading between the two peoples means that they were able to communicate with one another, as opposed to what Adam writes about the Finns (IV 32): *et loquentes ad invicem frendere magis quam verba proferre dicuntur, ita ut vix a proximis intelligi queant populis. Cf.* also Essay § 6.1.6.

9 Wegestaf According to Bugge, Vegestav, also called Ægestav, means 'the boundary mark by the ocean', an extensive promontory on the Murman coast of the Kola peninsula. It lies at the harbour entrance to Gandvik and corresponds to the present-day 'Sviatoi Nos' (or 'Svjatoj-nos') (Storm, note *ad locum*). **Biarmoniam** The reading of *A* is *Bearmoniam*, which might have been the spelling in the original, but *cf.* I 7 & 9: *Biarmones*.

10 profundissimus Septemtrionalis Sinus It is unclear which water he had in mind (The White Sea is one possibility); however, we read that it is found *ibi*, *i.e.* at Vegestav. This could be the fjord that, in line with the idea of how Greenland was connected to Europe, would have to be between these two areas. The author seems precise in his way of using the terms *sinus* and *mare*: *Solundicum Mare* (V 1) and *Petlandicum Mare* (VI 3) are both seas, whereas *Sinus Orientalis* (II 2) is a fjord. So the use of the term *sinus* for this water to the north indicates that he is thinking of a fjord. **Caribdim, Scillam** The notoriously dangerous whirlpool and sea-monster on each side of a strait (*The Odyssey* 12.101ff.). *Cf.* Honorius, who writes that Charybdis and Scylla are located in the straits near Sicily (I 35, *cf.* Virgil, *Aeneid* 3.420). They were first located in northern waters by Paulus Diaconus in his *Historia Langobardorum* I.6 (*c.* 790) who in turn inspired Theodoricus Monachus to treat them in an excursus in his Norwegian history (ch. 17, *cf.* Mortensen 1993).

11 promunctoria congelata *Cf.* commentary on I 10 (*congelatis scopulis*). For the spelling *promunctoria*, *cf.* commentary on I 4. **fluctiuomis inundacionibus** Literally 'vomiting waves'; *fluctiuomus* is a very rare poetical adjective. The same element of word formation occurs in *HN* VIII 11: *igniuomus*.

12 Viridam Above (I 10) the adjective is used in the nominative form *uiridis*; but it is not uncommon in ML for adjectives of the 3rd declension to display forms from the 1st/2nd declension, *cf.* Stotz vol. IV, p. 33. Hence the reading of *A* may have been original.

13 cete Greek neuter plural form of *cetos* (κῆτος), *cf.* Virgil, *Aeneid* 5.822, *Gn* I 21 and Adam IV 32 (*grandia cete*). The word also occurs in the masculine *cetus* with the plural *ceti* (as immediately below). This term includes larger sea creatures such as tunas, sharks, walruses, and whales. The Old Norse *Konungs Skuggsiá* (*King's Mirror*, *c.* 1250), ch.s 33–39 (ed. Holm-Olsen 1945, 14–17) discusses at length various species of whales and fish in northern waters. **diglutiunt** Ordinary spelling is *deglu(t)tiunt*, from *deglut(t)io* 4th, 'swallow down', a rare verb, which occurs in *e.g. Ion.* 2,1 and in *Ps* 124,3. For the spelling, *cf.* commentary on Prologue 3, *discribere*.

14 equini ceti monoculi Literally 'one-eyed horse-whales', perhaps referring to walruses. **profunda pelagi** Substantivized adjectives in the neuter plural are frequent in *HN*. They are often associated with the partitive genitive as here.

15 Illic The author breaks the anaphoric series of *ibi*. **pistrix** Or *pistris, pristix* or *pristis* f., from the Greek πρίστις, used to denote a sea creature such as a whale, walrus etc., *cf.* Pliny 9.3.2 §4 and Honorius (I 134). **hafstrambus** In folklore, the *hafstrambus*, in common with 'draugen' (or 'dødningen', *i.e.* a particular sea monster), warns people of danger by making an appearance. According to Fritzner 1886–96, a 'hafstrambr' is a creature (a merman) that lives in the water. Its upper body is shaped like a human head with a helmet, and its lower body tapers downwards like an icicle. This creature warns of storms and human death (*cf.* also *Kulturhistorisk leksikon* 1956–78 *s.v.* 'sjövette'). It is mentioned in *The King's Mirror* (ed. Holm-Olsen 1945, 27). **susum et iusum** Used for the sake of rhyme. *Iusum* is found *e.g.* in Ordericus Vitalis (*Historia ecclesiastica* IX.iii.539). *Susum* or *sursum* (see below IV 18) is a contraction of *subuorsum*, while *iusum* is a late Latin form of *deorsum* (Ernout & Meillet 1959). In ML we often see 'rs' shortened to 's' after a long vowel, *cf.* Elliot 1997, 32. **dissiliendo** From *dissilio* 4th, 'to burst', here 'to jump up and down', *cf.* I *Mcc* 9,48. Here it is in the ablative of the gerund standing for the present participle, *cf.* commentary on Prologue 5 (*postponendo*).

16 hafguua The name means 'ocean mist'. According to Fritzner 1886–96 it is a kind of sea monster. It is mentioned in *The King's Mirror*, ch. 39 (ed. Holm-Olsen 1945, 17). **haffkitta** Probably a kind of whale (Fritzner 1886–96). **pre** Used here in comparison, but *cf.* commentary on I 2.

17 Reuertentes a maritimis transferamur ad montana For this way of ending a chapter, *cf.* commentary on I 15–16.

III. On the mountain region of Norway

1 a metis For use of the preposition *a/ab* with the impersonal agent, *cf.* commentary on I 4 (*Finnis*).

2 IIII patrias et XII prouincias For law provinces and counties in the Uplands (the mountain region), *cf.* Essay § 6.1.3. **usque** Here a preposition with the accusative, *cf.* also XVIII 13, but *cf. e.g.* II 2 *usque ad*, where *usque* is an adverb. As a preposition it usually governs the ablative, *cf.* Elliot 1997, 30. It also occurs with the accusative in *e.g. De expulsione fratrum minorum* (ed. Gertz 1917–22, vol. II, 345, l. 2).

3 Conuallibus Albie *Albia* is originally the Latin name of the Elbe; here the term seems to be used for Storelvedalen (*i.e.* the Great River Valley) and Lilleelvedalen (*i.e.* the Small River Valley), *i.e.* Østerdalen (Bugge 1873, 44). It can also be regarded as an attempt to show that Norway has a large river like Saxony. *Cf.* the above-mentioned quotation (commentary on I 3) from Adam about the River Göta (*Gothelba*), which is also named after the Elbe. **Valles** Nom. sing., but in III 5 *uallis*.

5 incolatus *Cf.* commentary on II (heading).

6 fluuius [...] aureis rubens arenis *I.e.* the River Vorma, which gradually unites with the River Glomma and drains into the sea at Sarpsborg. *Cf.* also Honorius concerning the gold-laden River Hirnus (I 21): *ubi* [*sc. in Caria*] *fluit Hirnus fluuius, aureis arenis famosus.* For gold in the mountain region, *cf.* Essay § 6.1.4. and 8.6.

7 illo *I.e.* to the mouth of the river at Sarpsborg. **Saxones [...] furtim [...] detulerunt aurum** We are not familiar with this legend from any other source. **aduentantes et [...] deprehendentes** The present participle here stands for a missing past participle in the active voice and corresponds to a relative subordinate clause or a temporal clause, *cf.* Elliot 1997, 43–44.

8 ciuitatem Corresponds to both *urbs* and *oppidum*, *cf.* Elliot 1997, 7. In *HN ciuitas* is used for cities such as Bergen, Jomne (Jomsborg), London, Roda (Rouen) and Oslo and as a common designation of the cities along the coast. *Urbs* is used for Roda (Rouen), Dublin, coastal cities in Ireland, and in connection with the city-building of the Pents, *oppidum* about Fitjar, *locus* about smaller places like Rygjarbit, Vegestav, Agnafit, Oddesund, Himinheid, Rastarkalv, Håkonshella and Tryggvarøyr, *polis* about Holmgard and *incolatus* about villages in areas such as Valdres and Hallingdal. For this, *cf.* also Löfstedt 1936 pp. 174–75. For Oslo's role in *HN*, *cf.* Essay § 8.6. **magna copia argenti metalli** It has been suggested that the author was thinking about the silver mines at Kongsberg. For silver in the Uplands, *cf.* Essay § 6.1.4. and 8.6. See, however, Phelpstead 2001, 80 with further references, for the view that no mines are attested in Norway before the fifteenth century. **nimia** *Cf.* commentary on Prologue 4. **fluencia** *Cf. refluenta*, I 5. **uetita** 'forbidden', the expression suggests a divine will working in nature, *cf.* Honorius (I 11): *Ibi* [*sc. in Chrisa et Argare insulis*] *sunt et montes aurei, qui propter dracones et gryphes non possunt adiri.* **absconsa** From *abscondo* 3rd. Otherwise the participle form *absconditus* is used in *HN*, *cf.* IV 15 and VIII 20.

9 Peragratis [...] ingrediamur This form of chapter ending could have been influenced by Honorius (I 33): *Peragratis Africae finibus, ad insulas maris accedamus.* **siluas Finnorum** 'The forests of the Finns'. It is translated here by the Norwegian name 'Finnmarken', although much less precisely delimited than the present-day county of Finnmark, *cf.* Essay § 6.1.6. Nor must the term be confused with the Norwegian name 'Finnskogene', as Koht 1950, 16 and Salvesen 1969, 21 did. The name Finnskogene is used of a much smaller area which nowadays comprises Solør, the forested area between Kongsvinger and Trysil in the eastern part of Norway and takes its name from Finns (from Finland) settling down here in the seventeenth century. *Cf.* also commentary on IV 1. **perscrutatum** The only instance of the first supine in *HN*.

IV. On the Finns

1 Igitur *Cf.* commentary on I 1. **uastissima solitudo affinis Norwegie** For this huge wilderness, *cf.* Essay § 6.1.6. The precise meaning of *affinis* and the status of the Finns are difficult to grasp because in I 4 the Finns are inhabiting the third part of Norway, whereas here their land is bordering on Norway, *cf.* the discussion by Hansen 2000, 64–67. **diuidens eam per longum a paganis gentibus** For the division *per longum*, *cf.* commentary on I 4 where the same expression is used. Again, it seems to be implied here that the pagan Finns are living outside Norway.

2 que It is possible that *que* here is not a transitional relative, but rather introduces a relative subordinate clause. **Finnis et bestiis** For the agent in the passive without *ab*, *cf.* commentary on I 4 (*Finnis*). **quarum carnibus semicrudis uescuntur et pellibus induuntur** *Cf.* Adam (IV 32) concerning the pagan peoples to the north: *Qui ferarum pellibus utuntur pro vestibus. Cf.* also Honorius (I 11): *Quae* [*sc. Gog et Magog ferocissimae gentes*] *humanis carnibus vel crudis bestiis vescuntur.*

3 Sunt [...] transferuntur Here we have an example of how concentrated the style can be at certain places in *HN*. First there is a main clause with the appositions *soliuagi et instabiles* as well as the present participle *insidentes* referring to the subject (*uenatores peritissimi*). A relative clause (*que*) is joined to the main clause with a present participle (*inponentes*) acting as finite verb and an ablative absolute (*leuigatis asseribus pedibus subfixis*). To this relative clause is joined a new relative clause (*quod*). Finally we find yet another main clause, which contains an ablative absolute (*agitantibus ceruis*). For similar examples of this kind of compressed style, *cf.* IV 7, VI 8 and 11, VIII 2 and XVII 11 and 32. *Cf.* also Essay § 13.2. **tugurea corticea insidentes** *Tugurea* corresponds to classical Latin *tuguria*. The adjective *corticeus* derives from *cortex*, 'bark', but is attested in ML in the sense 'of skin' (*Dictionary of Medieval Latin from British Sources*, p. 504); Bugge's suggestion, accepted by Storm, *coriacea*, from *corium*, 'leather' is therefore hardly necessary. The verb *insideo*, 2nd, here takes the accusative, whereas in classical Latin it usually takes the dative. **leuigatis asseribus** From *leuigo* 1st, 'smooth'; *asser* m., 'a beam' or 'a plank'. **ondros** From Old Norse, 'ǫndurr', and not from Sami. It means the shorter of a pair of skis of different length. The plural should be 'ǫndrar' (nom.) or 'ǫndra' (acc.); *ondros* is either a latinization or a textual corruption. **condensa niuium ac deuexa moncium** For substantivized adjectives in the neuter plural associated with the partitive genitive, *cf.* commentary on II 14 (*profunda pelagi*). **agitantibus ceruis** *Ceruis* here must be a reindeer. The Latin term is *ceruus tarandus/tarandrus*, or just *tarandus/tarandrus*. According to Ernout and Meillet this is a Scythian word. It occurs *e.g.* in Pliny 8.34.52 §124 and Solinus 30. In the present translation the reindeer are perceived as domesticated reindeer, used by the Finns to pull their sledges when they are on the move. It does not seem to involve hunting here, since wives, children and tents were taken along. Furthermore, in the clause that follows, *enim* seems to explain why the Finns moved from place to place. **aue uelocius** *Cf.* Adam (IV 32): *Scritefingi vivere non possunt absque frigore nivium, qui etiam feras prevolant suo cursu per altissimas nives. Cf.* also Honorius, who writes about some sort of fairy-tale animals (I 13), saying that they are *velocius cursu quam avis volatu,* and the expression *aquilis velociores* in II *Reg* 1,23.

4 **prout [...] dictauerit** *Prout* occurs with both the subjunctive and the indicative in ML.

5 **infinita numerositas** Ellipsis of *est*. **ursorum, luporum, lyncorum, uulpium, sabelorum, lutrearum, taxonum, castorum** These animals, apart from *sabelus* and *taxo*, are mentioned *passim* in Solinus. Adam also mentions a number of animals in Norway (IV 32): *Ibi capiuntur uri, bubali et elaces sicut in Sueonia; ceterum bisontes capiuntur in Sclavonia et Ruzzia; sola vero Nortmannia vulpes habet nigros et lepores, martures albos eiusdemque coloris ursos, qui sub aqua vivunt quemadmodum uri.* The animals that are mentioned here in *HN* thus supplements those listed by Adam. The form *lutraea* is attested in *Dictionary of Medieval Latin from British Sources*, p. 1665, and needs no correction into the classical *lutra*; *taxo* or *taxus* m., 'badger' is a rare ML word, from German 'Dachs'. Solinus 40,16 and 18 uses *lynx* f. 3rd decl., but *lyncus* m. 2nd decl. is a common medieval alternative; hence, Storm's emendation of *lyncorum* into *lyncum* is not necessary.

6 **Que bestia mirabiliter cauta** Ellipsis of *est*. The striking description of the life of beavers is given in similar terms in *Chronicon Lethrense* and by Gerald of Wales, both roughly contemporary to *HN*; for further references *cf.* Essay § 6.1.7 and Phelpstead 2001, 80. Honorius employs a similar means of expression for certain fairy-tale animals (I 13): *Haec bestia nimis ferox.* **dum** Here used as the causal conjunction *cum* with the subjunctive. It also occurs with the indicative, *cf.* Elliot 1997, 37. In *HN dum* is often used instead of the temporal *cum* either with the subjunctive, *cf.* IV 16, 22 and 24, IX 13 and 26, X 3 and 7, as well as XIII 11, XV 10, XVII 5 and 39, or with the indicative, *cf.* IV 9, VIII 16 and XVII 22. *Dum* for *cum* is common in ML. **a ueltribus** From *ueltris* m. (ML from Celtic), 'hound', 'greyhound'. *Cf.* commentary on I 4 (*Finnis*) concerning the use of *a/ab* in connection with an impersonal agent.

7 **limpha** *I.e. lympha* f., poetical for *aqua* and very common in ML. **catellis** Diminutive of *catulus*, which in turn is the diminutive of *canis*. Here it means simply 'dogs'. **secus** *Secus* for *iuxta*, with the accusative, is common in ML, *cf.* Elliot 1997, 30. **unde [...] pateat** A final clause, therefore the subjunctive. **unde** used as *de quo* is common in ML in place of a pronoun with or without a preposition, *cf.* Löfstedt 1936, 180–81.

8 in [...] confidit *Confido* 3rd is usually associated in classical Latin with the dative or the ablative. With *in* + ablative, *cf. Ps* 10,1 and II *Par* 16,12. **meatibus** From *meatus* m., 'course', 'path'. It is common in ML, *cf. e.g.* Honorius I XLV. The beaver was probably intended by Adam (IV 32) when he writes about some *ursos qui sub aqua vivunt*.

9 Dum [...] insudauerint The author here shifts to the plural (*insudauerint*), in spite of the fact that the subject is an understood *bestia, i.e.* sing., as in the previous clauses. **plus** Here used as *multum*. **subere** *Suber* n., 'a cork oak', but here used as *cortex* for 'bark'. **uectigale** From *uectigal* n., 'tribute', but here used as *uehiculum*, 'means of transport'. **rectibus** *I.e. rictibus* from *rictus* m., 'jaw'. This is the reading of *A*, and it might well have been the spelling in the original. **trahendo** Here used as *trahentes*, *cf.* commentary on Prologue 5 (*postponendo*). **amminiculantur** From *adminiculor* 1st, written here with double 'm', but *cf.* Prologue 5 *aminiculis*.

10 haut Also written as *haud* in XVII 48. In ML texts 't' is often used interchangeably with 'd', *cf.* Elliot 1997, 4.

11 quam plures Corresponds to *perplures*, *cf.* I 7 and III 5. *Quam*, along with *per*, is frequently used as an intensifying adverb in the Middle Ages, *cf. quam saepe* in *Gesta Cnutonis Regis* II (ed. Gertz 1917–22, vol. II, 397, l. 14).

12 regibus Norwegie [...] maxima tributa For these kings, *cf.* Essay § 6.1.6. For the term *tributa*, *cf.* Essay § 6.2.6.

13 perfidia Here in the common Christian sense of 'superstition', 'pagan beliefs'; *cf.* Theodoricus ch. 11. **quantumue** *-ue* used as *et*. This shade of meaning is common in *HN*, *cf.* also VIII 12 (*mundumue*). **excerceant** The spelling *exc* instead of *ex* here is common in medieval manuscripts.

14 quidam ex ipsis A prepositional phrase containing *de* or *ex* + ablative often replaces a genitive in ML, *cf.* Elliot 1997, 17. **uenerantur** From *ueneror* 1st, in classical Latin usually a deponent, but here used as an active verb in the passive. It also occurs in this way in *e.g. Historia de profectione Danorum*, ch. XXV. In IX 4 below we see it as a deponent. For the reports about the Finns' beliefs, *cf.* commentary below (IV 16) and Essay § 6.1.6. **quoniam [...] predicent** From *praedico* 1st, here in the present subjunctive. Otherwise *quoniam*-clauses are with the indicative in *HN*, *cf.* Prologue 9 and VIII 20, XVII 34 and XVIII 15. *Quoniam* occurs with the indicative and the subjunctive in ML. **immundum spiritum** This expression also occurs in Honorius, who writes in the chapter entitled *De nominibus inferni* (I 37) about *acheronta, id est spiracula, scilicet immundos spiritus emittencia*. It occurs frequently in the New Testament. **gandum** The word 'gandr' is Old Norse for 'magic wand'. **percunctati** From *percunctor* 1st, usually a deponent, 'inquire', 'ask', but here used as an active verb in the passive.

15 prouinciis Here used as *regionibus*, but *cf.* commentary on II 1. **absconditos** For the form, *cf.* commentary on III 8 (*absconsa*).

16 Here begins the celebrated description of a shamanistic séance. Tolley 1994 offers an exhaustive reading of it with references to seventeenth- and eighteenth-century sources, recent theoretical literature etc. His general conclusion is that *HN* (153): "is striking as recounting an actual séance, rather than relaying general information about séances, and the detail it reveals is invaluable as a witness to the complexities of shamanism in practice [...] The parallels confirm the genuineness of the *HN* account, and serve to remind us how much we have lost in our knowledge of Lappish shamanism." **quadam uero uice** *Cf. aliqua vice* in, *e.g.*, *DN* vol. 5, 150 (1347 A.D.). *Cf.* also *Gn* 27,36: *altera vice. Vero* here appears in a weakened adversative sense, *cf.* also VIII 14, IX 3, 5 and 22, XV 2 (explanatory like *nam*) and 8, XVI 1 and 2, XVII 24 (explanatory), 26 and 40 (explanatory). **expirauit** *i.e. exspirauit.*

17 mortuam The subject is missing in this accusative with infinitive. **depredatam** From *depraedor* 1st. Here used as an active verb in the passive voice as often in later Latin, *cf. e.g.* Adam (III 13). Ellipsis of *esse.* **respondent** The historic present.

18 sub Tolley 1994, 136 & 141 defends the transmitted *sub* against Storm's alteration to *super* by pointing to indirect parallels and the sense of the space created by putting a cloth over your head rather than standing on it: the cloth may symbolize the heavens to be traversed. **profanas** Storm's alteration of the strange *profundas* ('deep') in *A*; the adjectives that are frequently coupled with *incantatio* in the Biblical and patristic literature are *Aegyptia* (see next note) and *diabolica*; Storm's suggestion is a very plausible variant of the latter. **incantaciones** From *incantatio*, often found in *Exodus* about the Egyptian sorcerers. It also occurs in Adam's description of pagan practices in the far north (IV 32): *Eos adhuc ferunt magicis artibus sive incantationibus in tantum prevalere, ut se scire fateantur, quid a singulis in toto orbe geratur.* **pepararet** It lies at hand to make the simple correction of *preparet* in *A* to *prepararet*, as Bugge 1873 and Skard 1930 suggest; this brings it in line with normal usage and the subsequent *uteretur*. The clause must be regarded as a final relative clause. In *HN*, however, there are surprising changes of tense, so *preparet* is, as suggested by Ekrem, possible. A third possibility would be to have the historic present *preparat*, as Bugge 1873 noticed and Storm accepted. **uasculum ad modum taratantarorum** The instrument in question is the ritual drum that was used by the 'noaidi', the most important religious functionary among the Sami. The drum consisted of a frame, usually made of wood, with a reindeer calfskin stretched over it, upon which were painted figures of various kinds (*Kulturhistorisk leksikon* 1956–78 *s.v.* 'runebomme' and Friis 1871, 15–47). **taratantarorum** From *taratantarum* or *taratantara*, a rare, onomatopoetic noun. According to Du Cange 1883–87 this is a Gallic word corresponding to *cribrum*, 'a riddle'. Zimmermann 1915 writes that *taratantara* is a 'Schallwort um den Ton der Tuba auszudrücken', *cf.* Ennius *Annales* 452; Ennius apud Priscian lib. 8: *At tuba terribili sonitu tarantara dixit.* **sursum** *Cf.* commentary on II 15 (*susum*). **occupatum** Here most likely in the sense 'decorated with', 'painted with'. **alta niuium [...] deuexa moncium [...] profunda stagnorum** For substantivized adjectives with the genitive, *cf.* commentary on II 14 (*profunda pelagi*). **quibus [...] uteretur** A relative final clause with the subjunctive.

19 incantando Here used as *incantans*, *cf.* commentary on Prologue 5 (*postponendo*). **saltasset** Contracted forms are frequent in *HN*. **humo tandem prostratus** For the locative both *humo* and *humi* are common in ML. **ethiops** Generic Greek and Latin ethnonym for all Africans of black skin. **spumans ora** *Ora* is poetical (or Greek) accusative. This is more prevalent in ML than in classical Latin, *cf.* Blaise 1994 § 71. The expression *spumans ora* has poetical inspiration, *e.g.* Virgil, *Aeneid* 12.372–73: *spumantia* [...] *ora.* **ut puta** It is also written *utputa* as one word, 'for example', 'like'. This expression occurs in Honorius (I 3) and *e.g.* in I *Cor* 14,10 and 15,37. **preruptus uentrem** *Ventrem* is poetical (or Greek) accusative. **cum maximo ⟨fremore⟩** A masculine word denoting a violent sound is clearly missing; the choice is between *fremor* (Storm & Skard, *cf.* VIII 16 on a natural phenomenon), *clamor* (Munch & Ekrem, *cf.* XVIII 21 on men shouting) or perhaps *rumor*; *fremor* is the more poetic and fits slightly better because of the sound pattern with *freneticus.* **emisit spiritum** *Cf. Mt* 27,50.

20 alterum *Alter* for *alius* is common in ML, *cf.* Elliot 1997, 36.

21 implens From *impleo* 2nd, here used as the finite verb. There is no reason to correct *A*, as Munch and Storm do, since the present participle is often used instead of a finite form in

HN (*cf.* Skard 1930, 9). **namque hospita sana surrexit** This phrase has been set between dashes to help bring out the point made by Tolley 1994, 137: "[...] that the shaman, not the hostess, is subject throughout, which the Latin leaves ambiguous. For the hostess to report what had happened on the spirit journey she would herself have to be a shaman, which neither this text nor Lappish tradition, which scarcely recognises female shamans, suggest". **intimauit** From *intimo* 1st, common in ML with the sense of 'make known', 'tell' etc.

22 inmaginatum From *imagino* 1st, in the sense of 'transformed' is post-classical Latin, and occurs *e.g.* in *Ps* 138,15. **ostico** *I.e. hostico*, equivalent to *hostili*. The dative is governed by *obuiasse*. **sudes** From *sudis* f., 'stake'. **quia [...] perforabant** This clause should probably be taken as part of the indirect statement in spite of the indicative. In *HN* all *quia*-clauses are with the indicative, *cf.* VI 10, XVII 21 and XVIII 2. For the manner of expression in the clause, *cf. Iob* 40,19: *et in sudibus perforabit nares eius.*

24 Finni unacum christianis etc. For another contemporary story of competing Christian and heathen fishermen see *Passio Olaui* (miracle 44, *cf.* the counting in Ekrem 2000 and in the forthcoming edition). The author obviously plays on the common ecclesiastical metaphor of catching souls (originating with the *piscatores hominum* of the Gospels, *e.g. Matth.* 4,19): *grex, carpere, uncus, de abysso.* The period entails a number of textual problems; perhaps a whole clause is missing somewhere. The two main problems are: what is the point of the story? what is the correlate of **quos**? From the context we should expect another instance of the evil magical powers wielded by the Lapps. The point may hide in the juxtaposition of two catching instruments **hamo** (unsuccessful) and **unco suo** (successful); *hamus* is the ordinary word for a fishing hook, whereas the heathen's *uncus* may be the *gandr*, his magic wand. The previous translations (Storm *in notis*, Koht, Salvesen, Kunin) take *quos* with the subsequent **sacculis** (*saccus*, 'a sack' in the diminutive, 'a fish trap' (ML)), *i.e.* the Lapps drew from the deep the almost full nets they had noticed in the Christians' sheds. Not only is this an awkward story but it is also very irregular to have the correlate long after the relative pronoun. It is tempting to look for a correlate in the previous sentence: it could be *hamus, i.e.* the heathens had seen a certain type of hook in the Christians' houses, but this would demand much textual surgery; a far easier correction would be to read *squamigerum* (subst. gen. pl.) instead of the adjective **squamigeram** (which in itself calls for attention because the two other instances of **grex** in *HN* are the standard masculine (VII 2, X 7)): thus the Lapps would have seen (a certain kind of) fish in the sheds of the Christians, which they then caught in nets. However, the logic or punchline of the story does not become much clearer. In addition **fere** is not a certain, although very good, emendation of *A*'s *ferre*, and it is strange to have a repetition of the subject (*Finni* [...] *pagani*). In this light it seems the better solution to provide the passage with a crux.

25 carptim excerpsi *Figura etymologica.* **secte** From *secta* f., in Christian Latin with a pejorative connotation of 'false doctrine'. **plus remotis** 'those farther away', *i.e.* from northern Norway or from Norway (or both); *cf.* Essay § 6.1.7.

26 pre Here used as *propter*, *cf.* also commentary on I 2. **Circumscriptis utcunque Norwegie finibus tendamus ad tributarias insulas** For this form of chapter ending, *cf.* commentary on III 9.

V. On the tributary islands

1 ergo *Cf. igitur* in commentary on I 1 and *itaque* II 1; for *ergo, cf.* also IX 29. **dictum** Understand *est.* For mention of the Solund Sea, *cf.* Essay § 6.2.2. **inter Norwegiam et Iberniam fluit** *Cf.* Adam (IV 35): *Igitur Orchades inter Nortmanniam et Britanniam et Hi-*

berniam positae. For the means of expression, *cf.* Essay § 6.2.2. *Iberniam* for *Hiberniam*, *cf.* commentary on Prologue 8 (*exorreo*). One would rather expect Scotland than Ireland, but perhaps the author is thinking in terms of sea-routes, as noted by Phelpstead 2001, 83.

2 numero plusquam XXX For the approximate number, *cf.* Essay § 6.2.3. **Orchano** The name is not known from any other source; it could be the author's own etymologizing, in line with Honorius and with his own liking for eponymic heroes, *cf.* the commentary to *Nor*, I 1. *Cf.* also Adam (IV 35), who claims that the barbarians called the islands *Organas*. For Orkan and the term Orkney Islands, *cf.* Essay § 6.2.3.–4.

3 diuersis incolis The preposition *a/ab* is missing in a number of places in connection with persons as agents in the passive, *cf.* commentary on I 4 (*Finnis*). For these inhabitants, *cf.* Essay § 6.2.3.–4. and 6.2.6. **Merediane Insule**. The Hebrides, in Norwegian 'Sudrøyene' (*i.e.* the Southern Islands). For the name *Hebrides*, *cf.* Essay § 6.2.3. **utrique** This 'both of them' refers to the *reguli* as well as the *comites*, as is agreed by all commentators and translators. Ekrem, however, proposes to read it as a possible reference to two earls of the northern isles, *cf.* Essay § 6.2.3; **regibus Norwegie** The plural is generic, see however Essay § 6.1.6 for another view. **non modica [...] tributa**. The chronological implications of the tribute and of the description of the southern and northern isles in this paragraph are a time of composition of *HN* between 1152 and 1195, or at least between *c.* 1150 and 1200, *cf.* Phelpstead 2001, 83 and Introduction p. 12 with further references. *Cf.* also Essay § 6.2.3.

VI. On the Orkney Islands

1 Peti The Pents (or Picts) were the pre-Norse population of Orkney, speaking a Celtic language. The name *Picti* is found in Roman sources (and is perhaps a Roman coinage — 'the painted people'). According to *HN* they constituted the first inhabitants of the Orkneys. *Cf.* also Essay § 6.2.4. **Pape** This is the term in Ari (*Íslendingabók*, ch. 1) for Irish Christian hermits in Iceland, *i.e.* for priests or monks, not a people, as here. For further references on these names *cf.* Phelpstead 2001, 84.

2 in structuris Munch's emendation of *instructuris* in *A* to *in structuris* is reasonable (Storm kept *instructuris* and noted, wrongly, that *instructura* was a common ML alternative to *structura*). **mira operantes** We find a similar construction about Harald Fairhair's son Ragnvald Rettilbeine in XI 7: *in eadem arte mira ut nutrix operatus est*. The present participle *operantes* is used here as a finite form of the verb. **meredie vero [...] in subterraneis domunculis [...] latuerunt** Adam writes (IV 41) about a people far to the north, *in antris subterraneis meridiano tempore latitantes*. The small, Bronze Age subterranean stuctures on the Orkneys (of uncertain purpose) gave rise to the belief that the former inhabitants were tiny; *cf.* Thomson 2001, 1–4. **meredie** *I.e. meridie*. **prosus** This is the reading of *A*. *Prosus*, for *prorsus*, might well have been the spelling in the original, *cf.* commentary on II 15 (*susum*). **pre timore** *Pre*, 'because of', *cf.* commentary on I 2.

3 Petlandicum Mare [...] quod seiungit The Pentland Firth, the strait between Orkney and Scotland; *cf.* Essay § 6.2.4. **omnium maxima uorago** The description of the whirlpool borrows directly from Honorius' explanation of the phenomenon in *Imago mundi*, I 41: *Hec autem vorago que totas aquas et naves absorbet et revomit, hinc fit*. The author of *HN* is probably responsible for placing this cosmic phenomenon firmly in the North Sea. *Cf.* also Essay § 6.2.4. **ledonem [...] malenam** *Cf.* Bede *De natura rerum* ch. 39 where it is spelled *malina*, 'flow'. In ML *ledo*, 'ebb', is also found as *lido*, *laedon* and *laedona*. **que fortissimas naues per ledonem attrahendo diglutit, earundem fragmenta [...] euomit.** Munch and Storm accepted the anacoluthic reading of *A*: *quas per ledonem attrahendo diglutit* (a relative clause here leaves *fortissimas naues* without a verb). Ekrem suggested a palaeographically elegant correction into *aquas per ledonem etc.*, thus avoiding the anacoluthon and bringing the phrase more in line with Honorius's words (see above) who talks of waters as well as ships being engulfed. However, as pointed out by Kraggerud, this spoils the very effective parallelism *per ledonem attrahendo diglutit* / *per malenam eructando euomit*; furthermore, the author had certainly made a choice of not following Honorius in the last clause as the *fragmenta* of course only refer to ships, not to waters. Deletion of *quas* is therefore more attractive. **diglutit** *I.e. deglut(t)io* 4th, 'swallow'.

4 **aduentasset [...] ignoramus** Classical sequence of tenses is not observed in ML, *cf.* Elliot 1997, 49. The pluperfect subjunctive is occasionally used in subordinate clauses for the imperfect subjunctive, *cf.* Blaise 1994 § 232. **penitus ignoramus** *Cf.* Essay § 6.2.4.

5 **albas** Understand *uestes*, 'priestly garbs'. It is the equivalent of the French word 'aube' f., 'an alb'. *Cf.* also *in albis e.g.* in *Vetus Chronica Sialandie* (ed. Gertz 1917–22, vol. II, 43, l. 26). **in Theutonica lingua** Here with *in*, *cf. Ps* 14,3 and *Prv* 31,26. In VII 1 (*patria lingua*) and IX 8 (*Norwaico sermone*), similar expressions are used without *in*. The author is here thinking of the Low German word 'pape' (Middle High German, 'Pfaffe'); for further references see Phelpstead 2001, 84.

6 **Papey** There are a number of islands by that name, both in the Shetlands and the Orkneys. *Cf.* Crawford 1987, 166 and 1996 pp. 10-11.

7 **habitum** From *habitus* m. Translated here by 'appearance'. It is not clear whether the Papes' appearance of dress or the books' appearance (or both) are envisaged. What is pictured on the so-called Bressay Stone could be representation of the Papes, with hooded cloaks, shoulder bags for books and shepherd's crooks. The Papes are thought to have left behind 'books, bells and croziers' (Crawford 1987, 170 (ill.)).

derelictorum From *derelinquo* 3rd. The double prefix is particularly characteristic of ML; *derelinquo* is a frequent word in the Vulgate. **Affricani fuerunt** This claim seems to be unique to *HN*, *cf.* Crawford 1987, 211. *Affricani* is a variant spelling for *Africani*. For various explanations of this surprising statement, see Phelpstead 2001, 85, *e.g.* that Honorius mentions Africa just after the Orkneys (*Imago mundi* I 29): *Britannia. Contra Hispaniam versus occasum sunt in oceano hee insule, Britannia, Anglia, Hibernia, Tanatos cuius terra quovis gentium portata serpentes perimit, Insole in qua fit solstitium, Orcades .xxxiii., Scotia, Thile cuius arbores numquam folia deponunt, et in qua .vi. mensibus videlicet estivis est continuus dies, .vi. hibernis continua nox. Ultra hanc versus aquilonem est mare congelatum et frigus perpetuum. Europam perambulavimus, ad Affricam transmigremus.* There must also be a connection with the author's conviction that one could reach the African Islands overland through Greenland, *cf.* I 11 above. **iudaismo adherentes** *I.e.* because of the Hebrew-like letter-forms, **apices**, found in the books. The author of *HN* does not agree with Ari (*Íslendingabók*, ch. 1), who writes that they were Christians and Irish. For this, *cf.* Essay § 6.2.4.

8 **Istas [...] subdiderunt** A long and heavy period, characterized by the subject (*quidam pirate*) being expanded with an apposition in the past participle (*progressi*) and a present participle (*transfretantes*), as well as a past participle (*exutas*) in apposition to the object (*istas* [...] *naciones*), all before the finite verbs *deleuerunt* and *subdiderunt*. **itaque** For this use, *cf.* commentary on I 1. **Haraldi Comati** Latinization of Harald's Norwegian nickname (Hårfagre). Theodoricus uses a more complete translation 'Pulchre-comatus' (ch. I). **pirate** In *HN* the term *pirata* is used alongside the term *tyrannus* and *predo* for a viking and a pirate. These terms, as well as *piratica* and *tyrannis*, can be understood in both a negative and a positive sense, *cf.* XII 6, XVII 5, 11 and 38, XVIII 2 (*pirata, piratica*), XVII 11 and 18

(*predo*), VI 9 and 13, (perhaps XV 12), XVII 15, XVIII 8 and 10 (*tyrannus, tyrannis*). *Pirata* is the common (neutral or positive) expression in Saxo (*passim*). Ordericus Vitalis uses the term *tyrannus* of 'viking' in a pejorative sense, coupled with *barbarus* (*Historia ecclesiastica* IV.ii.281). *Cf.* also Essay § 6.2.4. **Rogwaldi** Earl of Møre. He was given the Orkneys and Shetland by Harald Fairhair according to Snorri, *Heimskringla, Haralds saga ins Hárfagra*, 22. The spelling chosen here is that of *A*. It corresponds to *Rogualdi*, since 'w' is often written as 'u', *cf.* Blaise 1994, 133. Storm corrects it to *Rognwaldi*. It is probably more likely that *A* has the wrong spelling for *Rognaldi* or *Regwaldi*, which correspond to the western Norwegian 'Rognaldr' ('Raugnaldr') or 'Rægvalldr', *cf.* Hægstad 1919–20, 119–20. **de diuturnis sedibus exutas** In classical Latin *exuo* is not common in connection with *de*, but rather with a pure ablative or *ex*. **ex toto deleuerunt** *Cf.* Essay § 6.2.4.

9 Vbi [...] muniti This could either be taken as a temporal clause with ellipsis of the auxiliary verb (*e.g. sunt*): 'as soon as they had been ...', or as a participial construction with the *ubi* acting as a transitional relative: 'having been ... *there*'. **securius** The comparative is probably used here in the sense of 'reasonably safe'. **tyrannidem** From *tyrannis* f. *Tirannis* is used like *piratica* in the sense of 'viking raid', 'piracy', *cf.* commentary on VI 8 (*pirate*). **Northimbriam** *I.e. Northumbriam.* In *A* 'i' is sometimes used for 'u', *cf.* VIII 1 (*Tile*) and XII 4 and 5 (*Northimbrie* and *Northimbri* respectively).

10 De quorum collegio Rodulfus *HN* is the only Latin work that calls him *Rodulfus*. Otherwise it is *Rollo* (Storm, note *ad locum*). **Rodam** This is the Latinized Norwegian term for Rouen (Storm, note *ad locum*), *cf.* Essay § 6.2.4. It is interesting to note that the author of *HN* does not use the usual Latin name for Rouen, Rothomagus, as it was referred to at the very beginning of *Passio Olaui* and by Theodoricus (ch. 13); nor does he know of their story of Olav's baptism there derived from William of Jumièges' *Gesta Normannorum Ducum* — which was clearly regarded as an important fact in both those texts; see Mortensen 2000d for the possible conclusions to be drawn from the close relationship between *Passio Olaui* and Theodoricus on this point. The 'discovery' of William's testimony is likely to have been done by Theodoricus in the period *c.* 1170–1185 when the information also entered *Passio Olaui*. We have here further evidence of the lack of contact between *HN* on the one side and Theodoricus and *Passio Olaui* on the other. **ciuitatem** For the use of *ciuitas*, *cf.* commentary on III 8. **ingenio** 'talent', here 'trick', *cf.* Elliot 1997, 8.

11 Namque [...] progressi sunt Another long period: to the subject (*singuli quique naute*) are attached an apposition in the present participle (*latitantes*) and, asyndetically, another present participle (*precauantes*). In addition there is an absolute ablative (*tenuis glebis [...] simulantibus*) with the object *identitatem*; to the latter, a genitive (*campi spissitudinis*) is added in the form of an *abstractum pro concreto*. The period next contains an ablative absolute (*ordinata acie*) and an apposition (*parati*) to the subject, before we reach the main verb (*progressi sunt*). **tenuis** Here ablative with *glebis*. A 3rd declension adjective can have 1st/2nd declension forms in ML; hence Bugge's suggestion (followed by Storm) *tenuibus* is hardly necessary. *Cf.* note to II 12 above and Stotz vol. IV, p. 32 & 96. **concaua** A substantivized adjective in the neuter plural, *cf.* commentary on II 14 (*profunda pelagi*).

12 insecuntur This is the equivalent of *insequuntur*. The letters 'c' and 'qu' are often used interchangeably in ML, *cf.* Elliot 1997, 4.

13 illi [...] festinantes The subject, restated in **illi [...] Norwagenses tyranni**. **equites subsequentes [...] proruentes** The object, which is then restated as **eos. latencia precipicia** neuter plural; *latentia praecipitia* in standard spelling. **sonipedibus** From *sonipes* adj., 'with sounding feet' poetic Latin used for 'horses', *cf.* Virgil, *Aeneid* 4.135 and *passim*. It was used in ML prose as well, *e.g.* by Adam (IV 21). **tyranni** For the term, *cf.* commentary on VI 8 (*pirate*). **trucidabant** Classical Latin would have preferred the perfect.

14 Itaque Here in the first position in the sense of 'and so', but *cf.* commentary on I 1. **intrabant [...] obtinebant** In classical Latin the perfect would have been preferred.

15 adepta est Here the subject changes from 'they' (*sc. Norwagenses*) *obtinebant* in the previous sentence to *adepta est* (*sc. regio*) without this last word being mentioned.

16 comitis The term *comes* m. for 'earl', 'count' or 'duke' (*cf.* also VI 20), is quite common, especially during the eleventh century, and occurs alongside *dux* with reference to the conquerors in Normandy. Richard II (996–1026) was the first person to call himself *dux* (Bates 1982, 148–49).

17 Willelmum Longosped For the spelling of *Willelmum* here and in VI 19, *cf.* Cappelli 1995, 400; *Wilelmi* appears with a single 'l' in VI 18. This form of the nickname 'Longsword' (often understood as 'Longspear') probably derives from a French pronouncation (*longue espede*). The Latin form *longa spatha* is found *e.g.* in Robert of Torigni (William of Jumièges ed. and trans. van Houts 1995 II, *e.g.* Book VIII ch. 28. *Cf.* also Essay § 6.2.4.).

18 Iunior vero Ricardus habuit filium Robertum, qui Either a bit of text, like *habuit filium Robertum, qui* as Storm suggests, has disappeared, or the author's source was deficient. Here Richard II's sons are missing, Richard III (d. 1028) and Robert the Proud (d. 1036), who was the father of William the Bastard (the Conqueror).

19 Merlini regis For the term *rex* used about the prophet Merlin, *cf.* Essay § 6.2.4. Merlin is the Celtic prophet who was purported to have lived in the sixth century. His name is associated with a number of legends mentioned by Geoffrey of Monmouth in particular. For further references see Phelpstead 2001, 86. His suggestion that Ordericus Vitalis (see next note and Phelpstead *ibid.*) should be the direct source for the *HN*, however, is very unlikely, given the minimal contemporary spread of Ordericus's text. The massive attention drawn to Geoffrey's works from the 1140s and onwards in western and northern Europe must have engendered a great deal of oral and written material now lost to us. Ordericus and *HN* probably relied on similar digests of or references from Geoffrey. **leo iusticie** In the first variant version of Geoffrey's *Historia regum Britannie* (ed. N. Wright, Cambridge 1988) this prophecy begins (112 (11)): *Succedet leo iusticie ad cuius rugitum Gallicane turres et insulani dracones tremebunt.* Ordericus Vitalis quotes the prophecies in Book XII of the *Historia ecclesiastica*, composed around 1135 and adds a number of explanations (XII.iv.493), among which we find: *'Succedet leo iusticiæ' quod refertur ad Henricum.* For Henry I and the implications for the dating of *HN*, *cf.* Introduction p. 11 & Essay § 3 and 6.2.4.

20 Radulfus This is the reading of *A*. *Radulfus*, for *Rodulfus*, might have been the spelling in the original. In ML we sometimes find 'a' used as 'o' and vice versa, *cf.* Blaise 1994, 129. **comes** For this term, *cf.* commentary on VI 16 and Essay § 6.2.4. *Comes* here could allude to the Norwegian earl lineage or to Norwegian/Nordic association, *cf.* V 2 and 3, IX 25, XII 4, XVI 1 and 2, XVII 2, 26, 29, 40, 56 and 57 about, for example, the earl Orkan, the presidium of earls in the Orkneys, the Danish earl Ottar, Eirik Blodaxe, Håkon Jarl (earl) and the sons Eirik and Svein and the family of earls in Møre. **Fresones** *I.e. Frisones.*

21 posteritatis *A* has *posteritates*, but *A1*, an independent quotation from the exemplar of *A*, here reads the correct genitive *posteritatis*, which, in turn, may of course be a correction *in scribendo*. **excepto quod** For this expression, *cf. e.g. Gn* 9,4. **iure tributario** For the payment of tributes, *cf.* Essay § 6.1.6.

VII. On the Faroe Islands

1 in refluentis occeani For this expression, *cf.* commentary on I 5. **propria** *A* reads *prima*. Munch and Storm suggest *patria*, but if one is to emend *A* here, Bugge's *propria* seems better: the abbreviations of *propria* and *prima* are very much alike, *cf.* Cappelli pp. 257-8 and 261. At any rate the meaning of *propria* and *patria* will be 'mother tongue'. **Fereyiar** *A* has *farcar*. Bede and others call the Faroe islands *Farne*. This is quite close to *A*, but in *HN* it is the meaning of the Faroese name ('Islands of Sheep') that is important. *Cf.* also Essay § 6.2.5.

3 regibus nostris certis temporibus tributa persoluunt For payment of tributes, *cf.* Introduction p. 12 & Essay § 6.1.6. For the term *tributa*, *cf.* Essay § 6.2.6.

VIII. On Iceland

1 illa magna insula Ellipsis of *est.* **ab Italis** *Cf.* Adam (IV 36): *De qua [insula Thyle] tam a Romanis scriptoribus quam a barbaris multa referuntur digna predicari.* **Tile** This name may also be spelled *Thule* or *Thyle*. For the term *ultima Tile, cf.* commentary on I 11 (*Telensibus*). **quam magna** *quam* may be understood as intensifying adverb, *cf.* IV 11 (Adam (IV 36) calls Iceland *insula permaxima*), although this is unusual in comparison with *quam maxima*; perhaps one should read *cum* instead of *quam* (Kraggerud) **colonum** For *colonorum*, from *colonus* m. In ML the plural is often declined as *colones*, genitive *colonum*. **hominibus incognita** The author leaves out the fact that Irish monks (Papes) arrived there first, *cf.* Ari, *Íslendingabók*, ch. 1 and Essay § 6.2.6.

2 Tunc quidam Norwagenses [...] fugentes [...] ingredientes insulam, prius inventam [...] inquirendo [...] reperierunt To the subject (*quidam Norwagenses Ingwar et Hiorleifr*) are attached two present participles asyndetically connected (*fugentes* [...] *ingredientes*), a gerund in the ablative (*inquirendo*), which functions as yet another present participle, and finally the main verb (*reperierunt*), which, together with *inquirendo* takes the object *insulam*, with an apposition in the past participle (*inuentam*). **Ingwar** This is the name as given in *A*. Storm corrects to *Ingulfr*, but it is doubtful whether it is advisable to make a correction here. *HN*'s source could have had another name, *cf.* commentary on XVII 7 (*a quodam Olauo* [...]). **ob** For the use of *ob*, *cf.* commentary on Prologue 4. **reatus** *Reatus* m., 'guilt', also in the Christian sense of 'sin'. **fugentes** This is the reading of *A*. *Fugentes*, for *fugientes*, might have been the original spelling. In Christian Latin we find syncopated 'i' in, *e.g.*, *aspicentes (aspicientes)*, *cf.* Blaise 1994, 130. **post ab Oddo** *I.e.* Nadd-oddr (mentioned in *Landnámabók*). This is one of Storm's suggestions (note *ad locum*; cf. Phelpstead 2001, 87), and it seems reasonable, although somewhat uncertain. *A* has *post ab aubă* / *anbă*. Storm's suggestion assumes that the copyist has not been able to read the name correctly. One argument in favour of this suggestion is that it seems natural that the author of *HN* would mention either *Naddoddus* (Nadd-oddr) or Floke, both of whom were Norwegian, when he was already referring to Gardar, who was Swedish. All three left the island fairly soon, however. Storm also suggests the plausible *post ab Auda, i.e. Auðr djúpauðga.* This seems better than, for example, *post ab altero* (or *post ab alio*), which means that only the Swede Gardar is mentioned by name. The correction to *post a Flokone* (Munch's suggestion), on the other hand, means that *ab* must be changed to *a*. Nevertheless, in all these scenarios *post* remains in the insertion and not in the main clause together with the other temporal adverbs *tunc* and *tandem*. And this is preferable to *post ambo*, Bugge's suggestion (*cf.* Storm, note *ad locum*), since in this case there seem to be too many temporal adverbs in the main clause. A final suggestion could be *postea ambo*, since *post* in *HN* is nowhere used in the sense of *postea*, but rather always as a preposition. But we find *post* in this very sense — and with a preceding *prius*, as in *HN*, in *e.g. Passio Olaui* (ed. Metcalfe 1881, 115). For further references to the discovery of Iceland, *cf.* Phelpstead 2001, 87. **per pendulas pelagi undas** Alliteration. The adjective *pendulus* is poetical in classical Latin. It is quite common in medieval texts.

3 in quinquaginta fere annis According to Ari (*Íslendingabók*, ch. 3) it took 60 years. Here *in* + ablative for the time of duration, *cf.* Theodoricus (ch. 30): *Saxoniam, quam in annis triginta jugiter rebellantem*. Otherwise the pure ablative is preferred, *cf.* VIII 8, IX 21, XIII 4, XIV 1, XVII 8 and 57 and XVIII 11 and 27. The ablative of duration is post-classical Latin and is often found in the Vulgate and in ML. *Cf.* Elliot 1997, 22 and Löfstedt 1936, 51–56. For the accusative, *cf.* commentary on XI 3 (*LXXIII annos*). **ubique** *A* has *utrobique* ('on both sides'), which is unlikely, since the migrators established settlements all along the coast (unless the author wanted to say 'both on the north and the south coast'). The *ubique* goes well with the subsequent *ut nunc* ... which defines it: 'inhabited everywhere as it is now...'. Another suggestion for emendation is *est ubique* (Storm), or *ab utroque*, in the sense of 'by their respective kin' (Ekrem). **inhabitata** Ellipsis of *est*.

4 igitur [...] nuncupatur *Igitur* is a correction of *dicitur* in *A*. It is questionable whether this is legitimate, since *igitur* elsewhere in *HN* occurs in second position in the sentence, *cf.* commentary on I 1. If *dicitur* is retained, then *nuncupatur* must be rejected. **Islandia [...] glaciei terra** In the heading of this chapter (*De glaciali insula*) we find an approximate translation into Latin of the Norwegian name 'Island' (Iceland). Here the Latinized Norwegian name (*Islandia*) is explained. Adam uses the names *Thyle* and *Island* (IV 36–37).

5 habet namque eadem insula innumerabiles montes, uerum continua glacie contectos Here the author of *HN* disagrees with Adam (IV 36), who claims that the name 'Island' (Iceland) derives from the sea that has frozen over. **unde illis resplendentibus [...] per hos** Such a use of the ablative absolute is not customary in classical Latin, but it is common in ML, *cf.* Kaulen 1904, 300, Skard 1930, 34 and Elliot 1997, 20–21. A classical construction would be, simply, *per hos resplendentes*. Whereas the snow is shining in *HN*, Adam (IV 36) tells the reader that it is *nigra et arida*.

6 Mons Casule Actually 'Cabin mountain', but here *casula* is used for *cuculla* ('hood'). *Mons Casule* is a direct translation of the name 'Hekla', which means 'a hooded robe'. *Casula*, 'priestly garb', also occurs in *e.g.* Adam (III 45). **ad instar Ethne** *Ad instar* is post-classical Latin. Classical Latin uses only *instar*. Honorius uses the expression *ad exemplar* (I 2). About Etna he writes (I 35): *In hac [sc. in Sicilia] est mons Aethna cuius sulfurea exaestuant incendia*. Saxo also likens Hekla to Etna (here with readings of the forthcoming edition by K. Friis-Jensen, Præfatio II.7): *In hac itidem insula mons est, qui rupem Sicelicam perpetue flagrationis estibus imitatus incendia sempiterna iugi flammarum eructatione continuat*. **pruriens** From *prurio* 4th, 'tickle', 'itch'. **terrebili** *I.e. terribili*.

7 feruidi fonticuli Honorius speaks of some *fontes calidi* in connection with Sardinia (I 36). **operti** *A* has *aperti*; the use for 'a' instead of 'o' here by the author of *HN*, however, would be very confusing since the two spellings produce opposite senses: 'covered' and 'open'. **balnealia [...] lauacra** Pleonasm.

8 putei Honorius also mentions a *puteus* ('a well') in connection with the African city of Syene (I 36). **in quis** *I.e. in quibus*. **unius noctis spacio** The ablative is used here for the time of duration, *cf.* commentary on VIII 3 (*in quinquaginta fere annis*). **si lana aut pannus [...] immersi iaceant [...] conuertentur** The *si*-clause is in the subjunctive and the main clause in the future indicative, *cf.* Blaise 1994 § 304. *Cf.* also II 5, where the main clause is also in the indicative, but in the present tense. There is no justification for changing *conuertentur* to *conuertuntur*, as Storm does, since a certain flexibility in the use of tense and mood was pronounced throughout the Middle Ages. We should also note that the apposition *inmersi* and the verb *iaceant* are in the m. plural, in spite of the fact that the subject (*lana aut pannus*) usually requires the singular in classical Latin. As noted by Sandaaker 1985, 84, Saxo has a similar story in his geographical introduction on Iceland (Præfatio II.7): *Sane quicquid fumi huius exhalatione respergitur, in lapideæ naturæ duritiam transmutatur.* Saxo may have borrowed these details from *HN* (see Introduction p. 33 and *cf.* notes on VIII 6 and VIII 9).

9 fons quidam *Cf. The King's Mirror*, ch. 48 (ed. Holm-Olsen 1945, 21), which tells of a well in Hitardalr in western Iceland that does not satiate the one who drinks from it, but rather is easily digested and flows out like beer. If one drank enough from this well, one would become drunk. Saxo also reports about the beer (Præfatio II.7): *Sunt et alii fontes, quorum scatebra cerealis poculi proprietatem imitari perhibetur.* **scaturiens** From *scaturio* 4th, classical Latin *scateo*, 'bubble', 'spring forth'. *Scaturio* is common in ML, *cf.* also II *Mcc* 9,9. **ceruisie** *Ceruisia* or *cereuisia* f. is a Gallic word for beer which became common in ML. **adimplere** From *adimpleo* 2nd, 'fill completely'. For the use of the double prefix, *cf.* commentary on VI 7 (*derelictorum*).

10 nostra etate The account of this 'recent' eruption cannot be used for dating *HN*; see Phelpstead 2001, 87-88 and Introduction pp. 11–12. *Cf.* also Essay § 6.2.6.

11 tria miliaria The accusative of extent. *Miliaria* is sometimes spelled *milliaria.* **eurippi** From *Euripus* m., the straits between Euboea and Boeotia. It often occurs in ML (*e.g.* in Bede and William of Malmesbury) as a generic term for *abyssus* or *ledo*, *cf.* also Adam (IV 40). Thus it may best be translated by 'an abyss'. **quasi cacabus feruere cepit** *Cacabus* m. derives from Greek (κάκκαβος), was used in classical Latin, and became more frequent in ML (usually spelled *caccabus*) for 'cooking-pot', 'cauldron'. The phrase here is borrowed from Honorius who writes on *maximus oceanus* (I 33): *qui solis calore dicitur fervere ut cacabus.* **Cepit** *I.e. coepit.* **adhiscens** The inchoative of *hio* 1st, 'gape/stand open'. For the use of inchoatives, *cf.* commentary on I 13 (*albescunt*). **igniuomos** This adjective occurs *e.g.* in Lactantius, *Sermo de Ressurrectione Domini*, 3. *Cf.* also *fluctiuomis* in II 11. *Igniuomus* is common in ML. **undis** Ablative of separation.

12 monstris From *monstrum* n. Storm's correction to *monstri* (genitive) is questionable. The reason for preferring *monstris* (dative) is due to the fact that the plural form is retained in what follows with *mira* and *in talibus.* **mundumue** Here *-ue* used for *et*, *cf.* commentary on IV 13 (*quantumue*). **sui interitum** Customary ML expression for *suum interitum*, *cf.* II *Mcc* 5,8. In ML a distinction is often not made between the use of the possessive pronoun for objective and partitive genitives and the possessive adjective for pure possesion, *cf.* Elliot 1997, 34. **prefigurare** From *praefiguro* 1st, frequent in ecclesiastical Latin in the sense of 'foreshadow', 'prefigure'. **coniectant** The frequentative of *coniicio* 3rd, 'bring together', 'unite'. Here with an accusative with infinitive, as in classical Latin. **cum [...] exercent** It is a question whether this *cum*-clause is a temporal clause or a concessive subordinate clause. It has the indicative, but the flexibility in the use of the subjunctive (*cf.* commentary on I 9) makes a concessive subordinate clause possible. This is preferred because of the succeeding and explanatory *namque.*

13 Solinus Solinus's book is titled *Collectanea rerum memorabilium* in modern editions but was commonly known in the Middle Ages as *De mirabilibus mundi* or *Polihistor.* As first pointed out by Skard (1930, 78–79), however, most of the contents of 13–14 derive from Honorius, *Imago mundi* I 41 (*De voragine*): *Est in terra abyssus profundissima, de qua scribitur "Rupti sunt omnes fontes abyssi magnae". Iuxta hanc sunt cavernosa loca, et spelunce late* *patentes. In his, venti de spiramine aquarum concipiuntur, qui etiam spiritus procellarum dicuntur. Et hi suo spiramine aquas maris per patentes terrarum cavernas introrsus in abyssum attrahunt, et ea exundante iterum magno impetu repellunt. Cf.* Essay § 5.1.2. The author may have believed *Imago mundi* to be part of Solinus's work, or he may simply have confused his excerpts from the two works. The interesting discussion that follows now in *HN* on marvels of nature vs. portents of the end of the world is a good example of the importance and intricacies of the medieval discourse on the order of nature, brought forward well by Daston & Park 1998. **abyssum [...] existere [...] iuxta quam speluncas [...] uentos [...] in se continere** An indirect statement, in which *abyssum* [...] *existere*, appropriately enough, is in the accusative with infinitive. In the following sentence *iuxta quam speluncas* [...] *uentos* [...] *in se continere*, the indirect acc. plus inf. construction continues, and the *quam* must therefore be understood as a transitional relative. **abyssum** From *abyssus* f., Greek, *cf.* also the Honorius quotation above. **Rupti sunt fontes abyssi magne** From *Gn* 7,11 (on the Flood) as quoted by Honorius (see above). **spiritus procellarum** *Cf. Ps* 10,7: *spiritus tempestatum.*

14 spiracione From *spiratio* f. 'breath', 'breathing'. **meatus** For this word, *cf.* commentary on IV 8. **aquas maris ad se contrahunt et in thesauros abissi recondunt** *Aquas* is poet. plural. *Cf. Ps* 32,7: *congregans* [...] *aquas maris ponens in thesauris abyssos.* The treasures are not mentioned by Honorius.

15 terre motus 15–16 draws on the next paragraph in Honorius, I 42 (*De terre motu*): *De his ventis fit etiam terre motus. Nam venti concavis locis inclusi dum erumpere gestiunt, terram horribili fremore concutiunt, eamque tremefaciunt* (a number of early Honorius manuscripts read *tremere faciunt*, *cf.* Flint's edition, 1983, p. 69).

16 gliscunt From *glisco* 3rd, normally 'to swell', but the sense of 'to desire', 'to eagerly espouse' is also well attested. *Gliscunt* might be a misunderstanding of *gestiunt*, from *gestio* 4th, 'to long for', 'to desire', which we find in Honorius; but a comparison of these paragraphs with those of Honorius shows that the author of *HN* often strove to vary the wording of his source. Neither word is used elsewhere in *HN.*

17 spiritu ventorum introrsum cum igne concertante The text goes on to utilize Honorius; 17–18 is based on I 43–44 (*De hiatu & De Sicilia*): *Hinc etiam fit terre hiatus, dum loca cava et continuis aquis fragilia ventis concussa rumpuntur, et introrsus cadentia, in hiatum aperiuntur, de quibus et multe civitates devorate leguntur. Hoc est autem in terra tremor, quod in nube tonitruum. Hic hiatus quod ibi fulmen. Fiunt autem cum terre motu inundationes maris, eodem videlicet spiritu infusi vel residentis sinu recepti. (44) Unde tellus Sicilie, que cavernosa et sulphure ac bitumine strata, ventis pene tota et ignibus patet, spiritu introrsus cum igne concertante multis sepe locis fumum vel vapores vel flammas eructat, vel etiam vento acrius intumbente* [*i.e. incumbente*], *harenarum lapidumve moles egerit.*

19–20 This is the most philosophical passage in *HN.* It takes its cue from Adam IV 32 and mixes a number of approaches: one is the standard Christian rejection of human wisdom; our small spark of intelligence (*ingenioli igniculus*) cannot hope to achieve true understanding. On the other hand there is a more optimistic twelfth century trend of natural philosophy visible; the neo-platonizing focus on a divine Nature as expressed in the physical world is paralleled in the philosophy of Thierry of Chartres (d. 1155/56) and the didactic poetry of Bernardus Silvestris (d. *c.* 1160). (In contrast, Adam does not speak of *natura*, and concludes on a negative note that *phisici* of the past (Beda, Macrobius, and Lucanus) disagree). Thirdly, there is a poetological appeal (*inuocemus*) for divine understanding; the poet, or here poetic prosewriter, hopes to gain insights through divine inspiration. The author of *HN*, in this remarkable passage, seems to represent the more wordly, optimistic view of the cathedral schools rather than a typical monastic rejection of learning and science.

19 mirabilia Bugge's emendation of *A*'s *mutabilia* into *mirabilia* (and Storm's acceptance of it) seems justified from the contents: The author now sums up his discussion of the status of *mirabilia* after having quoted (he thinks) the major authority in this genre, Solinus. The scribe of *A* (or of its exemplar) could well have been influenced by the subsequent *immutabili mutabilium conditori* in the same sentence to make such a slip. **cataclismi** From *cataclysmus* m., Greek, 'flooding', *cf.* *Sir* 39,28 and 40,10; it was sometimes used in ML for the Biblical Flood, though the more frequent term was *diluuium*. **famulancia** The present participle in the neuter plural of *famulor*, with the dative *cognitori* and *immutabili conditori*. *Famulancia* is the subject of the sentence and refers back to *mirabilia*. **incognitorum Cognitori, immutabili mutabilium Conditori** Figura etymologica, probably with inspiration from the phrasing in *Dn* 13,42: *absconditorum es cognitori*.

20 corpulente From *corpulentus*, adjective, describing *caliginis*. **nostri ingenioli igniculus** These two diminutives also denote humility here. *Ingeniolum* is common in ML. **altissima profunda** An adjective that attaches itself to a substantivized adjective, *cf.* commentary on II 4 (*profunda pelagi*). **haut** *A* has *hauc*, *i.e.* 't' is interpreted by the copyist as 'c'. The spelling *haut* for *haud* is not uncommon in ML manuscripts, *cf.* commentary on IV 10. **ad inuestiganda [...] efficax** Here *efficax* occurs with *ad* + accusative instead of a pure genitive, *cf.* *Hbr* 4,12. *Cf.* also commentary on Prologue 2 (*imbecillem*). **qui illuminat abscondita tenebrarum spiritu intelligencie** Both *Absconditus* and *absconsus* is used in *HN*, *cf.* commentary on III 8. The wording derives from I *Cor.* 4,5: *(Dominus) illuminabit abscondita tenebrarum* and *Sirach* 39,8–10: *si enim Dominus magnus voluerit spiritu intelligentiae replebit illum, et ipse tamquam imbres mittet eloquia sapientiae suae, et in oratione confitebitur Domino, ipse diriget consilium eius et disciplinam doctrinae suae.*

21 tributarias insulas For the reason that Iceland is mentioned under these islands, *cf.* Essay § 6.2.6; *cf.* also Introduction pp. 12–13.

22 qui reges [...] rexerunt vel unde processerunt An interrogative subordinate clause where we might have expected the subjunctive, as in the other interrogative subordinate clauses, *cf.* *e.g.* I 8, IV 13 and 20, VI 4 and XVII 53. However, indirect interrogative subordinate clauses often take the indicative in ML, as in archaic Latin, *cf.* Elliot 1997, 49. *Cf.* also *Tb* 6,16 (Kaulen 1904, 293). **Nunc vero [...], qui reges [...] ad exponendum stilum uertamus** Honorius writes (I 52): *De profundis aquarum emergamus, et scriptoria penna in aera suspendamur.* Adam (II 23): *Nunc ad ea* [...] *calamum dirigamus.* For chapter endings, *cf.* also commentary on I 15-6, II 17 and III 9.

IX. On the lineage of the kings, from Yngve to Olav Tretelgje

De ortu regum Similar genealogies of the so-called Yngling kings are found in a number of Old Norse sources: Ari's *Íslendingabók* (the last unnumbered chapter called *Ættartala*), the poem *Ynglingatal*, Snorri's *Heimskringla (Ynglinga saga)*, among others; their interrelationship is the subject of a large debate. Major contributions are Ellehøj 1965 and Krag 1991. There is a useful synoptic survey in Ellehøj, 114–15 and the brief stories told about each king is commented on in detail by Krag, 99–143. For a systematic comparison the reader is referred to his fundamental work. Both these scholars state that *HN* almost certainly drew directly on Ari's work, in a version now lost. *Cf.* also Phelpstead 2001, 88ff.

1 Trondemia About Trøndelag as the first populated and most important area in Norway, *cf.* Essay § 8.1. **in Norwegia** Preposition instead of genitive.

2 itaque *Cf.* commentary on II 1. **Ingui** Since 'i' can be used interchangeably in *HN* with 'y', 'Ingui' in *HN* corresponds to 'Yngvi' in Ari and Snorri (*Heimskringla, Ynglinga saga,*

10). Yngvi's lineage is called the Yngling lineage. For Yngvi, *cf.* Essay § 8.1. **plurimi** 'A great many' or 'most'. Who these are is not known but the phrasing suggests that *HN* is deliberately avoiding Ari's explanation that he was a Turkish — *i.e.* Trojan — king, *cf.* Ellehøj 1965, 116. For the 'Asian' origin of the genealogy *cf.* also Krag 1991, 84–85.

3 Qui Here taken as a transitional relative.

4 tota illorum posteritas [...] uenerati sunt Here *ueneror* is used as a deponent verb, but *cf.* IV 14. *Constructio ad sensum* with the verb in plural in spite of the singular subject *posteritas* is common in the Vulgate and in ML, *cf.* Kaulen 1904, 285.

5 Froyr As Storm notes (1880, xix–xx) the author generally uses the Old Norse case forms. Therefore Storm corrected *A*'s repetition of the accusative from above (3) into nominative. This is supported by *BC* which both give a nominative (the corrupted form in *B*, *stroyer* — found several times in B — is due to a misunderstanding of the grapheme 'ff', *i.e.* capital 'F', and does not reduce the stemmatic weight of *BC* (equal to that of *A*) for preferring the nominative here). **Fiolni** Fjolne opens the genealogy in the poem *Ynglingatal* by Tjodolv of Kvin (traditionally dated around 900, but the exisiting version has recently been placed in the twelfth century, see Krag 1991). **medonis** From *medo* f. 'mead', a Germanic noun. It occurs in many ML texts, *e.g. Vita Gunneri episcopi Vibergensis* (ed. Gertz, 1917–22, vol. II, 272, l. 17 & 273, l. 20). **dimersus est** Variant spelling of *demersus est*, 'drowned', 'was drowned'. According to Snorri (*Heimskringla, Ynglinga saga*, 11), he himself was the cause of the accident.

7 demone From *daemon* m., Greek, 'a spirit', in Christian Latin 'an evil spirit', 'a demon'.

8 demoniorum From *daemonium* n., Greek, diminutive of daemon, but in Christian Latin simply 'an evil spirit'. **Norwaico** The adjective *Norwaicus* is only used in this one instance in *HN*. The author uses the adjective *Norwagensis* in VI 13, VIII 2 and 4, X 1, XVII 26 and XVIII 29, and *Norwegensis* in XVII 12. In Honorius Norway is written *Norweia* (*Imago mundi* I 24). **mara** A supernatural being, usually taken to be a female figure who tormented people and animals while they slept (*cf. Kulturhistorisk leksikon* 1956–78).

9 sui and **sua** refer to Wisbur. **cicius** *i.e. citius*. After **incenderunt** *C* gives the reading *ac familiam* which is superfluous (the *familia* presumably included in the *curia*) and not paralleled in any other source. This is one of a several additions made by the *C* redactor (see below, 10–11 and Introduction p. 36).

10 Cereri *Ceres* is the Roman goddess of fertility. One inspiration for using an *interpretatio Romana* here is, no doubt, Adam II 22, where he writes about Vulcan and Neptune in connection with Slavonic pagan practices. *Cf.* also IX 26 (*Diane*). *C* has *dee Cereri* — another glossing by the *C* redactor.

11 obiit *C* has *obiit morbo* ('died of illness'); Snorri (*Heimskringla, Ynglinga saga*, 16), writes that he 'died in Uppsala of a disease.' Storm followed *C*, probably because of Snorri, but perhaps also because the entire genealogy is composed after the scheme: 'a was son of b and met a death of type x'. On the other hand, the following sentence actually does not describe the way of dying and reads clumsily if we take *morbo* into the text. Furthermore, all sentences except those with *genuit* (following obvious Biblical models) and IX 15 and IX 32 (and, probably, IX 17) end with the verb. Finally, a private reading of *C* against *AB* carries very little stemmatic weight. In order to have made the addition, *C* must have known Snorri or a tradition derived from him.

13 Sciontanuath Storm preferred to include the alternative name found in *B*'s text *stotamuadh uel wapnawadh*. *A* gives only the first name in the corrupt form *scrotā uath*, but both are found in Snorri (*Heimskringla, Ynglinga saga*, 18; cf Krag 1991, 110–111) with the same phrasing: *Skjótansvað eða Vápnavað*. This no doubt convinced Storm, but he did not know what Bolin 1931 showed, namely that the Swedish genealogist around 1340 used Snorri and could thus easily have contaminated Snorri and *HN* at this point. There is also another reason to be sceptical: nowhere else does *HN* mention alternative names or spelling of names and it does not tally well with his otherwise assertive and authoritative style. There is one other instance of alternative spelling of a name, but also transmitted only in *B* (below IX 26), as well as an addition of a geographical name (IX 17: *Stockholm*); the same reasoning would apply there. **passeris iniurias** According to Snorri (*ibidem*) (*cf.* also *Ynglingatal* 18 and the comments of Krag 1991, 110–111) Dag had a sparrow he was very fond of because of its prophetic powers. It flew all over the world, but one day, when it was out searching for food, it was killed by a farmer in Gotland. Dag went there to avenge this injustice but was himself killed on the way back. **publico bello** *Bellum* in the sense of 'battle' is common in ML. It is not quite certain what is meant by *publico*: previous translations take it as an 'open' battle, but what would a 'closed' battle be? *Publicus* in ML does not have an obvious spatial reference; in most connections it refers to *res publica*, 'the state' or 'kingdom'. It is probably a technical term for a battle with the reign at stake; 'royal' seems to be the better suggestion. *Cf. e.g.* Lampert of Hersfeld, *Annales*, 1073 [ed. O. Holder-Egger, Hannover 1894, p. 199]: *Saxones comperto, quod elusis custodibus suis rex in alias regni partes evasisset, vehementer sunt contristati, arbitrantes, id quod res exigebat, nihil sibi deinceps ocii aut remissi habendum, nec pestem hanc ut hactenus intra domesticos parietes cohibendam, sed revelata facie bellum publicum cum hoste publico gerendum; ideoque sibi expedire, ut quantascumque possent gentes et regna adversus regem concitarent. Cf.* also XIII 6 below (*bella [...] publica*).

15 suus *Cf.* commentary to IX 9.

16 Agna *A* has *Hogana* with the first 'a' and the 'n' intertwined. The name is probably an error for *Agna* (acc.) as he is called *Agni* in Ari and Snorri (*Heimskringla, Ynglinga saga*, 19), and the place where he was killed is called *Agnafit*. Storm left *Hogna* in the text, perhaps because he thought the error was original; but *cf.* Ellehøj 1965, 116. In *B* we have *Ingimar*, perhaps the Swedish genealogist's attempt of reinterpretation, or simply the result of other graphemic troubles in the transmission. In Snorri Agni appears before Alrek, but Ari has the same order as *HN*; *cf.* Krag 1991, 111–12.

17 Agnafit In *B* there is an addition concerning Agnafit: *qui nunc Stokholmr dicitur*. This must have been added by the Swedish genealogist. See also Phelpstead 2001, 90 with reference to an argument that Stockholm is not mentioned in Swedish sources before 1252. **interfecit suspendendo ad arborem cum catena aurea** In *A* the sentence ends with *interfecit*. Is *B*'s longer description added on the basis of Snorri (*Heimskringla, Ynglinga saga*, 19; *cf.* Krag 1991, 111–12) or has it been lost in the *A*-transmission? This cannot be settled for sure, but as in other cases where we have sensible readings of *A* against those of *B* they have equal stemmatic value and must be decided on other criteria (as the alternative names in IX 13 above). Against the inclusion of *B*'s wording would speak the above consideration (IX 11, *obiit*) that the phrases in the genealogy almost all end with the verb. In favour, however, is the use of the gerund *suspendendo* as a present participle so typical for the author.

18 Ingialdr [...] ob infamiam uxoris Ingjald is called Yngvi in Ari and Snorri (*Heimskringla, Ynglinga saga*, 21). It has been suggested that *HN*'s name is a scribal error (*cf.* Krag 1991, 115), but one should keep in mind that it is attested by both branches of the transmission (*A* and *B*); consequently the error must go back to the time before the two branches split, *i.e.* possibly to the thirteenth century (see Introduction p. 43). Yngvi's brother was called Alv and was married to Bera. Since it was Ingjald/Yngvi, and not Bera, who was killed by Alv, *ob infamiam uxoris* is here translated by 'discredit on the latter's wife', *i.e. uxoris* is understood as an objective genitive. According to Snorri (*ibidem*), however, Yngve and Bera seem to have been equally guilty, since they both enjoyed the pleasure of one another's company. This passage can thus also be translated by 'the wife's indecent behaviour'.

20 Iorundr Understand *regnauit*. This seems to be the only place in *HN* in which the ellipsis implies a verb other than *esse*. **in loco** Here with a preposition, as in classical Latin, but *cf.* XV 1 and XVIII 12, where we have simply *loco*.

21 IX annis The author often uses an ablative of duration, *cf.* commentary on VIII 3 (*in quinquaginta fere annis*). **alimonie** From *alimonia* f. 'food'; while rare in antiquity it became a common ML alternative to *alimentum*.

22 Auchun He is called Aun by Ari and Snorri (*Heimskringla, Ynglinga saga*, 25). **Vendilcraco** 'Vendelkråke', *i.e.* 'Vendel Crow'.

23 pedissecus Or *pedisecus*, old spelling for *pedi(s)sequus*. This term was originally used about a slave who walks behind his master. For the spelling, *cf. insecuntur* in the commentary on VI 12. **bella commisit** For *bella cf.* commentary to IX 13.

25 Ottaro For some reason *HN* has made the two namesakes in contrast to the rest of the tradition where the earl is called Váttr, *cf.* Krag 1991, 121. **Danorum comite, et fratre eius Fasta ⟨in una⟩ prouinciarum Danie** Here we are confronted with two textual problems: *et fratre eius Fasta* is only transmitted in *B*. Furthermore the scribe of *A* has left a space of 4–8 letters between *comite* and *prouinciarum* (the only instance in the entire manuscript). Storm made a convincing conjecture of *in una*, a phrase that is used in exactly the same way in XVII 27. The two words *in una* would fit the space well, but it is odd that the scribe would, uniquely, baulk at these two easy words. It is more likely that he had trouble with the name *Fasta*, or perhaps some confusion of *fratre* and *Fasta*. Whether or not this was Storm's reasoning, the space left can be used as an argument for accepting *B*'s *et fratre eius Fasta*: *B* also omits the necessary *in una*, which indicates that this slip happened at an early stage of the transmission. **Wendli** *I.e.* Vendsyssel in northern Jutland.

26 Adils In *B*, *vel Adhisl* is added. It is not in keeping with the tenor of *HN* to add alternative spellings of names; the addition should be laid at the Swedish genealogist's door; *cf.* above IX 13. **ydolorum** From *idolum* n., Greek; in Christian usage about images of false gods, 'idol', *cf. e.g.* Adam (IV 28). **dum ydolorum sacrificia faceret**. The verb in this sentence is transmitted as *fugeret* (*A*) and *fugat* (*B*). Storm accepted *fugeret* (from *fugio*, 3rd, 'flee, shun'), *i.e.* Adils shunned the pagan rites. Apart from the fact that Diana's temple is not the ideal place to avoid idolatry, it is also strange that *HN* would not have him rewarded for resistance to pagan ritual, but rather punished. Furthermore neither Snorri nor *Ynglingatal* refers to any religious hostility on the part of Adils. Snorri says that he fell from his horse while taking part in the rites, *Ynglingatal* that an enchanting spirit (*vitta véttr*) caused his death (for these versions see Krag 1991, 70–72 & 122–23). The other received text, *fugat* (from *fugo*, 1st 'chase away', 'rout') is meaningless with *sacrificia* as object: you chase away people, soldiers, armies etc, but not sacrifices. If *HN* had wanted to express an act of hostility, it would have said that Adils chased away the priests or the people from the rite. Krag takes Storm's text for granted and uses it to interpret the other versions: *HN* and *Ynglingatal* state that Adils was struck down by a spirit because of his attack on the cult, whereas Snorri realizes that this was an anachronistic *interpretatio christiana* and consequently told the story as if the fall from the horse was an accident. Krag presses the point rather much and reads the king's hostility into *Ynglingatal* on the basis of *HN*. But the three texts rather say the same: Adils took part in the rites and fell fatally from his horse — probably caused by an evil spirit. Even apart from a combined reading with the other versions the illogicality of the Latin text demands attention: while shunning the pagan rites Adils fell from his horse — at the pagan rites. The problem is solved by Kraggerud's emendation: *faceret* instead of *fugeret*. It yields the passage not only readability and logic, but also Latinity: *sacrificia facere* is the standard idiom in classical Latin for performing sacrifices, rites etc. Moreover it is used in the Vulgate Old Testament (*III Reg.* 12.27; *Sap.* 14.23) and by the fathers about pre-christian religion, *e.g.* Augustinus, *De civitate Dei* XXII.10 (*sacrificia fecerunt*). **Diane** The Roman goddess for hunting is here used as an *interpretatio Romana* for the goddess Dis in Old Norse mythology. The religious event referred to is the so-called 'Disablot'. For the use of Roman divinities *cf.* commentary on IX 10 (*Cereri*) and Introduction p. 41. In connection with pre-Christian Nordic religion *Diana Scythica* is also referred to by Adam (IV 44) through a quotation from Lucan. **expirauit** *i.e. exspirauit.*

28 Canutus from *canus*, 'light', 'grey' is probably a Latinization of Yngvar's nickname in Old Norse; in *Ynglingatal* he is called 'ljóshamr', *i.e.* the 'fairhaired'. **Eycisla** *I.e.* the island of Ösel in the Baltic Sea. There is no reason to correct 'c' in *eycilla* in *A* to 's' (*Eysisla*), as Munch and Storm did; the spelling of names could well have varied in the original, *cf.* XVII 5 (*Eisisla* in *A*) and XVIII 5 (*Eysillam* in *A*) and Skard 1930, 10.

29 ergo *Cf.* commentary on *igitur* in I 1. **Siwardus frater eius** *HN* is alone in reporting that Sigurd slew his brother Braut-Ånund. **eius** There is no reason to change *eius* in *A* to *suus* as in *B* and in Storm. *Eius* and *suus* are sometimes used interchangeably in ML. **Himinheithy** *I.e. himinheiðr* as in Snorri, 'heavenly field'.

31 Withfadm 'Vidfadme', *i.e.* 'Widefathom'. **tunc temporis** The genitive of species, *cf.* XVIII 18 and *id locorum* XVII 11. This kind of expression is common in ML.

32 functus is found only in *B*. It is certainly right against *A*'s *firmiter in* which may have resulted from a false reading of an abbreviation. Without a verb *diu et pacifice* is left hanging in the air. **plenus** Here with the genitive, *cf.* Prologue 4 where *plenus* takes the ablative.

X. From Halvdan Hvitbein to Halvdan the Black

3 Bumbus or *Bombus*. For the alternate use of 'u' and 'o', *cf.* commentary on I 4 (*promunctoria*). The Norwegian nickname 'Fjert' (*i.e.* 'Fart') occurs only in Ari. *Bombus* is poetical Latin for 'dump', 'humming' or 'buzzing sound', as from a horn or from bees. In ML also for 'fart'. **uelificassent** should normally have been in the imperfect, since the action takes place at the same time as the action of the main clause, *cf.* commentary on VI 4 (*aduentasset*). *Velificor*, 'to make sail' is a deponent verb in classical Latin, but later it is often used actively, as here. **Eustein [...] uelificassent [...] percussus [...] disparuit** The change of subject from Øystein alone to Øystein and his men is somewhat surprising because the clause ends with singular again. Perhaps *uelificassent* should be emended to *uelificasset*. **alterius** Use of *alterius* for *alius* in the genitive is classical Latin, *cf.* commentary on IV 20. **percussus** Ellipsis of *est*. **undisque submersus** Poet. Latin, *cf.* Virgil, *Aeneid* 1.40: *submergere ponto*.

4 Auri Prodigus Cibique Tenacissimus Halfdan's Norwegian nicknames (Gullmilde and Matille, *i.e.* the Generous of Gold and Stingy of Food) are latinized. **stipendarios** In general 'a dependent person', in military language 'a soldier', 'a retainer'. As the spelling *stipendarius* is well attested in ML there is no reason to change it with Munch (and Storm) into *stipendiarius*.

5 **Regem Venatorem** Gudrød's Norwegian nickname (Veidekonge, *i.e.* the Hunter King) is rendered in Latin. *Venatorem* here functions as an adjective. **tironum** From *tiro, -onis* m., 'a young warrior', 'a recruit'. **latus lancia perforauit** *Lancia, i.e. lancea.* For the entire expression, *cf. Io* 19,34 on Christ *lancea latus eius aperuit.*

6 **Niger** Halvdan's Norwegian nickname (Svarte, *i.e.* the Black) is translated into Latin.

7 **Rond** *I.e.* Randsfjorden, a lake in the county of Oppland. **curribus et equitatu** *Cf. Ex* 15,19: *ingressus est enim equus Pharao cum curribus et equitibus eius.* It is not certain whether carts or sleighs are meant in *HN.* **adaquare** From *adaquo* 1st, 'water', *cf. e.g. Gn* 29,8 and *Ex* 2,16.

XI. Harald Fairhair and his 16 sons (late ninth–mid-tenth cent.)

1 **ob decoram cesariem** *Cf.* Virgil, *Aeneid* 1.590. For *ob*, *cf.* commentary on Prologue 4. **reguli** For these petty kings, *cf.* Essay § 8.2.

2 **multa et mirabilia** For the contents, *cf.* Essay § 8.2.

3 **LXXIII annos** Here the time of duration is in the accusative as in XII 3 and XVII 26, but *cf.* commentary on VIII 3 (*in quinquaginta fere annis*). Ari (*Íslendingabók*, ch. 1), like Theodoricus (ch. 1) and *Ágrip* (ch. 4), gives 70 years. Snorri adds three years in retirement (*Heimskringla, Haralds saga ins Hárfagra*, 42). *Cf.* also Phelpstead 2001, 92–93 for further references. **XVI filios** *Ágrip* (ch. 2) and Snorri (*Heimskringla, Haralds saga ins Hárfagra*, 17, 20, 21, 25 and 37) have here 20 sons and a slightly different order of arrangement. Jorund, Yngvar and Rolv are only listed in *HN.* On the other hand the names of Guttorm, Halvdan the Black, Halvdan the White, Sigfred, Rørek, Torgils, Frode, Ragnar and Dag are missing in *HN.* For the order and number, *cf.* Essay § 8.2. See also Phelpstead 2001, 93.

4 **Blothex** The Norwegian nickname (Blodøks) is translated into Latin (*Sanguinea Securis*). There is some doubt as to whether *Blothex* in *A* should be corrected to *Blothoex*. The *A* text has the dipthong 'oe' only at one place in *HN.* It is in XI 6 (*Hafoeta*). Immediately after that, in XV 2, the same name is written *Hafota.* Whether this is due to the author or the copyist is difficult to say.

6 **Gigas** Latinization of the Norwegian nickname, Risi. For Sigurd Risi, *cf.* Essay § 8.2. and 8.7. **Sextus Gunrodus. Septimus Guthrodus** *Gunrodus* and *Guthrodus* are both forms of one and the same name, but here for two different sons.

7 **Rogualdus** or *Rognaldus* is the reading of *A.* Storm corrects to *Rognvaldus*, but *cf.* commentary on VI 8. **Recilbein** This is the reading of *A. Recilbein*, for *Retilbein*, might well have been the original spelling, but it could also possibly be a copyist's error. *Retilbein* means 'Straight-limbed'. Storm added a *qui* after Recilbein in order to adjust the syntax to the pattern of the previous genealogical entries (name plus a relative clause); he may have been right, but the conjecture is not necessary. **fetonissa** This corresponds to *fitonissa* or *phitonissa* (a Greek noun), and in I *Par* 10,13 *pythonissa*, 'a fortune teller', 'witch'. For the use of 'e' and 'i', *cf.* commentary on I 5 (*meredie*). For the spelling with 'ph', *cf.* commentary on IV 18 (*profanas*). **Hatlandia** Modern 'Hadeland', north of Oslo and west of Hedmark. The spelling of *A* is retained against Storm's *Hathalandia*, *cf.* also XV 2. For 'Hetland' *cf.* also commentary on XVII 31 (*Hatlendenses*). **in eadem arte** *I.e.* in witchcraft. **mira** Here a substantivized adjective in the accusative plural (object). For the expression *mira* [...] *operatus est*, *cf.* commentary on VI 2. **nutrix** She was his mother, and named Snefrid, according to Snorri (*Heimskringla, Haralds saga ins Hárfagra*, 25); *cf.* Essay § 8.2.–3.

XII. Eirik Bloodaxe (mid-tenth cent.)

1 regnum ⟨optinuit⟩ [...] qui sibi ducens de Dania uxorem A verb with *regnum* as object is lacking and there is a good parallel for Munch's suggestion in X 6 (and in similar wordings, *passim*). Skard favoured no correction and used this as yet another instance of the author's predilection for ellipsis. Almost invariably, however, the ellipsis concerns some form of *esse* and this long period becomes strained without a finite verb. Bugge and Storm intervened more radically in the text because they did not like *ducens* functioning as the finite verb in the relative clause. Therefore they changed *qui sibi* into the (otherwise unattested) *acquisivit*. Skard 1930, 9 rightly dismissed their worries about *ducens*. **Gunnildam** Both *Ágrip* (ch. 5) and Snorri (*Heimskringla, Haralds saga ins Hárfagra*, 32) agree that she was a daughter of Assur Tote or Lavskjegg from Hålogaland and that she grew up in the Finnmark region in order to learn witchcraft (*cf.* Essay § 8.3). *HN* is the only source to give her a Danish royal origin and in this it is vindicated by modern historians. In any case this unique Danish information points to Danish connections or sources consulted by the author; see esp. Steinnes 1946–48, 31–32 and Phelpstead 2001, 93. **Gorms Stultissimi Danorum regis** For the nickname 'Foolish' (*Stultissimus*) instead of the usual 'Old' (*Gorm den Gamle*), *cf.* Essay § 8.3 and Phelpstead 2001, 93. **Thyri** cannot be the genitive feminine in Latin; in *HN* it is treated as an indeclinable (*cf.* also XVII 33). For the author's view of women and of the Danes, *cf.* Essay § 8.3. and 8.10.

2 sex filios Snorri (*Heimskringla, Haralds saga ins Hárfagra*, 43) mentions seven (Gamle, Guttorm, Harald, Ragnfrød, Erling, Gunnrød, and Sigurd Sleva), and *Ágrip* (ch. 5) mentions ten sons (in addition to Snorri's they are Halvdan, Øyvind and Gorm; *cf.* Driscoll's commentary to *Ágrip*, 1995, 88). **Siwardum Lioma** The Norwegian nickname is traditionally Sleva, whereas Ljome (*i.e.* the Radiant) is Gunnrød's nickname.

3 ob nimiam For *ob* and *nimiam*, *cf.* commentary on Prologue 4.

4 pedagogo In ML *pedagogus* does not have the classical connotation of servant, but of a superior, 'teacher', 'spiritual guide' etc. In *HN* it is together with *nutritor* used for 'fosterfather' *cf.* XVIII 31. **preficitur [...] eratque** There are a number of examples in *HN* in which there is a shift of tense (especially between the historic present and the perfect) within the same sentence, *cf.* in particular XVII 4, 13, 26, 51 and XVIII 11, 17, 19. For the use of tense in ML , *cf.* Blaise 1994 § 216–18 and 226–44. **quousque** Here with the subjunctive. We also find it with the subjunctive in the sense of 'until' in *e.g.* *DN* vol. 5, 11 (1278 A.D.) and *Tb* 6,6. **Gunnilda illo** *A* has *Gūn̄ illo*. It is questionable whether the original had only *Gunnilla*, but then that would be the only place where this name is written with two l's. Elsewhere it is spelled *Gunnilda*. Nevertheless this is not a clinching argument, since several names in *HN* are spelled in different ways, *cf.* Essay § 14.1.

6 in Hispanie finibus For this information, *cf.* Essay § 8.3 and Phelpstead 2001, 94. **piraticam** *Cf.* commentary on VI 8 (*pirate*).

XIII. Håkon Adalsteinsfostre (*c.* 935–960)

2 christianissimo Superlativus elativus. This form is common in ML. **detinende** Bugge and Storm emended *deinde* to *detinendae*. *Detineo* is used also in XVIII 11 to express 'holding on to' and makes excellent sense. *deinde* is not particularly troublesome (and was kept by Munch), but it is superfluous and there are no other temporal markers it can relate to. *detinende* is an elegant correction and it conforms better to the rhetorical and acoustic effects of an elaborate period (notice the alliteration on 'd' and 't'). **appostata** Alternative spelling of *apostata*. The sense of 'an apostate from Christianity' is in use from the early fathers. It is common in ML, especially in connection with the emperor Julian (361–363) who was well known to medieval historians and is mentioned at length *e.g.* in Theodoricus, ch. 8 (on Olav Tryggvason). For the presentation of Håkon in *HN*, *cf.* Essay § 8.4 and for comparison with the other sources, Phelpstead 2001, 93–99. **ydolorum** *Cf.* commentary on IX 26. **seruituti subactus** For this expression, *cf.* I *Cor.* 7,15. **deseruiret** There is no reason to correct *deseruiret* to *seruiret*, as does Storm, since this verb occurs in a similar context in VI 21 and XVI 3 and is clearly chosen to alliterate with *diis et non Deo*.

3 **eternaliter** 'eternally'. **cunctis [...] degentibus [...] regibus** Ablative of comparison spread out as an unusually comprehensive hyperbaton. **scita plebis** 'the decisions of the people' is expressed in a typical *interpretatio Romana*, the *plebiscita* originally referring to the decrees made at the plebeian assembly in contrast to those of the Roman Senate; the reference must be to lower or higher level things.

4 **deuotus** Here with the dative, 'faithful', 'devoted'. *Cf.* XVII 19, where it appears with *in* + ablative. In *Compendium Saxonis* (ed. Gertz 1917–22, vol. I, 368, l. 15) it appears with *ad* + accusative. **XXVII annis** *A* reads *ānū*. Here we must prefer the ablative **annis** because it usually signifies the time of duration, *cf.* commentary on VIII 3 (*in quinquaginta fere annis*). The same scribal error occurs below in XIII 5: *ultimis annis*. **defensabat** *Defendo* is not used in *HN*, only the frequentative *defenso*, *cf.* XVIII 21 and 23.

5–6 **bellum fuit. E quibus** The author here shifts from the sing. (*bellum*) to the plural (*e quibus*, sc. *proeliis*). **publica** *Cf.* commentary on IX 13.

6 **Northmore** *A* has *Northimore*. Storm's suggestion *Northmoere* does seem reasonable, since the name in Old Norse is 'Norðmœri' (the coastal region of Trøndelag); but we should remember that the author elsewhere uses the dipthong 'oe' in only one place, *cf.* commentary on XI 4 (Blothex). He also calls the county of Møre *Mor*, *cf.* II 4, so *Northmore* would seem to represent the best alternative. **loco** Here without *in*, but this could be due to the fact that *in* appears in the expression immediately preceding. In post-classical Latin and Christian Latin there are many examples of non-repeated prepositions, *cf.* Blaise 1994 § 199. *Cf.* also commentary on IX 20. **maxima pars [...] precipitati sunt** *Constructio ad sensum* with the subject in fem. sing. and the verb in m. plural, *cf.* commentary on IX 4.

7 **plurimi** Can also be translated as 'most' of their men. **hastam dirigens** The present participle here functions as the finite form of the verb.

10 **lippis et tunsoribus liquido apparet** 'Known to everyone'. A medieval school adage stemming from Horace, *Satira* I.7.2–3: *opinor / omnibus et lippis notum et tonsoribus esse. Lippus* designates a person with an eye disease, *i.e.* a visually impaired person; while on the other hand *tonsor* means a 'hair cutter', 'a barber', who is usually said to see (and hear) much. *Tunsor* is an acceptable medieval spelling. **ubi** Storm accepted the transmitted *ubi*. Ekrem suggested *uti* which has much in its favor. Firstly *ubi* elsewhere in *HN* is strictly local; and taken temporally, it still reads oddly. An explicative or consecutive (or causal) relation between the two clauses is what we should expect: '... it is clear through such an event that...', *tali euentu [...], uti* (*apparet* takes the accusative with infinitive). Against *uti* it can be said that *HN* never uses this form of *ut* elsewhere in our transmission. *Ubi* can be defended if we accept a causal or explicative connotation here: 'inasmuch as', 'since'.

11 **Alrecstathi** From the Old Norse name 'Álreksstaðir' m. plural. Here in the accusative plural. The farm was located just outside Bergen, now Årstad in Bergen.

genitus *A* has the meaningless double *genitus natus*. Bugge tried to save both words by emendation into *genitrice natus*, whereas Storm hesitantly preferred *genitus*.

XIV. Gunnhild and three of her sons (*c.* 960–975)

1 **XIIII annis** Ablative of duration, *cf.* commentary on VIII 3 (*in quinquaginta fere annis*). **subdita erat** Here *subdita* seems to function as an adjective. *Cf.* also commentary on XVII 42 (*munita erat*). This is customary in ML, *cf.* Elliot 1997, 49.

2 **exigente nequicia prelatorum** For the term *prelatorum cf.* Essay § 11.1.1. The idea that sins engendered natural or military disasters was often described with the verb *exigere* 'demand'. In twelfth-century crusading historiography the expression *exigentibus peccatis (nostris)* gained wide currency; for another Norwegian example and further references, see Skovgaard-Petersen 2001, 23.

3 **plebeis** From *plebeus* (variant spelling of *plebeius*), 'common person'. **Vorsorum** *I.e.* the inhabitants of the town Vors/Wors (now Voss) near Bergen. **consilio** There is no reason to correct *consilio* in *A* to *concilio*, as Storm does, since *consilium*, 'counsel', and *concilium* 'council' — already difficult to tell apart in classical Latin — were considered to be the same word in the Middle Ages. **uillula** Here a diminutive is used, but *cf. uillam* in XIII 11 concerning the same farm. **Alrecstadum** Here the dative plural of the Old Norse name 'Álreksstaðir'. **Bergonia** The city is usually called *Bergae* or *ciuitas Bergensis* in Norwegian Latin sources. Ordericus Vitalis calls it *Berga* (*Historia ecclesiastica* X.iv.27). *Cf.* the city of Lund in Skåne, which is called both *Lundae*, *Lundia* and *Lundoniae* in Danish sources (ed. Gertz 1917–22, vol. II, *Index III*), and *Lundona* by Adam (IV 7 schol. 111). **ciuitas** For the use of this word, *cf.* commentary on VI 10. **opinatissima** *Opinatus* is common in post-classical Latin for 'renowned'. For its use here, *cf.* Essay § 10.

4 **stipendariis** *cf.* X 4. **Senex** Latin translation of the nickname 'Gamle'. As suggested by Storm a passage about Harald Gråfell (Greycloak) (*c.* 960–970) has probably dropped out here before **Ast e magna** [...] in the next chapter (if due to homoioteleuton it is likely to have been brief). This Harald died after Sigurd and Gunnrød. For this, *cf.* Essay § 8.8. and commentary on XVI 1.

XV. The rest of Harald Fairhair's sons (late tenth century)

1 **loco** Here without *in*, *cf.* commentary on IX 20.

2 **uero** There is no reason to correct *uero* in *A* to *enim*, as Storm does here, since *uero* is often used in a weakened adversative sense, *cf.* commentary on IV 16, and in other places as an explanation for something preceding. **Regualdus** *A* has *Regnaldus*. Storm corrects this to *Rognvaldus*, but *cf.* commentary to VI 8. **inertissime artis** 'artless art', *i.e.* witchcraft. An instance of paradox or oxymoron. **Hatlandia** *Cf.* commentary on XI 7. **ingurgitatus** From *ingurgito* 1st, 'drown'. According to Snorri (*Heimskringla, Haralds saga ins Hárfagra*, 34), Ragnvald Rettilbeine was burned.

3 **admodum utilem** For the use of the positive with an intensifying adverb, *cf.* commentary on Prologue 2 (*satis proba[b]ili*). **sobolem** A variant spelling of *subolem*. **equiuoci** From *aequiuocus*, here 'namesake'. **celi luminaria** From *luminare -aris* n. The two luminaries are the sun and the moon in *Gen.* 1,16: *fecitque Deus duo magna luminaria.*

4 **educatus ibique** If we assume ellipsis of *est*, it is not necessary to change *ibique* in *A* to *ibidem*, as Storm does here (although it makes for a more fluent Latin).

5 **ualde elegantem** For the use of the positive with an intensifying adverb of degree, *cf.* commentary on Prologue 2 (*satis probabili*). *Elegans* here means 'outstanding', 'excellent',

cf. Svenonis Aggonis Filii *Brevis historia regum Dacie* (ed. Gertz 1917–22, vol. I, 102, l. 4). **Olauum perpetuum regem** For the notion of how Olav continued to rule the country after his death, *cf.* Essay § 8.13. This phrase points to a time of composition after 1153 as we know from other sources from the 1160s and 1170s that the notion of Olav as perpetual king gained currency in connection with the national religious centre at Trondheim, *cf.* Introduction pp. 14–15.

6 in matrimonium sibi copulauit *Cf. Ex* 36,10. **Scroffa** The Norwegian nickname (Syr, *i.e.* sow) is translated with the classical term for 'sow' (*scrofa*). For Sigurd Syr, *cf.* Essay § 8.7.

7 Siwardus Risi (id est Gigas) We have heard of this Sigurd before (XI 6), and we have a repetition of the name *Gigas*. For the translation of the Norwegian nickname (Risi), *cf.* Essay § 8.2. and 8.7.

8 sagacissimum *I.e.* 'with sharp senses', 'astute'. His Norwegian nickname is 'Hardråde' (*i.e.* Hardruler). For this Harald, *cf.* Essay § 8.7. Adam (III 17) admits that this Harald was a great warrior, but on the whole he is quite negative about him, probably because he neglected the Pope's instructions by allowing his bishops to be educated in France or England. He also sent away the papal legates *clamitans se nescire, quis sit archiepiscopus aut potens in Norvegia, nisi solus Haroldus.* **textus** From *texo* 3rd 'to weave', 'compose', *i.e.* 'texture', 'pattern'. **de quo quasi quodam filo textus** [...] For the translation of this passage, *cf.* Essay § 8.7. **protelatus** The author is clearly playing on the words *telum* (spear) and *tela* (a loom). *Cf.* also *retexere* in Prologue 3 and commentary on II 3 (*protelatur*). The lineage of the Norwegian kings is described in a metaphor from weaving underlining the importance of continuity. Here we catch a glimpse of the contemporary concerns of the author, *cf.* Introduction p. 10.

9 in prouincia Roumorum, ubi primitus regnasse dicitur According to Oddr, *Saga Óláfs Tryggvasonar* (ch. 1), Tryggve ruled first in Ringerike. According to Snorri (*Heimskringla, Hákonar saga Goða*, 2), he reigned over Ranrike and Vingulmark, but in *Ágrip* (ch. 16) we also hear that he ruled over Romerike. **Astridam** For her and the Uplands (mountain regions), *cf.* Essay § 8.6.

10 Orientalis Sinus used for Viken, *cf.* commentary on II 2. **penes** In classical Latin almost exclusively with persons ('in the power of', 'at'), but in ML, as here, often used locally: 'near' or 'by'. **firmare deberent** A modal verb is used instead of the imperfect subjunctive of the main verb (*firmarent*). This is a common way of expressing future time in ML, *cf. e.g. Compendium Saxonis* (ed. Gertz 1917–22, vol. I, 245, l. 21) and Blaise 1994 § 222.

12 imperialem From *imperialis*, 'which belongs to *imperium* or to an *imperator*, or, as here, 'imperious', 'dictatorial'. For the use of this word in connection with a *regulus* such as Tryggve, *cf.* Essay § 8.5. **ualerent** *Valere* is common in ML for *posse.* **indicto consilio** In *A* we have *in dicto consilio*, which would give the unacceptable meaning 'in the aforementioned council', no council having been mentioned. Storm's simple correction to *indicto consilio* 'having called a council' saves the sense rather elegantly. Its drawback is that this would be the only instance in *HN* of an absolute ablative functioning as a finite nexus; Skard 1930, 9 favoured it all the same, and parallels can be found in other ML texts, *e.g.* the near contemporary *Historia de profectione Danorum,* ch. VI (*cf.* forthcoming commentary by Skovgaard-Petersen with further references). Alternatives to Storm's emendation are: conjecturing an entirely new verb (or making *indicere* finite) or, better, expunging *in quo.* For *consilium* and *concilium* see commentary above at XIV 2. **tironum** Munch suggested the emendation of *tirannorum* ('lords', 'vikings', 'kings') in *A* to *tironum* ('recruits', 'squires', 'youths') and he was followed in this by Storm. They were no doubt thinking about the parallel in X 5, another hired murder: *ipsa enim quendam tironum precio corrupit, qui regis latus lancia perforauit.* Ekrem suggested that the *tiranni* might indeed be correct, namely in the sense of 'vikings', see commentary on VI 8. She writes "In *Ágrip* (ch. 16), the issue involves farmers who were no longer willing to put up with Tryggve's harsh rule, and so they killed him at the assembly ('ting'). But farmers were not just *tirones* (soldiers), they were also *tiranni* (vikings). According to Snorri (*Heimskringla, Haralds saga Gráfeldar,* 9) and Oddr, *Saga Óláfs Tryggvasonar* (ch. 1), Tryggve was killed by Gunnrød and his men before they themselves went off as vikings." But even if *tirannis* can be used for *piratica,* the sense of *tirannus* in *HN* as well as in *Passio Olaui,* Theodoricus and other contemporary Norwegian sources seems always to be connected to lordship or royalty. One would therefore tend to agree with Munch and Storm because the three names mentioned here are obviously minor figures and because the parallel with X 5 is very strong. But *tirannorum* can not be entirely ruled out. **Saxa, Scorra ac Screyiu** We do not find these names anywhere else. They may be nicknames, or they may be misspellings. **ipsum regem [...] necatum fecerunt** instead of *regem necauerunt* follows a common pattern in ecclesiastical Latin, *e.g. Eccl* 50,18: *et auditam fecerunt magnam vocem* and *Ps* 65,8.

13 siue ab istis siue ab illis Ellipsis of a verb, *e.g. factum est.*

14 Orchades *HN* is the only source claiming the Orkneys as Olav Tryggvason's birthplace (*cf.* Essay § 6.2.4). **enixa** From *enitor* 3rd, 'to exert oneself', often about labour, as here: 'gave birth to'. *A* has *enexa,* which might be the original spelling. **saluberima** *I.e. saluberrima.* **cepit** Here 'received'.

XVI. Håkon jarl the Wicked (*c.* 975–995)

1 ob For the use of *ob, cf.* commentary on Prologue 4. **Nequam** Latinization of the Norwegian nickname ('den onde', *i.e.* the Wicked). **tributiferis Sweonum** *I.e.* 'tributaries of the Swedes', 'those who paid taxes to the Swedes'. In Oddr, *Saga Óláfs Tryggvasonar* (ch. 52) we read that the Upland kings were subject to the Swedish kings in the time of Olav Tryggvason. **monarchiam** The author seems to emphasize that the kingdom of Norway is a monarchy and not an earldom, *cf.* Essay § 8.8. The term *monarchia* is also used in IX 2. Snorri (*Heimskringla, Óláfs saga Tryggvasonar,* 15–18) concedes him most of the country, but he had to fight for it. **usurpauit** The legitimate heir is thought to be Harald Gråfell (Greycloak, *c.* 960–70), the son of Eirik Bloodaxe, *cf.* Essay § 8.8. **secundum suos seniores** *Seniores* may mean 'predecessors' (as in Prologue 8), or 'ancestors'. In any case, they are his relatives.

2 Thoris Tacentis Latinization of the Norwegian nickname ('den tause', *i.e.* the Silent). Tore was the son of Ragnvald Mørejarl. **nobilissima ⟨Morensium⟩ ac Halogensium** *A* has *nobilissiū ac halogensuū.* It is debatable whether this should be emended to *nobilissima Moerensium (Morensium) ac Halogensium* (Bugge) or just to *nobilissima Halogensium* (Munch); if *ac* is not rejected a name is missing. For the choice of the spelling *Morensium,* and not Bugge's and Storm's *Moerensium, cf.* commentary on XI 4 (*blothex*) and XIII 6 (*Northmore*). The text of *Ágrip* ch. 11 is very close here, but not close enough to allow help in constituting the Latin wording. **prosapia** For Håkon's genealogy, *cf.* Essay § 8.8. and the survey at the end. **extitit oriundus** *I.e. ortus est.*

3 ydolatrie From *idololatria* f., a Greek noun, 'idolatry', common in ML in its contracted form *idolatria; cf. e.g.* Adam (IV 16). **plerasque patrias** If *patrias* is to be understood here in a restrictive sense, then it more likely means 'counties' than 'law provinces'. In the present translation it is understood in a broader sense, as expressed by 'areas'. We have just heard that Håkon took possession of the entire kingdom of Norway. The assertion here that he conquered *plerasque patrias* must be retrospective, and mean that he was awarded certain areas but had to fight for others, and thus arrogated the whole kingdom to himself. *Cf.* also Snorri (*Heimskringla, Óláfs saga Tryggvasonar*, 15–18). **perampliauit** An intensifying *per*, analogous to the classical adjective *peramplus*, 'very large'.

XVII Olav Tryggvason (995–1000) and the sons of Håkon jarl (1000–16)

1 Sed Storm amends *sed* in *A* to *Sed cum*, probably on account of the asyndeton with the following sentence. But asyndeton is commonplace in *HN*, *cf. e.g.* VIII 2, XVIII 17 and 19, and the sentence works quite well as it stands. **pupillum puerum** Phelpstead 2001, 96 suggests that Olav Tryggvason is here implicitly compared to the Christ-child and, consequently, Håkon jarl to Herod; this parallel is worked out by Oddr, but there is nothing in the Latin wording of *HN* that comes directly from *Mt* 2,1–18, although of course the plot is somewhat similar.

2 quamquam Here with the subjunctive as very often; in the Vulgate we find it almost entirely with subjunctive, *cf. e.g. Io* 4,2 and *Phil* 3,4. **tenerrime diligeret** From the adjective *tener*. *Tenerrime* is post-classical Latin in the sense of 'fervently', 'deep', and occurs in *Gn* 44,20: *tenere diligit.* **comperuit** This perfect from *comperio* instead of *comperit* is attested in other medieval texts, and it is used again in XVII 19. **prouidente** The alternating use of 'e' and 'i', also in the ablative sing., is typical of ML, *cf.* Blaise 1994, 129. **sequestrando** The gerund in the ablative used as the present participle, *cf.* commentary on Prologue 5 (*postponendo*). *Sequestro* for 'hand over', 'deliver', is common in ML. **Thorolfo** Inserted by Storm on the basis of Oddr Munk or Snorri.

3 Quem [...] suscipiens Notice the unsignalled change of subject from *mater* in the previous sentence to *Thorolfus* here. Storm classicized the syntax by changing the transitional phrase to *qui eum*, wrongly as pointed out by Skard 1930, 10: this is typical for *HN*. **proprio sinu imponens** Literally 'putting on his own lap', *i.e.* by way of the ritual for adoption. *Imponere*, 'to put', usually occurs with *in* + accusative or with the dative, and quite rarely with *in* + the ablative. Here it seems to be used with a locative ablative, but *sinu* can also be a variant form of *sinui* (dative), *cf.* Blaise 1994 § 53. For the mention of Olav Tryggvason, *cf.* Essay § 8.9. **confinia** From *confine* or *confinium* n., 'border'. The plural form is common in ML.

4 moram gessit per horam The expression *moram gerere* in the sense 'to stay' seems to be rare in ML — we have found no parallels. The usual form is *moram facere*. Nor is *Per horam*, 'a while', an ordinary expression. The author no doubt wanted a rhyming effect on *moram [...] horam [...] Rusciam [...] Eistriam.* **deuenit** *Deuenire* is often used in classical Latin in the sense of 'to arrive in a place', 'to come to'. Here the prefix has the sense of 'off the beaten path', *cf.* XVII 11 (*deuiatur*), since Olav and his friends were taken by surprise before they came to Estonia.

5 uela tenderet A poetic expression that we find *e.g.* in Virgil, *Aeneid* 3.268 and in Adam (II 22). **tenderet [...] predantur [...] necantur** Change of subject from Torolv to Torolv and his companions. **piratis** For the use of this term, *cf.* commentary on VI 8. **predantur** From the deponent *praedor*, 'plunder', used here as an active verb in the passive, *cf.* commentary on IV 17 (*depredatum*).

6 capite plectitur is ordinary legal Latin for 'suffers capital punishment'; but here the legal connotation is probably weaker: 'is put to death'. **Eistriis** This expression can mean both 'to the Estonians' and 'by the Estonians', since both pirates and the persons who purchased Olav were Estonians according to Snorri (*Heimskringla, Óláfs saga Tryggvasonar*, 6).

7 a quodam Olauo suo cognato According to Snorri (*Heimskringla, Óláfs saga Tryggvasonar*, 7) and Oddr, *Saga Óláfs Tryggvasonar* (ch. 8) the name of the relative was Sigurd (Eiriksson Bjodaskalle), and he was the brother of Olav's mother, Astrid. *Ágrip* mentions that he is a kinsman, but does not give his name. Storm's emendation to *a quodam Olauus suo cognato* is questionable since the name Olav (of the kinsman) might have occurred in *HN*'s source. The nominative *Olauus* certainly creates a very strained hyperbaton, and one does not need a repetition of the subject here; what one expects is the name of the secondary character introduced by *quodam* as is often the case in *HN*. **redimitur [...] legatus fuit** The historic present and the periphrastic perfect used in the same sentence. The use of such a 'double perfect' is commonplace in ML and is known also in classical Latin, *cf.* Elliot 1997 pp. 49-50. *A* has *ligatus* and this might be the original spelling. **tributa** For this term, *cf.* Essay § 6.2.6.

8 aliquot annis The ablative of duration, *cf.* commentary on VIII 3 (*in quinquaginta fere annis*).

9 XII annorum The genitive of quality in connection with numerals, here in connection with age. **Holmgardie** *I.e.* Novgorod. **pedagogum** For this term, *cf.* commentary on XII 4.

10 duodennis adj. 'of twelve years'. **intonuit** *Intonare* originally means 'to make a thunderous noise', but the sense 'to speak of resoundingly' or 'make an impression upon' is well attested in ML, *e.g.* in Sven Aggesen's *Brevis historia Regum Dacie*, 11 (ed. Gertz 1917-22, vol. I, 126, l. 15): *rumor regibus auribus intonuit.* **presentatur** Change of subject from *inaudita ulcio* in the previous sentence to *presentatur (sc. puer).*

11 factus [...] exercens [...] perlustrando [...] existendo [...] inscius deuiatur The sentence is concentrated, with two appositions to the subject (*ille magnificus predo*) in the past and present participle respectively (*factus* [...] *exercens*), two appositions to the same subject as gerunds in the ablative (*perlustrando* [...] *existendo*), as well as an adjective (*inscius*) also in apposition to the same subject. **piraticam** For this term, *cf.* commentary on VI 8 (*pirate*). **gentilibus** From *gentilis*, 'countryman', or 'relative', but here in the usual Christian sense of 'pagan'. The words *gentilis, profanus/prophanus, paganus* are used interchangeably, *cf.* IV 1, 18, 24 and 25, as well as XVII 25 and XVIII 4. **id locorum** The adverbial accusative and the genitive of species here form a rare, but probably acceptable idiom, 'of that place' or 'in that place'; the only parallel we have managed to find is from Theodoricus Monachus, ch. 28: *ab id locorum.* **magnificus predo** For *predo*, *cf.* commentary on VI 8 (*pirate*). For *magnificus*, *cf.* commentary on Prologue 9 (*magnificencias*).

12 ciuitate For the use of this word *cf.* commentary on III 8. There is no reason to insert *in*, as Storm does. The author of *HN* often makes use of a pure ablative without *in*. This could be due to the influence of poetry or the Vulgate, *cf.* Blaise 1994 § 108. **Iomne** This piece of information stating that Olav Tryggvason often wintered in Jomsborg is only found in *HN* and in *Ágrip* (Ellehøj 1965, 216). *Iomne* is described by Adam II 22. **inter Sclauie urbes** The preposition *inter* is used instead of a partitive genitive, *cf.* also commentary on IV 14 and XIII 9. **frequentabant** Iterative imperfect.

13 Hinc tetendit in Frisiam [...] nulli parcens in Hybernia Hanssen 1949, 28–31 tries to show traces from Hallfred Vanrædaskald's *Ólafsdrápa*. Munch's correction (accepted by

Storm) of *A*'s *hic* to *hinc* seems reasonable. It is not impossible to read *hic* as a restatement of the subject, but it is unneccesary and the focus on locomotion even makes it awkward. **post hanc** There is no need to change *post hanc* in *A* to *posthac*, as Storm does. Skard 1930, 10 calls it a brachyological use of *post*, one that is not uncommon in late Latin, and he mentions Tacitus, *Annales* IV.40 as an example: *Post Drusum* ('After (she had been married to) Drusus'). Furthermore it is used in just the same way in many places in Honorius, *cf. e.g.* I XX. **Flandream** Storm's insertion of *in* is not necessary, since ML is liberal with pure accusative in connection with countries, *cf.* Blaise 1994 § 75. The author may have left out the second *in* to achieve poetic variation, *cf.* Skard 1930, 10.

14 depredans [...] parcens Another instance of the author's preference for the present participle; here it results in a strained parallelism between the first and the second participle, the action of the first being concluded before the successive events described by **gessit** and **parcens. perperam** Bugge and Storm did not like *perperam* ('misguided') and changed it to *perquam* ('as much as possible'), thus spoiling both the alliteration and the sense; *cf.* Skard 1930, 11.

15 tirannum For this term, *cf.* commentary on VI 8 (*pirate*). **per uiscera misericordie** 'the inmost of his mercy'; this and the following wording draws on *Lc* I 78-79: *per viscera misericordiae Dei nostri, in quibus visitavit nos oriens ex alto inluminare his qui in tenebris et in umbra mortis sedent.* **uisitando** The gerund in the ablative used instead of the present participle, *cf.* commentary on Prologue 5 (*postponendo*). **eo tenus** *Tenus* is a postposition with the ablative, common in ML. **umbra mortis operuerat** From Luke as above and *Ps* 43,20: *et operuisti nos umbra mortis.* **stola claritatis eterne indueret** Quotation from *Sir* 6,32: *stolam gloriae indues eam* and *Sap* 10,14: *et dedit illi claritatem aeternam.*

16 debacharet From the deponent *debacchor* 1st, 'rage', but used here as an active verb. **anachoritam** from *anachoreta* (Greek), 'hermit'. **penes** For the use of *penes*, *cf.* commentary on XV 10. **Britannia** *I.e.* 'Celtic' Britain (Wales, Cornwall etc.). See further Phelpstead 2001, 96–97.

17 uernaculum From *uernaculus* m., 'which belongs to a *uerna*' (*i.e.* a slave who was born in the house).

18 predonum For this term, *cf.* commentary on VI 8 (*pirate*). **properauit** *A* has *proparauit*, which might have been the spelling in the original, *cf.* Blaise 1994, 129. **quem iam Dei prophetam non dubitauit; et ab eo multa futura audiuit, que paulo post in re comperuit** Storm's restitution of a *locus desperatus* of which the sense, however, is quite clear. *A* reads: *quem iam Dei prophetam non dubitatum et ab eo multa futura audiendum que paulo post in re comperuit.* Instead of *dubitatum* and *audiendum* one needs finite verbs with Olav Tryggvason as subject (or to assume several lost words including a finite verb). Storm straightens out the Latin and preserves many of the original letters; his worst problem is *audiendum* which he simply changes into *audiuit.* Here, Ekrem's suggestion of *audit, eademque* deserves credit, but the present tense is somewhat odd. Storm's solution also gives a rhyme on four verbs in *-uit* (beginning with *properauit*), an effect that accords well with our author's style. The entire story is very similarly told in *Ágrip* ch. 19, but again it is not close enough to provide help in constituting the Latin wording.

19 deuotissimus Superlativus elativus. Used here together with *in* + ablative, but *cf.* commentary on XIII 4.

21 habeto The future imperative, *cf.* commentary on Prologue 7 (*accipito*). **naues excesseris** From *excedo* 3rd, 'leave', which here takes an object in the accusative. In classical Latin it usually takes the dative. **ad** The received text gives the senseless *nisi ad.* By leaving out *nisi* Storm gave a very probable solution; Bugge and Ekrem have offered various attempts to make some palaeographical sense of *nisi*, but none of them are quite convincing. Alternatively an entire clause introduced by *nisi* has dropped out. **conspexeris [...] agnoueris** Here the future perfect in the main clause, *cf.* Blaise 1994 § 229. In classical Latin the future is preferred. **idque dolo actum agnoueris** Ellipsis of *esse*. **insidiaberis** From the deponent *insidior* 1st, 'ambush', but here as an active verb in the passive.

22 plagaberis From *plago* 1st, 'wound', 'beat'. **vixque** The sentence works quite well without inserting *vivus*, as Bugge and Storm do. *Vivus* is a repetition of the immediately preceding *fere ad mortem*. **fonte uite** *Cf. e.g. Prv* 13,14 and *Sir* 21,16.

24 beatus Olauus For this term, *cf.* Essay § 8.13. **per salutarem dextre excelsi mutacionem** The expression derives from *Ps* 76,11: *Et dixi: nunc coepi; haec mutatio dexterae Excelsi.* **bap̊tismi** From *baptismum* n., a variant form of *baptisma*, *cf.* commentary on XII 4 and *Mt* 21,25. It is common in ML. **transfretauit** From *transfreto* 1st, 'cross (a strait)'. *Cf.* the same expression about St Olav in XVIII 33. **Iohannem** The same name as in Adam (II 37) and Oddr, *Saga Óláfs Tryggvasonar* (ch. 26 & 83) but against the rest of the tradition. Ellehøj 1965, 256 argued that this was a common borrowing from Adam through Ari; Andersson 1985, 208 uses this passage as an example of the difficulties involved, and suggests that Sæmund might be the common source. **Glaciales** *Glaciales*, 'the Icy Ones', here used as a variation for *Telenses*, *cf.* I 11. *Cf.* also *Orientales*, 'people in Viken', XVII 35. **misit predicare** Final infinitive is widespread in ML. For the contents, *cf.* Essay § 6.2.6 and Phelpstead 2001, 97 with further references.

25 omnes unanimes uno ore This formula of the unanimity of believers comes from *Rm* 15,6: *ut unianimes uno ore honorificetis Deum et Patrem Domini nostri Iesu Christi.* **ewangelizare Christum gentilibus** *Cf.* Adam (I 59): *euangelizans verbum Dei gentilibus.* For *gentilibus*, *cf.* commentary on XVII 11. For the spelling *ewangelizans* with 'w' instead of 'u', *cf.* commentary on VI 8 (*Rogwaldi*). **cepere** *I.e. coeperunt.*

26 Norwagenses For this term, *cf.* commentary on IX 8. **regem constituunt** For this expression, *cf.* commentary on X 1. **XXXIII annos** Here the accusative is used for the time of duration; otherwise the author prefers the ablative, *cf.* commentary on VIII 3 (*in quinquaginta fere annis*).

27 in una prouinciarum The partitive genitive, but *cf.* XVII 12 and IV 14, XIV 4 and XVIII 22.

29 Sweinone *I.e.* the Danish king Svend Tveskæg (Forkbeard) (d. 1014). **pacifice recepti sunt** For this reception, *cf.* Essay § 8.3. and 8.9.-10.

30 reconsilians From *reconcilio* 1st, 'unite'. There is no reason to correct this to *reconcilians*, as Munch, Bugge 1873 and Skard do, *cf.* commentary on XIV 3 (*consilio*). Nor is there any reason to correct it to *reconciliat*, as Storm does, since the present participle is often used for a finite verbal form in *HN*. For the double prefix, *cf.* commentary on VI 7 (*derelictorum*). **compatriotos** From *compatriota* m. This reading of *A* may be a copyist's mistake, but the more rare masculine nouns of the first declension do display some wavering in several medieval texts, *cf.* Stotz vol. IV, p. 5. Therefore the reading of *A* may be original. **nobilem cum ignobili** *Figura etymologica.* **subiugauit** For this verb, *cf.* commentary on VI 9.

31 Hatlendenses, Orchadenses, Fereyingenses ac Tilenses For these, *cf.* Essay § 6.2.4. *Hatlendenses* means here 'the population of Hetland'. Hetland is an old term for Shetland, or Hjaltland, as it is also called. Thus there is no reason to correct *Hatlendenses* to *Hialtlandenses*, as Storm does. **fide preclaros, spe gaudentes, caritate feruentes** From *Rm* 12,10–12: *caritatem fraternitatis invicem diligentes [...] spiritu ferventes [...] spe gaudentes.*

32 Vnde [...] multiplicatus [...] referta [...] circumducti [...] reuehuntur A heavy period with two subjects (*currus* and *quadriga*), each with its own apposition in the past participle (*multiplicatus* and *referta* respectively), as well as a common apposition in the past participle m. plural (*circumducti*) and a main verb in the plural (*reuehuntur*). The intertwining of physical and spiritual geography and the use of scriptural phrases in this passage is striking; such a poetic crescendo is well timed for the first wave of Christianization in Norway. **currus Dei decem milibus multiplicatus** The metaphor derives from *Ps* 67,18: *currus Dei decem millibus multiplex.* **quadriga** As the 'chariot of the Lord' *cf. Is* 43,17 & 66,15. **eiusdem** *I.e.* 'His own' (Christ, not the king). **in fines orbis** A key passage on 'the ends of the earth' for medieval and renaissance scholars was *Ps* 18,5: *in omnem terram exivit sonus eorum, et in fines orbis terrae verba eorum.* **ad patriam** *Patria* in the sense of 'heaven', 'eternal life' is common in ML. **Paradisum** Paradise, or the Garden of Eden, was often placed in the Far East, sometimes as an island east of the Asian mainland. Honorius writes in connection with his reference to Asia (I 9): *Huius prima regio in oriente e paradiso; locus videlicet omni amoenitate conspicuus, inadibilis hominibus, qui igneo muro usque ad coelum est cinctus.* See von Brincken 1992, pp. 158-160.

33 autem *Cf.* commentary on I 2. **Sweinonis** It is natural to take *A*'s reading *Swein* as an error because all the other ten instances of this name are declined from the latinized *Sweino* (of one we cannot be sure, namely immediately below XVII 34 where *A* abbreviates to *S.*), including the genitive in XVII 45. **Tyri** For the form *cf.* commentary on XII 1. **dux quidam de Sclauia** Boleslaw the Brave of Poland (992–1025), *cf.* Phelpstead 2001, 98.

34 contra Danos bellum instituit *Cf.* Adam (II 36), who claims that Olav started the war after being goaded on by his wife (*cuius instinctu bellum Danis intulit*). For this, *cf.* Essay § 8.9.

35 Orientalibus For the use of this term, *cf.* commentary on *Glaciales* in XVII 24 and *Orientalis Sinus* in II 2. **in confinio** From *confinium* n., 'border'; *cf.* commentary on *confinia* in XVII 3. **expectabat** *i.e. exspectabat.*

37 At ille metas patrias transire nolens [...] **reuersus est** The subject is *exercitus*. For the contents *cf.* Essay § 11.2.1.

38 se [...] illusum Ellipsis of *esse.* **piratica** For this expression, *cf.* commentary on VI 8 (*pirate*).

39 dum iuxta Selandiam iter ageret The famous battle of Svold, now following, took place outside Sjælland; this accords also with Adam (II 40) and *Ágrip* (20). Further references on the battle are given by Phelpstead 2001, 98. **a lupis** The preposition *a* is used here to signify impersonal agent, *cf.* commentary on I 4 (*Finnis*). **insidiatus** Here as the passive of an active verb, *cf.* commentary on XVII 21.

40 Cum [...] audierat [...] accersierat This is a temporal *cum*-clause with the indicative, *cf.* also XVIII 12, but otherwise, temporal *cum*-clauses take the subjunctive in *HN*, *cf.* commentary on I 9. **in manu forciorum** In classical Latin one would have written *cum manu* or just *manu* instead of *in manu. Forciorum, i.e. fortiorum*, is comparative for positive. **regem Sweonum Olauum** *I.e.* Olof Skötkonung (*c.* 980–1021/22). **aduenturum** Ellipsis of *esse.* **nauale [...] bellum** *I.e. proelium nauale*, *cf.* commentary on IX 13.

41 ⟨xxx⟩ nauibus This number is inserted in accordance with *Ágrip* (ch. 20). **xi** This number is the same as St Olav's, *cf.* XVIII 23 and Essay § 8.13.

42 lxxx spaciolis In *Ágrip* (ch. 20) there are 32 sections in all. In Snorri (*Heimskringla, Óláfs saga Tryggvasonar*, 88), there are 34. **munita erat** *Munita* seems to function as an adjective here, *cf.* commentary on XIV 1 (*subdita erat*). **instar** here 'figure', 'imitation', is the object of *gestabat*. **puppi prora** *I.e.* 'in the stern, in the prow', ablative, asyndeton and alliteration. The use of the pure ablative here is an influence from poetry. *Cf.* XVII 12 (*ciuitate*). The expression is found in other texts, though with *et*, *e.g. puppi et prora* in the anonymous *De rebus gestis in Majori monasterio* (PL 149, col. 416B).

43 insimul *I.e. simul.* **mansiunculas** *Mansiuncule* seems to mean 'seats' or 'places' here, but *cf. Gn* 6,14 which mentions *mansiunculae* as small rooms in the Ark. **CLX remiges** According to Oddr, *Saga Óláfs Tryggvasonar* (ch. 53), there were 104 oars.

44 XL in XX spaciolis A reads *XL in XXX spaciolis*. Storm suggested in a note *ad locum* that the number of sections, XXX, should be amended to XX, so that the sections altogether number 100 (80 + 20) and the rowers and priests altogether number 200 (160 + 40) persons; but for some reason he kept the received text all the same. Snorri (*Heimskringla, Óláfs saga Tryggvasonar*, 94) writes that there were 8 men "in each half compartment" and 30 in the forward compartment. **indocti ad pugnam** In classical Latin *indocti* would have taken an objective genitive. *Cf.* also commentary on Prologue 2 (*imbecillem*). **plus in deprecando quam debellando laborabant** *A* reads *defensando* instead of *deprecando*. Storm's emendation is excellent and probably correct. But one should remember that *defensando* is not defenceless. The idea that priests were on board to pray matches well with the picture *HN* wants to give of the pious Olav Tryggvason. But priests did fight in those days, and one wonders why so many priests were necessary if they could only pray. *Defensare* does yield a contrast to *debellare* which in ML and in *HN*'s usage is aggressive, 'to attack', 'to wage war against' (IX 20, XVI 3, XVIII 13). For this passage see also Essay § 8.9.

45 depopulatis Here from *depopulo* 1st, 'plunder'. In the Vulgate it occurs as a deponent in *Gn* 34,27 and as an active verb in *Ez* 36,4 and *Ioel* 1,10. The latter use is not uncommon in ML.

48 acerime *I.e. acerrime.*

49 resistendo The gerund in the ablative is used as the present participle. *Resistere* here takes an accusative object (*eosdem proteruos rebellantes*), whereas in classical Latin and in the Vulgate the dative is customary. **quippe** *A* reads *quibus* which cannot give any sense. One might consider the nominative *qui* resulting in the use of *incipiens* as a finite verb (somewhat awkward on top of the *resistendo* construction). But such a *qui* would at best be superfluous. Bugge and Storm emended to *suis* (linked to *uiribus*) which is a rather large intervention in palaeographical terms. It also entails a new problem: although hyperbaton is often used by the author of *HN*, he never uses it to have a preposition split the central governed noun and its specification (adjective, pronoun, or genitive). This is a poetic practice rarely found in prose (except with the relative pronoun which insists on taking first place, *e.g. quem ad modum*). For the author of *HN* it is always *per unius anni spacium* (II 5), *a paganis gentibus* (IV 1), *in infimum confert latibulum* (IV 7), *ad uillam suam* (XIII 11) etc. Furthermore *pro uiribus* works well on its own. If we do not want to leave out the word, which is possible, or make greater rearrangements, *quippe* would answer palaeographical considerations as well as give good sense: 'inasmuch as he ...' / 'for he ...'. In this way the word is used twice in *HN* (XV 3, XVIII 23).

50 ore gladii The expression *os gladii* for the 'edge of the sword' stems from the Vulgate (*cf. Nm* 21,24 & *Ios* 10,28) and became widespread in medieval historiography.

53 coequeuis From *coaequaeuus*, 'of the same age' or, as here, 'contemporary'.

54 diffiniendo *i.e. definiendo.* **pretereamus** The author avoids making a final decision as to Olav Tryggvason's death. For this presentation, *cf.* Essay § 8.13. *Cf.* also a similar reflection in Adam (I 61): *Sufficit hoc scire, ne, si plura dicimus, mentiri velle dicamur. 'Melius enim est,* *ut ait beatus Ieronimus, vera dicere rustice, quam falsa diserte proferre*'. For other sources on Olav's legendary uncertain fate see Phelpstead 2001, 98.

55 Ast coniux intemperanter uiri mortem ferens dolore deperiit For this, *cf.* Essay § 8.13.

56 Tiuguskeg The heir to Norway was Tryggve Olavsson, but according to Snorri (*Heimskringla, Óláfs saga helga*, 248–249) he was killed by King Svend of Denmark before he could ascend the throne.

57 XIIII annis The ablative for the time of duration, *cf.* commentary on VIII 3 (*in quinquaginta fere annis*).

58 beatus Olauus *I.e.* Olav Tryggvason. For this term, *cf.* Essay § 8.13. **plantauerat [...] rigauerat [...] eradicauerunt** *Cf.* I *Cor* 3,6: *ego plantavi, Apollo rigavit, sed Deus incrementum dedit* and *Mt* 15,13: *omnis plantatio quam non plantavit Pater meus caelestis eradicabitur.* The first two verbs in the pluperfect tense seem to have affected *eradicauerunt*, which has thus been written as *eradicauerant* in *A*. For the substance of the sentence and the honour of Christianizing Norway, *cf.* also Essay § 8.13.

XVIII. Olav Haraldsson (1015–1030)

1 Olauus [...] clarus habetur *HN*'s summary of Olav's viking career before he returned to Norway to claim the throne, is peculiar, and perhaps very valuable as an historical source in several respects. A key point of disagreement between *HN*, *Ágrip* (ch. 26), and William of Jumièges on the one hand and *Fagrskinna*, Snorri (and partly Adam II 52) on the other, is the relationship between Olav and Knud the Great before Olav's reign. Until Krag 1995, 137–41, Norwegian historians followed Snorri and traced the conflict between them — that would eventually lead to Olav's death at Stiklestad — back to this period. But now *HN*'s account of a viking partnership between the two in the English campaigns has begun to be taken seriously again. Krag draws on the thorough investigation by the Swedish historian Ove Moberg (1941, esp. 25–87). *Cf.* also Friis-Jensen 2000, 251. For the presentation of Saint Olav, see also Essay § 8.12.-13.

2 herili solo Corresponds here to the substance of *hereditariam* [...] *patriam* in XIII 4. **pyraticam** For this expression, *cf.* commentary on VI 8 (*pirate*). **exercere necesse habebat** *Cf. Lc* 14,18.

3 ea poli *A* reads *eo poli*. There would be nothing particularly odd in having *polis* as masculine, as *metropolis* sometimes is, but then the subsequent *quam* must be corrected to *quem*! For the stay here, *cf.* Essay § 8.12.

4 gentiles *Cf.* commentary on XVII 11. **depredando lacessendo** Two gerunds in the ablative used for the present participle in a somewhat strained asyndeton. One is tempted to add a *-que*.

6 colonum For the declension of this word, *cf.* commentary on VIII 1.

7 in finibus Curorum This area corresponds approximately to present-day Latvia. For the plundering of Kurland, *cf.* Essay § 8.12. with note. **de ipsis [...] trihumpho** *De ipsis* probably belongs to *trihumpho*, and we have an uncommonly comprehensive hyperbaton. It is not very likely that *de ipsis* goes with *dans strages*. In Ordericus Vitalis's *Historia ecclesiastica* we find a similar construction with *triumphus de* + ablative (IX.iii.553). *trihumpho* is an acceptable medieval spelling. **celeberimo** *I.e. celeberrimo.*

8 tirannidis For this term, *cf.* commentary on VI 8 (*pirate*).

9 Canuto Canute the Great (Knud den Store), king of Denmark and England 1016–1035. For Olav's cooperation with him, see note above XVIII 1.

10 beatissimi tiranni 'most holy viking' or perhaps to be taken as an oxymoron, 'most blessed tyrant'. *Cf.* Essay § 8.13.

12 Cum [...] repatriauit For temporal *cum*-clauses in the indicative, *cf.* commentary on I 9. **patris loco** Here without *in*, *cf.* commentary on IX 20.

13 Britones The inhabitants of Brittany. **usque** Here a preposition with accusative, *cf.* commentary on III 2. **partes** Equivalent to *fines, regiones*, *cf.* Elliot 1997, 9. **multum honorifice** *Cf.* commentary on Prologue 2 (*satis probabili*).

16 Olauum The first is Olof Skötkonung, the second Olav Haraldsson. **illo** *I.e. illuc*. **concitauit** Bugge's and Storm's choice instead of *A*'s unintelligible *cogitauit*. It seems to be better in sense ('spurred on') and sound (alliterating with *consortem [...] comitari*) than Skard's *rogitauit* which does not make for an easier correction; *concitavit* and *cogitauit* are very close when pronounced in (auto)dictation. **pollicendo** The gerund in the ablative used for the present participle, *cf.* commentary on Prologue 5 (*postponendo*). **amminiculis** is written here with a double 'm'. For this expression and for the spelling, *cf.* commentary on Prologue 5. **posset** Perhaps there is no reason to amend *A*'s *possit* to *posset*, as Storm does, since the alternation of tenses within the same sentence is not an uncommon phenomenon in *HN*, *cf.* XII 4 (*preficitur* [...]) and below XVIII 17 & 19 (*cf.* Skard 1930, 12); on the other hand the author seems to be consistent in cases such as this with past tense in an indirect clause governed by a past tense verb (*cf.* also the dubious case in IV 18 (*prepararet*)).

17 Pergunt [...] tenuerunt Asyndeton between the two parts of the period. **millenis** From the distributive *milleni*. **plenis uelis prosperis uentis** A display of poetical effects with asyndeton, rhyme and two ablatives — and, in addition, the initial letters p, u, p, u. **Iarmuthiam** Yarmouth, on the Isle of Wight.

18 Londonias For the form, *cf.* commentary on XVIII 25. **tunc temporis** The genitive of species, *cf.* commentary on IX 31. **Etelredo**. Æthelred II 'the Unready' (978–1016) (also written *Adelredus*, *cf.* XVIII 11); on his and King Edmund's (reigned and died 1016) whereabouts see Phelpstead 2001, 99.

19 conuocat [...] iussit Asyndeton.

20 dicta factis This proverb occurs in writings of all periods of Latinity. **prouinciis** Here most likely in a broad sense of 'regions', but *cf.* commentary on II 1.

21 appropiantes *Appropio* 1st, 'approach' is common in ML. **ceperunt** *I.e. coeperunt*.

22 per totam diem *Dies* is feminine here. We also find this in classical Latin, but the masculine is more common. In the Vulgate it is often feminine.

23 cum undecim nauibus For the number, *cf.* Essay § 8.13. and XVII 41. **subeuntes** Here 'attacking'. Bugge's suggestion *subeuntes* would seem to be the best emendation of the error *subematus* in *A*. **ipse eiusque** This is the emendation of Bugge 1873. *A* has *ipsi enimque*. The emphatic form of *enim* is *enimuero* and not formed with *-que* (like *nam / namque* and *ita / itaque*). Although ML allows for a number of abundant *-que* suffixes (*cf.* Stotz vol. IV, pp. 471–72), *enimque* is so singular that it must be rejected as a scribal error (probably as a false rendering of an abbreviation). Olav (*ipse*) was surely meant to be present on one of the ships and he is the subject of the previous sentence. Furthermore Storm's *ipsi namque*, and Skard's (1930, 11) *ipsi denique* are slightly less convincing because we already have *quippe* establishing the explicative connection. **tutancium testudinum tegmine protecti** Alliteration. **defensantum** The form in *A* is retained, since the distinction between *-um* and *-ium* in the genitive plural is not strict in ML, *cf.* Blaise 1994 § 51. **pertransiere** Storm's elegant emendation of *pertransire*. According to Snorri (*Heimskringla, Óláfs saga helga*, 13), the event took place as they rowed up close to the bridge and tied their ropes to the piles supporting the bridge, whereupon they rowed down the river and pulled the piles — and thus the bridge — along with them, so that the defences collapsed.

24 tota obtenti triumphi ascribebatur fama perhaps there is an allusion to II *Rg* 12,28: *ne cum a me vastata fuerit urbs nomini meo adscribatur victoria.*

25 Lundoniam For the name *Lundonia*, *cf.* XVIII 18 *Londoniae*, and *Lundona* in Adam (IV 7 schol. 111). **quinquies in IX mensibus** *Cf. Liber de legibus Angliae* II, 235 (Storm 1880, 122 note to l. 19), where the same thing is asserted.

27 priuatur [...] possedit [...] duxit The historic present alternates with the perfect. **Elfigeuam** This was Knud's first wife (or rather concubine). The lacuna of approximately one line probably mentioned Knud's wife from 1017, Emma, with whom he had Harde-knud (see below). Svend was a son of Knud and Elfgiua. *Ágrip* mentions Ælfgifu as queen, but not Emma (ch. 27). *Cf.* Phelpstead 2001, 99. Storm presumed a lacuna of the following content (p. 123): *quæ et Emma, soror Roberti Normannorum ducis. Cuius instinctu in hæredes Angliæ constituit duos* etc. **Durum** Latinization of the Scandinavian nickname ('hard'). Hardeknud was king of Denmark from *c.* 1030 to his death in 1042, and king of England 1040–42. Theodoricus also mentions the sons Svend and Harde-Knud (ch. 22), and so does *Ágrip* (ch. 36).

28 sanciuerat A variant conjugation for *sanxi* in the perfect. **fratrem** his brother Harald (2) was king of Denmark from the death of Svend Tveskæg (1014) to his own death in 1019. **socium** *i.e.* Olav. **omni mercede laborum frustratos abire permisit** The expression may be influenced by *Sap* 10,17: *et reddidit iustis mercedem laborum suorum.*

29 sororem Olaui Sveonensis, nomine Margaretam For her, *cf.* Essay § 8.12. **digna vicissitudine** 'in worthy reciprocity'. **intimi amoris priuilegio** *I.e.* 'by the rights of the deepest love'. **disponsauit** *I.e. desponsauit.*

30 Iarezlafus de Ruscia Jarislav the Wise (978–1054), ruler of the Kievan Rus from 1019. *Cf. Ágrip*, ch. 25.

31 maximum odiorum atque discordiarum fomitem *Fomes*, 'tinder' is often used as *peccatum* in ecclesiastical Latin, *cf. e.g. Gn* 37,8: *invidiae et odii fomitem* and Hugh of St Victor *De vanitate mundi* (PL 176, col. 707): *odii et discordiae fomitem subministrat. Fomes* is used only here in *HN*, but there is no other support for its being feminine; hence *maximam* in *A* must be corrected to *maximum*. **nutritoris** We do not know who he was, but according to Snorri (*Heimskringla, Óláfs saga helga*, 88) the foster-father of Olof of Sweden's daughter, Astrid, was a person by the name of Egil, who lived in Västergötland. **redintegraret** It is hardly necessary to correct *redintegraret* in *A* to *redintegrasset*, as Storm does. The use of tense vacillates somewhat in *HN*, *cf.* commentary on VI 4 (*aduentasset*) and X 3 (*dum* [...] *uelificassent*).

32 Ex qua genuit According to Snorri (*Heimskringla, Óláfs saga helga*, 91 and 180), Olav was married to Olof of Sweden's daughter, Astrid, and they had a daughter, Ulvhild. According to *Ágrip* (ch. 25) he was married to the same Astrid, but their daughter's name was Gunnhild. For further references see Phelpstead 2001, 99–100. Storm established a lacuna here. The missing text may have been just a line or so, or it may have been a longer passage, perhaps involving a whole campaign. The final remarks of our text about the bishops Olav took with him from England is unprepared — one would have liked some narrative link to his Christian faith. *HN* does not seem to have known William of Jumièges's information about his baptism around 1013 (subsequently taken up by Theodoricus Monachus and *Passio Olaui*, *cf.* Mortensen 2000d), but some other version about his piety may originally have been in this missing part. It is probable that the Orkney excerptor skipped something here and hastened to the end of the book.

33 transfretauit *Cf.* the same expression about Olav Tryggvason in XVII 24. **quatuor episcopi** For the number, *cf.* Essay § 8.12. Adam writes (II 57): *Habuitque (sc. Olauus) secum multos episcopos et presbyteros ab Anglia* [...] *Quorum clari doctrina et virtutibus erant Sigafrid, Grimkil, Rudolf et Bernard.* **Explicit** For this conclusion of Book I, *cf.* Introduction 9–10 and Essay § 9.3. and 12.

Essay on Date and Purpose

Contents

1. Introduction 157

2. Previous research 158

3. The present theory 161

4. The Nordic and the Norwegian archdioceses 162
- 4.1. The Nordic archdiocese
- 4.2. Towards a national archdiocese of Norway
- 4.3. *HN* and the Norwegian archdiocese-to-be

5. The Prologue 168
- 5.1. Sources
  - 5.1.1. Adam of Bremen. 5.1.2. Honorius of Autun and Julius Solinus. 5.1.3. Marcus Tullius Cicero
- 5.2. Contents

6. The geographical description of Norway 176
- 6.1. The mainland
  - 6.1.1. Location and borders. 6.1.2. The inhabitants. 6.1.3. The jurisdictional division. 6.1.4. Natural resources. 6.1.5. The coastland. 6.1.6. The Finns. 6.1.7. *Mirabilia*
- 6.2. The tributary islands
  - 6.2.1. Previous research. 6.2.2. The Solund Islands and the Solund Sea. 6.2.3. The Orkney kingdom. 6.2.4. The Orkney Islands. 6.2.5. The Faeroes. 6.2.6. Iceland

7. The scope of the archdiocese 194

8. On the kings' lineage 194
- 8.1. The Yngling kings. 8.2. Harald Hårfagre and his sixteen sons.8.3. Eirik Blodøks. 8.4. Håkon Adalsteinsfostre. 8.5. Tryggve Olavsson. 8.6. The Uplands. 8.7. The direct line of the contemporary reigning kings. 8.8. Håkon jarl the Wicked (den onde). 8.9. Olav Tryggvason. 8.10. The Danes and English in *HN*. 8.11. Eirik and Svein jarl. 8.12. St Olav. 8.13. Olav Tryggvason and St Olav

9. The question of whether *HN* was ever completed 210
- 9.1.The geographical description. 9.2. The kings' lineage. 9.3. A possible Book II of *HN*? 9.4. A possible Book III and IV of *HN*? 9.5. Paganism and Christianity

10. Place of origin 217

11. Commissioner, dedicatee and author 218
- 11.1 The dedicatee
  - 11.1.1. Agnelle/Angnelle/Anguelle. 11.1.2. Augustinelle. 11.1.3. Other alternatives
- 11.2. The author
  - 11.2.1. Archbishop Øystein. 11.2.2. Other alternatives. 11.3. Conclusion

12. Final comments 223

1. Introduction

Hardly any work in Latin from the Norwegian Middle Ages has been studied and dissected as stringently and as often as the seemingly insignificant work *Historia Norwegie*[1] (hereafter referred to as *HN*). Ever since the first edition of P. A. Munch in 1850 it has been a challenge for Norwegian and foreign researchers alike, whether they be historians, Old Norse and classical philologists, palaeographers etc. This is true for a number of reasons: it is one of the few Latin works we have that deals with the history of the Norwegian Middle Ages; it contains information that we do not find in the more familiar and larger sagas; it is written by an anonymous author; dedicated to, for us, an unknown *Agnellus, Angnellus* or *Anguellus*;[2] written at an unknown location; and it is difficult to date.

What is certain is that the manuscript consists of a Prologue (approximately one page) and one book: *liber primus* ("the first book"). This book consists of about 25 pages, whose contents fall into two main categories:

1. A geographical description of the Norwegian realm (c. two-fifths of the text), specifying first the location and surroundings of the mainland, then its character, the tripartite settlement, the Norwegian and non-Norwegian population, the religious situation (Christians and pagans), and the jurisdictional subdivisions ("lagdømmer" (*i.e.* law provinces) and "fylker" (*i.e.* counties)). Along with mainland Norway, Greenland, Bjarmeland, "the Land of Giants", "the Land of Maidens" and "the Land of the Skrælings" are mentioned. Then the tributary islands are listed: first a relatively long chapter about the Orkney Islands, which primarily deals with the population's Norwegian descent and their conquering of Normandy; (briefly) about the Faeroe Islands, and finally a relatively long chapter on Iceland that tells of the Icelanders' descent from the Norwegians – but primarily about various natural phenomena. All these islands pay some form of tax to the Norwegian monarchs. Animal life at sea and on land is mentioned, and anecdotes about the kingdom's various *mirabilia* ("wonders") are sprinkled throughout.

2. An account (*c.* three-fifths of the text) of the Norwegian kings in chronological order from the first Swedish Yngling monarchs to St Olav's voyage from England to Norway in the year 1015. While the first kings are mentioned only summarily, the account becomes more detailed after their transference to Norway, and culminates in the account of Olav Tryggvason and St Olav. We hear of an unbroken genealogical line of kings that stretches all the way to the author's day. Moreover they (but Olav Tryggvason in particular) deserve credit for Christianizing the area (including the Orkney Islands, the Shetland Islands, the Faeroe Islands, Iceland and Greenland). The ways in which the two Olavs are presented have many parallels.

These two sections, a geographical and a historical, are already mentioned in the Prologue. Here the author also maintains that he deals with the arrival of

[1] The work is usually known by the title *Historia Norwegiæ* or *Historia Norwegiae*. This corresponds to the manuscript's spelling *Ystoria N[orwegie]*.

[2] The name in the copy appears as *āguelle* or *āgnelle*, though it could have been misspelled.

Christianity, the flight of paganism, and the status of both at the time of writing. Furthermore we understand from the Prologue that *HN*, or at least the extant copy of *HN*, cannot have been completed.

2. Previous research

Thus far no one has been able to provide a satisfactory answer to all the questions that *HN* raises as to its origins. The various studies — of which some are quite comprehensive and thoroughgoing — have tended to concentrate on three approaches: an attempt to find the sources for the work (especially by Aðalbjarnarson 1937 and Ellehøj 1965), a detailed study of individual historical facts in the work (by most of the researchers), and, finally, two researchers (Skard 1930 and Ulset 1983) have done purely linguistic analyses. Ulset 1983 attempts to determine its genetic relationship to *Ágrip* (around 1190) and to Theodoricus Monachus's work *Historia de antiquitate regum Norwagiensium* ("The History of the Ancient Norwegian Kings") (before 1180). In addition, Hægstad 1919–20 studied the text with a view to reconstructing the wording of names in the original. The aim of all the researchers was to fix the date of authorship.

In time two main groups of views emerged (see the survey in Ekrem 1998a, 88). There were those who believed that *HN* originated during the thirteenth or fourteenth century (Munch 1850,[3] Bugge 1873,[4] Maurer 1875,[5] Meissner 1902,[6] Jónsson 1923, Kválen 1925, Aðalbjarnarson 1937 and Nordal 1953,[7] to mention the most important ones). With this supposition as a point of departure, the attempt was made to find a person who fitted the one to whom the book was dedicated. Munch himself believed that the person in question might be a bishop.[8] Other suggestions put forward were Lambe (*Agnellus*) from the Elgeseter monastary,[9] a French Franciscan monk, Agnellus, who came to England in 1224,[10] Agnello da Pisa, who died in 1232, and Agnellus, the patriarch of Jerusalem, who died in 1277.[11] *HN* was roundly condemned by some of these researchers. In fact it was characterized by Meissner in 1902 as a "*mönchisches Machwerk*" written by a highly unskilled person in a "*lächerlich hochtrabende Sprache*" that was in marked contrast to a "*dürftig*" and "*flüchtig*" account.[12] Bugge 1873[13] and Jónsson 1923[14] share much the same view. All these researchers' hypotheses and arguments for dating *HN*

[3] If it had not been for the two brief Swedish excerpts of the 1300s from the same text, Munch would have dated *HN* to after 1422, since a volcanic eruption such as the one we find described in *HN* then took place in the ocean off Iceland, according to Icelandic annals. [4] P. 37.

[5] P. 8. He sets the date at after 1266, when the king of Scotland began to pay taxes to Norway. Maurer is the most radical when it concerns *HN*'s age. According to Koht 1919–20, 101, Maurer goes so far as to claim that it must have been written in the fifteenth century.

[6] P. 43. [7] P. 205. [8] Munch 1850, v.

[9] Bugge 1873, 34. Meissner 1902, 40 disputes this claim, because he believes that *HN* was written for a foreigner. Aðalbjarnarson 1937, 2 also disputes this claim.

[10] Paasche 1924, 432. [11] Kválen 1925, 200. [12] Pp. 39 and 43. [13] Pp. 24–29. [14] *E.g.* p. 602.

were convincingly contested and refuted by the other group.[15] In fact there was only one argument with any apparent value (see § 6.2.1. and § 6.2.6. below).

The other group claimed that *HN* had to be from the last half of the 1100s (among whom the more significant are Storm 1873a and b and 1880, Koht 1949–51, Hægstad 1919-20, Berntsen 1923, Schreiner 1927, Steinnes 1946–48 and 1949–51, Hanssen 1949, Ellehøj 1965 and de Vries 1967 II). From the survey at the end we see that in the 1870s Storm dated *HN* at the end of the 1100s, and he nominated an archdeacon, Agnellus of Wells, as the best — and only — suggestion he could come up with as the person for whom the book was written. Storm pointed out that this was merely a suggestion.[16] For many years, no one came up with a better proposition, and a number of attempts were made to find some sort of connection between this Agnellus and *HN*.[17] Only with the arrival of Hanssen 1949 did doubts begin to emerge. Nor did many of this group of researchers think very highly of *HN*; rather they viewed its value more in terms of an ancient historical document.

Most of those who were occupied with *HN* long believed that, at the very least, *Agnellus / Angnellus / Anguellus* had to be a foreigner, and that the book had been written by a Norwegian, *e.g.* someone from the Uplands,[18] or a Westerner,[19] — or at least by a foreigner *in* Norway. During 1946–51 the debate resumed with a vengeance with Steinnes' article 1946–48 about one of the sources of *HN*, the so-called Sorø manuscript (lost). This study was later followed up and elaborated by Ellehøj 1965.[20] The Sorø manuscript seems to have contained, among other things, three works by Adam of Bremen, Honorius Augustodunensis (from Autun) and the geographer Julius Solinus, respectively, which might well have been just those versions that are used as some of the sources for *HN*.[21] According to Steinnes the Sorø manuscript was once located in the diocese of Roskilde, probably as early as 1140, and later made its way to Sorø, ending up at the University Library in Copenhagen, where it disappeared in the fire of 1728. After Steinnes' contribution in 1946–48, Koht (1949–51) appeared on the scene once more, along with Hanssen (1949) and finally Steinnes once again (1949–51). An interesting debate among these three men led to the dating of *HN* as early as 1152–63. Agnellus now alternated with *Anguellus* or similar as the Latin designation for the personal Norwegian name Orm (*i.e.* serpent, *anguis*). They took no position on whether this person was Norwegian (Orm, Abbot of Munkeliv in 1146), Danish (Omer, bishop of Ribe and Børglum in 1179), or perhaps bishop of the Faeroe Islands (in 1139). In fact there were other candidates as well.

Suggestions for the sources of *HN* are many, but no one has been able to point to sources that are earlier than the time around 1150 (probably rather around

[15] For example, Koht 1919–20. [16] Storm 1880, xxiii.

[17] Koht 1919–20, 109–10 concurs with Storm's suggestion. *cf.* also Koht 1927b, 182–86, Steinnes 1946–48, 40, and Mogk 1904 , 810.

[18] Storm 1873a , 23, 1873b, 385 and 1880, xix–xx. [19] Koht 1919–20, 112.

[20] Pp. 146–47 and 159.

[21] For manuscripts of Adam's work, *cf.* Nyberg 1984, 302–7.

1140).[22] Everyone agrees that parts of Adam of Bremen's work are one of the sources and, apart from Storm,[23] that *Ágrip* and also the monk Oddr Snorresson's saga of Olav Tryggvason (*c.* 1190) and *HN* share common sources.[24] And many believe that this must be the Icelander Ari's (1068-1148),[25] or his and his countryman Sæmund's (1056–1133) lost works.[26] A few (Berntsen 1923, Aðalbjarnarson 1937 and Beyschlag 1950) lean towards the view that a lost Upland saga might be involved.[27] Bugge believes that a saga of St Olav, albeit not the so-called "Legendary" one, is the basis for parts of *HN*,[28] and Lindqvist 1936 believes that a Latin Yngling saga by Torgeir Avrådskoll was one of the primary sources of *HN*.[29] Munch and Maurer felt confident that *Kongespeilet* (*Speculum regale*) (*c.* 1250) had been the source for part of *HN*. Most researchers no longer share this last view, although it is recognized that both works have a number of details in common.[30] Many researchers thought that additional (English/Norman) sources also contributed to parts of the contents of *HN*,[31] while Ellehøj 1965 refutes them. Most researchers, Holtsmark 1938 and Beyschlag 1950 in particular, reckon that oral sources are somehow involved; and there are some, including Storm, Hanssen and Lange, who believe that in places *HN* reflects the influence of the poems of Tjodolv of Kvin, Hallfred Vandrædaskald and Ottar Svarte (all from the tenth or eleventh centuries).[32] There seems to be a consensus that Theodoricus's work and *HN* do not derive from a common source.

It should be pointed out that few of those who have studied *HN* seem to have any opinion as to why *HN* was written. Anne Holtsmark suggested that it might

[22] The source for the reference to King Henry I as "a righteous lion" and to the prophet Merlin as "king", which I have in view here, could be Ari's lost *Íslendingabók* (Ellehøj 1965, 171) or an oral source. It has so far been claimed that the expression *rex*, used about Merlin, comes from the poem *Vita Merlini*, which is thought to have been written by Geoffrey of Monmouth around 1148–51: *Ergo peragratis, sub multis regibus, annis / Clarus habebatur Merlinus in orbe Britannus. / Rex erat et vates* [...] (ed. San-Marte 1853, 273 v. 19–21). *cf.* also Skard 1930, 77 with note, for the knowledge in Norway of Merlin.

[23] 1873a, 22, 1873b, 385 and 1880, xxii–xxiii (in the latter it is clear that Storm also believes that Odd Snorresson has borrowed from *HN* for his own Olav's saga).

[24] For example, Bugge 1873, 4 (the source is Norwegian) and Maurer 1875, 8.

[25] For example, Bugge 1873, 13–6 and Ellehøj 1965.

[26] Gjessing 1896, 134ff., Mogk 1904, 810, Lange 1989, 155.

[27] Berntsen 1923, 53–94 and Aðalbjarnarson 1937, 48. Schreiner 1927, 77 opposes this view.

[28] 1873, 22.

[29] P. 270. The statement in *HN* about Trøndelag being the most important area (which has nothing to do with the Yngling kings) is explained by Lindqvist on the basis of the fact that this Torgeir was a Trønder. For this reason, Koht 1949–51, 54 also suggests the possibility of the author of *HN* being a Trønder, from Sunnmøre. But according to *HN*, Sunnmøre was not a part of Trøndelag at this time.

[30] Munch 1850, vi, Maurer 1875, 9. The opposite of Jónsson 1923, 597.

[31] *Cf.* Bugge 1873, 40, Storm 1873b, 367 and 1880, xxi–xxii, Koht 1919–20, 105–6, Paasche 1924, 432, Steinnes 1946–8, 40–5, Koht 1949–51, 55–6 concerning English sources.

[32] Storm 1873a, 23 and 1873b, 385, Hanssen 1949, 29, Lange 1989, 143–44.

have been a school assignment.[33] This suggestion found favour with Ellehøj, but was rejected by de Vries.[34]

All in all, Hanssen seems to be correct when he writes:[35] "Opinions as to when the work (*i.e. HN*) was written vary from the 1260s to *c.* 1170. What makes dating this work especially difficult is the fact that it does not contain any references to events that could be used as points of reference with which to determine any "terminus post quem" and "ante quem". The views that arise in the course of the discussion are thus of a more general nature, and can be applied in any number of ways. In my opinion the date of origin remains uncertain."

In the light of this comment by Hanssen a fresh attempt at dating the work seems in order.

3. The present theory

As stated before, the Prologue shows that *HN* deals with three subjects: 1. A geographical description of the Norwegian realm. 2. The Norwegian kings' lineage and history. 3. The arrival of Christianity, the flight of paganism, and the status of both at the time of writing. There is a general consensus that only section 1 is complete, as *HN* presents it to us today.[36] However, it was precisely in connection with section 1 that something caught my attention, something that no one had apparently taken much notice of in the many years since Storm dated *HN*.

The last of the dukes of Normandy mentioned in *HN*, and who according to the author had their roots in the Orkney Islands and in turn were descended from the earl of Møre, is a certain Henry (ch. VI 19). We know him as Henry I, who was also king of England from 1100 to 1135. Thus *HN* must have been written after Henry had become king. However, if the list of Norman dukes in *HN*, which belongs to section 1, is brought forward to the author's day and age, why then does he conclude with Henry? Of course, this could reflect the author's source; but for the recent past and his own time there would have been no need of a written source. Henry's immediate successors were also dukes of Normandy, and it seems odd that the author does not mention Stephen, who was king of England from 1135 to 1154, nor Henry II, king of England from 1154 to 1189. Storm, who suggested Agnellus, the archdeacon of Wells, as the dedicatee writes that the latter had written a *Libellus de morte et sepultura Henrici regis Angliæ junioris* ("A little book about Henry, the Young King of England's, death and burial") in 1183, *i.e.* for a son of Henry II.[37] If Storm's Agnellus were truly the person to whom *HN* is dedicated, one would at the very least expect Henry II to have been mentioned in connection with the list of dukes in *HN*. Stephen and Henry II were clearly not in the male line of succession after Henry I, since Stephen was son of William

[33] 1938, 162. [34] 1965, 143–44 and 1967 II, 254, respectively. [35] Hanssen 1949, 3.

[36] Gjessing 1896, 134, Mogk 1904, 809 and Ellehøj 1965, 142 do not believe that *HN* was completed or preserved in its entirety. Indrebø 1922, 50 seems to hint that *HN*, like Sæmund's work, ended with Magnus the Good (den gode). Steinnes 1946–48, 4 is tempted to believe that *HN* did not continue beyond the preserved copy, and Ulset 1983, 148 that its coverage could have extended to *c.* 1155. [37] Storm 1880, xxiii.

the Conqueror's daughter, and Henry II was son of Henry I's daughter. Nevertheless, their reigns were a fact. So was the reign of Håkon jarl, who represented the maternal lineage of the Norwegian kings, but is mentioned all the same in *HN* (see 8.8. below). The fact that the author does not mention a king as great and mighty as Henry II, who moreover was of the Møre lineage, could well mean that Henry II was unknown to him. In other words *HN* could have been written after 1100, but before 1135 (or possibly before 1154). If we now combine this with the above observations concerning the sources (before *c.* 1140 or *c.* 1150) for *HN* and the debate around 1950 that pushes back the dating of *HN* to the time-frame 1152–63, it would seem that a good point of departure for dating *HN* is the period from 1140 (or *c.* 1150) to 1152 (or 1154). Whatever the conclusions, the present work has taken this as its vantage point.

The present edition is based upon a new theory which attempts to place *HN* within a contemporary and unified framework. In particular this is reflected in this Essay and in the Commentary, but mostly by way of references to the Essay. The theory is based on the following tenets:

1. That *HN* must have a specific purpose or a specific message. The commission was not given without reason; yet it could be fictitious.

2. That it is not without reason that the author received, or took upon himself, this commission; he must have commended himself as particularly well-suited to the task, or as having a special interest in the matter. So I take him at his word, where possible, and trust him.

3. That *HN* should be read on the background of Adam of Bremen, Honorius and Solinus.

4. That my own observations seem to show that the date of authorship can be pushed all the way back to 1140 (or *c.* 1150)–1152 (or 1154), and that the commission can have been related in some way to the establishment of the archdiocese in Nidaros in 1152/1153.

4. The Nordic and the Norwegian archdioceses

4.1. The Nordic archdiocese

If we cast a glance at the politics of Church and state in Europe as well as in Norway during the first half of the 1100s and ask ourselves what are the major, crucial events that characterize these years, we shall, among other things, discover the following:[38]

Until 1102/1104 the three Nordic countries all belonged to the Hamburg archdiocese, with its seat in Bremen. As national unification in the eleventh century gained momentum in these three Nordic countries, it became common practice for the king to be in charge of building and expanding the Church in each country, not the remote archbishop. From the monarchy's standpoint a need was felt to wrest free of the archbishop. This also happened to be in the interests of each country's national Church: an independent archdiocese meant greater independ-

[38] What follows is based to a high degree on Gunnes 1996.

ence for the Church. To begin with, a Nordic archdiocese was requested. Denmark, with its close proximity to the German realm, was the first to apply. It is not known whether this was the result of a Danish initiative, but the application could have come in the wake of a Nordic royal council in Konghelle (at the common border of Sweden, Denmark and Norway) in 1101.

With the rift between the papacy and the German emperor in 1076, the archbishop of Hamburg took sides with the emperor, and the Papal State felt the need to curtail the Hamburg archbishops' power in order to strengthen its own hold over Scandinavia. The Danish application for a Nordic archdiocese thus seems to fit hand in glove with the wishes of the pope, and the application was granted in 1104 (possibly already in 1102). The archdiocese was located in Lund (in Skåne, which at that time belonged to Denmark), but with jurisdiction over Sweden and Norway as well. With the arrival of a new pope, along with a new emperor, this resolution was rescinded — only to be reinstated once again. And in order that there should be no doubt about the new Nordic archdiocese, a Nordic synod was finally held in Lund in 1139 under the auspices of a cardinal legate from the pope, among others, attended by Bishop Sigurd of Bergen and Bishop Orm from the Faeroe Islands. However, the issue remained unsettled. In Denmark a virtual state of civil war raged between two rivals for the throne, both of whom sought help from the German kingdom as well as assistance from the archbishop of Hamburg-Bremen.[39] At the same time, the German emperor, with support from the very same archbishop, consolidated his power vis-à-vis the pope. It is against this background that we must view the English cardinal Nicholas Breakspear's visit to Scandinavia in 1152. He arrived with instructions from the Pope to strengthen the power of the Church in Scandinavia by dividing the internordic archdiocese into national archdioceses. He had brought with him two *pallia*, making it clear that from the Pope's point of view the matter was settled.[40]

4.2. Towards a national archdiocese of Norway

The question arises as to whether the Norwegians knew in advance of the cardinal's arrival, and whether any Norwegian initiative was taken with respect to a national archdiocese. Let us take a look at the political situation in the country at that time. Starting in 1136, Norway was ruled by two brothers: Inge Krokrygg (Hunchback) (died 1161) and Sigurd Munn (Mouth) (1133–1155). Inge, who was only two years of age, had "lendmenn" (*i.e.* vassals) to govern for him. Although it is unlikely that there was any permanent sectionalization of the kingdom at that time, Inge seems to have resided at times in Bergen and Sigurd at times in Trøndelag. In 1142 a third brother, Øystein (died 1157), appeared on the scene. Apparently he was often in eastern Norway. These three brothers seem to have co-reigned with no major conflicts until about the middle of the 1150s, despite the

[39] *Cf.* Engels 1992 concerning the relationship between the German kingdom and Denmark at that time.

[40] *Pallium* actually means "a cloak", but here it is a white woollen ribbon with black (or red) crosses woven into it. An archbishop is permitted to wear it on certain occasions.

fact that they were all quite different by nature: Sigurd was a philanderer, Øystein was wild and reckless, but little Inge — largely on account of his handicap — stuck mostly to reading books. There is considerable evidence, however, to indicate that all three shared a preference for a Norwegian archdiocese and thought that it should be located in Nidaros, where St Olav's shrine was. As early as 1111, the Norwegian King Sigurd Jorsalfare (the Crusader or Jerusalemfarer) had made a vow in the Holy Land that he would work towards a separation from the archdiocese in Lund and for an independent archdiocese in Norway.[41] Furthermore, it is not hard to imagine where the kings believed the archbishop of Lund's sympathies and support would lie in the case of a conflict between Denmark and Norway.

The Norwegian monarchy had powerful interests in the western islands. A Norwegian archdiocese that included them would, in turn, strengthen the king's sovereignty there. Norwegian kings had participated in the election of the bishop of Greenland, and they could well have been involved when the Faeroes gained their own bishop. But the archbishop of York claimed the Orkney Islands, and he enjoyed the Pope's support. Nevertheless it seems that the English candidate during the 1120s never gained much power there. The islands had their own bishop, who was supported by the Norwegians.[42] In addition, the Scottish bishop at St Andrews, who answered to York, wanted an independent archdiocese for Scotland. The Scottish king was urged on towards this end, with the backing of the pope's legate during the latter's visit there.[43] This archdiocese was to include the Orkney Islands, and probably also the Isle of Man and the Hebrides.[44] But the Norwegian kings also laid claim to these islands, and they had every reason to maintain a high profile in this matter.

During these years we find a lively activity in the relationship between these very islands and Norway.[45] Ever since 1139 the Orkney Islands had been divided between the earls, Ragnvald and Harald. We find both of them in Norway in 1148,[46] or, according to Gunnes,[47] with King Inge at Bergen in 1149. In 1151 this same Ragnvald and his bishop, William the Old, set sail with the Norwegian magnate Erling Skakke on a crusade to the Holy Land. They had barely begun their journey when King Øystein left for the Orkney Islands. Whether this was due to financial greed, a spirit of wanderlust, or whether it was done with his brothers' blessing in order to take the islands, is not for us to say. The journey can also be interpreted as a sign that people in Norway — or, at any rate, King Øystein himself — were unaware of an impending visit by the cardinal. Historians regard

[41] *Cf. Ágrip*, ch. 54.

[42] *Latinske dokument*, ed. Vandvik 1959, 38 and 139. For Celtic bishops on the Orkneys, *cf.* Kolsrud 1913, 374–9.

[43] As late as 1151, the papal legate Johannes Paparo weighed this option (Seegrün 1967, 166).

[44] For Celtic bishops on Man and the Hebrides, *cf.* Kolsrud 1913, 357–74.

[45] What follows about the Orkney earls builds on Clouston 1932, 90–108 and Gunnes 1996. Some of the information, especially the dates, is questionable.

[46] Clouston 1932, 92.

[47] 1996, 67.

the cruise as an unabashed pillaging raid.[48] In the Orkney Islands he conquered Earl Harald who, in Ragnvald's absence, ruled over the entire group of islands. Harald had to purchase his freedom with three marks of gold, after which he received the islands as a fiefdom from King Øystein. That same year, a certain Erlend Haraldsson laid claim to half of the islands, and to buttress his claim he travelled to King Øystein in Norway. Erlend was assigned Harald's portion, and in September 1152 Earl Harald was compelled to relinquish it. Erlend and Harald ruled the islands (Harald ruling Ragnvald's half) until Ragnvald returned home himself. Nevertheless Harald is said to have travelled to Norway in 1153 to petition for help. Ragnvald also seems to have arrived in Norway early in 1153 after his crusade, where he is reported to have remained until just before Christmas of that year, and perhaps until the end of Breakspear's visit. The earls' visit to Norway in 1148/1149 and later in 1153, along with King Øystein's raid on the Orkney Islands, can be regarded as a countermove to the Scottish and English kings. Moreover, the fact that Gudrød, king of the Hebrides, swore an oath to Inge in 1152/1153, perhaps in connection with the cardinal's visit, can be interpreted along these same lines. Concerning Gudrød, in *Chronica Regum Maniæ*, it is said that *In proximo autumno venit* [...] *de Norvegia cum quinque navibus, et applicuit apud Orcadas* ("the following autumn he came from Norway with five ships and anchored at the Orkney Islands").[49] According to Munch, Johnsen and Broderick, this took place in 1153.[50] He returned with his newly ordained bishop, the Norwegian clerk Ragnvald. There can be no doubt that both the Orkney earls and the king of the Hebrides went to Norway voluntarily — whether they were summoned or not. From their standpoint a remote Norwegian king was preferable by far to a Scottish king nearby.

For the Norwegian clerics a separate archdiocese foreshadowed a strengthening of the Church's influence, so there is every reason to believe that ecclesiastical and secular forces shared a common cause here. Gunnes writes,[51] "Some historians have thought in terms of a deliberate reform-minded "Church party", organized around the legitimate King Inge. But all traces of proof have vanished." We should note that any reform-minded tendencies among Norwegian clerics could have been enhanced by the establishment of the Cistercian monastery, Lyse, at Bergen in 1146 by Bishop Sigurd. Shortly thereafter followed Nonneseter at Bergen and the monastery in Hovedøya at Oslo — both most likely of the same order. The Cistercians were in the service of the universal Church; moreover, Pope Eugenius III (1145–53)[52] was a representative of the same order. Gunnes continues: "There is far more reason to believe that in Sigurd Munn's and Øystein's circles the office of archbishop was considered to be an honour worthy of sacrifice." Later, Øystein and Sigurd had to pay a fine to Breakspear because the latter had become indignant with them. We do not know the reason for this. As to Øystein, it could be

[48] *Cf. e.g.* Johnsen 1965.
[49] *Chronica Regum Manniæ*, ed. Munch 1860, 9.
[50] Munch 1860, 78–9, Johnsen 1966, 7 with note and Broderick 1973, 14–6.
[51] Trans. from Gunnes 1996, 60.
[52] Johnsen 1945, 29–30 and Johnsen 1967.

due to his pillaging raid. According to Johnsen 1965, Øystein plundered a wealth of Church property in Scotland and England. This was forbidden after the Council of Rheims in 1148, which called for excommunication of anyone expropriating or plundering Church property.[53] However, the call for a fine might also have originated with the legitimate Inge, Breakspear's preferred king. In the first place the earls on the Orkney Islands, which Øystein had ravaged, seem to have been allied with Inge. And as for Sigurd, two crimes appear to have played a part: he was accused of having impregnated Erling Skakke's fiancee/wife, and of having killed Ottar Birting. Both Erling Skakke and Ottar Birting were King Inge's men. Ottar Birting was also married to Inge's mother. The demand for a fine could thus have been Inge's condition for sitting down at the negotiating table with his brothers, but it could also be due to Sigurd's and Øystein's illegitimacy and constitute a prerequisite from the cardinal for the continuance of the joint monarchy. With the next king, Magnus Erlingsson, the joint monarchy, as we shall see, came to an end; it was also the end of the right to succession on the part of illegitimate heirs. Since both fines were paid, we may interpret this not only as signalling a wish for the continuance of the joint monarchy, but also as an indication that all the kings were in accord over the archdiocese issue.

The sources for this period are anything but abundant, yet another sign of Norwegian initiative for the establishment of a separate ecclesiastical province could be the following: the Icelandic annals speak of an "Archbishop Reidár", who was "the first archbishop of Norway" and who died in "Sydlandene" (the South) in 1151 on his way home from his ordination by the Pope.[54] If there is any truth to this, it could suggest that Norway followed the advice of the Pope that the Irish had previously been given – namely, that all the bishops of the land, as well as clerks and prominent men, should come together for a Church council meeting.[55] Then they were to seek the *pallium* in accordance with everyone's wishes and consent, and the application would then be granted. This describes the situation up to 1152/1153.

4.3. HN and the Norwegian archdiocese-to-be

From the foregoing we see that there are good reasons to take a closer look at the years before 1152/1153. My hypothesis is now that *HN* could have been written around 1150 — and no later than 1152/1153. On the one hand, *HN* could have been written for purely literary reasons, or it could have sprung from the notion of a separate archdiocese and have been written solely on the basis of a sense of need for a work of history that would "put" Norway on the map in relation to European Christianity in general. We shall return to this later; for the moment we shall pursue another option: in my opinion *HN* might well be an official Norwegian ecclesiastical-political work for the occasion, written in advance of the establish-

[53] Johnsen 1965, 8.

[54] *Islandske annaler*, ed. Storm 1888, 114, 253, 322 and 474 and Gunnes 1996, 61.

[55] According to Kolsrud 1958, 186, a Church council was convened in Bergen during the spring of 1150. Unfortunately this claim is undocumented.

ment of the archdiocese in Nidaros. I consider it a possibility that *HN* might be an important – perhaps the most important – document, which shows that on the Norwegian side forces were at work to ensure the establishment and the scope of this archdiocese. As far as I can determine, *HN* could have been written with a view to persuading the Pope/cardinal that the Norwegian kingdom was not only in need of and worthy of a separate archdiocese, but that it should also have the scope that it ultimately attained. As we know, Cardinal Breakspear's visit not only saw the establishment of the archbishop's seat at Nidaros, but ten whole dioceses were put under its jurisdiction: Bergen, Stavanger, Oslo, Hamar (which was new), the Faeroe Islands,[56] the Orkney Islands, the Hebrides,[57] Iceland (2) and Greenland. Since Hamar was a new diocese and the king of Man and the Hebrides left for home with a newly ordained bishop, we should be on the alert for some trace of this in *HN*. But not only that, we should also note the account of Olav Tryggvason: *HN* could, as far as I can deduce, contain an attempt to justify his candidacy as a saint. But be that as it may, the account in *HN* of him and his work on earth, compared with the account of St Olav, is remarkable indeed. The canonization of great and highly regarded kings was in full accord with prevailing attitudes throughout European countries. Here at home St Olav had been declared a saint by Bishop Grimkel as early as one year and five days after his death, *i.e.* the third of August 1031, when his body was transferred to Klement's church in Nidaros. This was accepted by the Trønders (the local inhabitants), fully in accordance with the custom of the times. Like St Olav, Olav Tryggvason was a highly regarded king, and when he died, his life history was embellished in a manner that customarily presaged sainthood: conversations with angels were ascribed to him; an exceptionally beautiful light descended upon him when he jumped into the sea; he saved himself from drowning and lived alone for many years abroad, etc.[58] The only problem, however, was that, in actual fact, he disappeared in the sea and his body was never found. As a result there was no place to make pilgrimages to; nor did any miracles take place at the site of his presumed drowning. Before a *pia fraus* (a pious fraud) was devised, this place was occupied by St Olav. Olav Tryggvason was eclipsed by St Olav, with respect to whom Olav Tryggvason was regarded as a mere forerunner. But he was forgotten abroad.[59] St Olav himself was not canonized by the Pope (see 8.13. below); nevertheless a number of official documents prove that he was acknowledged as a saint.[60] To begin with, the king administered his holy dwelling. But as the bishops gained their own permanent seats, and the Norwegian Church's ties to the Curia grew more tight-knit, the trusteeship passed increasingly into the hands of the Church. By the time of Magnus Erlingsson's

[56] Believed to have fallen out by mistake of the Pope's Letter of Foundation of 28 November 1154, *cf. Latinske dokument*, ed. Vandvik 1959, 157.

[57] The Hebrides are mentioned in the Pope's Letter of Foundation as *Suthraie Insulas* (*Latinske dokument*, ed. Vandvik 1959, 54). The Isle of Man is not mentioned. [58] Daae 1879,16.

[59] Daae 1879, 17. In Odd Snorresson's *Saga*, Olav Tryggvason is presented in relation to St Olav as a kind of John the Baptist figure in relation to Christ (Daae 1879, 91 and Odd's *Saga* Prologue, 19). [60] Daae 1879, 18.

coronation around 1163 the Church had relegated the kings to positions of mere vassals of St Olav.[61]

With Adam of Bremen's work in mind we shall also see that the author of *HN* is perhaps sending indirect signals to the Pope/cardinal to the effect that a Norwegian archbishop would represent a counterbalance to the Hamburg Church and provide invaluable support for the Pope. Furthermore, we should keep in mind Solinus's and Honorius's works to see what potential significance they might have had in the formation of *HN*. Finally we have good reason to take a closer look at certain attitudes expressed in *HN* which can be traced back to resolutions that were possibly made during Breakspear's visit, resolutions with major consequences for Norway, both in sacred and secular affairs during the latter half of the 1100s.

Many earlier researchers believed that *Agnellus / Angnellus / Anguellus*, to whom *HN* is dedicated, was a foreigner. I believe that with equal justification he could be identified as Norwegian, but that the author might have had a particular foreigner in mind when he wrote *HN* — namely, a cardinal legate or the Pope. We shall discuss below (§ 12) whether *HN* was written with Reidar's possible journey to the Curia in mind (*c.* 1150), or whether it was finished around the time of Breakspear's arrival in 1152, or yet again whether it might have been written during his visit. At all events, if my theory is valid, *HN* must have been finished sometime during the period 1150–53. Whether the Norwegians knew of an impending visit by a papal emissary or whether they knew it was Breakspear himself who was coming will also be discussed below (12). We can only guess at the importance *HN* had for the entire archepiscopal issue; but it surely did not have a deleterious effect. And it is this very point that I shall attempt to demonstrate.

5. The Prologue

5.1. Sources

5.1.1. Adam of Bremen

As a model for *HN* the author has chosen Adam of Bremen's account of the Hamburg archdiocese, *Gesta Hammaburgensis ecclesiae pontificum* ("The Achievements of the Archbishops in the Hamburg Archdiocese") in four books dating from *c.* 1076. This includes geographical, historical and ecclesiastical-political strains — in short, that which is made clear by the Prologue of *HN*:

1. A geographical description of the Norwegian kingdom (including the mainland and islands towards the west).

2. The Norwegian kings' lineage and history (which ends when St Olav sets sail from England for his homeland in the year 1015.)

3. An account of the introduction of Christianity, the flight of paganism, and the situation of both in the author's lifetime.

These elements had also previously been dealt with by Ari, and we find a similar division later in Oddr Snorresson's *Saga* (though in a different order).[62] But

[61] Daae 1879, 19.

[62] Bugge 1873, 19–21, Gjessing 1896, 149, Ellehøj 1965.

on the whole a disposition based on geographical introductions (on the location, scope and population of the country) was commonplace in history writing during the Middle Ages. Yet in *HN* it is unusually long and constitutes not an introduction, but rather an important and integral part of the work. This might indicate that the author had something else than a mere chronicle of kings in mind.

Adam's name is not mentioned, but allusions to his work are many, both substantively and linguistically, in the Prologue as well as in Book One itself. For this reason Bugge felt justified in accusing the author of *HN* of "lack of independence" and of being a person "bereft of an awareness of his calling".[63] However, this form of imitation was traditional during the Middle Ages and Bugge's assertion lacks validity. We shall see that the author of *HN*, in part, corrects statements in Adam's work that he finds unsatisfactory; in part he contradicts him; in part he supplements him when he knows more; and in part he omits material in his own account that he considers satisfactorily or "harmlessly" presented by Adam. Adam's work is partly based on Danish sources (in Book IV about Scandinavia, in particular), *HN* often on others, and the author of *HN* makes only eclectic use of Adam. In addition Adam represents the Hamburg archbishop, so that a potential contradiction of Adam can be interpreted as Norwegian support for the Pope. *HN* can thus be read as a Norwegian rejoinder and as a supplement – but also as a counterpart to Adam's work. The choice of Adam as a model is no doubt deliberate, because Adam's work was both known and appreciated by many learned persons – at any rate in the northern part of Europe. With my theory as a vantage point, we can also surmise that the author of *HN* might have wanted to make the learned reader aware of the fact that in *HN* the reader could expect a Norwegian counterpart to Adam's Church history of the Hamburg archdiocese; if not exactly a *Historia ecclesiae / archiepiscopatus Trudensis* ("The History of the Church/Archdiocese of Nidaros"),[64] at least a basis and prerequisite for the Norwegian archbishopric.

5.1.2. Honorius of Autun and Julius Solinus

In the Prologue, however, the author of *HN* alludes — in fact even more directly — to another author, an author of the twelfth century. Unfortunately the copy in our possession today begins with a torn upper left-hand corner, a missing part which extends for a distance of twelve lines — which means that, among others, the initial word which contained a large capital is partially gone. It is quite clear from the context, however, that it contained the name of a person. And by reading further we see that this person in his *Philistratu* (which is clearly a work by him) sings the praises of friendship and tells of how (Prol. 1)"no difficulties will exist between loving friends" (*inter [ca]ros amicos nichil fere difficile fore*). We also understand that this person is (Prol. 2) *tantus philosophus* ("such a great philosopher"). Gustav Storm emends *Philistratu* to *Philostrato*. He, however, errs when he writes that the initial name ends with *tus* (*...tus in Philostrato suo*): We are only

[63] Bugge 1873, 24.

[64] *Trudensis* is the name used in the Pope's Letter of Foundation of 28 November 1154 (*Latinske dokument*, ed. by Vandvik 1959, 54).

able to read ...*us*.[65] In front of *us* we see the remnants of a small vertical line, which could be an "i" without the dot or the last vertical line in "u", "n" or "m", but the copy is so unclear here that other letters might also be relevant.

There can be no doubt, however, that Honorius of Autun is the author whom *HN* draws on for these lines. But whether he has written Honorius's name is less sure. If we try to insert the name [*Honori*]*us in Philistratu suo*, we shall discover that this does not work, for the simple reason that there is no room for it in the aforementioned lacuna in *HN*. It is possible, however, that the author has written *Hōrius*, even though it seems strange that the scribe wouldn't write out the first word in *HN*. He does not start using a nasal stroke until the last word on the fifth line. The name of *Henricus*, as Honorius also calls himself,[66] is also too long a word to insert. One factor that could speak in favour of the author of *HN*'s having written Honorius's name is the fact that Honorius was a well-known representative of Pope Gregory's Church reform and a supporter of the universal Church. By starting his work with Honorius's name, the author of *HN* is showing his colours.

One of *HN*'s presumed sources, the so-called Sorø manuscript, apparently contained the following texts, among others, in the order indicated:
(*a*) Adam of Bremen's *Gesta Hammaburgensis ecclesiae pontificum* from *c.* 1076.
(*b*) Honorius Augustodunensis's *Imago mundi* ("Image of the World") from *c.* 1110.[67]
(*c*) Julius Solinus's *Collectanea rerum memorabilium* ("A collection of memorable things") from the third century A.D.[68]

Of these texts we find direct traces in *HN* only of the first two. However, the author only refers to Solinus's name and to his book "on the wonders of the world" (*de mundi mirabilibus*). This occurs in the chapter on Iceland (VIII 13). But it later becomes apparent that, as in so many other places in his account, the author of *HN* has taken words, phrases and other material from Honorius.[69] In the opinion of some previous researchers this could be due to the fact that the author believed that both *Imago mundi* and *Collectanea rerum memorabilium* were written by Solinus. But, as far as I can see, this cannot be the explanation. Naturally, the fact that the author, so to speak, quotes from one book, such as *Imago mundi,* while referring to another *de mundi mirabilibus*, could possibly indicate that the two works had at some point merged to become one; but a more likely explanation is that Solinus's name, along with the expression *de mundi mirabilibus*, appeared in a scholium in connection with Honorius's work in the author of

[65] Koht 1919–20, 115 and Lehmann 1937, 76–77 discuss the possibilities of who this person could be, but they convince neither themselves nor anyone else by their suggestions.

[66] *Cf. Lexikon des Mittelalters* on Honorius.

[67] Flint 1972, 226–27.

[68] This work became very popular. During the course of the Middle Ages it was given different titles, and was heavily edited, but always under Solinus's name. A number of manuscripts and editions that go under Solinus's name bear the title *Polyhistor* (*cf.* Solinus, ed. Mommsen, xxv–lviii).

[69] Skard 1930, 78–83 and Steinnes 1946–48, 18–29.

HN's source, so that he had the impression that Honorius, in the relevant passage, builds upon Solinus. There might, however, also be another explanation.

Solinus's name fits perfectly into the above-mentioned lacuna in the Prologue. But if the author of *HN*, in good faith, has written Solinus there (and not Honorius), this means that the introductory letters in Honorius's *Imago mundi*, in the form in which we now have them, must have undergone a change: from the epistle dedicatory of Honorius's *Imago mundi* the author of *HN* has lifted a large number of expressions for his Prologue. In fact part of the Prologue appears to be based upon it. Some of these passages have caught the attention of previous researchers.[70] However, the edition of Honorius's work in Migne's *Patrologia Latina*[71] (hereafter referred to as PL) shows, in addition, that the epistle dedicatory has the following heading: *Epistola Honorii ad Christianum, de eodem* ("Honorius's letter to Christian about the same"). Just before this letter we also find *Epistola Christiani ad Honorium Solitarium de Imagine mundi* ("Christian's letter to the monk Honorius concerning *Imago mundi*"). As we see, both headings contain Honorius's name. In the text of the epistle dedicatory it is also written that Honorius calls his work *Imago mundi*. In other words, there seems to be only one reason for the author of *HN* not knowing Honorius's name: the headings and the title *Imago mundi* have disappeared from his source. This sounds unlikely, and there is also another reason: the words on friendship introducing the Prologue of *HN* must be a paraphrase of Honorius's words in the epistle dedicatory: Honorius complains that *Laboriosum* (*sc. negotium*) *quidem mihi in aliis occupato* ("the commission (*i.e.* of writing *Imago mundi*) is indeed difficult for me who have been dealing with other things"), but *charitas vincit omnia* ("charity overcomes everything").[72] Neither Solinus, nor for that matter Adam, has anything about friendship in his work. But in spite of this it is not unthinkable that the author of *HN* knows very well what and whom he is dealing with and that he is deliberately referring to Solinus and his book on the wonders of the world. We must remember that in a number of places, Adam also mentions Solinus. One might think that a work is getting off to a bad start if the author starts quoting one author while referring to another. But this is too modern a way of looking at it, for we find the same procedure among many of his contemporaries, *e.g.* Theodoricus.[73]

What, then, does the author of *HN* eventually hope to achieve by this? As far as I can see, he is trying to make the learned reader aware that he can expect *HN* to provide a Norwegian contribution and supplement to Solinus's work on the wonders of the world, *i.e.* a description that also contains characteristic Norwegian *mirabilia* which associate the Norwegian kingdom with the rest of the civilized world. Norwegian and Nordic *mirabilia* are understandably a neglected area with Solinus; he knew too little about them. An argument in favour of this assumption is the fact that words from the same root, such as *mirus, mirabilis* and *mirificus*, are used in some form or other fifteen times in *HN*. Perhaps we should also note that the author of *HN* does not refer to Solinus's work by *Collectanea*

[70] *Cf.*, for instance, Skard 1930, 78–84.
[71] 1844–91, vol. 172 col. 119.
[72] *Cf.* also Commentary on Prologue 1.
[73] *Cf.* also Skard 1930, 81–82.

rerum memorabilium, Polyhistor or, for example, by *De rebus mirabilibus* ("On wonders"), but rather confuses Honorius's and Solinus's titles and perhaps stresses the word *mundi* ("the world's"). Both Solinus's and Honorius's works were quite popular in the Middle Ages, and if the author of *HN* does not retain Honorius's name, this could, as far as I can tell, be due to the fact that he feels he is killing two birds with one stone: a reference is made to "the classicist" Solinus, but the learned reader knows and recalls that the source is Honorius. For that matter both works have much in common, and in some places Honorius builds on Solinus. So it is not unreasonable that the author of *HN* perceives Honorius's and Solinus's works as belonging to the same category, so that for him the term *imago/imagines mundi* ("image(s) of the world") is virtually identical with *mirabilia mundi* ("world wonders").

This leads us to the next question — namely, the connection between Honorius/Solinus and, according to Storm and later researchers, a book called "Philostratus" (*in Philostrato suo*). We know of no work by the name of *Philostratus* or, as our manuscript reads, *Philistratus*. But we recognize *Philostratus* as a personal name, and there are many who go by that name. The closest conjecture I can make is that the connection could be between Honorius's *Imago mundi* (*Image of the World*) and Flavius Philostratus's presumed work *Εἰκόνες* (*Pictures*) in Greek dating from *c.* 200 A.D. This work of Philostratus, however, deals with paintings. Honorius's work appeared in several editions after the year 1110, each time with new additions.[74] It is not known whether the author of *HN* had one of these before him, or whether he perceived these additions to be additional *Imagines* and whether the work can thus be perceived as a Latin reply to Philostratus's Greek work. Still, all in all the connection between these two works of Honorius and of Philostratus is hard to imagine.

There is, however, another — and better — suggestion[75] for emending *in philistratu suo* than the one Storm made: *philistratu* could be a misreading by the Scottish copyist (or the copyist of his exemplar). *Philistratu* could well have been two words which, in the exemplar, appeared close together and shortened with abbreviations, like this: *phiē trātu*. According to Cappelli, this is a common way of abbreviating the expression *philosophie tractatu*.[76] The expression *in philosophie tractatu suo* ("in his philosophical treatise") makes good sense at this point in *HN*. It does not, however, resolve the question of whether the initial word was "Honorius" or "Solinus", because the works of both men could appear under this description.[77] And yet the former seems to be the more likely, since the expression *philosophia*, along with other similar expressions, is also used in those letters which introduce Honorius's work. However, if my dating of *HN* is right, Honorius might still have been alive when *HN* was written, and even if he was dead, it would be quite a surprise if the name of Honorius (or Henricus) appeared at

[74] Flint 1981. [75] The suggestion comes from Peter Fisher. [76] Cappelli 1929, 272 and 380.
[77] The term *philosophus* ("philosopher") was used in a broad sense at that time, and could also designate a geographer and a grammarian. Adam of Bremen uses it, for example, in connection with "the apostle of the North", Ansgar (I 15).

the beginning of *HN*: as far as we know, Honorius's name is not mentioned or referred to in any other works in the Middle Ages,[78] whereas Solinus and his work are mentioned many times throughout the centuries, among others by Adam.

5.1.3. Marcus Tullius Cicero

A third possibility of the lost name introducing the Prologue of *HN* should also be discussed here: could it have been Cicero, often referred to as *Tullius*?[79] The words on friendship certainly lead the thoughts to his philosophical treatise, *De amicitia*. Nevertheless the most interesting passage in this connection we find in his *Orator* 10.33 (spoken to Brutus): *Sed nihil difficile amanti puto* ("But I think that nothing is difficult for friendship"). *Amanti* (here in the dative) is a common expression for friendship or brotherly love (*charitas*) in medieval Latin.[80] This saying of Cicero's seems to have been quite popular in the Middle Ages, especially in the eleventh and twelfth centuries, and we find it quoted in *e.g.* Petrus Damianus's *Sermo XXIX De Sancta Maria Magdalena*, in Petrus Abelardus's *Ethica* and in Rabanus Maurus's *De vita B. Mariae Magdalenae et Marthae*.[81] The question is now whether the author of *HN* would go to the length of using Cicero's name, as well as transcribing his famous sentence. Well, that might have been the case, as this, as mentioned above, is a traditional form of imitation in the Middle Ages. But another question is what signals the author of *HN* would send out by using Cicero. Certainly something about philosophy (in our current sense of the term) and rhetoric. But the author of *HN* is more concerned about the truth, and his work is first and foremost a work of ecclesiastical-political, geographical and historical statements and facts. That means in turn that Adam, Honorius and Solinus, but not Cicero, would be the right authors to allude to at the beginning of a work like *HN*, even though all four of them could have been called "great philosophers". Furthermore, there are no direct linguistic traces of any of Cicero's works.[82]

The conclusion must be that unless the copyist has forgotten a letter in the name of Honorius/Henricus, or unless the author of *HN* has used an abbreviation or another, and shorter, name for Honorius/Henricus, whom he is actually using in parts of both his Prologue and in Book One, Solinus's name which is quoted later in Book One, is so far preferable to both Honorius and Cicero. This in spite of the fact that Solinus does not seem to have been directly used by the author of *HN*. But the whole issue is debatable, and there might be other alternatives.

5.2. Contents

Not only is the torn corner of the first folio leaving a missing part of the text a headache for the reader of *HN*, but the Prologue as a whole leaves many open questions as to who the author and the dedicatee, *Agnellus / Angnellus / Anguellus*, are. A second question, which so far has never been put forward, rises from the

[78] *Cf. Lexikon des Mittelalters*. I owe the reference to LBM.

[79] The suggestion comes from LBM whom I also thank for the reference to Cicero's *Orator* 10,33.

[80] *Cf. e.g.* PL *Auctor incertus* 184 col. 598.

[81] PL 144 col. 665, 178 col. 659 and 112 col. 1471, respectively.

[82] *Cf.* Skard 1930, 69.

fact that *HN*, like Honorius's work, but in contrast to Adam's work, seems to have been commissioned (*negotium*, Prologue 4), conceived by someone other than the author himself. We hear nothing of the reason for the commission, however; in fact, both the commission and the commissioner could well be fictitious. We find many of the same expressions as we do in the epistle dedicatory of Honorius, who claims that he was commissioned by a certain *Christianus*. This might be a personal name, or it might just mean "a Christian fellow brother"; it might also be a fictitious name. We shall return to this. The question now is whether the dedicatee and the commissioner of *HN* are one and the same person, or whether they are two persons. The author of *HN* writes, to begin with, *about* the commissioner, but soon he turns to speak directly *to* the dedicatee. This might indicate two persons. Honorius speaks only *to* his commissioner who is also the dedicatee. A third question would be what role this commissioner might have played in the writing of *HN*. As all these are delicate issues which concern the whole work, we shall leave them to the end of this Essay. Until then we shall have to treat the original writer of *HN* as the author, and the commissioner and *Agnellus/Angnellus/Anguellus* as one person, as the dedicatee of *HN* (though all this is not a foregone conclusion), and concentrate on other issues in the Prologue.

As Adam wrote to his archbishop, so the author of *HN* could have been writing for the Pope or a cardinal. And like Adam, and also Honorius Augustodunensis, the author of *HN* takes up a number of commonplaces (*topoi*) in his Prologue. In *HN* these include the recurring theme of modesty, the fear of envy (and also of danger), the difficulty with and scope of the work, lack of experience, gratitude and sense of obligation towards one's commissioner, the claim to be producing groundbreaking work (in Latin) and invoking of sources, linguistic and stylistic deficiencies, the eschewing of renown as a writer of history, the request for the dedicatee's protection, as well as the work's usefulness for later generations. These are all commonplaces in keeping with the spirit of the times, employed in antiquity and further developed in the earlier Christian era and during the Middle Ages.[83]

When the author of *HN* writes in the Prologue that there is no Latin work corresponding to *HN*, we are justified in taking this to mean, by implication, "as far as he knows". We must also add "by a Norwegian", because the author might have been familiar with the Icelander Sæmund's Latin chronicle and certainly was, as we know, with Adam's work. Gjessing's suggestion that the author of *HN* was thinking about Latin works with a similar tripartite division of the material we can keep in mind,[84] but this might not be the most important thing. On the other hand the author of *HN* says nothing about whether there were similar works in Old Norse. We shall return to this subject at the very end.

There has been a discussion as to whether the expression (Prol. 5) *nostris aminiculis fretus* ("trusting to such resources as I/we have") alludes to oral or written sources, or both. In my opinion, the latter without a doubt. The expression quite simply means "aids" or "means" here. The same uncertainty has surrounded

[83] Simon 1958 and 1959/60.

[84] 1896, 133.

the expression (Prol. 8) *seniorum asserciones secutus* ("followed the statements of my/our elders"). Here we must enlist the help of Honorius's epistle dedicatory: *Hic nihil autem in eo* (*sc. libello*) *pono, nisi quod majorum commendat traditio* ("But I put down in this (*i.e.* book) only what ancient report has passed on") and Adam's Prologue: *pleraque omnia seniorum, quibus res nota est, traditione didici* ("I have learned nearly everything from the accounts of the elders who have known about the matter"). *Asserciones* means, actually, legal assurances or assertions to the effect that someone ought to be free. Here *seniorum asserciones* must correspond to the above-quoted *majorum/seniorum traditio* and, as far as I can tell, include both older written and oral accounts, *i.e.* from both deceased and contemporaneous persons. In other words the author of *HN* has certain books at his disposal, but at the same time lives in a place where he is in contact with, or belongs to a circle of learned and/or older men who serve as his knowledgeable supporters; and he has benefited from their knowledge. It will suffice in this regard to mention, for example, Bergen, which was home to both the bishop's see and two to three monasteries and, on occasion, the king and his men. Furthermore we should bear in mind that the Icelander Eirik Oddsson, for example, who wrote the now-lost *Hryggjarstykki*, a chronicle about the Norwegian kings which started with the year 1130, in the years around 1150 seems to have travelled back and forth between Iceland and Norway in order to collect information for his chronicle. It is easy to imagine that, in exchange for such information, he might have told what he knew from Iceland. For that matter he might also have brought with him Ari's and Sæmund's now-lost chronicles to Norway. We know, for example, that Eirik was one of King Inge's men and obtained information from his housecarls.[85]

Furthermore, the author of *HN* invokes the truth (Prol. 8), *cum nichil a me de vetustatis serie nouum vel inauditum assumpserim* ("since I have incorporated on my own account nothing new or unheard of from earlier ages"), and says that he himself has merely added contemporary, memorable exploits. It is important for the author that *HN* should come across as a truthful, reliable historical document. Nevertheless we must bear in mind that this is also a traditional way of expressing oneself, thus leaving the responsibility of truth to the sources and not to the user of them.

Concerning his own times, where the author builds on his own observations, he maintains that he has included what he found worth remembering; the reason for this is that he has seen (Prol. 9) *multorum magnificencias cum suis auctoribus ob scriptorum inopiam a memoria modernorum cotidie elabi* ("many men's splendid feats, together with their performers, sink daily into oblivion among our contemporaries owing to the shortage of written records"). Nevertheless it is on this very point that many researchers believe the author of *HN* falls short (see § 9.3. below). We should also note that the last part of the Prologue is cast in the perfect tense, *i.e.* the author seems, naturally enough, to have written *HN* *before* the Prologue was conceived.[86] But a number of researchers do not believe that this is the case. This will also be discussed below (§ 9.3).

[85] *E.g.* Kválen 1925, 158–59. [86] *Cf.* Aðalbjarnarson 1937, 2 and Holtsmark 1938, 162.

6. The geographical description of Norway

6.1. The mainland

6.1.1. Location and borders

Book One starts with a description of the mainland. With simple strokes the author draws a map that is easy to visualize for a person who is unfamiliar with the country. He specifies the exact borders and the form and location of the country, and this map tells us that the country stretches practically to the uttermost limits of the world. We also notice that Jämtland is outside the country's borders, and many researchers have tried to use this to date *HN*; some believe that Jämtland paid taxes to Norway as far back as the 1130s,[87] others from Magnus Erlingsson's (1161–84) or Sverre's time (1184–1202).[88] Aðalbjarnarson and Steinnes believe that it was the geographical, not the political, border that was in question.[89] But Paasche points out that a distinction was also made between Jämtland and Norway in *Egil's saga* (after 1200).[90] In my opinion tax payment is an important issue here, but might not be the only one (see 7. below). Just what did the author of *HN* have in mind when delineating borders here? He might have had the new archdiocese in mind. For this same reason, perhaps, it is said of Greenland that we can thank the Icelanders (whom we later discover to be Norwegians) that Greenland was discovered, populated and Christianized. Thus the implication is that it naturally belongs to a Norwegian archdiocese. We read elsewhere (not in *HN*) that in his day Sigurd Jorsalfare assisted in the election of the bishop there.[91] The fact that Greenland is mentioned at this point in *HN*, and not under the "tributary islands", could be due to the fact that the author regards Greenland as a continent (in contrast to Adam)[92] which (I 11) *terminus est ad occasum Europe* ("marks the western boundary of Europe"), and is so large that it *fere contingens Affricanas insulas* ("almost touches the islands off Africa"). With these words the Norwegian kingdom is represented as a virtual world monarchy.[93] Nevertheles, the mention of Greenland at this point, and not under the tributary islands, is most probably due to the fact that the population did not pay taxes at the time *HN* was written. There are valid reasons for believing that the same was the case with Jämtland. As we shall see the author of *HN* is ready to mention tax payments wherever he can. Thus the fact that Greenland first began to pay taxes to Norway in 1261 is relevant for dating it before this year.[94]

6.1.2. The inhabitants

Just as he did with the matter of location and borders, the author of *HN* delineates the country's natural divisions of settlements in terms of a broad coastal zone, an inland zone and a forested zone where the Finns (*i.e.* the Lapps, see § 6.1.6. below)

[87] Hanssen 1949, 8.
[88] Koht 1919–20, 108 and 1949–51, 52.
[89] 1937, 24 and 1946–48, 35, respectively. Koht 1949–51, 52 disagrees.
[90] 1924, 432.
[91] Gunnes 1996, 59.
[92] He calls it an island in IV 37.
[93] A similar presentation of Greenland, its size and location, is found in the Icelandic Abbot Nikolaus's *Itinerarium*. Nikolaus died in 1158. For this geographical theory, *cf.* Bjørnbo 1909, 229ff.
[94] *Cf.* Bugge 1873, 32–3.

lived. This is in contrast to Adam (IV 24 & 32) who writes that the Finns partly belong to Sweden, partly to Norway, and partly live in between. At the same time, the author of *HN* deals with the status of religion in the country: in the first two belts, the coastland and the Uplands ("Opplandene", *i.e.* the mountain region), we understand that the native Norwegians (thank God) are now Christians; but the Finns in the forested zone and some peoples towards the north (alas) are still pagans. They come from the east and are termed Kirjalers, Kvens, Horned Finns and the two kinds of Bjarms. In other words they are presented as non-Norwegian, but might represent an object of missionary activity. And this mission field lies just outside Norway's living-room door, on Christian Norwegian ground as it were. "Norway was one of those countries whose turn it was to be conquered by the missionary order", Paasche tells us.[95] The fact that he believed this would be done by the Franciscans is another matter. The land of Norway is admittedly hostile to habitation in some areas, but nowhere in *HN* is it intimated that its location or nature was or had ever been a hindrance to Christianity. On the contrary, in spite of this land being far-flung, with its mountains, forests and cold temperatures, the native Norwegians have all been Christianized. The author merely makes the reader understand that all native Norwegians are Christians in his time. As we shall see, he takes the subject up again later. This seems to suffice at the outset, however, and perhaps he is assuming that those who are familiar with Adam's work will remember his long narrative (IV 31) about what good Christians Norwegians were — in the eleventh century, no less!

The accounts of the "Land of Maidens", "Land of Giants" and "Land of the Skrælings" might be designed to buttress the impression that Norwegians are not isolated from the outside world, but are on a par with other civilized nations; they are wide-ranging merchant sailors who come into contact with the most remote and unlikely places on earth; and if anyone is traditionally familiar with Europe's northernmost and westernmost area, it is the Norwegians. That is probably why the author of *HN* finds it necessary to give a different account of these areas from Adam, and corrects the latter's combination of Kvenland and the "Land of Maidens" (IV 17 & 19). Furthermore Adam recounts (IV 39–41) that Harald Hardråde, and afterwards some noblemen from Friesland, made an expedition for the purpose of studying these regions more closely. In *HN* it is the Norwegian merchants who are credited with studying them. The mission field might be enlarged with these "alien" creatures.

6.1.3. The jurisdictional division

The coastland and the Uplands are divided into clearly-defined "law provinces" ("lagdømmer") and adjoining "counties" ("fylker") in an orderly way. The author of *HN* is well-orientated in judicial matters, and specifies the exact numbers and extent of these legal divisions. We may note that even Hålogaland, where many pagan Finns live, constitutes a separate law province.[96] In other words, from a legal standpoint, Norway is a fully developed society.

[95] 1924, 432.

[96] This leads Maurer 1875, 9 to date it far later. But Hålogaland is also a separate law province in Oddr's *Saga Óláfs Tryggvasonar* ch. 22.

A number of researchers have been puzzled by the way the author, in connection with the reference to the country's concrete jurisdictional divisions, makes use of the word *patria*[97] ("fatherland", but here "law province"). There are those who believe that this is due to French influence,[98] while others point out that it is used for larger legal districts in Denmark,[99] and Robberstad 1949–51 is concerned with defining the contemporary meaning of the word more closely. For researchers, the problem associated with the use of *patria* has been that this expression is not only employed for what we nowadays understand by the law provinces of Borgarting, Gulating, Frostating and Hålogaland, but that it is used in connection with the Uplands which, *HN* asserts, consist of four *patrie*. Under all *patrie* there are several *provincie*[100] in the Uplands, as in the three first-mentioned law provinces. As for the large law provinces, their constituent *prouincie* correspond to the Norwegian term "fylker" nowadays (here translated by "counties"); but this does not fit for the Uplands. Robberstad concludes that the term *patria* in *HN* points to a larger jurisdictional area which corresponds to the Old Norwegian word "lǫg" and has its own "ting" (*i.e.* court assembly). *Prouincia*, on the other hand, is a smaller jurisdictional area with a "ting" inferior to that of the *patria*. He writes further,[101] "Here one has to consider that the Norwegian author of *HN* might have had a greater knowledge of the juridical structure of his day than the Icelandic saga writers." When we consider this together with everything else we discover about the author's knowledge, Robberstad's last statement seems reasonable. But with respect to the former, we should also bear in mind that the terms *patria* and *prouincia* were also used in the 1100s, for example by Theodoricus and in *Passio et miracula Beati Olaui* (*St Olav's Passion and Miracles*) (hereafter referred to as *Passio Olaui*, written before 1188),[102] about a larger or smaller area in general, without reference to legal jurisdictions at all. In *HN*, for example, we see *patria* used in connection with Greenland, while *prouincia* is used in *Passio Olavi* about Norway.[103] We should also note here that *HN*, if it reflects the reality of its author's time, could be the oldest document that tells us that Viken, *i.e.* the law province of Borgarting, at that time comprised four counties. We know only of Ranrike, Vingulmark and Vestfold. Not until Snorri do we meet grounds for the assertion that Grenland belonged to Viken around 1164.[104] All the same, we should note the following: by using the terms *patria* and *prouincie* for the Uplands as well, the

[97] II 1 and elsewhere. [98] Storm 1880, xxiii, Koht 1919–20, 113–16, de Vries 1967 II, 253.

[99] Steinnes 1946–48, 31. Koht 1949–51, 50 accepts this. [100] III 2. [101] Robberstad 1949–51, 191.

[102] It was published in 1881 by F. Metcalfe, but at first in a shorter, composite version by G. Storm in 1880 under the title of *Acta Sancti Olavi Regis et Martyris*. While Metcalfe had a manuscript copy from *c.* 1200 at his disposal (Oxford, Corpus Christi College, 209, ff. 57–90), Storm's edition rests for the most part on printed editions from the 1400s and 1500s and even later.

[103] *HN* I 11 and *Passio Olavi*, ed. Metcalfe 1881, 68. The term *provincia* is also used of Europe, but this could also reflect a misunderstanding on the part of the copyist (*Passio Olavi ibid.*, 100).

[104] Storm 1880, 77 note 3. *cf.* Snorri (*Heimskringla, Saga Magnús konungs Erlingssonar*, 2).

author of *HN* draws a parallel with the large law provinces of the coastland. This could well be quite deliberate on his part; he wants to show that in this way the Uplands are on an equal footing with the coastland. We should merely note this point about the Uplands; we will return to it later.

There is, however, another matter of interest to discuss. If we look at the figures that are given in connection with the jurisdictional division of Norway, we find the following:

The law provinces of		
Viken	=	4 counties
Gulatingslag	=	6 counties
Trøndelag	=	11 counties
Hålogaland	=	1 county[105]
Uplands	=	12 counties

Assuming that the borders more or less correspond, both Viken and Gulatingslag at this time were also bishoprics, one (with 4 counties) and two (with a total of 6 counties) respectively. If we consider Trøndelag and Hålogaland as a unit, we have Trøndelag bishopric (with a total of 12 counties). After the Church and national council in 1153 we also find the Uplands as a separate bishopric (with 12 counties). The lowest common denominator for these figures is 12, and 12 is the exact number of *hinna vitrasto manna or hueirium biskupsstole i Norighi* ("those wisest men from every bishopric in Norway"), who convened at the Church and national council in 1153.[106] Altogether this makes sixty persons from all the bishoprics in Norway, provided the Uplands are represented. And the latter seems to be the only reasonable conclusion, in particular if the new bishop of Hamar (in the Uplands) had already been appointed before the Church and national council. We know that Bishop Arnald of Greenland, the first bishop-to-be of the Uplands, was present, and probably in this latter capacity (see § 6.2.6. below). With a newly established diocese and new guidelines for the Church in general, there was a conspicuous need for those in responsibility in the Uplands to be informed about the matter. So if we now look at *HN* and imagine twelve persons being sent off from each of the five law provinces of Viken, Gulating,[107] the Uplands, Trøndelag and Hålogaland, this also represents a total of sixty people. The question now is whether this is coincidental or whether a connection can be made with *HN* from the naming of *tolf hinna vitrasto manna or hueirium biskupsstole i Norighi.* The fact that it was decided in 1153 that the twelve men were to come from each dio-

[105] In *HN*, the number of counties in Hålogaland is not specified. In our copy of *HN* it is written that in the coastland there are a total of XXX. This seems to be an error for XXII, which Munch has already corrected in his critical apparatus. I choose to follow Munch and regard Hålogaland as one continuous county and law province.

[106] NGL I 447, A and Johnsen 1945, 179. In another place it is said that these appointed men were *or løgum ollum* ("from all the law provinces") (NGL I 182 and Johnsen 1945, 178).

[107] To which Valdres, Hallingdal and probably Numedal belonged, but these are not reckoned as separate counties in *HN*.

cese, and not from the separate law provinces as listed in *HN*, is understandable from the standpoint of fairness, consideration for the population density and the number of Christians; Gulatingslag as a law province gained only twelve representatives, but as two dioceses twenty-four; similarly, Hålogaland as law province would also have twelve; but taking the above account as our point of departure, it would only have one representative. If it is a legitimate argument that there is a relationship between the jurisdictional division in *HN* and the twelve appointed men who were to attend the Church and national council in 1153, then this means, in turn, that it is possible, quite literally, to calculate exactly how many men were intended from each county: three from each county in Viken (3 x 4), four from each county in Gulatingslag ((2 x 6) x 2), one from each county in Trøndelag (1 x 11) (as well as one representative from Hålogaland) and one from each county in the Uplands (1 x 12). This does not seem unreasonable, considering the population and populated areas.

6.1.4. Natural resources

The country is rich in natural resources: plenty of fish in the sea and many kinds of fur-bearing animals that the Finns paid taxes on. Here we can make comparison with Adam, who in two places relates how attractive and expensive fur was (IV 18 and 21). There were deposits of silver some distance from Oslo (perhaps it was just a matter of digging it up), and gold in the river Vorma in eastern Norway. In *HN* an otherwise unknown legend tells of how some Saxons in their day discovered gold there and took it all away (III 7) *furtim* ("stealthily").

The abundance of natural resources, in other words, meant good growth conditions for Church incomes and church construction — in fact, even for the Pope,[108] and there is not a single word about the greedy clerics, such as we find in Adam (IV 31). The information about the richness of the country might be read in contrast to Adam, who relates that the Swedes are rich, but the Norwegians poor (IV 21 & 31).

We note that Oslo is admittedly mentioned by name (Stavanger is not), but we should also note that the deposits of silver were not located in Oslo, but (III 8) *iuxta ciuitatem Asloiam* ("not far from the town of Oslo"), since the silver deposits are mentioned in connection with the Uplands and found in the mountains there. In other words, deposits of the two precious metals occurred in the Uplands.

6.1.5. The coastland

The coastland is called by a Greek word (II 1), *Decapolis* ("the land of ten townships"), which suggests a civilized society of faithful believers; we find this term used in the Bible and in medieval literature about part of the Holy Land. The account of Hålogaland probably rectifies Adam's confusion about this part of the country: he calls it *Halagland* and is not sure whether it is an island or the most northern part of Norway (IV 38). Trøndelag, too, belongs to the coastland and is

[108] *Cf.* the exact wording in Magnus Erlingsson's coronation oath of 1163/1164 concerning "Peter's pence" introduced with Breakspear's visit (Johnsen 1945, 249).

the most important law province in the country according to *HN*. Later in the narrative we hear, perhaps, the reason for this (see 8.1. below). The author of *HN* could be the first Norwegian to put down in writing the widespread perception among the population that Trøndelag was the most important area.[109] This attitude persisted; we find it both in *Heimskringla* and later works.

As the Uplands will be dealt with in a later chapter (8.6.), we shall now pass over to the third inhabited area of Norway.

6.1.6. The Finns

A relatively long chapter (IV) deals with the third inhabited area of Norway, the *silue Finnorum* (in the present edition translated by "Finnmarken") or the *uastissima solitudo affinis Norwegie* ("immense wilderness on the borders of Norway").[110] We gather that this wilderness divides Norway into two parts, separating the Christian native Norwegians from the pagan peoples. In this wilderness live the *Finni* (in the present edition translated by the Norwegian term "Finns"), *i.e.* the Samis or the Lapps, not to be confused with the people of Finland.[111] We do not hear who they are, or where they come from. They have just lived there, it seems, from of old in a separate part of the Norwegian kingdom. Nor do we hear of the exact location or the exact borders of this area, and the question is now, where in Norway this third inhabited zone might be according to *HN*. It is quite clear that the wilderness lies inside the border of Norway. But where, and bordering what? The following might serve as an answer: at the beginning of *HN* the author writes that Norway borders on Sweden in the east, but no Swedish area is mentioned north of Jämtland and Ångermanland. Further, that the Norwegian coastland, the first inhabited zone, takes up the whole area from the Danish border (the River Göta) in the south to Vegestav and Bjarmeland in the north. In the coastland, Trøndelag, which in *HN* consists of eleven counties, takes up the whole area between the coast and the Swedish border, as far as I can see. No Finns are reported in *HN* as living here. But the eastern border of Hålogaland, north of

[109] *Cf.* also Adam IV 33 concerning the city of Nidaros.

[110] *Cf.* commentary on III 9 and IV 1 for the translation of *silue Finnorum* and *affinis Norwegie*, respectively.

[111] "Finn" is the old Norse term designating the Sami people, who formerly were widely called "Lapps" in the international scholarly literature. As such it must not be confused with the modern use of "finner" in Norwegian and "Finns" in English, which of course relates to the inhabitants of Finland. The term "Lapps" seems to have its origin in a more easterly context, and was extensively used on the Swedish side and in some medieval Latin texts. In early modern times the Norwegian authorities also used it to distinguish the reindeer-herding mountain Samis ("mountain Lapps") from the settled Sami population along the coast and the terms "finner" and "lapper" were to a certain extent used interchangeably by the Norwegian population. After World War II the Norwegian and English renderings of the Samis' own name for themselves, in the forms "samer" and "the Samis" respectively, have gained ever stronger foothold, and are now widely accepted both among Norwegians and by international scholarship (I owe this piece of information to Lars Ivar Hansen, *cf.* also his article on "Samer" in 1999).

Trøndelag, is not defined clearly. In Hålogaland Finns live together with Christians, but they all represent the first inhabited zone. So far it looks as if there is some room left for the Finns east of Hålogaland and north of Trøndelag, Jämtland and Ångermanland.

The Uplands, the second inhabited zone, take up the inland area, stretching all the way across the interior behind the coastland and along the Swedish border to the east (along Götaland) to Trøndelag in the north. No Finns are reported in *HN* as living here either. Before we move on, it must be added and emphasized that the fact that the Finns are only mentioned in connection with Hålogaland and the third inhabited area in *HN* does not mean that they did not live elsewhere in Norway. The author just does not mention it.[112]

In paragraph I 7 the author writes that the Kirjalers, the Kvens, the Horned Finns and the two kinds of Bjarms live east of Norway, *i.e.* probably in the area stretching from both sides of the White Sea over the area around the northern part of the Gulf of Bothnia to Karelia in eastern Finland.[113] That means that the third inhabited zone, the *solitudo* or *silue Finnorum*, seems to be the area north of Trøndelag in Norway and north of Jämtland and Ångermanland in Sweden, covering the interior east of Hålogaland as far as these pagan peoples in the east, and to Vegestav and Bjarmeland in the north. That means in turn that the *silue Finnorum* or *solitudo* where we find the big concentration of Finns in *HN*, cover largely the huge area which was called "Finnmarken" in the Middle Ages and which was thought of as the northern part of the Scandinavian peninsula, stretching all the way north of Trøndelag and Jämtland from the Norwegian coast to the White Sea. This area was of old regarded by Norwegians as belonging to Norway; we find the same expansionist attitude in the time of Håkon Håkonsson, in the thirteenth century.[114] We also find this wilderness delineated with all its borders in *Egil's saga*.[115] They correspond to those mentioned here in *HN*. No wonder that the author of *HN* calls this *solitudo uastissima* ("immense wilderness").

As for the terms *solitudo* and *silue*, they both cover the Norwegian word for a forested wilderness, namely "mark" (Old Norse "mǫrk") as we find it in "Finnmark" (Old Norse "Finnmǫrk") (*i.e.* "the Finns' forests" or "wilderness").[116] This area was also known as just the "mark", as we understand it from *Egil's saga*.[117] One might ask why the author of *HN* did not use the Latinized Norwegian term *Finmarchia* which *e.g.* Saxo used in his *Gesta Danorum* around 1200.[118] The answer might be that the author of *HN* probably knew it, but that according to one tradi-

[112] Except perhaps for the *fetonissa* ("sorceress") in Hadeland (XI 7) who is a Finn, without it being said so, *cf. Ágrip* ch. 2 where her descent is mentioned explicitly.

[113] *Cf.* Commentary on I 7. [114] *Cf. Kulturhist. leksikon* 1956–78 (*s.v. Finnmark*). [115] Ch. 14.

[116] We have the same word in *e.g.* Hedmark, Telemark and above all in "Markir" (pl., the forested region on the Swedish border in eastern Norway). The term is also used as the opposite of cultivated land, which fits in with ch. I 4, where it is said that the Finns do not cultivate the earth. The term also seems to mean "border" or "bordering forest" in Norway (cf. *Kulturhist. leksikon* 1956–78 (*s.v. mark*)). [117] Chs. 14 and 17.

[118] Book V.13.1 (*Finmarchia*) and IX.4.23 (*Finnimarchia*).

tion, the tradition Saxo reports, *Finnmarchia* was a kingdom of its own, independent of Norway. This would not fit into *HN*'s design, as the author claims it is a part of the Norwegian kingdom. And what a kingdom, stretching from the utmost west and south (Greenland, Africa) to the Great Ocean surrounding the whole world to the utmost north and to the far East, so far away that its eastern neighbours seem to live at the back of beyond; *que gentes post istos habitent, nichil certum habemus* ("we know nothing for sure about the races living beyond these") (I 8).

We understand that good contact had already been established between the native Norwegians and the Finns through commerce and fishing. The language was not a problem (contrary to Adam's belief in IV 32); and if it were possible to communicate with the Finns, this should provide one means of Christianizing them. And what a huge area to incorporate under the Church! That it was now the Finns' turn to be Christianized becomes clear from the macabre account of their dreadful magic gand ('magic wand', here also 'unclean spirit') and the anecdote about their fishing with the Christians. Furthermore, we also come to see that these Finns pay (IV 11) *maxima tributa omni anno* ("a large tribute every year") to *regibus Norwegie, quibus et subiecti sunt* ("the Norwegian kings, who are their overlords"). Put another way, the authorities controlled also the pagan Finns. It would seem from the foregoing that the author of *HN* is well informed about the country's tax revenue (the taxes were annual), and that there was more than one king in Norway at this time. A closer reading of *HN* shows that the expression *regibus* ("kings") recurs in the plural everywhere the payment of taxes is mentioned, and that paying taxes is associated each time with the present tense form of the verb. However, this could also be a historic present (used as a perfect), and it is a convenient occasion for its use just here. Nevertheless, it is also possible that it is the Kings Inge, Sigurd and Øystein who are being mentioned here. Yet it should be emphasized that *regibus Norwegie* could also be a kind of idiomatic expression.

After this chapter about the Finns we hear nothing more in *HN* of the third inhabited zone and its people. The coastland and the Uplands, however, are mentioned throughout the historical part of *HN*, and nearly always kept apart from each other.

6.1.7. Mirabilia

The mention of various legends from the whole country points out its manifold characteristics. In some of these legends — for example, the one about the farm at Møre and the story about the beaver — there could be allusions to known works from the Middle Ages. We find parts of these legends in Giraldus Cambrensis's (Gerald of Wales) *Topographia Hibernica* ("Irish Topography") from 1187, in *Chronicon Lethrense* ("the Lejre-Chronicle") from *c.* 1170, and in the Norwegian *Konungs skuggsiá* ("King's Mirror") from *c.* 1250; however, no researcher has succeeded in demonstrating any direct connection between these and *HN*. The legends could also derive from oral traditions which the author of *HN* was personally familiar with. In general the mention of a variety of fish and land animals should be seen in the light of Solinus, Honorius and Adam; animal life often featured prominently in their works. The author of *HN* emphasizes those stories which are particularly characteristic of the Norwegian nation. Other legends, such as the one about "the Land of Maidens" and the one about "the Land of Giants", resemble those we find in Adam and might, as mentioned above, be read against this background (IV 19 & 41). All in all, these improbable anecdotes remind us of Solinus's *mirabilia.*

Finally it should be mentioned that when the author of *HN* says that he recounts these small stories (IV 24) about the Finns' *profana secta* ("unholy band") for *plus remotis* ("those who live farther away"), the latter expression could just as well be directed towards people in southern Norway as the inhabitants of Rome; but it can also be understood as an answer to Adam's challenge (IV 32): *Cumque diversa prorsus et insueta nostris multa ibi videantur, ab eisdem patriae incolis haec et alia plenius dicenda relinquo* ("And since many things there seem to be quite different and unusual for us, I leave it to the natives to give a more detailed account of this and other matters").

6.2. The tributary islands

6.2.1. Previous research

In chapter V *De tributariis insulis* ("On the tributary islands") and those following in *HN* we find the Solund Islands, the Hebrides, the Orkneys, the Faeroes and Iceland. The placing of the Orkneys and Iceland in the text is the same as in Adam, but the latter also includes Greenland in the islands towards the west (IV 35–37). In *HN*, as was noted earlier, Greenland is not a tax-contributing island. We have now come to that part of *HN* which has been a real problem for researchers, partly because of its length — particularly with regard to the Orkneys — but also on account of a host of points that are perceived as unclear. Maurer dates *HN* on the basis of the chapter about Iceland; he believes that *HN* had to have been written after 1264, since it was only then that Iceland began paying taxes to Norway.[119] Meissner believe much the same.[120] Bugge 1873, and also Maurer 1875 and Jónsson 1923, believe that it had to have been written after the year 1211, since the Icelandic annals tell of a similar volcanic eruption in the ocean off Iceland to the one we hear about in *HN*.[121] Meissner, who broaches the same subject, nevertheless considers it strange that this volcanic eruption is not mentioned elsewhere.[122] For his part, Storm asserts that *HN* can only have been written after 1152, when the Hebrides began to pay taxes to the Norwegian king.[123] Some researchers claim that the author of *HN* was a highly uninformed person who did not know about the Shetlands and mistakenly grouped the Hebrides under the Orkneys.[124] Then again, others saw in this long chapter on the Orkneys an indication that the author of *HN* came from there, that he died before he had finished *HN*, and that this is why a manuscript remained in the Orkneys.[125]

[119] Maurer 1875, 9. [120] 1902, 40. [121] P. 37 and 596. [122] Meissner 1902, 39.

[123] 1880, 88 note 4. Hanssen 1949, 18 agrees with him.

[124] For example, Bugge 1873, 41 and Meissner 1902, 42.

[125] Munch 1850, II and VI and Mogk 1904, 810.

6.2.2. The Solund Islands and the Solund Sea

I shall attempt here to show that in these chapters we have perhaps arrived at the crux of the matter, but that it is well packaged and thus well hidden. These are the chapters in which the author of *HN* seems to get down to business. If it is true that *HN* was written in connection with the establishment of an archdiocese in Norway, then on the basis of the aforementioned claim on the Hebrides and the Orkneys from the bishop of St. Andrews and the archbishop of York, we should expect that the author would do his utmost to show that they belonged to Norway. To start with it should be mentioned that it is of particular interest to read *HN* with Adam as a backcloth (IV 35–36). One would have thought that the author of *HN* would have benefited from Adam, especially with respect to such out-of-the-way islands. But no; for the most part the author of *HN* only takes the number of islands from Adam — and barely at that. The remainder is left unused and uncontested. Why is this? As far as I can tell, the answer must be that Adam here is completely "harmless" in his statements, and what he has to say is of no interest or use to the author of *HN*'s purpose. Here the latter wants to draw on other facts.

At first glance it seems perplexing that it is the Solund Islands that are mentioned out of the many islands off the Norwegian coast, considering the fact that many islands or clusters of islands (such as Karmøy, Stord and Lofoten) could just as well have been specified. Furthermore it is strange that the Solund Islands are named in connection with the tributary islands. Geographically and historically they have always been considered a natural part of mainland Norway, and no one else staked a claim to them. Mention of these islands seems merely to be a pretext for introducing the term *Solundicum mare* ("the Solund Sea"),[126] which lies just inside and just outside this cluster of islands. According to the author it was the Norwegians who gave the name to the sea. This must have been done in the remote past when names began to be used. It indicates an historical claim. The sentence about the Solund Sea can be read against the background of Adam who merely calls it *infinitum occeanum, qui totum mundum amplectitur* (IV 35). In *HN* V 1 this sea *inter Norwegiam et Iberniam fluit* ("flows between Norway and Ireland"). To be sure, the author does not say explicitly that it stretches all the way to Ireland, but this is the impression he gives — quite deliberately no doubt;[127] in this way a firm connection with the islands in the west is established, which is of greater interest to us in this context. The objection could be made that the sentences related to the Solund Islands and the Solund Sea should have appeared just before the heading *De tributariis insulis* and have been incorporated in the last part of the previous chapter, in which the author has mentioned the many islands which lie just off the Norwegian coast, but then the heading would break the very connection with the tributary islands that the author perhaps wished to establish.

[126] Ch. V 1, *cf.* also Meissner 1902, 41.

[127] In Adam's time, it was thought that Ireland was situated due west of the Orkneys (Bjørnbo 1909, 156–57 and Adam IV 35).

6.2.3. The Orkney kingdom

In this, so to speak, "Norwegian" sea, the Orkneys lie (V 2), *numero plusquam XXX* ("totalling over thirty"). That the number is approximate is probably due to the fact that the author's sources diverge: in Honorius's *Imago mundi* (I 31) is written: *Orcades triginta tres* ("the Orkneys comprise thirty-three islands"), whereas Adam writes (IV 36 schol. 150): *Orchadae sunt insulae, quarum XX sunt desertae, XVI coluntur* ("Of the Orkneys, twenty are uninhabited, sixteen are inhabited"). The exact number in Honorius and Adam can only apply to the Orkneys, since (the Isle of) Man and the Hebrides alone constitute thirty-two islands,[128] but we cannot automatically assume that the author of *HN* knew this. It would seem that it was important for him to delineate the area for the new archdiocese and include the two other island clusters, the Shetlands and the Hebrides. Together with the Orkneys they would include "more than thirty in number", which is correct. In *HN* the term *Orchades*, earlier researchers believe, includes the Orkneys, the Shetlands and the Hebrides. If we read *HN* carefully, we will see that this is only partly correct, and the joining together of these three clusters of islands is hardly due to a lack of knowledge on the part of the author. It is true that the Shetlands are not mentioned explicitly in this chapter, and this might be deliberate; the author could see no purpose in doing so. Moreover this is quite justifiable, since the Shetlands at the time in which the author seems to be writing were part of the Orkney kingdom. They were not "separated" until 1195.[129]

The author of *HN* writes that the Orkneys in his time consisted of two domains (V 3): *Que quidem diuersis incolis acculte nunc in duo regna sunt diuise: Sunt enim merediane insule regulis sublimate, brumales vero comitum presidio decorate, qui vtrique regibus Norwegie non modica persoluunt tributa* ("They are populated by different peoples and now split into two domains; the southern isles (*i.e.* the Hebrides) have been elevated by petty kings, the northern graced by the protection of earls, both of whom pay no mean tribute to the kings of Norway"). Here the reader may assume, implicitly, that they formerly constituted a single kingdom, as opposed to *nunc* ("now"). The author's choice of words and expressions is quite ingenious in the above quotation, for here he kills two birds with one stone, a fact which has escaped the notice of a number of earlier researchers; instead of calling the one kingdom — the southernmost of the three island clusters — the *Hebrides*, which is the Latin name for it (this expression is used by Bede, among others), he translates the corresponding Norwegian name "Sudrøyene" literally — and quite correctly — as *merediane insule* ("the southern isles"), the cluster of islands that lies to the south of the Orkneys, but also south of Norway. Thus he not only gives a closer connection to Norway, but this expression must be understood to mean that the islands constitute the southernmost of the Orkneys, as opposed to *brumales* ("the northern"), *i.e.* the Orkneys and the Shetlands. And, politically speaking, this is quite right, because down the years the Hebrides at various times were subject to the Earl of Orkney; but at that exact

[128] Johnsen 1966, 5–6.

[129] *Cf.* Koht 1919–20, 108.

time it had its own Norwegian petty king.[130] We must also bear in mind – and this is important — that these *merediane insule* are mentioned under the heading *De tributariis insulis*, not under *De Orcadibus insulis* ("On the Orkney Islands"). Only afterwards does the chapter about the Orkney Islands appear, and when it does, the Hebrides are not mentioned, *i.e.* the chapter entitled *De tributariis insulis* seems to deal with the three island clusters as nation(s), but the chapter entitled *De Orcadibus insulis* with the Orkneys themselves as a geographical island cluster. In other words, the name *Orchades* is used both for the Orkney kingdom (which by then was divided in two) and for the geographical island cluster the Orkney Islands. As we shall see, this gives the author a great deal of leeway.

There are even more things we should note. For one, the author writes that these tributary islands were populated by *diuersis incolis* ("different peoples"), but he doesn't dwell on the term; this can be interpreted to mean that the author is not interested in emphasizing the fact that quite a few Celts lived there. Another feature is the lofty expressions he uses in connection with the kingdom and earldom on the Hebrides and the Orkneys respectively; these kingdoms are *sublimate* ("elevated") with petty kings and *decorate* ("graced") with earls. This could redound to the glory of the king of the Hebrides and the Orkney earls, whom we recall were perhaps all present in Norway in 1153. If that is not the case, these expressions, at the very least, indicate respect and good will on the part of the author. A similar "grand style" is not employed when writing about the other tributary islands, where payment of taxes and/or the Norwegian proportion of the population and the Christianizing process are emphasized.

Furthermore, *HN* seems to indicate that both island kingdoms paid taxes to *regibus Norwegie*. Not only that, but it was *non modica* ("no mean"). Here the author shows, once again, that he is well-informed about his subject. In fact, it would not be surprising if he also knew the exact size of the tax! Storm claims that the people of the Hebrides first paid taxes from the time of their king's visit in 1152/1153, but in the same note he concedes that nothing is written about this, only that the king swore allegiance to King Inge.[131] This claim of Storm's caused Koht and Hanssen to fix upon the year 1152 as the earliest possible date for the *HN*. Storm seems, however, to have been mistaken here, for by the time Magnus Berrføtt conquered the Orkneys, the Hebrides and the Isle of Man around the year 1100, the Norwegian kings' claim of sovereignty had been established. Not only did the Orkney earls have the islands as a fiefdom from the Norwegian king, but for quite some time the king of the Isle of Man and the Hebrides had paid ten marks in gold at each new accession to the throne.[132] Just how circumstances were in the turbulent 1130s we do not know with any certainty. In general we know very little about the payment of taxes from here in the first half of the 1100s.[133] But that does not mean that it did not take place. King Øystein's aforementioned trip to the Orkneys in 1151 could have been intended to strengthen connections. But

[130] Storm 1873a, 22 and 1880, xxiii–xxiv believes that *HN* had to have been written before 1265 because it makes mention of these Norwegian petty kings.

[131] 1880, 88 note 4. [132] Gunnes 1986, 337–38. [133] *Cf.* Helle 1974, 124–25 and 198.

if Storm should nevertheless prove correct in his assertion that taxes were paid for the first time (in later years) starting with the king of the Hebrides' visit in 1152/1153, this could mean that the author of *HN* must have known ahead of time that it would take place, or it could mean that he himself was present during the king's visit. If so, then *HN* must have been written exactly during that time. A completely different explanation, one that has apparently been totally neglected, is the thesis that the taxes mentioned in the above quotation were perhaps only paid by the persons referred to, namely the two earls, since the expression *utrique* ("both") could perhaps in reality point back just to *comitum presidio* ("the protection of earls"), and not also to *regulis* ("petty kings"), as has previously been the conclusion of earlier researchers. During the years 1090–1158 the Orkneys were ruled by two earls. In other words the two-earl rule, for the author of *HN* and his contemporaries, was an established practice; they had not experienced anything else, and the author could assume as a matter of course that this was something everyone knew. But it could also be that his intention was to create the impression in the mind of his readers that both the Hebrides and the Orkneys paid taxes to the Norwegian kings. The author of *HN* had a wonderful way with words and used this gift purposefully. Grammatically speaking it is completely justifiable to let *utrique* refer back just to the earls, of whom there were only two at this time. In this way the author could perhaps create an impression of something other than what he seemed to be saying, and yet do so without having to eat his words.

But now we come to the point: we know that the Orkney earl had his bishop with him on his trip to Norway, perhaps in 1153, after their journey to the Holy Land; but the king of the Hebrides appeared without one. Why? Because no doubt he had his own kingdom, but no bishop who was acknowledged by the Norwegians. What, then, was the result of Breakspear's visit? The king of the Hebrides left for home with a newly-ordained Norwegian bishop. The unit that the author of *HN* speaks of in connection with the Orkneys, the Shetlands and the Hebrides and their relationship with the Norwegian kingdom seems to be a political unit, with payment of taxes to Norway. Nevertheless, these few lines could also be referring to Church politics; both island clusters had to belong to a potential Norwegian archdiocese, as we saw in connection with the mainland; Jämtland did not belong, but Greenland did. We certainly cannot call the author of *HN* an ignorant or unskilled person, and he was far from being "without any appreciation of his own work".[134] He managed to present the three island clusters as a political unit, but one that had now become subject, as two kingdoms, to the Norwegian king, as far as the payment of taxes was concerned. Before we leave the little chapter *De tributariis insulis*, we should also note that the term *Orchades*, according to *HN* (V 2), stems from the otherwise unknown Earl *Orchanus* ("Orkan").

6.2.4. The Orkney Islands

After this the author moves on to discuss the Orkneys, the richest and most important of the three island clusters. As we already know, he has noted that these

[134] Bugge 1873, 24.

islands, along with the Hebrides, were populated by *diuersis incolis*. Once again bringing up the question of population in connection with the Orkneys, he first mentions the Pents and the Papes, and ends with the Norwegians. This could be deliberate on the author's part, with his purpose accomplished without having to finesse the truth, the Celts were not to be mentioned. The Pents were pygmies, it is pointed out clearly, and we do not know (VI 4) *penitus* ("at all") where they came from. Neither the English nor the Scots, then, could claim descent from them, or vice versa. The Pents gave its original name to the island cluster, *terra Petorum* ("Pentland"). One indication that the author is speaking the truth here is the name of the Pentland Firth, which is duly mentioned. Likewise, we should note that this *omnium maxima uorago* ("most gigantic of all whirlpools) *seiungit* ("separates") the Scots from the Orkneys on account of its water spouts, just as *profundissimus septemtrionalis sinus* ("the immensely deep fjord to the north") with its (VI 3 & II 10) *ineuitabiles uoragines* ("inescapable whirlpools") separates Norway from Bjarmeland, whereas on the other hand we saw that the Solund Sea in some way or other seemed to knit Norway together with the islands. In other words the Orkneys more naturally belonged to Norway than to Scotland. A further emphasis on the close connection the author tries to make between Norway and the Orkneys lies in his use of the Latinized Norwegian term *Peti* ("the Pents"), instead of the usual Latin *Picti* ("Picts", "the painted ones").

For their part the Papes, from whom the island Papey is named (mentioned as yet another piece of evidence that the author of *HN* is telling the truth) were of African origin and were supporters of the Jewish religion, so here too, the Celts must be left out of the picture. Where the author gets his version of the Papes from is unknown.[135] Ari Frode uses the term "Papes" to describe Irish monks in Iceland (ch. 1).

But then the Norwegians arrived in the Orkneys, even as early as Harald Hårfagre's (Fairhair's) time. This occasioned the total destruction of the natives (VI 8), at any rate in the Orkneys, and here the narrative broadens markedly in scope; the Norwegian vikings were descended from the Earl of Møre, conquered the islands and settled down, overcame the Irish, Scots and English and took part of their land; and one of them, Gange-Rolv (Rolf the Walker), conquered Normandy and gave it its name. It must have been around this time that the island cluster, according to *HN*, changed its name from Pentland to the Orkneys. In other words the earl, Orkan, appears to be of Norwegian descent. If this observation is valid, it means that not only the names Iceland, Greenland, "Sudrøyene" (the Hebrides), the Faeroes and Normandy are of Norwegian origin, but also the name "the Orkney Islands". This emphasizes their Norwegian identity.

We also note the use of the Latinized Norwegian name *Roda* (VI 10) for Rouen, instead of the Latin *Rothomum, Rodonum* or *Rotomagum*, as well as the use of the Norman nickname (VI 17) *longosped* ("Long spear", Norwegian: "Langspyd") for the Latin *longa spatha*. This use might well derive from the sources,[136] but it fits very well with the author's purpose none the less. We should also bear in

[135] *Cf.* Crawford 1987, 168, and, 211 in particular.

[136] *Cf.* Ellehøj 1965, 170–71.

mind that Gange-Rolv was made (VI 20) *comes Normandie* ("count/earl of Normandy"). The term *comes* and not *dux*, which alternated with *comes* during the eleventh and twelfth centuries,[137] is surely due to the author's source, but it, too, fits quite well, as it suggests associations with Rolv's Norwegian lineage and the earl lineage at Møre. Gange-Rolv also made inroads all the way into Friesland, where he died. We should note that the term *tyranni* (VI 13), used of him and his men, means vikings, and in *HN* this could be a positive thing. It could hardly be used in that sense later in the century, when the civil wars had started, for by then this word had acquired a bad odour. But most important of all, we understand that Gange-Rolv's descendants took over the English throne. The last-mentioned of these is Henry I (1100–35). And what a king he would be, according to the Englishmen's own major prophet, Merlin, a *leo iusticie* ("Lion of Justice"). Furthermore, in the Orkneys the populace to that very day were subject to *illorum posteritatis dominio* ("the lordship of their descendants"), yet (VI 21) *iure tributario regibus Norwegie deseruiunt* ("with the proviso that they are bound to pay tribute to the Norwegian kings"). Thus the connection with Norway remained intact. We note the emphasis that the author puts on this; he repeats that the Orkneys paid taxes to Norway. This is one of the few places in *HN* where we find repetition.

In addition, later in Book One the author has the great Christian king, Olav Tryggvason, being born in the Orkneys (XV 14), as opposed to another tradition, which says that he was born in Norway.[138] The author's version, with which we are unfamiliar from any other source, strengthens the connection between the Orkneys and Norway. Furthermore he credits this same Olav with having Christianized everyone in Norway, along with everyone in the tributary lands, *i.e.* (XVII 31) *Hatlendenses, Orchadenses, Fereyingenses ac Tilenses* ("the people in Hetland (an older Norwegian name for Shetland), the Orkneys, the Faeroes and Iceland"). Here it must be added that by terming the population of the Shetlands *Hatlendenses*, the author probably indicates the connection with Norway again[139]. The claim for Olav's Christianizing the Shetlands tells us that the author of *HN* knew these islands well, and it is the first time we find what — on the surface — seems to be a slip on his part: having previously linked together the following island clusters, the Hebrides, the Shetlands and the Orkneys, stressing their unity, he now splits off the Shetlands. Yet this is hardly done without reason; in fact it can be explained by saying that this all took place in Olav Tryggvason's time, not at the time of writing, and that his source related it this way. We find this very same list in Oddr's *Saga*;[140] and, as mentioned above, they have a common source. Yet we also find Greenland mentioned by Oddr, but the author of *HN* had already told about its Christianization. We can see how he sticks to his approach exactly; there is little room for repetition. If the Shetlands are mentioned because this is

[137] Bates 1982, 148–49.
[138] For example, *Ágrip* ch. 17.
[139] *Cf.* the name *Hatlandia* ("Hadeland"), the name of a Norwegian county, XI 7.
[140] Oddr, *Saga Óláfs Tryggvasonar* ch. 54.

how the source read, then this is a good example of how faithful the author of *HN* is to his sources. Even in *Ágrip* we find the same names.[141] As for the sources for *HN*, earlier researchers have noted how its author calls the prophet Merlin *rex* ("king"), and Henry I a *leo iusticie* ("Lion of Justice") (VI 19). We find the latter expression in Ordericus Vitalis's *Historia ecclesiastica* (1114–41),[142] while the former, as mentioned in an earlier note, occurs in the poem *Vita Merlini*, which is thought to have been conceived in 1148–51 by Geoffrey of Monmouth. This alone, however, does not justify the claim that *HN* must have been written after that time, since its author could well have derived the term *rex* concerning such a well-known prophet as Merlin from an oral source.

6.2.5. The Faeroes

No one else but Norway claimed the Faeroes, which could be why they do not receive as much mention as the Orkneys. The Scots and English cannot claim that the residents of the Faeroes are their descendants, but according to *HN* the Norwegians can; the name of the Faeroes in their "own" language is "Fereyiar" (or "Færeyjar"), and "fær" is Old Norse for "får" (*i.e.* sheep), and "eyjar" for modern Norwegian "øyer" (*i.e.* islands).[143] This is further pointed out in the heading *De insulis ouium* ("On the Islands of Sheep") and proves Norwegian descent. A point is also made of the Faeroes consisting of a total of eighteen islands.[144] There is apparently no doubt about the number here. Moreover, we are given to understand that they *certis temporibus* ("at set times") paid taxes to *regibus nostris* ("our kings") (VII 3). The islands were rich enough for that, since the populace made a living from sheep farming; some even had thousands of sheep and, as we know, from these we get wool, which, according to Adam, was highly valued for the sake of barter (IV 8). Once again the author of *HN* shows his familiarity with the Norwegian kings' tax revenues.

6.2.6. Iceland

The last of the tributary islands to be focused on is Iceland. According to the author it was the Norwegians who named the island Iceland, because it was they who discovered the island, settled there, and populated it as it is today, all during the course of just fifty years, and their descendants still live there — quite a historical claim. We note that the author does not claim that the Norwegians Ingolv and Hjorleiv were the first to discover the island; it was the Swede Gardar and the Norwegians Nadd-oddr and Floke who did, but they soon left the island.[145] The author does not mention, however, that Irish hermits preceded them, which he surely must have known about. We see here again that he does what he can to exclude the Celts. In other words he credits the Norwegians with Christianizing the island; this took place, as we just saw, in the time of Olav Tryggvason, who

[141] *Ágrip* ch. 19. [142] PL 188 col. 920.

[143] *Fereyiar* is my emendation of *A*'s *farcar*; for a discussion of this see Commentary on VII 1.

[144] If the number "eighteen" (which Munch inserted) was not originally there, some other exact number is missing. [145] Ari, ch. 2–4.

sent the priest Tangbrand there. In *HN* this comes across as though it were the first thing that King Olav did after he arrived in Norway. The author could well have been trying to give this impression deliberately, as it emphasizes not only Olav's zealous piety but also the close contact between Iceland and Norway.

We note that Iceland appears in the section on the tributary islands, even though it is not explicitly stated (as in the chapters about the Finns, the Orkneys, the Hebrides and the Faeroes) that the Icelanders paid taxes to Norway. In the chapter on Olav Tryggvason, however, we hear once again that the Icelanders, together with the inhabitants of the Shetlands, Orkneys and Faeroes, are reckoned as *tributarios* ("tax-liable") (XVII 31). This, together with the above-mentioned chapter heading, cannot be explained by saying that it was only true of Olav Tryggvason's time. We must bear in mind, however, that the Old Norse word for "skatt" (*i.e.* tax) is a broad term, one that can encompass both duties in general, fiefdom tribute (the so-called *relivium* or *relevamen*), customs duties on goods and conscription for war service (*tributum*).[146] In *HN* only the term *tributa* is used, which would seem to include the Old Norwegian word for tax in general. During the 1100s the Icelanders paid a rather large fee, called "landøre", when they came to Norway to do business, and they were liable for conscription for military service if they stayed on the mainland during times of war.[147] Such an agreement on Norwegian-Icelandic relations was already entered into under St Olav. It lasted a couple of centuries and was confirmed twice.[148] This must be why the Icelanders are mentioned under *tributariis insulis*. It also explains why the author does not write explicitly about the Icelanders' payment of taxes. It was not a question of an agreed service at an agreed time, such as with the Finns and the inhabitants of the Faeroes, but did include any duties or liability to military conscription for individual Icelanders if and when they came to Norway.

Iceland constituted an ecclesiastical entity which, during the first half of the 1100s, was subject to the archbishop of Lund. The Icelanders had their own dioceses, two in all. Moreover the Icelanders constituted a sort of settler colony from mainland Norway, in what we might call a "semi-subject" relationship.[149] And it seemed only natural to the Norwegians that these two bishops should be subject to a Norwegian archbishop-to-be. But was it the wish of the Icelanders? Hanssen believes the author of *HN* knows little about Iceland and regards this as a sign that *HN* is denoting pre-Icelandic historical record-keeping, as opposed to Theodoricus, who writes completely differently and in detail about, for example, the Christianizing of Iceland.[150] As far as I can tell, the few facts recorded about Icelandic society might also be due to the fact that the author of *HN* is keeping some of his knowledge secret, for fear of presenting Iceland in too independent a light, independent enough to have a claim to an archbishop of its own; after all, the Icelanders certainly had chieftains and their own "allting" (*i.e.* national assembly), and they enjoyed local autonomy. The author of *HN* must surely have known this. If nothing else, he could have chosen to make use of Adam's detailed account,

[146] *Cf.* Johnsen 1966, 9–10. [147] Gunnes 1986 II, 335. *cf.* also Ari, ch. 1.
[148] *Cf.* Gunnes 1986, 335. [149] Storm 1880, xxv. [150] Hanssen 1949, 35.

which, among other things, has this to say about the Icelanders (IV 36): *Episcopum suum habent pro rege; ad illius nutum respicit omnis populus; quicquid ex Deo, ex scripturis, ex consuetudine aliarum gentium ille constituit, hoc pro lege habent* ("They count their bishop as king; the entire population obeys his will; what he decrees based on God and the Scriptures, or based on the customs of other nations, they regard as law"). My impression of the author of *HN*'s attitude here is also consistent with the fact that Iceland does not seem to have been represented by any bishops at the Church and national council in 1153.[151] Neither were the Faeroes or Greenland, in all probability.[152] This is consistent, in turn, with the fact that these four dioceses were not made liable for Peter's pence after the council. The opposite was the case with respect to the Orkneys, the Hebrides and the Isle of Man.[153]

We hear a great deal more about Iceland in *HN*, but this additional information has nothing to do with the archbishop issue or with national legal issues. Rather, it deals with natural phenomena, which we might interpret as a clear-cut diversionary tactic. Much of the content derives verbatim from the contemporaneous Honorius Augustodunensis, even though the author of *HN* refers to Solinus's name and work.[154] This could represent an attempt to associate the island – and thus the Norwegian kingdom — with *mirabilia mundi*.

With regard to Honorius and the author's own time, we read about an underwater volcanic eruption that resulted in a new island, *nostra etate* ("in our own time"), as it says in *HN* (VIII 10). A number of researchers who believe that *HN* was written in the thirteenth century have, as previously stated, used this very event as an argument for claiming that *HN* was written after 1211, since we find this event recorded in the Icelandic annals as the first of its kind. The strange thing is, however, that none of the other and later sagas or documents make any mention of it; only *HN* does. In addition, Koht refuted this theory convincingly in 1927(a) after studying the old annals. His article shows that the farther back we go into the 1100s, the less reliable are the annals. They were recorded quite irregularly. It is easier to believe that this is something the author of *HN* might have had from an oral source — most likely an Icelander. Hanssen suggests that it could have been made up, drawing a comparison with a passage in Seneca, and Koht 1919–20 that it was the Etna eruption in 1169 which was being referred to.[155] In fact Mt Hekla is compared with Etna in the passage just before this. True enough this passage is borrowed from Honorius (who compares Etna with Gehenna),[156] but the comparison also fits well with an account for a pope/cardinal. The chapter concludes with a lengthy discussion about these kinds of mysterious events and with a prayer to God to enlighten our minds so that we can understand them. Here we get the first "religious-minded passage" in *HN*, which is otherwise penned in a secular style. This shows that *HN* was written by a good Christian. The passage corresponds to Adam's reflections in IV 42.

[151] Johnsen 1945, 169–70 and 328.

[152] Yet Arnald, the bishop of Greenland, was present; but he had been or was elected bishop for the Hamar diocese and thus did not actually represent Greenland.

[153] Johnsen 1945, 251–52. [154] Skard 1930, 78–81.

[155] Hanssen 1949, 11 with note and Koht 1919–20, 109. [156] Skard 1930, 80.

7. The scope of the archdiocese

We have now come about two-fifths of the way into *HN*, and so far I have attempted to point out those places which, in my view, partly show the Norwegian demand for a separate Norwegian archdiocese, and partly illustrate the scope of it vis-à-vis the claims of St. Andrews and York; such a Norwegian archdiocese should comprise mainland Norway (though not Jämtland), Greenland, the Orkneys (including the Shetlands), the Hebrides and the Isle of Man, the Faeroes and Iceland. In this connection the author seems to build upon three criteria: an historical, an ecclesiastical-political, and a secular-political. If an area fulfilled at least one of the following requirements, it seemed according to the author to belong to a Norwegian archdiocese: 1. Norwegian origin (the Orkneys, the Faeroes, Iceland, Greenland); 2. The recipient of a Norwegian Christian mission (the Orkneys, the Shetlands, the Faeroes, Iceland, Greenland); and 3. The payment of taxes to Norway (the Orkneys, the Hebrides, the Faeroes, Iceland, the Finns). From this we understand that the Orkneys, the Faeroes and Iceland are strong candidates. The fact that the author uses the expression *Orchades* of the Orkneys both politically and geographically, might be interpreted with the idea that the author also includes the Hebrides in all three criteria. Jämtland clearly does not satisfy any of these. In fact Jämtland did not belong to Norway in an ecclesiastical sense either, but rather to Sweden. Only after the Reformation, in 1570, did it come under the diocese in Nidaros.[157]

Thus it must be concluded that the chapters so far in *HN* quite rightly form a geographical description, but a description that gives to weight the historical, political and ecclesiastical affairs of Norway from their very first beginning to the time of writing.

8. On the kings' lineage

8.1. The Yngling kings

Thus far in *HN* the Danes have not been mentioned. When we move on to the Norwegian list of kings, we must also look for further traces that would suggest a Norwegian demand for a separate archdiocese, *i.e.* a secession from Lund. We shall be taking a close look at Dano-Norwegian relations to see what kind of impression we get of the Danes as we continue our reading of *HN*. In a work such as this, and at a time such as that, we must nevertheless constantly bear in mind that Norwegians are being emphasized at the expense of others, since the Norwegian sense of national pride had already taken deep root by the 1100s. Moreover, from our experience with the author so far we would expect that a possible aversion to the Danes would suggest a political stratagem. We shall continue to keep an eye on Adam's work, since he often depends on Danish sources and, in general, represents the view of the Hamburg Church. Further, with my theory as a point of departure, we shall also note the way in which the Uplands are presented (the diocese-to-be), as well as the way Olav Tryggvason is depicted.

[157] Kolsrud 1958, 189.

The kings of Norway, the author writes, have roots that can be traced all the way back to the old world of the Swedish gods. This is consistent with Adam's account (IV 26). In other words it is a long list. The first kings were Yngve, Njord and Frøy. The author of *HN* seems to have obtained from Ari this long list of heathen kings that we are now being confronted with.[158] Yet in the preserved *Íslendingabók* of his we find, among other things, that Yngve was a "Turkish king" (*i.e.* a Trojan king).[159] In *HN* he is the first king of Sweden (IX 2). This could also have occurred in Ari's lost *Íslendingabók*, but it could also mean that in *HN* the author is demonstrating his unwillingness to compete in the race to discover which nation had the most ancient kings. This is not his concern at this point. Against the background of the Muslim conquests and their many battles against Christian populations, it would have been written with the risk of being misunderstood and thus in the Pope's/cardinal's eyes stigmatize the Norwegian kings; this was the last thing that the author of *HN* wanted!

We should note that the author seems to rest on two traditions about the country's first king; right at the very beginning of Book I the author mentions that Norway took its name from a certain King Nor, a tradition that we also find in the *Saga* of Oddr (and later in Peder Claussøn Friis (d. 1614)). Adam writes that the name of Norway is due to the country's location in the farthest north (IV 31). In ch. IX in *HN*, *De ortu regum* ("On the lineage of the kings"), Yngve, however, is mentioned first.[160] The Yngling kings themselves had nothing to do with Trøndelag. According to *HN*, when they left the Uppsala region they settled in the Uplands. But while they were still in Sweden, *HN* relates that Trøndelag was populated from there. This could represent an attempt to establish some sort of connection between them and Trøndelag, but the purpose could also be to relate how early Trøndelag was populated. Then we have the mention of Nor. Taken together, as far as I can tell, these bits of information could have a specific purpose: it is one thing that the author likes to make use of etymology (Nor — Norge), in line with the customs of the time, but also through the story about Nor and others who came there from Sweden, Trøndelag becomes the oldest populated area of the country. Based on the attitude that "oldest is best", the author has yet

[158] *Cf.* Krag 1991.

[159] This piece of information must surely be read against the background of similar accounts that we find in Jordanes (wrote c. 550), Dudo (wrote *c.* 1000), William of Jumièges (wrote *c.* 1050–1070), Orderic Vitalis (d. 1142/1143) and Robert of Torigni (d. 1186), about how the Goths (who were thought to be descendants of Noah via his grandson Magog, and thus staked a claim to being the most ancient of peoples) settled in Skåne in Sweden (*Scanza*). From here they spread in part to Scythia *ulterior* (which lay to the north and east of the Black Sea), in part to *Dacia* (north of the Alps) which, according to William of Jumièges, is identical to *Danamarcha* (named after *Danaus*). The inhabitants there called themselves *Daci, Danai* or *Dani*, but were also called *Nortmanni*. Among their leaders was the Trojan Antenor, who fled there with many men after the fall of Troy (Dudo, *De moribus et actis primorum Normanniae ducum*, I.1–3 and William of Jumièges, *Gesta Normannorum Ducum* I.1–3(4)).

[160] *Cf.* Gjessing 1896, 138 and Oddr, *Saga Óláfs Tryggvasonar,* 22.

another argument for Trøndelag to be the seat of an archdiocese-to-be (apart from the additional fact that St Olav's shrine was located there).

8.2. Harald Hårfagre and his sixteen sons

Then we follow a summary account of the Swedish list of kings until we come to Halvdan Hvitbein (Whiteleg), who moves to the Uplands and becomes king, and further on to Halvdan the Black (Svarte), at which point the narrative line broadens somewhat. This broadening becomes more marked as we move on, culminating at last in the two Olavs. Up to and including Harald Hårfagre, the Danes are only mentioned in connection with three of the Yngling kings who were killed by the Danes in Denmark. It might seem that the author passes over Harald Hårfagre lightly, but he intimates that he knows many incredible things he can say about him (XI 2): *nunc longum est narrare per singula* ("it would take too long now to relate individually"). The author seems to be in a hurry; his goal is to arrive at the Christian kings. The pagan ones serve merely as a kind of prelude, showing that the genealogy of the Norwegian kings is very long and unbroken.

However, the author makes his most important point about Harald: with him the Hårfagre family line begins. Harald subjugated the entire coastal area, and although petty kings still ruled in the Uplands, they were (XI 1) *quasi sub eius dominio* ("seemingly governing under his lordship"). It is not completely clear whether the author here is thinking about the sons to whom, as he grew older, he delegated more and more power, or whether he had other petty kings, or whether he had both in mind. This vagueness could have been quite deliberate, for we should note that this passage does not mention the exact number of petty kings. One natural way to regard this would be to surmise that the author was not giving Harald full credit for having united all of Norway, as we find stated in *Ágrip*, the *Saga* of Oddr and other sagas later on.[161] Contrariwise it could also be because the author of *HN* would rather emphasize the Uplanders, who so far in the story have been able to hold their own with their own petty kings. Thus it is important to get across the names and the order of Harald's sixteen sons. And here we should perhaps note Gjessing's point with respect to the number and order in which they are listed.[162] In *Ágrip* there are twenty sons, who are listed in another order, grouped around the various mothers.[163] *HN* does not mention that the sons had different mothers, including a concubine and a Finn whom he titles (XI 7) *nutrix* ("foster-mother") in spite of her being the real mother. The first two sons mentioned are Eirik Blodøks (Bloodaxe) and Håkon Adalsteinsfostre (Æthelstan's foster-son), both of whom became kings governing the coastland. The next ones are the petty kings, Olav, Bjørn and Sigurd Rise (the Giant). The first two of these excel because they gave rise to Olav Tryggvason and St Olav, respectively, and Sigurd achieved renown because he established the lineage that led to the author's time, *i.e.* to the kings Inge, Sigurd and Øystein, according to my theory. Of the last

[161] *Ágrip* ch. 2. Oddr makes first Harald Hårfagre and later Olav Tryggvason unite the Norwegian kingdom (Gjessing 1896, 137 and Oddr, *Saga Óláfs Tryggvasonar,* 22–23).

[162] 1896, 143–44.

[163] *Ágrip* ch. 2.

eleven that are mentioned, two died before they could assume the throne; the remaining nine all became petty kings in the Uplands. Along with Olav, Bjørn and Sigurd Rise this makes twelve. This corresponds in *HN* to the number of counties in the Uplands. Or, to put it another way, the Uplands are an important area which, even after the time of Harald Hårfagre, have seemingly had a king in each county.

One of Harald Hårfagre's sons is, as mentioned above, Sigurd Rise (*Gigas*). His Norse nickname was actually Hrísi, which meant "a bastard". In those days, this corresponded to the Norwegian Rísi, but the accent was traditionally not written. As I see it (and as we shall see later), the author of *HN* chooses, probably deliberately, to write it as "Risi", *i.e.* "Rise" (Giant).[164] A number of researchers have seen evidence here that the author either had oral sources, written sources, or that he did not know Old Norse.[165]

8.3. Eirik Blodøks

At first Eirik Blodøks is the most interesting of Harald Hårfagre's sons. Now the author of *HN* no longer seems to be in such a hurry. Eirik is discussed against the background of his Danish wife (XII 1), *Gunnildam quandam maleficam et iniquissimam, Gorms stultissimi Danorum regis filiam ac Thyri mulieris prudentissime* ("Gunnhild, cruel and double-dyed in wickedness, daughter of the Danish King, Gorm the Stupid, and his very clever wife, Tyra"). Gunnhild receives all the blame for Eirik's banishment by the Norwegians. He fled to England, where he was baptized. Then he became an earl over the whole of Northumberland and was well liked by everyone until his (XII 4) *improba uxor* ("villainous wife") came over. People found her (XII 5) *pestiferam rabiem* ("pernicious fury") unbearable; he was once again banished. He left on a viking expedition to Spain, where he was killed.[166] Gunnhild returned to Denmark, where she was received by her brother, the Danish king. *HN* is the only Norwegian medieval work that tells us she was of Danish stock (we also find this claim in the bishop of Bergen, Anders Foss's, genealogy of the Danish kings (1592)). According to Adam (II 3 & 28) she was a Danish queen, married to Harald Blåtann (Blue-tooth), both of whom were baptized. But the Norwegian tradition is that she came from Hålogaland. We note that her father was Gorm "the Stupid" — not "the Old" — two nicknames that referred to the same person.[167] Again and again we hear about Gunnhild and her demented behaviour in Norway. Her sons recede into the background and die

[164] *Cf.* also Hanssen 1949, 4–5, who, however, does not give any arguments for his view.

[165] Bugge 1873, 41 sees an indication here that *HN* could have been written on the Orkneys; Koht 1919–20, 108 that *HN* rests on written sources; Meissner 1902, 43, and Jónsson 1923, 599 that the author of *HN* was not a Norwegian; Berntsen 1923, 70, that *HN* depends on a Norse saga in Norwegian; Holtsmark 1938, 153ff., that an oral source could be at play; Koht 1919–20, 108, and Koht 1950, 40–1 that *HN* relies on written Norwegian sources.

[166] This last piece of information occurs only in *HN* and in *Ágrip* (ch. 7).

[167] He is called both "the Old" and "hinn heimski" in Jomsvikingesaga (*Soga um Jomsvikingane*, ed. Joleik 1931, 10).

on the battlefield, one by one, while she occupies the limelight and thrives there. There is no regret, no sensitivity to the loss of her sons (in sharp contrast to Olav Tryggvason's Norwegian mother Astrid in *HN*). Rather it seems to be a matter of having enough sons to sacrifice. The fact that Gunnhild is given such a prominent place in the Norwegian list of kings (compared, say, to Harald Hårfagre: five to six lines)[168] could be interpreted as a countermove to the retention of the Nordic archdiocese in Lund; the Danes are stupid (Gorm), and bring misfortune (Gunnhild), and the Danish king (Gunnhild's brother Harald) supports these types of people. In other words, how could one expect the archbishop of Lund to be an unbiased judge in the case of controversies between the two countries?

While still on the subject of Gunnhild we should note the way in which the author of *HN* speaks about women in general. All women — both Norwegian and Danish — are given Latin declension endings.[169] This could be because their names are so easy to Latinize, but in *HN* it seems that every name that a foreign reader was meant to notice was written with a Latin declension form. Of important persons this applies first and foremost to the Norwegian kings from Halvdan the Black onwards, and the English bishops and kings; and among Danish persons *Sweino* and *Canutus*, and perhaps also women; the Norwegian name forms from the time after Harald Hårfagre denote less important persons from both pagan and Christian times.

As for the role of women in *HN*, it is tempting to pose the following questions: do we see here the same attitudes about the elevation of woman as an individual and as a guardian of moral life, and about marriage as a holy and peace-making institution that found expression, partly, in the Law of Succession of 1163/1164, partly in Canons 8, 9 and 10?[170] The latter are part of a collection of sixteen *canones* which, according to many researchers, stem from Archbishop Øystein's hand later that century. In *HN* the woman — especially as wife and mother — is spoken of with respect. The author seems to recognize her strength as well as the political role a number of women played in the course of history. Moreover he lets the men in *HN* take care of their wives. In brief the author stresses the legitimacy of marriage and its fundamental value: he lets those Norwegians who fled or emigrated take along their wives (except, understandably enough, Eirik Blodøks); he conceals the many different women (including a concubine and a Finn) of the sons of Harald Hårfagre; he translates Risi as "Rise" (*i.e.* Giant),

[168] She is one of the few persons who is often emphasized, being mentioned eight times by name. By comparison Eirik Blodøks is only named four times. In four places their sons are called "Gunnhild's sons", and in only two places are they called "Eirik's sons". Olav Tryggvason is mentioned thirteen times and St Olav eleven times, whereas Harald Hårfagre, admittedly, is mentioned seven times by name, but four of these are in connection with his sons, and two in connection with conquest (of the Orkneys) and emigration (to Iceland) during his time, without his having anything to do with these events directly.

[169] With the apparent exception of *Thyri/Tyri* (genitive), which cannot however be the genitive feminine in Latin.

[170] *Latinske dokument*, ed. Vandvik 1959, 46–51.

and not as "Bastard"; he is keen on mentioning the Norwegian kings' legitimate marriages (Eirik Blodøks, Harald Grenske (the Grenlander), Sigurd Syr (Sow), Tryggve Olavsson, Olav Tryggvason and St Olav); and in some places he tells of rapes that end with the death of the perpetrator.

8.4. Håkon Adalsteinsfostre

Next in succession after Eirik was his brother Håkon Adalsteinsfostre, who was baptized in England. The fact that he was born of a concubine is kept secret. In *HN* he becomes an *appostata* ("an apostate") (XIII 2 "religous-minded passage" No. 2). According to some scholars this seems to be an early version of Håkon's life.[171] In Theodoricus he is a pagan and presented favourably (ch, 4). In *HN* baptism (and perhaps his English upbringing, see § 8.10. below) must nevertheless have helped him, because he is praised as a righteous king, one who upheld the law and respected the decisions of the people. He was constantly at war with Gunnhild until finally, after a victory, he was killed, as a punishment from God, by a young boy; the one who had denied the young Christ was himself slain by a young boy ("religous-minded passage" No. 3). For fourteen years Gunnhild and her sons wielded power, and (XIV 2) *sub istorum imperio exigente nequicia prelatorum maxime oppressa est Norwegia fame ac qualibet iniuria* ("under their dominion Norway suffered hardship from hunger and all kinds of injustice, in accordance with the negligence of these overlords").

8.5. Tryggve Olavsson

The rest of Harald Hårfagre's sons and their fate are given only brief mention. Perhaps at this point the way in which Tryggve Olavsson's rule is spoken of may be noticed; the author calls it an *imperialem rigorem* ("harsh dictatorial rule"). *Imperialis* is a rather grand word to use about such an insignificant petty king in Ranrike, and this inevitably leads our thoughts to the term *imperator*, and thus to the German emperor and his reign. On the other hand the author of *HN* uses the term *imperium* in a number of places in connection with Norwegian dominion, so we should not attach too much significance to his use of *imperialis*.

8.6. The Uplands

None the less, two of Hårfagre sons are emphasized, Bjørn and Olav, who later gave rise to (XV 3) *illi salutares equiuoci duo Olaui, qui quasi clara celi luminaria suam sacre luce fidei illustrabant patriam* ("those two benefactors of the same name, Olav, who like bright celestial stars illuminated their country with the light of the Holy Faith") ("religious-minded passage" No. 4). We see here that the two Olavs are spoken of as equals and in the same breath. But let us pause just a moment at the Uplands, because this is where much takes place in this chapter. A number of researchers (*e.g.* Berntsen 1923 and Aðalbjarnarson 1937) have suggested that the Uplands figure prominently and frequently in *HN*. Storm sees this as an indication that the author of *HN* came from there,[172] while others, as mentioned before,

[171] *Cf.*, for example, Hanssen 1949, 24–27.

[172] 1873b, 385.

believe that the author's knowledge rests on an oral or written Upland saga no longer extant, either in Latin or Norwegian.

There may well be something to this, but in my view this is not the important point here. It is correct to say that the Uplands "are showcased" (to use a modern media expression) in *HN*, for example in comparison with Viken. Up to now we have heard that the Uplands constituted a separate geographical part of the country, that they were populated by Christians, that they had "law provinces" and "counties" just like the coastal areas; furthermore, they were rich in gold and silver, and it was here that, according to *HN*, the Norwegian royal line was established, with Halvdan Hvitbein as progenitor. Halvdan the Black had his headquarters here, many petty kings asserted their dominion here, and the fathers of the two Olavs resided here. Moreover the Uplands are spoken of in connection with Astrid, the mother of Olav Tryggvason. She came from here (according to Snorri, the Saga of Olav Tryggvason, ch. 1, she was from Jæren), Olav Tryggvason was conceived here, and it was here that St Olav was born and raised. Briefly, in *HN* the Uplands, more than any other area, were the "royal lair" for the Norwegian royal family, and thus symbolically also the original seedbed of Christianity in Norway. Is there then anything at all that the Uplands lacked? Indeed, they lacked a diocese such as the coastland had, where there were four. As we have seen, conditions were ripe for it. In the event, as we all now know, a diocese was established near Lake Mjøsa, at Hamar, with Cardinal Breakspear's visit. The first bishop to be ordained there (as mentioned in a previous note) was the Greenland bishop, Arnald. The fact that only Mjøsa is mentioned, and not Hamar, could be due to the fact that the cardinal, with papal authorization (and perhaps by personal inspection) determined which location was worthy of the seat of a new diocese. For the same reason, perhaps, the city of Nidaros is not mentioned, only the law province of Trøndelag. As far as I know, it does not appear clearly from any extant document whether Breakspear inspected the Uplands in order to seek out the most appropriate sites, or whether he made his decision during the negotiations.[173] At this time Hamar must have been an insignificant little trading post, a market town, whereas the court was previously located near Vang rectory at Åker. The choice of Hamar could be due to the fact that on the site where Hamar Cathedral was later built a stone church already existed. Recent archaeological excavations suggest that this is the case. Now we understand better why Stavanger is not mentioned by name (it is included in the term *Decapolis*), and Oslo only barely mentioned (in giving directions for the location of the silver in the Upland mountains); both cities already housed a bishop. Thus there was no need to advertise them. Again, we see that the author of *HN* seems to choose his subjects with care and adheres to a rigorous structure.

8.7. The direct line of the contemporary reigning kings

After the author has told his readers about the death of Harald Grenske, St Olav's father, he mentions that his "most excellent wife" (XV 5), Åsta from the Uplands

[173] Johnsen 1945, 90 and 115–16 is of the view that Breakspear visited the Uplands, but *cf. Historisk-topografiske skrifter*, ed. Storm 1895, 134–35.

and Olav's mother, remarries with Sigurd Syr from the same place. Next (seemingly superfluously), the author takes up the lineage of Sigurd Syr (who, of course, was not St Olav's father) and shows that he is actually descended from Sigurd Rise (see the survey at the end). Next, when the author traces the time in the opposite direction, we hear that Sigurd Syr, along with this same Åsta, had a son named Harald (XV 8), *uirum sagacissimum et in bellica arte peritissimum* ("a man of deep perspicacity, a great expert in the science of warfare"). This extra piece of information about Harald could perhaps prove to be a detail from the author of *HN* (see 11.2.1. below), but it could also be read against the background of Adam, who speaks negatively of the same Harald.[174] This Harald would later become the Norwegian king, Harald Hardråde (Hardruler) (1046–66). However, the author leaves out his nickname; instead he draws a line from him all the way to his own time with the following sentence (XV 8): *de quo (sc. Haraldo) quasi quodam filo textus genealogie regum Norwegie hucusque protelatus gloriose descendit* ("From him (*i.e.* Harald), as if along a thread, descended the glorious Norwegian royal line in its genealogical pattern up to the present"). With my interpretation as a vantage point, this seems to be a tribute to the reigning kings, Inge, Sigurd and Øystein. After all, who is this Harald Hardråde? In fact, he is their great-great-grandfather through his son Olav Kyrre, who in turn farthered Magnus Berrføtt (Barefoot), who in turn sired Harald Gille (Gilchrist), the father of the three royal brothers. Not only were they descended from the Hårfagre family line via Harald Hardråde on the male side, but via Åsta the connection is also drawn on Hardråde's mother's side directly to St Olav. Of the reigning royal brothers, Inge, as mentioned above, was the only legitimate son. Thus we understand why the author of *HN* chose to interpret Sigurd Rise's nickname as *Gigas* ("Rise"), and not "Bastard"; it was not especially flattering to have a bastard as progenitor on the throne; neither was it warranted (anyway not in every European country), nor especially tempting to have to tell a pope or cardinal about it. And perhaps more importantly, do we see here a connection to the Law of Succession under Magnus Erlingsson, which claimed that the eldest legitimate royal son headed the line of royal succession?[175] Here the reader can also question whether the author intends to take up the thread of the king's list again in *HN*, or whether this is his way of dispensing with it up to his own time (this issue will be discussed in§ 9.2.–4. below).

8.8. Håkon jarl the Wicked

After the death of Gunnhild's sons, Håkon jarl (Earl) *usurpauit* ("appropriated") the whole Norwegian kingdom (XVI 1) (*totius Norwegie monarchiam*). According to *HN* he preferred to call himself *comes quam rex secundum suos seniores* (here translated traditionally with "jarl to king because of his descent").[176] We might assume, implicitly, that with this title he was an exception to the rule of kings. In fact Håkon's use of the earl title is repeated in *HN*, and repetitions in *HN* usually indicate that the author attaches importance to the issue in question.

[174] III 17, *cf.* also Commentary on ch. XV 8.

[175] Steen 1949–51, 8.

[176] *Cf.* Koht 1950, 42 and Salvesen 1969, 32.

The author continues with an account of Håkon's descent; he came from the famous earl family of Møre and Hålogaland. Sigurd was Håkon's father and Bergljot his mother, Bergljot being the daughter of Tore the Silent (den tause). As we know from elsewhere, Tore himself was married to Ålov Årbot, the daughter of Harald Hårfagre, *i.e.* Håkon was descended from him on his mother's side (see the survey at the end). It seems important to the author to point out the Hårfagre family's continued rule through Håkon jarl, and that Norway was a *monarchia* ("a kingdom") ruled by kings, even though Håkon called himself earl. The whole chapter might be understood against the background of Adam, who maintains that Håkon was descended from the Yngling kings and from giants, and that Norway so far had been ruled by chieftains (*ducibus*, II 25). That is why the translation of the passage *comes quam rex secundum suos seniores* with "but preferred that title (*i.e.* jarl) to being known as king, in the same way as his predecessors" is preferred in the present edition. The passage seems to be an answer to Adam, since the author of *HN* underlines Norway's traditional rule of kings, whereas Håkon jarl is an exception through his title.

We note that Håkon is credited as being the first person to rule all Norway, and for the first time in *HN* the coastland and the Uplands are not kept apart. Whether Håkon's absolute monarchy as the first one in the history of Norway is an early version (we also find it in Theodoricus, ch. 5), or recorded here as a compensation for his descent from Hårfagre on the female side, is hard to say. But traditionally Harald Hårfagre is credited with the role of the first absolute monarch. On the other hand Håkon is said in *HN* to have usurped the kingdom. We know from elsewhere that he was helped by conspiring with Danish king, and that he had not inherited the monarchy legitimately.[177] The legitimate heir was Harald Gråfell (Greycloak), the son of Eirik Blodøks, but he was killed by the Danish king, Harald Gormsson, and his fellow-conspirators, Gull-Harald and Håkon jarl. This might also have stood at the end of chapter XIV in *HN*, in a passage which seems to have fallen out due to an error of the copyist. In this chapter the author mentions the brothers Sigurd, Gunnrød and Harald (*i.e.* Gråfell), and afterwards describes the death of the former two, but we are not told of Harald's death. The missing passage was most probably not longer than the mention of his brothers' death, but there are grounds for believing that it might have contained a mention of the Danish king and perhaps Håkon jarl. This would be consistent with the author's atttude to the Danes, and he was probably not willing to let this pass without comment.[178] It would also be consistent with the way Håkon jarl's sons came to power (XVII 56). This leads the thoughts once more to the above-mentioned Law of Succession under Magnus Erlingsson, which claimed that the eldest legitimate royal son headed the line of royal succession. Be that as it may, the fact that Håkon jarl reigned over the whole kingdom certainly heightens the

[177] *Cf.* Snorri (*Heimskringla, Óláfs saga Tryggvasonar*, 9–14) and *Ágrip* ch. 14.

[178] *Cf.* also Storm 1880, 107–8, note to line 17. Aðalbjarnarson 1937, 32 does not agree on the grounds that Håkon jarl would then have been mentioned as in *Ágrip* ch. 10.

glory of Olav Tryggvason; whereas Håkon usurped power, according to *HN* Olav Tryggvason was the first king ever in Norway to be elected by all the Norwegians.

Nevertheless, and in spite of being evil and a heathen, Håkon is at least reported in *HN* as a brilliant warrior, who expanded his reign far and wide. This virtue, besides piety (*i.e.* Christian faith) and justice, is a returning theme in the account of the kings in *HN*.

Håkon is also said in *HN* to have reigned for thirty-three years; Adam has thirty-five years (II 25), but we do not hear in what year he died. To this it may be added that the author of *HN* puts the main emphasis on a genealogical and relative, chronological presentation of the Norwegian kings within a strictly Norwegian framework. He pays no attention to universal chronology; there is not a single date to indicate how far along in the universal history the narrative has come.

8.9. Olav Tryggvason

When Håkon heard that Olav Tryggvason had been born in the Orkneys, he feared that Olav would take away his kingdom, so he prepared for war with him. With this the account shifts its attention to Olav Tryggvason He is the person in *HN* who is mentioned the most; indeed, what a strong contrast there is between him and the previous kings! He is presented as an example in the best biblical spirit: God's care for him, his trials as a child, his bravery even at a tender age, his monumental escapades on viking raids where he holds sway throughout the entire Baltic region, Friesland, Flanders, Scotland, England and Ireland, how he is leader of Norwegians, Danes, Götars and the Wends, only at the end to receive his calling from God through a hermit on an island near England. In Olav's power struggle with the Norwegian earl sons, the latter were doomed to lose. They fled to Denmark, where they (XVII 29) *a rege Sweinone pacifice recepti sunt* ("were received in friendly fashion by King Svend"). The Danish king does not show solidarity with his Norwegian counterpart. Even worse, he breaks his vow concerning Zealand as a dowry in connection with Olav's marriage to his sister. A battle ensues — not at Svolder (as in later sagas) — but off Zealand,[179] where both the Danish and the Swedish kings, despite superior strength in terms of ships and men, have to surrender, and where Olav can only be defeated by a Norwegian, Eirik jarl. We note that Adam equips Olav with a very large fleet (II 40). In *HN* Olav has only eleven ships, the same number as Eirik jarl, but far fewer than the fleet of the Danish and Swedish kings. The Danes are perfidious and cowardly warriors in *HN*'s story.

In connection with the naval battle we are told that Olav's ship was called "Ormen den lange" ("the Long Serpent"), and we are given a rather detailed description of it — not just because the author is impressed with its size, but perhaps because he is more interested in making the point that there were forty priests on Olav's side. Their task was not to fight, but to pray. It might seem absurd that these forty priests, who had not been trained for war, should have

[179] *Cf.* also Adam II 40.

to perish, while conscripted farmers from Gulatingslag and Trøndelag failed to appear. One wonders whether the author of *HN* is indirectly telling us that these priests should have stayed at home — precisely in order to pray. If this is the author's point, then he is expressing an attitude that we find in *canon* 2, in which everyone who serves in the Church, is exempt — by and large — from military conscription.[180]

The author of *HN* especially contradicts Adam who, in his account of Olav Tryggvason (II 40), claims that Olav was to blame for the war. Furthermore, Adam questions Olav's Christian faith, and in one place at least mainly credits the Germans with the Christianizing of Norway. The English only continued their work (IV 34). Moreover Adam maintains in one place that Olav was baptized by Germans (II 36); and while the author of *HN*, after Olav's death, allows his wife to die of sorrow, Adam has her dying from hunger and want. Adam takes much of his information from Danish sources, particularly from the Danish king, Svend Estridsen. Adam's critical attitude towards Olav Tryggvason could be due to the fact that Olav carried out independent religious policies vis-à-vis the Hamburg Church and belonged to that Church's competitor – namely, the Anglo-Saxon Church.[181]

8.10. The Danes and English in HN

While this issue involves the author of *HN*'s relationship to Adam, we could also add that even if we cannot speak of a clear-cut hatred of the Danish, the author of *HN*'s aversion to the Danes often comes to the fore. We read only negative things about them (apart from *Thyri prudentissime* (genitive)).

Concerning the Irish, the Scots and the English, however, we find nothing disparaging and — in the light of my interpretation — this is despite the fact that both the English and the Scots were the Norwegians' competitors in the matter of the archdiocese. Nevertheless the reader is left in no doubt that the Norwegians have been far superior to them all in war. The English are mentioned in connection with Norwegian conquests in that country; in one place we even read that the English tried to resist as best they could (XVIII 21). At other points the Celts could have been mentioned, but they are passed over in silence. In addition, when *HN* tells us that Olav Tryggvason was baptized in England, that English bishops helped both him and St Olav in their Christianizing of Norway, and that several English kings were involved in having Norwegians baptized, we begin to suspect that the Norwegians had known that it was the English cardinal, Breakspear, and not another cardinal, who would be coming to Norway in 1152. But this pro-English stance could, with equal validity, be interpreted as a counterweight to the archbishop of Hamburg-Bremen and his attitude towards the Pope. On the other hand it might just reflect the author of *HN*'s own positive attitude towards the

[180] *Latinske dokument*, ed. Vandvik 1959, 42–45, and Johnsen 1945, 238ff. (*canon* 3).

[181] Hallencreutz 1984a, 361–62. *cf.* also Bagge 1992 and Mortensen 1994 for accounts of Olav Tryggvason, and Hallencreutz 1984b, 22–27 for Adam's account of the opponents of Hamburg-Bremen's traditional missionary activities.

English, and towards *Agnellus/ Angnellus/ Anguellus*, if he is English, and a corresponding aversion to the Danes. For example, could the author have resided in England and perhaps studied there?

Some researchers have attempted to show that the author of *HN* might have been influenced by the French.[182] In one place he also demonstrates a knowledge of the German language. However, he could easily have learned some German in a Norwegian city, such as Bergen. At this stage of my investigation there is nothing in terms of content, attitudes, linguistics or stylistics that points to a specific school or a specific order. A separate, thorough study of the question of educational sites must, in my opinion, be undertaken before we can answer this with any satisfactory degree of certainty.

8.11. Eirik and Svein jarl

After the death of Olav Tryggvason, Norway was ruled for fourteen years by Håkon jarl's sons. They were put on the throne by the Danish King Svend, *i.e.* they, too, were not legitimate heirs, but had the support of a treacherous Danish monarch. They nearly managed to eradicate the holy Church (XVII 58), *quam beatus Olauus egregie plantauerat, Iohannes rigauerat* ("which this holy man Olav (*i.e.* Olav Tryggvason) had planted so painstakingly and John had watered"). In this way the author of *HN* gives Olav Tryggvason and his English Bishop John the honour of having Christianized Norway. This conflicts with Adam, who allows the Danish King Svend to introduce Christianity and St Olav to complete the process.[183] We shall return to the presentation of Olav Tryggvason in *HN*, but first let us finish with the last king in *HN*, St Olav.

8.12. St Olav

If we look at the account of Olav Tryggvason before his arrival in Norway, we shall notice that in terms of length it corresponds largely to that of St Olav, where the story stops just before his arrival in his homeland. The content, as well, has many parallels. St Olav was also bereft of his homeland and began his adult career as a viking, who brutally pillaged the entire Baltic region.[184] En route to his fatherland, he arrived in Denmark, at which point he was persuaded to accompany King Svend on a raiding mission to England, where they won all their battles, thanks to Olav's prowess in war. Olav continued to fight in England and went as far south as Spain after Svend died, while the latter's son, Knud, was in Denmark, where he was elected king. Later on Olav left for Denmark but was persuaded by Knud to accompany him once again to England. Knud's promise to Olav and Olof of Sweden was to give them half the English empire, if they were victorious. London was taken, thanks to St Olav's great courage but the Danes were unsuccessful. However, Knud neglected his promise to Olav, and Olav decided to return home.

182 Storm 1880, xxiii.

183 II 41 and 57. Hanssen 1949, 27, believes that *HN* thus fits better before 1163 than afterwards. Theodoricus lets Olav Tryggvason plant and St Olav water (ch. 16).

184 *HN* alone has St Olav wintering at Holmgard and ravaging Kurland (Ellehøj 1965, 156).

Before that happened Olav became engaged to Olof of Sweden's *soror Margareta* (XVIII 31). This seems to be incorrect, based on our knowledge of the tradition that says he was engaged to Olof's daughter. Nevertheless we should be careful about deprecating the author of *HN*, as Bugge does, for "carelessness and unreliability".[185] Storm claims that this assertion in *HN* is due to a combination of two different traditions:[186] Adam writes (II 54) that Knud gave his sister Margareta in marriage to the Norman duke, Richard, and in a scholium that his sister Estrid was given in marriage to the Russian king, whereas the tradition we find in, for example, Theodoricus (ch. 16) and in *Ágrip* (ch. 25) has one of Olof of Sweden's daughters marrying Olav and the other marrying Jarislav of Russia. It is easy to understand how there could be a confusion, since the two kings, Knud and Olof of Sweden, were half-brothers, as we read in *HN*. Concerning Olav, Adam writes only that he was married to Olof of Sweden's daughter, without identifying her by name (II 61). Nevertheless it is not certain that Storm is right. The view that a confusion had occurred does not square with one's overall impression of the author of *HN*. Nor does it square with yet another factor: if the author of *HN* had read in his source that Olav's bride-to-be was actually Knud's sister Margareta, he would surely have preferred this solution, if for no other reason than the fact that this would have given him yet another direct parallel to Olav Tryggvason, who was also married to the sister of a Danish king. We should also note the parallel between these two women, both of whom are forced into an engagement or marriage against their will. Even if Knud's sister really was Olof of Sweden's half-sister, there would have been no reason to "switch" her over to Olof of Sweden. It seems more likely that the source contained what the author of *HN* writes here, that Olav became engaged to Olof of Sweden's sister Margareta.

The contrast with Adam is not so significant in the account of St Olav as was the case with Olav Tryggvason Still, Adam does not mention Olav's role in King Svend's victory in England, and he claims that Olav did not participate in the second expedition to London with King Knud (II 51–52). In fact, the two of them were at war, Adam tells us, and in his opinion Olav might have been assassinated by his own countrymen to curry favour with Knud (II 57 & 61).

The narrative and Book I (see 9.3. below) in *HN* ends with St Olav's voyage home from England with two large merchant vessels and four English bishops. Here we should bear in mind that while Adam writes that Olav took many bishops home with him (II 57), the author of *HN* claims that there were only four; the names he gives are from Adam. One wonders whether this number was used on purpose and that it was meant to symbolize the dioceses that were eventually established. Is St Olav, the four bishops' superior, meant to be perceived as their "archbishop", and are they, taken together, meant to represent the number of bishoprics in Norway? This gives the author of *HN* a good argument for establishing an archdiocese, as well as yet another bishopric — the one that was eventually founded at Hamar. We note that when the archdiocese at Nidaros was established, the Hamar bishopric was also initiated. Can the number five be substantiated in

[185] Bugge 1873, 28–29. [186] 1873b, 363–64.

connection with the dioceses and the archdiocese throughout the Catholic period, based on Olav and the number of bishops that *HN* says he took home with him?

8.13. Olav Tryggvason and St Olav

From the foregoing we see that the two Olavs — Olav Tryggvason and St Olav — are spoken of together in connection with the mention of their fathers, *i.e.* the point is made that they are related, that both had to flee the fatherland, both were preceded by evil and pagan earls who were not legitimate heirs but helped to the throne by Danish kings, and who thus made the two Olavs more outstanding, both resided for a time in Russia (where they made a positive impression), both won reputations as prominent vikings, both pillaged the Baltic region, and both paid visits to Holmgard (*i.e.* Novgorod). Both were better warriors than the Danes, both finished up in England before returning home to Norway, both fought with eleven ships in a crucial battle, both were deserted by Danish kings, Olav Tryggvason is called *beatus* and St Olav *beatissimus,*[187] both are called *tyranni* (*i.e.* vikings),[188] both marry "sisters" of Danish kings, and both take English bishops home with them. It should be mentioned here that the expression *beatus* was actually used about a saint who had not been canonized by the pope. Not until the time of Alexander III (pope 1159–81) did the Curia explicitly reserve the right to declare someone a saint, a practice which later became standard. A saint who had not been canonized by the Pope was relegated to a lower class of saints; the other saints were called *sancti*. For most of the Middle Ages, however, the two expressions were used interchangeably.[189]

While the account of Olav Tryggvason in several passages is related in a legendary style,[190] the account of St Olav is narrated in another style altogether — soberly descriptive and down-to-earth; Olav Tryggvason is presented as the man of the Church, St Olav as the viking warrior. Above all, Olav Tryggvason is presented as a Christ figure: Håkon jarl comes across like another Herod, who fears the infant Christ,[191] Olav's mother Astrid like the Virgin Mary, the recluse like an angel bearing glad tidings about the birth of Christ,[192] and Christ is represented by Olav, who, it is predicted, will become a great king, one who will multiply the number of Christians. Olav came to a turning point when he was twelve years old and showed his gifts in public for the first time by taking revenge on his foster-father's murderer. Jesus was the same age when he was found in the temple of Jerusalem publicly disputing with the scribes and teachers for the first time. Olav leaves for Norway and immediately upon arrival starts the process of Christianization. Even the ending has elements in common with the Christ-figure; just as Christ was betrayed by Judas, one of Olav's own men, Eirik jarl, is the cause of Olav's demise.

[187] XVII 24 & XVIII 10. [188] XVII 15 & XVIII 10. [189] Daae 1879, 5.

[190] As *e.g.* ch. XVII 15, 19–20, 24–5 and 30–2. In the account of Olav Tryggvason we also find direct speech for the first (and last) time in *HN*.

[191] Ellehøj 1965, 149. [192] *Ibid.*, 150.

We should note that this Christ-like presentation was traditionally associated with St Olav. The fact that Olav Tryggvason is given the honour of having Christianized the entire country (as opposed to the account of Oddr Snorresson, who lets St Olav complete the process of Christianizing the country),[193] and as it is said of him that he "had planted" (*plantauerat*) the Church while his bishop, John,[194] is credited with "having watered" (*rigauerat*) it, this is all apparently at the expense of St Olav. Moreover, the fact that the author of *HN* mentions the uncertainty surrounding Olav Tryggvason's disappearance (in a monastery, escaped by boat, swam ashore, drowned, helped by an angel) and refrains from offering a conclusion, we may justifiably ask whether Olav Tryggvason is being deliberately promoted as a candidate for canonization. There seems to be no doubt that *beatus Olauus* (*i.e.* Olav Tryggvason) is already a saint in the author's eyes, that he is eager to defend Olav against Adam's critical presentation of him, and that he wants to ensure a favourable posthumous reputation for this good Norwegian Christian king. But why the seemingly relentless parallelism with St Olav in the author's presentation of their earthly lives? Could this not be understood as an indirect attempt to tell the reader that Olav Tryggvason was as worthy a saint as St Olav? Or is it merely to portray Olav Tryggvason's life as an example for edification, one to be followed, as Sverre Bagge suggests is the purpose of Oddr's *Saga*?[195] Or is it because Icelandic or national ecclesiastical interests are involved, as Lars Lönroth (among others) claims is the case with the same saga?[196] According to Lönroth, as well as Hilde Fagerheim, this saga is not an attempt to get Olav Tryggvason officially recognized as a saint; but Jan de Vries is of a different opinion.[197] One crucial difference between Oddr's work on Olav Tryggvason and *HN* (apart from their length, of course) is that Oddr takes a definite position on the outcome of the battle of Svolder: Olav Tryggvason survives, flees on a Wendish ship and lives the rest of his life as a monk in a monastery.[198] In *HN* the author discusses the various rumours but does not take a stance on any of them. As far as I can tell, we cannot simply claim that he gives himself away when he tells how Olav Tryggvason's wife died of sorrow over her husband's death:[199] This was what she had been told — at least according to the story as it has been handed down to us in Oddr.[200] In any case she never saw her husband again, since it was Olav Tryggvason's previous wife, the Wendish princess Astrid who, according to this same story,[201] helped rescue him. With my interpretation in mind, it is tempting to ask whether the author of *HN* deliberately chose not to take a positive position on Olav Tryggvason's death in the absence of a direct parallel to St Olav's death and *translatio* (*i.e.* the transfer of his body by Bishop Grimkel to Klement's church) (see 9.3. below). Moreover, while *HN* calls Olav Tryggvason *beatus*, Oddr does not seem to call him "holy" anywhere.

[193] Oddr, *Saga Óláfs Tryggvasonar*, 54.

[194] This name also occurs in Adam (IV 34) and in Oddr (*Saga Óláfs Tryggvasonar*, for example ch. 26 (Jon) and 83 (Jon, also called Sigurd)).

[195] 1992, 23.

[196] 1963, 66.

[197] Lönroth 1963, 66, Fagerheim 1995, 61–65 and de Vries 1967 II, 245.

[198] Oddr, *Saga Óláfs Tryggvasonar* ch. 80.

[199] Ellehøj 1965, 153–54, claims that this is so.

[200] *Saga Óláfs Tryggvasonar* ch. 78.

[201] *Ibid.* ch. 80.

Be all that as it may, St Olav's reputation is not adversely affected, notwithstanding the emphasis on Olav Tryggvason St Olav's reputation is secure, since he had already been declared a saint in the eleventh century, and this could not be taken away from him. Furthermore, it is possible that *HN* did not end with the first book (see 9.3. below). Thus we see that St Olav is called *Olauus rex perpetuus* ("Olav the eternal king") in *HN* (XV 5). This appellation, in turn, leads our thoughts towards Magnus Erlingsson's Letter of Privilege (Norwegian: "Privilegiebrev"), drawn up by Archbishop Øystein around 1163, in which Magnus vows to take the Norwegian kingdom as a fiefdom from St Olav and, as his deputy, vassal and knight, to govern it well:[202] *Deo namque in hac die gloriose resurreccionis me cum regno in perpetuum et glorioso martyri regi Ola⟨u⟩o [cui] integraliter speciali deuocione secundo post dominum regnum assigno Norwegie, et huic regno, quantum deo placuerit, velut eiusdem gloriosi martyris possessioni hereditarie sub eius dominio tamquam suus vicarius et ab eo tenens presidebo. Porro quoniam prefatus martyr pro lege dei sui, pro salute subiectorum, pro presentis regni conseruacione intrepidus inimicis occurrit, et non dubitans manibus tradi nocentum presens regnum sui preciosi sanguinis effusione consecrauit, eius cupiens sicut in regno successor, sic et, in quantum vires suppetunt, adiutus a deo et ab eodem martyre fieri quoque uirtutum imitator, quecunque me uocauerit necessitas, tribulacio siue angustia, pro lege et iusticia tenenda, pro patria tamquam sancti Olaui possessione tuenda, diuino et eius tutus munimine ad certamen ipso preduce tamquam eius miles et in suis castris pugnaturus intrepidus accedam, et si consistant aduersum me castra, non timebit cor meum.* [...] ("So then, on this glorious day of resurrection, I bequeath my person and my kingdom to God for ever and ever; and by a special act of sacrifice I commit the kingdom of Norway wholly to the noble martyr King Olav, who is next after the Lord. And God's favour permitting, I shall manage this kingdom as the noble martyr's inheritance, under his feudal majesty and as his deputy and vassal. And because this martyr fearlessly went to meet his enemies in battle to uphold the law of his God, for the salvation of his people, and to safeguard this kingdom, and because he unhesitatingly gave himself into the hands of evil people, he sanctified this kingdom by his precious blood. I therefore wish to be his follower in ruling this kingdom and, as far as my strength will allow, to imitate his virtues with help from God and this same martyr; and whatever need, lacks or tribulations I may encounter, I will fearlessly fight for the cause of justice and defend the country as St Olav's property, confident through God's and his protection, and I will fight under his leadership, as his knight and in his army; and though a host should rise up against me, my heart shall not fear [...]".[203]

The Letter of Privilege is representative of current ideas. Ever since the eleventh century many countries, as previously mentioned, tried to acquire a royal guardian saint; and in the twelfth century we see that some of them were success-

[202] *Cf.* Magnus Erlingsson's *Privilegiebrev* (Letter of Privilege), ed. Vandvik 1962, 13–4 and 44. Gunnes 1996, 118, believes that, on the contrary, this letter should be placed in the 1170s.

[203] Trans. from *Latinske dokument*, ed. Vandvik 1959, 60–61.

ful.[204] Their initiatives sprang from the old concept of *rex iustus*. In Norway St Olav not only became an example, but also protector of the monarch and of the realm. The term *Olauus rex perpetuus* was a common concept long before 1163 and, as such, does not set any *status ante quem*, as Koht claims.[205] My assertion is confirmed by Paasche, who points to the content of some poems from the eleventh century.[206] Even Koht later concedes that the story of how Olav continued to rule over city and country after his death was already circulating in 1032 in a poem by Toraren Lovtunge.[207]

These are the most important things I have been able to find in *HN* concerning the justification for establishing an episcopal seat in the Uplands and for breaking away from Lund's authority in Church matters. Nevertheless, one important query remains: where does Nidaros enter the picture as the seat of the archdiocese-to-be? We shall soon return to this. As for the way in which Olav Tryggvason is presented, in my opinion it is an open question whether an attempt is being made to promote official recognition of him as a saint. At all events, the effort did not succeed. According to my interpretation, *HN* seems in general to contain many of the thoughts we find in other documents we have related to the Church and national council in 1153, Magnus Erlingsson's coronation in *c.* 1163 and the regulations, *canones*, which were adopted for the Norwegian Church in the latter half of the twelfth century. *HN* also has certain traits in common with *Passio Olaui* (see 9.3. below). The principle agent behind these documents is thought to be Øystein Erlendsson, who was archbishop from around 1160 to 1188. However, recent research on *Passio Olaui* concludes that Øystein was the author of only the last group of miracles here.[208] Though it is not an undisputed fact that he was the author of all the other documents, one might at least say that *HN* seems to be consistent with the Norwegian thinking of the time.

9. The question of whether *HN* was ever completed

9.1. The geographical description

According to my interpretation, the author of *HN* shows in his geographical description (point 1) which areas Norway as a nation had a historical claim to in connection with the establishment of a national archdiocese. Partly related to this is a justifiable wish for a new bishopric for the Uplands. Further, that the desire for a new archdiocese is justified on the basis of the fact that the Norwegian kingdom, with its faith, its well-developed society and its abundance of natural resources, is worthy of such an archepiscopal seat. The fact that the geographical description takes up nearly half of *HN* also seems to show that *HN* was not a mere chronicle og kings. I believe that this part of the account — again based on my own interpretation — has been completed.

[204] Gunnes 1996, 121–22. [205] Koht 1919–20, 109.
[206] 1922, 3–4. *cf.* also Hanssen 1949, 9. [207] 1950, 40.
[208] *Cf.* Ekrem (2000) and Mortensen (2000c).

9.2. The kings' lineage

Then, in the chapter about the lineage of the kings (point 2), the author of *HN* attempts, according to my interpretation, to show that even the constitutional aspect of the question was valid, by means of a long series of independent kings, which was the true driving force in the Christianizing of the country. One king, St Olav, had already been declared a saint. Another, Olav Tryggvason, was worthy of it by virtue of his earthly life. At the time of writing, the Norwegian kings wielded power over a large area, from which they collected taxes. Furthermore, the author seems to show how desirable it was from a Norwegian standpoint for a separate archdiocese vis-à-vis Denmark, with a new diocese in the Uplands. The important role that *HN* assigns to the Uplands would seem to indicate that *HN* was not merely written out of a general need to put Norway on the map, as it were, for others abroad; this kind of marketing of the Uplands has no purpose with respect to foreigners in general. The account, however, constitutes a strong argument to the Pope for the establishment of a diocese. This emphasis on the Uplands, based on my interpretation, suggests that *HN* was written before the establishment of the Nidaros archdiocese and the Hamar bishopric; if *HN* had been an attempt to provide an overview of the extent of the archdiocese after 1152/1153, then the Oslo and Stavanger dioceses should have been given as much attention as the Uplands. Furthermore, if *HN* was meant to constitute a mere chronicle of kings, the author would probably have underlined the unity of the Norwegian kingdom in quite another way; the keeping apart of the coastland and the Uplands, not only in the geographical section, but almost throughout the whole book, certainly diminishes, more than heightens, the reputation of the Norwegian kings.

9.3. A possible Book II of HN?

Whether my dating and interpretation of *HN* is accepted or not, it does not seem that point 2 about the lineage of the kings could have been completed with the version of *HN* that is available to us. Quite certainly the author of *HN* nowhere writes that he intended to update the royal lineage to his own time (although he does so anyway, albeit only briefly); but he writes in the Prologue that he has told about *multorum magnificencias* ("many men's splendid feats") in his time, recording everything he has found worth mentioning. Of these we hear nothing. Moreover, the author of *HN* owes St Olav greater coverage. After all, it is as a beatified royal that he lives on. But our copy gives us only Book I, which concludes with the viking king, St Olav's, journey to Norway, *i.e.* before his most important effort on behalf of Christian Norway began. The book ends, so to speak, with a kind of prelude to a potential Book II. Confirming this claim is the heading of the first chapter after the Prologue: *Incipit liber primus in ystoria Norwegie* ("Here begins the first book of the History of Norway"). There was little reason to write this if the work only included (or was intended only to include) a single book.

But more important still, provided it is true that *HN* was written in connection with the establishment of the archdiocese, there is only weak support for this archdiocese having its seat in Nidaros. And who could be a better argument for that than St Olav — but to be sure, only after he arrived in the fatherland and gradually earned the title *Rex perpetuus Norwegie*? We hear little about Trøndelag in *HN*; in fact, no connection whatsoever is drawn between this area of the country and St Olav. All this could mean that the Prologue was written before *HN* was completed. And if indeed *HN* finished at the end of Book I, this could be due to the author's (or his commissioner's) death. But according to my interpretation of *HN*, this could just as well be due to Breakspear's sudden arrival. Such a possibility must be considered, because after his departure there was no need for a continuation of *HN*, as I interpret it. The purpose was already achieved.

On the other hand, if we assume that the Prologue was written after *HN* was completed and if we take the wording literally, we would expect a Book II at the very least; and it is reasonable to assume that such a book would have begun with Olav's continued exploits in Norway and that an account of him would conclude with his death and perhaps with a number of miracles. Further, it is reasonable to assume that this would occupy an entire book, or the better part of one. Such a book, according to my theory, would automatically constitute the climax of the entire work; and it could well have had a different character. Since the subject is St Olav, we cannot altogether discount the possibility that it could have been composed as a legend. However, it could also have been written by being based on the same principles of historical writing as *HN*.

If we continue the train of thought from Book I, in a potential Book II we might expect a parallel account with that of Olav Tryggvason in the *vita*-section, apart from the viking enterprises abroad, *i.e.* some mention of St Olav's conversion and baptism. Furthermore, we would expect Olav's Christian missionary work in Norway to be given equal emphasis with Olav Tryggvason's. As Olav Tryggvason's son, Tryggve, is not mentioned in Book I,[209] we might not expect St Olav's son, Magnus, to be mentioned in a Book II, though he actually became king after St Olav. The real climax surely must have been an account of Olav's death, which took place in the Nidaros area itself, an important argument for an archdiocese there. As for good reasons there was no *translatio* of Olav Tryggvason, we might not expect to find mention of St Olav's. Finally, we cannot exclude the possibility that the book, which must have expressed a generalized pro-English, anti-Danish attitude, could have ended with a number of the miracles that we perhaps see reflected in the poem *Geisli* from *c.* 1153 and in the oldest part of *Passio Olaui* (see below). At least one of these miracles might correspond to the information about Olav Tryggvason's possible rescue by angels.

It is thought that the oldest Olav saga was penned during the years around 1150.[210] Perhaps we could assume that a Latin version of this work, or of a correspondingly early edition,[211] was actually Book II of *HN*? If this were so, then it would be easy to understand how it could have been separated from Book I and in a short time have begun to circulate as an independent book, as an Olav legend.

[209] *Cf.* Commentary on XVII 56.

[210] For fragments of the oldest Olav saga and their nature, *cf.* de Vries 1967 II, 241 and Louis-Jensen 1970, 60.

[211] *Cf.*, for instance, Schreiner 1926, 13ff.

If we take my theory as a point of departure, on Breakspear's visit Book I of *HN*, as mentioned, could already have outlived its usefulness and become obsolete; it was a commissioned work, prepared with a specific purpose in mind. Book II, on the other hand, could easily have been reworked and given its own introduction,[212] such as for instance the introduction to the *uita*-section found in Metcalfe's edition of *Passio Olaui*. This introduction would be superfluous and unfit in a Book II of *HN*, because *HN* has its own geographical description of the Norwegian realm, and because Olav Tryggvason is credited here with the Christianizing of the country. But what about an earlier version of *Passio Olaui* than Metcalfe's manuscript? Here, indeed, we might find something interesting. Fortunately enough we have an earlier version at our disposal: *Codex Duacensis* from *c.* 1170–90,[213] which represents the most reliable and probably the oldest extant Latin version of *Passio Olaui*.[214] If we take a closer look at it, we shall find the following in the *vita*-section: it is much shorter than Metcalfe's manuscript of *Passio Olaui*, but reflects it nearly *verbatim*; the highly legendary tone and the use of many scriptural passages are drastically reduced; and it deals exclusively with Olav's life and work on earth, as well as his death. The same is true of *Codex Neoclaustrensis* (sixteenth century).[215] Neither of them contains anything which is not found in Metcalfe's manuscript. An introduction like that in *Codex Duacensis* fits better than the one in Metcalfe's *Passio Olaui* as a continuation of *HN* Book I, but this is not to say that it was necessarily such a continuation.

However, some features of *Codex Duacensis* connect this legend and *HN*. Moreover they are all common to the Latin manuscripts and editions of Olav's breviaries and legends that we know of, so we can keep the term *Passio Olavi*.[216] Olav's main antagonist in *Passio Olaui* is the Danish King Knud. In *Gammelnorsk Homiliebok*, which was written in Old Norse and partly builds on the Latin, partly on the Old Norse tradition, it is the name of the Norwegian land-owner Kalv Arnesson which is mentioned in this connection.[217] Reference to Knud in the Latin versions might indicate an original author who sympathized with the Norwegian land-owing aristocracy, and not at all with the Danish king nor the Danes, as the author of *HN* might have done (see 8.10. above and 11.2.1. below). On the other hand, one might say that both Olav Tryggvason and St Olav were in a way betrayed by the Trønders without it being said so directly: Olav Tryggvason

[212] *Cf.* also Holtsmark 1956, 20–24. She dates the first version of *Passio Olaui* to before 1150 (p. 24).

[213] Bibliothèque municipale in Douai, 295, fol. 94–108.

[214] *Cf.* Ekrem 2000.

[215] Located in Wiener-Neustadt, Neukloster XII. Signature: D 21 fol. 1–6.

[216] The editions of Storm 1880 and Metcalfe 1881, the manuscripts mentioned as well as *Liber Laurentii Odonis* (Dresden, Sächs. Landesbibl. A 182, fol. 172–77) and *Vita Sancti Olaui* (Oxford, Bodl. Rawlinson C 440, fol. 187v–94r). The fragments *Stockholm, Riksarkivet*, Fr 596, 614 and Br 256 diverge somewhat from these, but not in any of the matters discussed (I thank Eyolf Østrem, Uppsala, for copies of the three last items).

[217] *Cf. Gammelnorsk Homiliebok,* trans. Salvesen 1971, 143.

because they didn't join him on his expedition against the Danish king, and St Olav because they were his actual opponents and killers in the battle at Stiklestad. However, the mention of Knud's name makes him the main person to blame.

Furthermore, while we are on the subject, we find the same aversion to the Danes in miracle no. 4,[218] in which "the villain" is a prominent Danish personage, while good relations with England can be deduced from miracle No. 8,[219] in which "the victim" is an English priest who is rescued by Olav. It is also worth stating that the first ten miracles of *Passio Olaui* seem to have taken place before the Norwegian archdiocese was established.[220] These same miracles seem to form the oldest part of *Passio Olaui*, the first of which (about the celestial ladder just before the death of St Olav) corresponds in a way to the miracle, referred to in *HN*, of angels at the death of Olav Tryggvason. Also significant might be the following: neither the son of Olav Tryggvason nor the son of St Olav is mentioned in *HN* Book I. The reason for leaving out the latter might be an obvious one; he was not born until some years after Olav came to Norway. But he is not referred to in any of the Latin versions of *Passio Olaui* either, and here he could have been mentioned when he fled with his father to King Jarislav, since this event forms part of the legend. Thus the reason for leaving out Olav Tryggvason's son in *HN* Book I might be due to a missing parallel account to St Olav in a Book II or vice versa. This might also be the reason for the omission of St Olav's *translatio* (see 8.13. above) in all the Latin versions of *Passio Olaui*. It is mostly mentioned in works which build on Old Norse tradition.

The best indication of a connection between *HN* and *Passio Olaui* in an older version, might, however, be the following: in spite of all the parallel accounts of Olav Tryggvason and St Olav in *HN*, one important issue is missing, St Olav's baptism. We are only told that he, like Olav Tryggvason, brought clerics with him back to Norway, so that we understand that he was already a Christian. We know from other medieval works that according to one tradition St Olav was baptized in Ringerike in the eastern part of Norway by Olav Tryggvason when he was three years old.[221] But Theodoricus also knows of another version:[222] Olav was said to have been converted to Christianity in England and have been baptized in Rouen. Moreover in another place Theodoricus narrates that during Olav's stay in England a recluse predicted that he would become a saint (ch. 15). This last piece of information is nearly the same as the account of Olav Tryggvason's meeting with the recluse in *HN*. One might say that in a way it is transferred to the latter. But the account of St Olav's conversion in England, most probably known also to the

[218] Storm 1880, 136–7 and Metcalfe 1881, 78–79.

[219] Storm 1880, 138–9 and Metcalfe 1881, 80–82.

[220] As the numbering of miracles might differ in various articles, it must be emphasized here that I mean up to and including the miracle of Olav's cutting shavings on a Sunday (Storm 1880, 139–40 and Metcalfe 1880, 83–84).

[221] *Cf. e.g. Óláfs saga Helga* ch. 8, Snorri, *Heimskringla, Óláfs saga Tryggvasonar*, 60 and Theodoricus ch. 13.

[222] Theodoricus ch. 13, *cf.* also William of Jumièges's *Gesta Normannorum Ducum* V.12.

author of *HN*, would fit excellently into *HN*. Why then, did the author not say anything about it, or about Olav's baptism at all? The reason might be that it was to be mentioned, or already was referred to in a Book II. And this is exactly the case with *Codex Duacensis*. This work not only recounts this episode, but even begins with it: *Gloriosus rex Olauus ewangelice ueritatis sinceritate in Anglia comperta fidem toto admisit pectore et ad baptismi gratiam in urbe Rothomagi deuota animi alacritate conuolauit* ("The renowned King Olav perceived in England the sincerity of the evangelic truth, admitted the faith with all his heart, and, pious and devoted, he hastened to be baptized in the city of Rouen").[223]

Whereas the Danish kings in *HN* and *Passio Olaui* were a threat to both Olav Tryggvason and St Olav, the Russian kings supported them; in *HN* Olav Tryggvason in his exile as a boy, is adopted by the Russian king (no name stated), and in *Passio Olaui* St Olav spends his exile with King Jarislav (his brother-in-law according to *HN*). They were, so to speak, both related to these kings. Finally, the style in which both works are written comprises both legendary passages and matter-of-fact passages based on the principles of historical writing, while the attitude of the author(s) seems to be the same in both works.

Whatever the conclusions, the resemblance between *Passio Olaui* and *HN* is remarkable and seems too great to be merely coincidental. But there are also differences. The most important is that Olav Tryggvason was not forced to flee to Russia after he had become king. Whereas he is described as the conqueror of heathendom, the account of St Olav is a *passio*. And whereas Olav Tryggvason dies, or disappears, for a justified, but materialistic, cause, St Olav dies also for his faith. That means that Olav Tryggvason fought for Christianity, but he did not die for it. Furthermore, he disappeared in the sea and his body was never found. Right here lies the problem of the author of *HN*; in spite of many parallels he is unable to form the account of Olav Tryggvason as a *passio*. Instead he tries to emphasize Olav Tryggvason's laborious effort in the cause of Christianity, probably hoping to make him worthy as a saint. Another difference between *Passio Olaui* and *HN* is that in *Passio Olaui* the exact place and date of St Olav's death is mentioned, *i.e.* Stiklestad, 29th of July 1028. The author of *HN* does not give a corresponding specification concerning Olav Tryggvason's death, but dates, as mentioned above, are not found in *HN* at all. The results of my research into all known Latin versions of *Passio Olaui* thus seem to indicate a connection with *HN*. But that does not mean that *Passio Olaui* was written as a Book II of *HN*; a Latin version of an Olav saga/legend might already have been available, and *HN* might have been written as its Book I. If that is the case, such a version has merely functioned like — though was not in fact — a Book II of *HN*. This last possibility does not seem at all improbable. If so, the author might be vindicated for writing *explicit* ("the end") at the end of the first book.

Again this is conditional on his being the author of both works; if there is anything to the claim that the source for an older version of *Passio Olaui* corresponds to Book II of *HN*, then it might be said that *HN* continues up to the time around

[223] *Cf.* also Ekrem 2000.

1152, when the miracles were still taking place, and then St Olav, along with the many people whom he healed by virtue of faith and deeds, can be linked with *multorum magnificencias* ("many men's splendid feats"), which we heard about in the Prologue of *HN*.[224] Thus the Prologue must have been composed after *HN* Book I and Book II were written, and both books must have been written by one and the same person. Then, in my opinion, we have to eliminate Øystein (see below).[225] When the author uses the expression *multorum magnificencias*, he is not thinking of mighty princes and prominent men and their exploits, as one might think, but rather the saint-king himself and the many believers in Christ. But then again, *HN* was not, in my opinion, written as a chronicle of kings in the usual sense of the term, but as a national history, a *Historia Norwegie*, conceived against an ecclesiastical-historical backcloth, and springing out of an ecclesiastical-political need.

As the whole issue of a possible Book II is rather questionable, we must leave it here, but I have found the theory of a possible connection between *HN* and *Passio Olavi* so interesting that I decided to publish it.[226]

9.4. A possible Book III and IV of HN?

Whether there might have been still another book, beyond the one about St Olav, is impossible to say, but using my interpretation and dating as a hypothesis, such a book would seem to be superfluous as far as the author's purpose was concerned. Nor, for that matter, is there anything that even points in that direction. Theodoricus's chronicle, "The History of the Ancient Norwegian Kings", could in fact have been written to compensate for such a missing continuation of the list of kings.

One reason for a continuation of *HN* could be that the kings would have felt slighted if the royal line were not updated in a more detailed form. If this is the case, then the author had to pick up his account where he left off after St Olav, and update the list in greater detail up to the time of the three kings of his own day. The fact that Harald Hardråde is the last reigning king whom the author refers to by name could be due to his source. For example, Gjessing believed that Sæmund the Learned left off his history when this king was to take over after the death of Magnus the Good (den gode).[227] But this very same Magnus is not mentioned at all in *HN* — in any case, not in Book I. Granted, he represented a "blind alley", since the line of kings continued with his half-uncle, Harald Hardråde. Nevertheless (again, with my theory as a point of departure), this seems strange, partly because Magnus, if anyone, provided a useful argument in the battle for an independent archdiocese vis-à-vis the Danes, since for a time he ruled over both Norway and Denmark — and partly because he, and also Olav Kyrre and Magnus, are mentioned in Adam. The author's reason for not including these three

[224] The term *magnificencias* is used only this once in *HN*. It could also have been used in Odd's Latin and original saga of Olav Tryggvason, as an expression of "the greatest feats", which in turn seems to point to Christian deeds and virtues (Fagerheim 1995, 68).

[225] *Cf.* Ekrem 2000. [226] *Ibid.* [227] 1896, 128.

kings could be that his primary intention was not to write a chronicle or to retaliate against Adam. But it might nevertheless be a good reason to follow up Adam. The next king, Magnus Berrføtt, by conquering the western islands could play a part in strengthening the Norwegians' ecclesiastical candidacy there. But all this remains speculation. The fact that neither the Danish nor the Norwegian kings in *HN* are listed by name any later than Harald Hardråde (died 1066) is not necessarily surprising. We might today view the matter in too modern a fashion, for during the 1100s people had a different and a stereotypical way of thinking.

My conclusion is that the author of *HN* prioritized that portion of Norwegian history which constituted the actual basis and source for what was significant for him; Trøndelag was the oldest and most important area, the Uplands were home to the oldest Norwegian kings, and their descendants were still ruling the kingdom of Norway; the people of the Orkneys, the Faeroes and Iceland were direct descendants of the Norwegians, and the payment of taxes from the various parts of the kingdom was mentioned as proof of its current scope. In addition we have the extensive account of Olav Tryggvason. As early as his time a solid Christian foundation was laid in Norway. In other words, the foundation was laid for a national archdiocese of a certain size, an episcopal seat at Hamar, and for the potential beatification of Olav Tryggvason. If we follow this interpretation, there does not seem to have been any reason to continue the list of kings after a possible Book II. Nor are there any signs to show that the author of *HN* may have had a work of four volumes in mind, similar to that of Adam's.

9.5. Paganism and Christianity

With respect to point 3 concerning paganism and Christianity, it would seem to be answered – not as a separate point, but integrated in the text at various places. Gjessing is right in pointing out that the author of *HN* describes the volcanic eruption near Iceland in terms of contemporaneous events and the Finns' pagan beliefs.[228] But Gjessing errs in believing that a *historia ecclesiastica* is missing.[229] Indeed we hear of the situation for both religions at the time of writing (Christians along the coast and in the Uplands, pagans in Hålogaland and in the forested zone), as well as the introduction of Christianity and the expulsion of paganism in connection with the accounts of the Norwegian kings, and especially of Olav Tryggvason According to my interpretation, we can say that, in a certain sense, *HN* also contains a Norwegian *historia ecclesiastica*, though insignificant.

10. Place of origin

Hægstad 1919–20, independently of any other research on *HN*, determined that the language was very much like Munkeliv's *Jordebok* (from *c.* 1175, Bergen). If we look at the political scene around 1150, there is much there that points to Bergen and to the circle around King Inge. We can also consider the expression *in villula Alrecstadum, iuxta quam nunc sita est Bergonia ciuitas opinatissima*[230] ("at the manor Alrekstad, close to the present site of the famous city of Bergen"), which

[228] 1896, 133. [229] *Ibid.*, 134. [230] XIV 3.

is no proof in itself, since Bergen was a large city in Norway at the time; but it could support it as a place of authorship. This is, in fact, the only place in *HN* in which an extra definition of a smaller place is associated with a city. Moreover, the addition to Bergen of *ciuitas opinatissima* ("the famous city") is unique in *HN*.[231] According to my theory we should not, however, exclude Nidaros as a possible place of origin; Nidaros would have had special interest in the matter of an archdiocese-to-be.

11. Commissioner, dedicatee and author

11.1. The dedicatee

11.1.1. Agnelle / Angnelle / Anguelle

It is time for an attempt to answer the following questions. Who is the commissioner of *HN*? Who is the dedicatee? Are they one and the same person? And who is the person who conceived *HN*? Whether the latter is the actual author of *HN* is, as previously mentioned, an open question, but we have no choice but to assume that he was. As for the commissioner, we shall also have to leave that an open question for the moment and concentrate on the dedicatee.

Over the years a number of persons, as previously mentioned, have been discussed as possible candidates for dedicatee (see the survey at the end), but no researcher has been able to pin it down. Everyone has accepted Munch's and Storm's reading of the form of the dedicatee: *āgnelle / āguelle*, which they spell out as *Agnelle / Angnelle / Anguelle*. Storm goes further with the name Agnellus and suggests, as stated above, that this could be Archdeacon Agnellus from Wells, of the end of the 1100s, and many later researchers follow Storm. However, this is to ignore the line over "a" that both Munch and Storm took to be a nasal line. Thus this suggestion would seem, at first glance, less acceptable, even if the spelling *Angnellus* for *Agnellus* was no doubt used as well. The form *Anguelle*, in the sense of "dear Orm", would seem to be a better suggestion, and this also accords with my interpretation of *HN*. *Anguelle* is thus a form for the diminutive in the vocative (form of address), used as an expression of intimacy, of the nominative *anguis*, which, like the Norwegian personal name Orm, literally means "a serpent", "a snake". The actual diminutive is *anguiculus* ("a little worm/snake"), so this could not be used. Furthermore, forms with *-ellus* seem to have been popular in the Middle Ages.[232] The intimate form of address corresponds to the second person singular that the author uses when addressing his dedicatee, and would seem to indicate that the dedicatee and the author must have been quite close friends, and that the distance between them, from a professional standpoint, could not have been very great. There does not seem to have been any real pupil-teacher relationship. With the name Orm, Abbot Orm comes to mind, who was at the Munkeliv monastery in 1146, as Hanssen suggested.[233] Against this, perhaps, is a written reply from the Pope addressed to him in the same year, in which Orm

[231] This expression is also found in the Book of Judith 2,13.

[232] *Cf.* Elliot 1997, 12.

is called by the Norwegian name *Ormo*.[234] This means that Orm himself probably used this form in his previous (now lost) letter to the Pope. But it would have been odd for him to sign his letter *Anguis*.

There is yet another reason for believing that this Orm could be the dedicatee; it depends on what the author means by the expression (Prologue 7) *iure didascalico mi prelate* (translated here by "you, who have been set over me with a teacher's authority").[235] The term *prelatus* ("a leading person", "a superior") was used in the Middle Ages, among other things, to designate an abbot or a bishop. If the aforementioned Abbot Orm was *HN*'s dedicatee, this could mean that he was *didascalus* in Bergen, *i.e.* the canon in charge of the school at the chapter.[236] This sounds reasonable, but we should remember that a *prelatus* in *HN* is also used to denote petty kings and rulers in pagan times.[237] In other words this term need not allude to a cleric. Moreover, *prelatus* actually means "a person who is preferred" (here: "my preferred master teacher"). But the fact that the adjective *didascalicus* can be used also in a broader sense, ("very learned" or "apt to teach"), and the fact that we know nothing else about Abbot Orm make it impossible for us to determine with any certainty whether he is the dedicatee of *HN*. But if he is, then he must have been Norwegian, or perhaps English — but he could not have been Danish, considering the attitude of the author of *HN* towards the Danes. Nevertheless it is not impossible that Abbot Orm could be the same Orm who is called a prior in Ringsted monastery (Denmark) in 1139. This was a Benedictine monastery, founded in *c.* 1082. It also housed the burial site of the Danish martyr, Knud Lavard. And we could also add that Robert Elgensis, perhaps an English Benedictine monk (from Ely) at the Ringsted monastery, wrote *Vita sancti Canuti ducis*, *i.e.* about Knud Lavard, during the period 1134–37. This work was written in order to promote the cult of Knud as a saint, and Orm, as prior, must have known of this. A position as abbot at the monastery in Bergen meant, at that time, a promotion for this same Orm. It is only a short distance between Ringsted and Roskilde, where the Sorø manuscript, according to Steinnes, was located. So Orm could have known about this. For all we know, he might even have been the copyist! All this remains in the realm of speculation; nevertheless it shows us that it is easy to make a connection between Bergen and Roskilde if that is necessary. Orm could also, though no document says so, be the same person who later became bishop of Hamar, the second bishop ordained there, though we do not know exactly when.[238]

11.1.2. Augustinelle

There is another possibility. Both Munch and Storm may have misinterpreted the name in the copy of *HN*. If we look closely, and take the copy quite literally, we see that it does not say *āgnelle* / *āguelle*. The line over the "a" is not an unambigu-

[233] 1949, 18. [234] *Latinske dokument*, ed. Vandvik 1959, 38.

[235] *jure* means "on account of"/"by virtue of"/"by the right of".

[236] According to Steinnes 1965, 28.

[237] *Cf.* the quotation above (8.4.) on the sons of Gunnhild and their tyrannical rule.

[238] *Cf.* Hanssen 1949, 18.

ous nasal line that shows the disappearance of "n" or "m"; rather it seems to be an abbreviation in the form of a line that also stretches over most of the letter "g." And this gives a different turn to things: such an abbreviation is used in connection with the names August (the month), *Augustus*, and *Augustinus*.[239] If we add *-elle*, we get *Augustinelle* ("dear Augustine"), a form of the diminutive in the vocative, used as an expression of intimacy, for the name *Augustinus*. And just who might this *Augustinus* be? 1. We are fortunate enough to possess at least two writings in which this name is used for one and the same person; Theodoricus dedicates his work to *Augustino Nidrosiensi archiepiscopo*[240] ("Archbishop Øystein of Nidaros"), and this same Øystein calls himself *Augustinus* in *Passio Olaui*.[241] In other words we might be dealing with the later Archbishop Øystein. The name *Augustinus* alludes to Øystein's great examplar, the Church Father Augustine (354–430). An indication that *HN* was written before Øystein became archbishop (around 1160) could be the missing title *Archiepiscopus* in the address in the Prologue. On the other hand the word *prelate* occurs. 2. An alternative to Archbishop Øystein is King Øystein who was a *prelatus* in the sense of "petty king". He, too, is called *Augustinus* in one of the miracles in *Passio Olavi*[242] and is interesting here as his scald, Einar Skulason, was the one who wrote *Geisli*.

Unfortunately we cannot make any further headway in our speculations at this point. The fact is we cannot be completely sure that the reading *Augustinelle* is correct; the difference consists of just a few millimetres of a horizontal line, which might even simply be the copyist having drawn the line a bit too far to the right. If that is so, it would not be the only place in the copy that this occurs. Moreover, as I see it, the letter after "g" seems more closely to resemble a "u" than an "n" in our copy. But if this is the case, it could easily represent a misinterpretation on the Scottish copyist's part. He was not all that skilled.

11.1.3. Other alternatives

The name of the dedicatee might simply represent a Norwegian or an English and otherwise unknown cleric in Norway. Finally, the possibility of a misspelling or confusion of the name of the dedicatee must not be ruled out; then, for example, *Anguilla* ("Åle") and, interestingly enough, *Ynguelle/Inguelle* ("dear Inge") *i.e.* King Inge, could be a likely alternative. But all in all, we must conclude that we have reached the end of the line regarding sure conclusions about the dedicatee.

11.2. The author

11.2.1. Archbishop Øystein

In view of everything else that has come to light in the present study, the question arises whether Øystein as an author might have had a hand in the forming of *HN*. He would then seem to have begun his literary activity earlier than otherwise thought. Around the year 1150 Øystein was King Inge's curate and "fehirde", *i.e.* royal treasurer. This might explain why *HN* talks so precisely about the taxes from

[239] Cappelli 1929, 10–11. [240] Theodoricus, Prologue, 3.
[241] In Metcalfe 1881, 104. [242] Metcalfe 1881, 103.

the Finns and the western islands, and illuminates the view of *Olauus rex perpetuus* which, as mentioned earlier, we recognize in Øystein's Letter of Privilege. Before Øystein entered the Norwegian political scene in earnest there is little we know about him. He came from a line of landowners in Trøndelag and was born perhaps around the year 1120. His great-grandfather was Ulv Uspaksson, who served as King Harald Hardråde's brother-in-arms and marshal.[243] Perhaps this might also explain, in part, why Harald received the aforementioned additional description (XV 8) *uirum sagacissimum et in bellica arte peritissimum* ("a man of deep perspicacity, a great expert in the science of warfare") in a paragraph of *HN* that in all other respects deals only with genealogy. As already stated, the author leaves out his nickname Hardråde ("Hardruler"). It is possible that he was trying to conceal it on account of the ruling kings who were descended from him in a direct line. The praise could, as mentioned, merely be a tribute to the three royal brothers, perhaps on account of the fact that Øystein — if, indeed, he is the author — on the basis of his relatives' accounts, had got a different impression of Harald from what the nickname Hardråde would suggest. But, as noted above, he might also have omitted it as an answer to Adam.

Ellehøj 1965 takes up the question as to whether the author of *HN* could be a spokesman for the view of the Norwegian magnates and an opponent of the king's encroaching power; he shows no wrath towards those farmers from Gulatingslag and Trøndelag who failed Olav Tryggvason by refusing to go to the war with him, and who consequently returned home. Did the author know that a levied force was not bound by duty to a war of attack, and did he excuse them for this reason? asks Ellehøj.[244] This may possibly be the reason, but it could also be due to the fact that the author here was in a dilemma and thus passed over the matter lightly; on the one hand, he doubtless did not want the great Christian king, Olav, to be let down; on the other hand, he and the farmers might well have belonged to the same circle — all of which is consistent with the view that Øystein could have written *HN*.

After his schooling in Nidaros, Øystein probably studied abroad, although we do not know where. If Abbot Orm is the dedicatee, and Øystein the author, this could imply that the latter had had some connection with the school in Bergen before his residence abroad; but in my view it also means that as curate he was in a subordinate position with respect to the canon, Orm, although the distance between the two could not have been very great. Around 1160 King Inge appointed Øystein as archbishop of Nidaros, where he served in this post until his death in 1188. The many ecclesiastical and national political documents of his that have been preserved suggest a "statesman and church builder"[245] of rank and of corresponding vigour. Furthermore, Øystein seems to have been a friend of England. It could, for example, be mentioned that, after their defeat of Magnus's forces at the hands of Sverre, Øystein chose to flee to England, while King Magnus himself chose Denmark.

[243] Gunnes 1996, 17. [244] 1965, 151. [245] *Cf.* the title of Gunnes 1996.

On the basis of my interpretation, Øystein, or a person of the same background or view, would seem to be a reasonable candidate for author, since *HN*, on the surface, appears to be a chronicle that praises the Norwegian kings' greatness and exploits, yet all the while seems to be inspired by the wishes and interests of the Church. In my opinion, *HN* first and foremost has an ecclesiastical purpose. But all in all I am forced to conclude that it is not possible at the present time to confirm or disprove whether Øystein is the author of *HN*.

11.2.2. Other alternatives

If Øystein is not the author, then, in my opinion, the person who did compose *HN* must have had thoughts and attitudes similar to Øystein's. It is difficult to say who such an author could be, since the same attitudes were probably typical of many within the Norwegian clergy and among the Norwegian élite in general at that time. It is not improbable that a monk could have been assigned the task of writing *HN*.[246] Learned monks good at writing were often used as clerks at that time, and monasteries were consulted for advice and were involved in diplomatic activity. One suggestion, put forward without any documentation and mostly for want of alternatives, could be the above-mentioned Ragnvald Klerk who, during Breakspear's visit, was ordained bishop of the Hebrides and the Isle of Man and who followed the king of Hebrides home, perhaps in 1153. They stopped en route at the Orkneys and could have brought a manuscript with them (see also 12. below). But this is all mere speculation.

11.3. Conclusion

Skard 1930 concluded that the author of *HN* was a Norwegian, had been abroad and studied, and had been thoroughly trained in all the stylistic and rhetorical arts. *HN*'s knowledge of the Vulgate was so good that Skard believed there were valid reasons for assuming that the author was a prominent cleric. According to Skard it is not possible to show where he studied abroad.[247] For the most part this strengthens my own impressions. The author of *HN* is austere in his approach. He wishes to stress allusions to the Vulgate and to contemporary literature, probably for the purpose of showing that *HN* was being written by a trustworthy Christian, a learned and enlightened man, thus rendering *HN* a legally reliable document.

Its writing in Latin alone shows that *HN* was also intended for a foreign audience. This, too, might be reflected in the way of presenting personal and geographical names (see 8.3. above and 13.1. below), but *Agnelle / Angnelle / Anguelle / Augustinelle*, to whom the book is dedicated, might well have been Norwegian. The book was almost certainly written by a Norwegian; he shows a continuous train of Norwegian thought and an equally profound knowledge of Norwegian affairs. However, in my opinion it is not possible, on the basis of the text, to determine what part of the country the author was most familiar with. The author presents himself as truth-loving (in the sense that the truth is in the sources), he weighs his words with care, and he makes eclectic use of his sources. This is par-

[246] *Cf.* also Ekrem 2000.

[247] Skard 1930, 84–85.

ticularly evident in his use of Adam's work. The author knows how to make his case by means of a subtle treatment of the material and a sober, down-to-earth style. He shows both clerical and worldly sides and is both a theoretician and a practitioner. He is extremely thankful to his commissioner on account of *crebrorum munerum beneficio* ("all those many kind favours", Prologue 2) on his part, and there seems to be a close friendship between the two of them. It must have been in his capacity as superior, benefactor and good friend that the commissioner gave his author the assignment to write *HN*. The relationship between the dedicatee and the author bears the same stamp. That might be an indication that the commissioner and the dedicatee are one and the same person.

One argument that seems to speak in favour of author and dedicatee being two local persons is as follows: the Prologue in *HN* is penned in the first person singular, except for the expressions (5) *nostris aminiculis* ("our/my resources") and *si quid nostra refert* ("if they (*i.e.* the envious persons) are at all capable of doing us/me harm"). This could be interpreted to mean that the author is in the same location as his dedicatee and belongs to the same learned circle. And we might add that the Prologue as a whole does not give the impression of any great distance in space between the author and his dedicatee. Nevertheless it should be pointed out that the Latin expression in the first person plural does not necessarily include persons other than the author himself.

All in all the commissioner/dedicatee does not seem to be a fictitious person. But ultimately we should ask whether one and the same person might have been both commissioner/dedicatee and author of *HN*. This option leaves many questions unanswered and is highly speculative. The possibility must nevertheless be mentioned, since this kind of fictitious commission was not uncommon during the Middle Ages.

The conclusion must be that it is not possible at the present time to pin down one or more particular persons as the commissioner, dedicatee or author of *HN*.

12. Final comments

I have attempted to show that there is no reason why *HN* could not have been written before 1152/1153, and that there are positive reasons for believing that indeed it was. The many questions that researchers have posed over the past 150 years have, in my opinion, now found an answer that is subsumed in an overlying issue: the establishment of the archdiocese at Nidaros. Since all answers can easily be refuted, it is not their quality but their quantity that makes the theory interesting. Whether, taken together, they represent the actual truth cannot be determined; but if nothing else, they will hopefully reinvigorate the debate about *HN* and its age. If I should be proved right in my hypothesis, then *HN* must be characterized as a well-thought-out, purposeful work, penned by a learned and skilful person. It does not seem likely that *HN* is just an ordinary school assignment. *HN*, which in its day and age was surely considered to be a reliable legal document but which, during the past 150 years, has been regarded by many as an innocuous, incomplete and superficial small chronicle of kings — even a botched piece of work — could turn out in reality to be a subtle "application" to the cardinal/Pope. By this I do not necessarily mean that *HN* was sent to the Pope with an application, even though that is within the realm of possibility. But in that case, *HN* would more probably have taken the form of a rhetorical address with direct argumentation, although we cannot be sure of this either. The requirements for accuracy in a work of history are far more stringent than those for a piece of writing filled with rhetoric. What I am proposing is that *HN* seems to reflect Norwegian interests in connection with a separate archdiocese, and could have been conceived with a view to a potential contact with the Pope or his representative. It is basically from the perspective of such interests that I believe *HN* can best be understood: 1. A national archdiocese, with its seat in Nidaros. 2. The scope of this archdiocese. 3. A new diocese in the Uplands. 4. A possible canonization of Olav Tryggvason. We find the justification in *HN*, which must be read against the background of Solinus and Honorius, and especially of Adam. Regarded in this way, the author is vindicated when he writes in the Prologue that such an assignment (implicit, as far as he understood it) has never before been written in Latin and, we could add, certainly not by a Norwegian. We understand his foreboding. It is pointless to ask whether a similar work was ever written in Old Norse, because the cardinal/Pope, for understandable reasons, would not have comprehended it.

Furthermore, it did not seem certain, when *HN* was written, that Norway would get its own archdiocese. This could indicate that *HN* was written in connection either with a Church council, or with Reidar's trip south (cf. § 4.2.), where he was ordained as archbishop, *i.e. c.* 1150. This sounds quite reasonable. It means, in turn, that the question of whether any Norwegian initiative was taken with respect to the establishment of an archdiocese must be answered in the affirmative.[248] On the other hand there are many factors which tend to suggest that the decision to send a cardinal envoy to Scandinavia came quickly from the Curia — so quickly, in fact, that it took the principle actors in Norway by surprise.[249] Moreover if they did know of the visit in advance, it is hard to say whether they knew that it would be the Englishman Nicholas Breakspear who was coming as *HN*'s pro-English bias could also symbolize how the author takes sides with the Pope against Hamburg-Bremen. If *HN* was written for a cardinal envoy/Breakspear and not for the Pope in the first instance, then *HN* might have been written in 1151–52, *i.e.* after Archbishop Reidar's company finally returned home (for he could not have left alone) with information about his death and the results of his visit to Rome, and before Breakspear arrived on 20th July 1152.

There is a third possibility, however: *HN* could have been written while Breakspear was in the country and possibly at his suggestion or commission, *i.e.* it could have been formulated in 1152–53. This option seems to be somewhat less likely.

Pope Anastasius IV (1153–54) confirmed the Norwegian archdiocese in a Letter of Privilege of 28 November 1154. He died only a few days later, and Breakspear was elected to be the new Pope, taking the name Hadrian IV.

In any case, if *HN* was written in connection with the establishment of a national archdiocese, this also readily explains how a manuscript copy found its

[248] If there is anything to this, then it is natural to ask whether the oldest Olav's saga, or a Latin version of it (or a possible Book II of *HN*), was written down as a result of this move.
[249] Johnsen 1945, 55–59.

way to the Orkneys; in addition to the above-mentioned possibility involving Ragnvald Klerk, it could have been brought back by Earl Ragnvald himself (who, incidentally, had poetical gifts)[250] and his learned bishop, William the Old (or "the good Paris clerk", as he was also called),[251] after meeting the cardinal. For, as we recall, these two remained in Norway until just before Christmas, probably in 1153. But even if this is the case, it is far from certain that it was the original they brought back with them. It could have been a copy, from which our own copy originates. This could also explain why we only have Book I today; perhaps the earl was only interested in Book I, which mentioned the Orkneys, and had a copy made of it. Another possibility is that the Scottish copyist who wrote on commission from the Sinclair family, previously earls of Orkney, about the year 1500 in order to record as much information as possible about the latter's lineage, had no use himself for a Book II, nor an Olav saga/legend, and might therefore have decided not to copy it.

But if the original did not come to the Orkneys, where was it? As far as I can tell, it might possibly have been in Bergen,[252] or it could also have been taken to Rome. This, in turn, might explain why Theodoricus did not know about *HN*. When Koht writes:[253] "Historia Norvegiæ was not a work that left any great mark", he is correct as far as its being a source for other works is concerned, but perhaps not so correct where it concerns the major changes that took place in Norwegian Church history immediately afterwards, and in Norwegian Church politics in general.

Finally, it should be mentioned that if *HN* ever included a Book II, then the word *Explicit* ("The end"), which concludes our copy of Book I of *HN*, must have been added by the copyist; or he could have been using only a part of the expression *Explicit liber I* ("Here ends the first book"). The third possibility in case of a connection between *HN* and an older version of *Passio Olavi* was suggested above.

In any case, there is much to suggest that *Historia Norwegie* was conceived before the Norwegian archdiocese was established in 1152/1153, and in this regard Halvdan Koht was not exaggerating when, in 1919–20, he called it "Den fyrste norske nasjonalhistoria" (*i.e.* "The First Norwegian National History").

[250] de Vries 1967 II, 24–33.
[251] *Flateyjarbók*, ed. 1862 II, 475.
[252] The Danish bishop here, Anders Foss, seems to have been familiar with it (Storm 1880, xxx). *Cf.* his surveys from 1592 of the Danish kings in which Gunnhild is the Danish king's daughter as in *HN*, the only place from which we know it. *Cf.* also his son-in-law Henrik Høyer, who is known for his collection of manuscripts. Unfortunately, most of it was destroyed in a fire at Copenhagen University in 1728. We find the same pedigree of Gunnhild in Peder Claussøn Friis, who also includes the comment about how Norway got its name from Nor (Aðalbjarnarson 1937, 40). Further, we also find Gunnhild's Danish descent in Arild Huitfeldt (around 1600) and Claus Lyschander (the 1600s) (Storm 1876, 4). Aðalbjarnarson 1937, 7 claims that the Swedish excerpts from the basis manuscript of *HN* are proof that copies of it existed in Norway. Chesnutt 1986, 67–68 writes that an exemplar of *HN* was at Kirkwall in the first half of the 1400s. Steinnes 1965, 27 mentions how Anders Foss could have seen the copy in Roskilde. But none of the foregoing precludes the possibility that the original or a copy of it was in Bergen.
[253] Koht 1919–20, 118.

Bibliography

Abbreviations

General

ML — Medieval Latin
KLNM — *Kulturhistorisk leksikon for nordisk middelalder*
DN — *Diplomatarium Norvegicum*
PL — *Patrologia Latina*
NGL — *Norges gamle love indtil 1387*

Books of the Vulgate

Act — Actus Apostolorum
Cor — Epistula Pauli ad Corinthios
Dn — Danihel Propheta
Est — Liber Hester
Ex — Liber Exodi
Ez — Hiezecihel Propheta
Gn — Liber Genesis
Hbr — Epistula Pauli ad Hebraeos
Io — Evangelium secundum Iohannem
Iob — Liber Iob
Ioel — Iohel Propheta
Ion — Iona Propheta
Ios — Liber Iosue
Is — Isaias Propheta
Lc — Evangelium secundum Lucam
Mc — Evangelium secundum Marcum
Mcc — Liber Macchabeorum
Mt — Evangelium secundum Mattheum
Nm — Liber Numerorum
Par — Liber Paralipomenon
Phil — Epistula Pauli ad Philippenses
Prv — Liber Proverbiorum
Ps — Liber Psalmorum
Rg — Liber Regum
Rm — Epistula Pauli ad Romanos
Sap — Liber Sapientiae
Sir — Liber Iesu filii Sirach
Tb — Liber Tobiae
Tim — Epistula Pauli ad Timotheum
Tit — Epistula Pauli ad Titum

Sources

Manuscripts

BRUXELLES, Bibliothèque royale, 10862–10865 (*cf.* p. 19).

DOUAI, Bibliothèque municipale, 295 (*cf.* p. 213 & Mortensen 2000d).

EDINBURGH, National Archives of Scotland, Dalhousie Muniments, GD 45/31/1 (*cf.* pp. 28–31 and Chesnutt 1986).

EDINBURGH, National Library of Scotland, T.D. 209 (*cf.* p. 30).

OXFORD, Bodleian Library, Arch. Selden B. 24 (*cf.* p. 30).

OXFORD, Corpus Christi College, 209 (*cf.* p. 178).

STOCKHOLM, Kungliga Biblioteket, B 17 (*cf.* pp. 31–32).

Stockholm, Riksarkivet, A 8 (*cf.* p. 32).

Stockholm, Riksarkivet, Fr 596 (*cf.* p. 213 & Østrem 2000).

Stockholm, Riksarkivet, Fr 614 (*cf.* p. 213 & Østrem 2000).

Stockholm, Riksarkivet, CCM Br 256 (*cf.* p. 213 & Østrem 2000).

Wiener-Neustadt, Neukloster XII D 21 (*cf.* p. 213).

Uppsala, Universitetsbiblioteket, C 699 (*cf.* p. 19).

Editions, translations and commentaries

Ágrip af Nóregskonungasǫgum. A Twelfth-Century Synoptic History of the Kings of Norway, ed. and trans. M. J. Driscoll (Viking Society for Northern Research. Text Series vol. X). London 1995.

Adamus Bremensis, *Gesta Hammaburgensis ecclesiae pontificum*, ed. Bernhard Schmeidler. Hannover & Leipzig 1917.

— *Adam av Bremen. Historien om Hamburgstiftet och dess biskopar*, trans. by Emanuel Svenberg with commentaries by C. F. Hallencreutz, K. Johannesson, T. Nyberg & A. Piltz. Stockholm 1984.

Ari Thorgilsson, *Íslendingabók*, ed. Jakob Benediktsson (Íslenzk fornrit I 1). Reykjavik 1968.

Biblia Sacra iuxta vulgatam versionem, ed. R. Weber *et al.* Vols. I-II, Stuttgart 1975 (1st ed. 1969).

Chronica Regum Manniæ et insularum. The Chronicle of Man and the Sudreys, ed. P. A. Munch, Kristiania 1860.

— *Chronica regum Manniae et insularum. Chronicle of the Kings of Mann and the Isles* I, ed. and trans. G. Broderick, and B. Stowell, Edinburgh 1973.

De Profectione Danorum in Hierosolymam, ed. M. Cl. Gertz in *Scriptores minores Historiæ Danicæ Medii ævi* vol. II, pp. 443-92, Copenhagen 1922.

— *Historia De Profectione Danorum in Hierosolymam* Ed. and comm. K. Skovgaard-Petersen, trans. by P. Fisher. Copenhagen, forthcoming.

Diplomatarium Norvegicum vol. 1-22. Kristiania / Oslo 1847–1995. Electronic access through the Documentation programme (www.dokpro.uio.no).

Dudo de St. Quintino, *De moribus et actis primorum Normanniae ducum*, ed. M. J. Lair. Caen 1865.

Egils saga Skallagrímssonar, nebst den grösseren Gedichten Egils, ed. Finnur Jónsson. Halle 1894.

Flateyjarbók. En samling af norske konge-sagaer med indskudte mindre fortællinger om begivenheder i og udenfor Norge samt annaler udgiven efter offentlig foranstaltning, vols. I-III. Kristiania1860–68.

Foss, Anders, *Fire taffler eller stam register: Om Danmarckis oc Norgis konger ordentlig som her efftterfølger beskreffune*. Trans. by Jacob Mattssøn. København 1592.

Galfridus – see Geoffrey.

Gamal norsk homiliebok. Cod. Am 619, 4to, ed. G. Indrebø, Oslo 1931.

— *Gammelnorsk homiliebok*, trans. A. Salvesen, introduction and notes by E. Gunnes. Oslo, Bergen, Tromsø 1971.

Historisk-topografiske Skrifter om Norge etc. – see Storm 1895.

Geoffrey of Monmouth, *Historia regum Britannie*, ed. N. Wright: *The Historia regum Britannie of Geoffrey of Monmouth II. The First Variant Version: a critical edition.* Cambridge 1988.

Guillelmus – see William.

Historia Norwegie, ed. P. A. Munch 1850, 1–18.

— extract of *HN* ed. D. Laing 1855, 33–34.

— ed. and comm. G. Storm 1880, xiv–xxx, 69–124.

— trans. and comm. H. Koht 1950.

— trans. and comm. A. Salvesen 1969, 15–49.

— trans. D. Kunin, comm. C. Phelpstead in Phelpstead 2001, ix–xxv, 1–25, 75–100.

Homilieboken – see *Gamal norsk homiliebok.*

Honorius Augustodunensis, *De imagine mundi*, in *Patrologia Latina* vol. 172, col. 115–46.

— ed. Valerie I. J. Flint, 'Honorius Augustodunensis Imago Mundi', *Archives d'Histoire Doctrinale et Littéraire du Moyen Age* 57 (1982) 7–153 [1983].

Islandske Annaler indtil 1578 – see Storm 1888.

The King's Mirror – see *Konungs skuggsiá.*

Konungs skuggsiá, ed. L. Holm-Olsen. Oslo 1945.

Latinske dokument til norsk historie – see Vandvik 1959.

Magnus Erlingssons privilegiebrev og kongevigsle – see Vandvik 1962.

Norges gamle love indtil 1387 I, eds. R. Keyser & P.A. Munch. Kristiania 1846.

Oddr Snorresson, *Saga Óláfs Tryggvasonar* , ed. Finnur Jónsson. København 1932.

— Trans. M. Rindal: *Soga om Olav Tryggvason* (Norrøne bokverk no. 46). Oslo, 1977.

Ordericus Vitalis, *Historia ecclesiastica*, ed. Marjorie Chibnall: *The Ecclesiastical History of Orderic Vitalis*, vols. I–VI. Oxford 1968–1980.

Passio et Miracula Beati Olaui, edited from a twelfth-century manuscript in the library of Corpus Christi College, Oxford, with an introduction and notes by F. Metcalfe. Oxford 1881.

— ed. G. Storm, *Acta Sancti Olavi regis et martyris* in Storm 1880, xxxi–xxxxi, 125–44.

— trans. D. Kunin, comm. C. Phelpstead in Phelpstead 2001, xxv–xlv, 26–74, 101–22.

Profectio Danorum – see *De Profectione Danorum.*

Saxo Grammaticus, *Gesta Danorum*, eds. J. Olrik & H. Ræder: *Saxonis Gesta Danorum*, vols. I-II with an *Index verborum* by F. Blatt. Copenhagen 1931–57.

— ed. K. Friis-Jensen with a Danish trans. by P. Zeeberg. Copenhagen, forthcoming.

Scriptores minores historiæ Danicæ medii ævi – see Gertz 1917–22.

Snorri Sturluson, *Heimskringla*, ed. Bjarni Aðalbjarnarson, vols. I–III, (Íslenzk fornrit XXVI–XXVIII). Reykjavik 1941–51.

Soga um Jomsvikingane, ed. and trans. A. Joleik. Oslo 1931 (1st ed. 1910).

Solinus, *Mirabilia*, ed. Th. Mommsen: *C. Iulii Solini Collectanea rerum memorabilium.* Berlin 1895.

Sverris Saga etter Cod. AM 327 4°, ed. G. Indrebø. Kristiania 1920.

Theodoricus Monachus, *Historia de antiquitate regum Norwagiensium*, ed. Storm 1880, i–xiv, 2-68.

— Trans. and comm. D. & I. McDougall, with an introduction by P. Foote (Viking Society for Northern Research Text Series vol. XI). London 1998.

— Ed. and comm. E. Kraggerud, trans. by P. Fisher. Copenhagen, forthcoming.

Vulgata – see *Biblia sacra*.

Vita Merlini, ed. in San-Marte 1853.

William of Jumièges, *Gesta Normannorum Ducum*, ed. and trans. E.M.C. van Houts: *The Gesta Normannorum Ducum of William of Jumièges, Orderic Vitalis, and Robert of Torigni*, vols. I-II (Oxford Medieval Texts). Oxford 1992–95.

Studies

Aðalbjarnarson, Bjarni 1937, *Om de norske kongers saga* (Skrifter utgitt av Det Norske Videnskaps-Akademi i Oslo II. Hist.-Filos. Klasse 1936. No. 4). Oslo.

Andersson, Theodore M. 1985, 'King's Sagas (*Konungasögur*)', pp. 197–238 in Carol J. Clover & John Lindow, *Old Norse-Icelandic Literature. A Critical Guide* (Islandica XLV). Ithaca.

Bagge, Sverre 1989, 'Theodoricus Monachus – Clerical Historiography in Twelfth-century Norway', *Scandinavian Journal of History*, pp. 113–33.

— 1992, 'Helgen, helt og statsbygger – Olav Tryggvason i norsk historieskrivning gjennom 700 år' pp. 21–38 in S. Supphellen (ed.), *Kongsmenn og krossmenn: Festskrift til Grethe Authén Blom*. Trondheim.

— 2001, *Da boken kom til Norge (1000–1537)* (Norsk idéhistorie I). Oslo.

Bates, David 1982, *Normandy before 1066*. London & New York.

Benediktsson, Jakob 1960, 'Geografisk litteratur – vestnordisk' in KLNM, vol. V, 263–68.

Berntsen, Toralf 1923, *Fra sagn til saga. Studier i kongesagaen*. Kristiania.

Beyschlag, Siegfried 1950, *Konungasögur. Untersuchungen zur Königssaga bis Snorri. Die älteren Übersichtswerke samt Ynglingasaga* (Bibliotheca Arnamagnæana VIII). Copenhagen.

Bjarni – see Aðalbjarnason.

Bjørnbo, Axel Anthon 1909, 'Adam af Bremens Nordensopfattelse', *Aarbøger for Nordisk Oldkyndighed og Historie*, 2. Rk., 24, 120–244.

Blaise, Albert 1994, *A Handbook of Christian Latin: Style, Morphology, and Syntax* trans. Grant C. Roti, Turnhout (French ed. 1955).

Bolin, Sture 1931, *Om Nordens äldsta historieforskning : studier över dess metodik och källvärde*. Lund.

Boserup, Ivan 1981, 'The Angers Fragment and the Archetype of *Gesta Danorum*', pp. 5–26 in K. Friis-Jensen (ed.), *Saxo Grammaticus. A Medieval Author between Norse and Latin Culture*. Copenhagen.

— 2000, 'Ærkebiskop Erik Ivarsson og abbed Wilhelms brevsamling', pp. 303–23 in I. Ekrem, L. B. Mortensen & K. Skovgaard-Petersen (eds.), *Olavslegenden*. København.

Brincken, Anna-Dorothee von den 1992, *Fines Terrae. Die Enden der Erde und der vierte Kontinent auf mittelalterlichen Weltkarten* (Monumenta Germaniae Historica Schriften vol. 36). Hannover.

Broderick 1973 – see Sources, *Chronica regum Manniae et insularum*.

Bugge, Sophus 1873, 'Bemærkninger om den i Skotland fundne latinske Norges Krønike', *Aarbøger for Nordisk Oldkyndighed og Historie*, 1–49.

Cappelli, Adriano 1929, *Lexicon Abbreviaturarum. Dizionario di abbreviature Latine ed Italiane.*

Chesnutt, Michael 1986, 'The Dalhousie Manuscript of the Historia Norvegiae', *Bibliotheca Arnamagnæana* 38 (1985), *Opuscula* VIII, 54–95.

Clouston, J. Storer 1932, *A History of Orkney*. Kirkwall.

Crawford, Barbara E. 1977, 'The fifteenth-century 'Genealogy of the earls of Orkney' and its reflection of the contemporary political and cultural situation in the Earldom', *Mediaeval Scandinavia* 10, 156–78.

— 1987, *Scandinavian Scotland* (Scotland in the Early Middle Ages 2). Leicester.

— 1996, 'Holy Places in the British Isles: some Parallels to Selja', pp. 7–29 in M. Rindal (ed.), *Two Studies on the Middle Ages* ed. (KULTs skriftserie 66). Oslo.

Daae, Ludvig 1879, *Norges helgener*. Kristiania.

Daston, Lorraine, & Katharine Park 1998, *Wonders and the Order of Nature 1150–1750*. New York.

Dictionary of Medieval Latin from British Sources, fasc. I–V [letters A–L] (ed. R.E. Latham, D. R. Howlett *et al.*). Oxford 1975–97.

Du Cange, Charles Du Fresne, *Glossarium mediæ et infimæ Latinitatis* I-X. Niort 1883–87 (1st ed. 1678).

Ekrem, Inger 1998, *Nytt lys over Historia Norwegie. Mot en løsning i debatten om dens alder?* Bergen.

— 1999: 'Historia Norwegie og erkebispesetet i Nidaros', *Collegium Medievale* 11 (1998) 49–67.

— 2000, 'Om *Passio Olavis* tilblivelse og eventuelle forbindelse med *Historia Norwegie*', pp. 109–56 in I. Ekrem, L. B. Mortensen & K. Skovgaard-Petersen (eds.), *Olavslegenden*. København.

Ekrem, I., L.B. Mortensen & K. Skovgaard-Petersen (eds.) 2000, *Olavslegenden og den latinske historieskrivning i 1100-tallets Norge*. København.

Ellehøj, Svend 1965, *Studier over den ældste norrøne historieskrivning* (Bibliotheca Arnamagnæana vol. XXVI). København.

Elliot, Alison G. 1997, 'A Brief Introduction to Medieval Latin Grammar', pp. 1–51 in *Medieval Latin* by K.P. Harrington, revised by J. Pucci. Chicago and London (1st ed. 1925).

Engels, Odilo 1992, 'Friedrich Barbarossa und Dänemark', pp. 353–85 in A. Haverkamp (ed.), *Friedrich Barbarossa. Handlungsspielräume und Wirkungsweisen des staufischen Kaisers*. Sigmaringen.

Ernout, A. & A. Meillet 1959, *Dictionnaire étymologique de la langue Latine. Histoire des mots*. Paris (4th ed.; 1st ed. 1932).

Fagerheim, Hilde 1995, '*Odd munk Snorreson og Soga om Olav Tryggvason*', unpublished dissertation, University of Bergen.

Finnur – see Jónsson.

Flint, Valerie I.J. 1972, 'The Chronology of the Works of Honorius Augustodunensis', *Revue Bénédictine* 80, 215–42.

— 1981, 'World history in the early twelfth century; the "Imago Mundi" of Honorius Augustodunensis', pp. 211–38 in H.C. Davis et J.M. Wallace-Hadrill (eds.), *The*

Writing of History in the Middle Ages. Essays Presented to Richard William Southern. Oxford.

— 1983 – see Sources, Honorius.

Friis, J.A. 1871, *Lappisk mythologi, eventyr og folkesagn.* Kristiania.

Friis-Jensen, Karsten 2000, 'Olav den hellige hos Saxo', pp. 250–62 in I. Ekrem, L. B. Mortensen & K. Skovgaard-Petersen (eds.), *Olavslegenden.* København.

Fritzner, Johann 1886–96, *Ordbog over det gamle norske sprog* I-III. Kristiania (1st ed. 1867).

Gertz, M. Cl. (ed.) 1917–22, *Scriptores minores historiæ Danicæ medii ævi,* vols. I–II. København.

Gjessing, G.A. 1896, 'Sæmund frodes forfatterskab', pp. 125–52 in *Sproglig-historiske studier tilegnede professor C.R. Unger.* Kristiania.

Gunnes, Erik 1986, *Rikssamling og kristning ca. 800–1177* (Norges historie vol. II ed. K. Mykland). Oslo.

— 1996, *Erkebiskop Øystein. Statsmann og kirkebygger.* Oslo.

Hallencreutz, Carl Fredrik 1984, 'Adam, Sverige och trosskiftet. Det missionsvetenskapelige perspektivet', pp. 355–78 in *Adam av Bremen. Historien om Hamburgstiftet och dess biskopar* (trans. E. Svenberg). Stockholm.

— 1984b, *Adam Bremensis and Sueonia. A fresh look at Gesta Hammaburgensis Ecclesiae Pontificum* (Skrifter rörande Uppsala universitet. C, Organisation och historia 47). Uppsala.

Hansen, Lars Ivar 1996, 'Interaction between Northern European Sub-arctic Societies during the Middle Ages: Indigenous peoples, peasants and state builders', pp. 31–95 in M. Rindal (ed.), *Two Studies on the Middle Ages* (KULTs skriftserie 66). Oslo.

— 1999, 'Samer', pp. 360–67 in *Norsk historisk leksikon* (ed. S. Imsen and H. Winge). Oslo (2nd ed.).

— 2000, 'Om synet på de "andre" – ute og hjemme. Geografi og folkeslag på Nordkalotten i følge *Historia Norwegiae*', pp. 54–87 in I. Ekrem, L. B. Mortensen & K. Skovgaard-Petersen (eds.), *Olavslegenden.* København.

Hanssen, Jens S.Th. 1949, *Omkring Historia Norwegiae* (Avhandlinger utgitt av Det Norske Videnskaps-Akademi i Oslo. II. Hist.-Filos. Klasse 1949, 2). Oslo.

Helle, Knut 1974, *Norge blir en stat 1130–1319* (Handbok i Norges historie, vol. 3). Bergen, Oslo & Tromsø.

Hemmingsen, Lars 2000, 'Middelaldergeografien og *Historia Norwegie*', pp. 26–53 in I. Ekrem, L. B. Mortensen & K. Skovgaard-Petersen (eds.), *Olavslegenden.* København.

Holtsmark, Anne 1938, 'Om de norske kongers sagaer', *Edda. Nordisk tidsskrift for litteraturforskning* 38, 145–64.

— 1956, 'Sankt Olavs liv og mirakler' pp. 15–24 in A. Holtsmark, *Studier i norrøn diktning.* Oslo (first printed pp. 121–33 in *Festskrift til Francis Bull,* Oslo 1938).

Hægstad, Marius 1919–20, 'Tillegg. Det norske skriftgrunnlaget i "Historia Norwegiæ"', *Edda. Nordisk tidsskrift for litteraturforskning* vol. 12, 118–21.

Jakob – see Benediktsson.

Janson, Tore 1975, *Prose Rhythm in Medieval Latin from the 9th to the 13th Century* (Acta Universitatis Stockholmiensis XX). Stockholm.

Johnsen, Arne Odd 1939, *Om Theodericus og hans historie de antiquitate regum Norwa-*

giensium (Avhandlinger utgitt av Det Norske Videnskabs-Akademi i Oslo II. Hist.-Filos. Klasse, 3). Oslo.

— 1945, *Studier vedrørende kardinal Nicolaus Brekespears legasjon til Norden*. Oslo.

— 1951, *Om erkebiskop Øysteins eksil 1180–1183* (Det kgl. norske videnskabers selskabs skrifter 1950, 5). Trondheim.

— 1965, *Er Einar Skulesons fyrstedikt "...lutter historiske og historisk nøjaktige;.."?* (Det kgl. norske videnskabers selskabs skrifter 1965, 2). Trondheim.

— 1966, *Betalte Suderøyene og Man skatt eller lensavgift til Norges konge (1153–1263)* (Avhandlinger utgitt av Det Norske Videnskaps-Akademi i Oslo II. Hist.-Filos. Klasse. Ny Serie, 10). Oslo.

— 1967, *On the Background for the Establishment of the Norwegian Church Province. Some New Viewpoints* (Avhandlinger utgitt av Det Norske Videnskaps-Akademi i Oslo II. Hist.-Filos. Klasse. Ny Serie. No. 11). Oslo.

Jónsson, Finnur 1923, *Den oldnorske og oldislandske litteraturs historie*, vol. II. København (1st ed. 1901).

Kaulen, Franz 1904, *Sprachliches Handbuch zur biblischen Vulgata. Eine systematische Darstellung ihres lateinischen Sprachcharakters*. Freiburg in Breisgau.

Koht, Halvdan 1919–20, "Den fyrste norske nasjonalhistoria", *Edda. Nordisk tidsskrift for litteraturforskning* 12, 90–118. (Repr. in Koht 1921, 197–231).

— 1921, *Innhogg og utsyn i norsk historie*. Kristiania.

— 1927a, 'Um upphave til dei islendske annalane', *Historisk tidsskrift* 5. rk. vol. 6, 31–45.

— 1927b, 'Erkedegnen Thomas Agnellus', *Historisk tidsskrift* 5. rk. vol. 6, 182–86 (Oslo).

— 1946–48, 'Litteratur' [review], *Historisk tidsskrift* 34, 645–48.

— 1949–51, 'Historia Norvegiæ', *Historisk tidsskrift* 35, 49–56.

— 1950 (trans. of *HN*), *Den eldste Noregs-historia* (Norrøne bokverk 19). Oslo (1st ed. 1921).

Kolsrud, Olav 1913, 'Celtic Bishops in the Isle of Man, the Hebrides and Orkneys', *Zeitschrift für Celtische Philologie* 9, 357–79.

— 1958, *Noregs kyrkjesoga I. Millomalderen*. Oslo.

Krag, Claus 1991, *Ynglingatal og Ynglingesaga. En studie i historiske kilder* (Studia humaniora 2). Oslo.

— 1995, *Vikingetid og rikssamling, 800–1130* (Aschehougs Norgeshistorie, ed. K. Helle, vol. 2). Oslo.

Kulturhistorisk leksikon for nordisk middelalder fra vikingtid til reformasjonstid, vols. I-XXII (ed. F. Hødnebø *et. al.*). Oslo 1956–78.

Kválen, Eivind 1925, *Den eldste norske kongesoga. Morkinskinna og Hryggjarstykki*. Oslo.

Laing, David 1855, 'Extracts from a Manuscript Volume of Chronicles, in the Possession of the Right Honourable Lord Panmure', *The Bannatyne Miscellany* III (Bannatyne Club 19). Edinburgh.

Lange, Gudrun 1989, *Die Anfänge der isländisch-norwegischen Geschichtsschreibung* (Studia Islandica 47). Reykjavík.

Lehmann, Paul 1937, *Skandinaviens Anteil an der lateinischen Literatur und Wissenschaft des Mittelalters*. 2. Stück (Sitzungsberichte der Bayerischen Akademie der Wissenschaften. Philosophisch-historische Abteilung, Jahrgang 1937, Heft 7). München.

Lexikon des Mittelalters, vols. I-IX & Registerband. München & Zürich 1977–99.

Löfstedt, Einar 1936, *Philologischer Kommentar zur Peregrinatio Aetheriae. Untersuchungen zur Geschichte der lateinischen Sprache*. Oxford, Uppsala and Leipzig (repr. of 1911 ed.).

Lönroth, Lars 1963, 'Studier i Olaf Tryggvasons saga', *Samlaren* 84, 54–94.

Louis-Jensen, Jonna 1970, '"Syvende og ottende brudstykke". Fragmentet AM 325 IV α 4to', *Bibliotheca Arnamagnæana* 30, *Opuscula* IV, 31–60.

Luckhardt, Jochen & Nierhoff, Franz 1995, *Heinrich der Löwe und seine Zeit. Herrschaft und Repräsentation der Welfen 1125–1235. Katalog der Ausstellung, Braunschweig 1995, Bd. 2: Essays*. München.

Marold, E. 1999, 'Historia Norvegie', pp. 621–28 in *Reallexikon der germanischen Altertumskunde* Bd. 14. Berlin.

Maurer, Konrad 1875, 'Die Entstehungszeit der älteren Frostaþíngslög' (*Abhandlungen der philosophisch-philologischen Classe der königlich bayerischen Akademie der Wissenschaften* vol. 13, Abt. 3, 1–84). München.

Meissner, Rudolf 1902, *Die Strengleikar. Ein Beitrag zur Geschichte der altnordischen Prosalitteratur*. Halle.

Moberg, Ove 1941, *Olav Haraldsson, Knut den Store och Sverige*. Lund.

Mogk, Eugen 1904, *Geschichte der norwegisch-isländischen Literatur*. Strassburg (2nd ed.).

Mortensen, Lars Boje 1993, 'Det 12. århundredes renæssance i Norge: Teoderik Munk og Romerriget', pp. 17–35 in Ø. Andersen and A. Aarseth (eds.), *Antikken i norsk litteratur* (Skrifter utgitt av Det norske institutt i Athen vol. 4). Bergen.

— 1994, [Review of *Adam av Bremen, Beretningen om Hamburg stift, erkebiskoppenes bedrifter og øyrikene i Norden*. Overs. og komm. af B.T. Danielsen & A.K. Frihagen. Oslo 1993], *Klassisk Forum* (1994) 1, 79–82.

— 1999, 'Philosophical Learning on the Edges of Latin Christendom. Some Late Twelfth-Century Examples from Scandinavia, Poland, and Palestine', pp. 301–13 in S. Ebbesen & R. L. Friedman (eds.), *Medieval Analyses in Language and Cognition. Acts of the Symposium 'the Copenhagen School of Medieval Philosophy', January 10–13, 1996* (Det Kongelige Videnskabernes Selskab, Historisk-Filosofiske Meddelelser 77). København.

— 2000a, 'The Nordic Archbishoprics as Literary Centres around 1200', pp. 133–57 in K. Friis-Jensen & I. Skovgaard-Petersen (eds.), *Archbishop Absalon of Lund and His World*. Roskilde.

— 2000b, [Review of *Theodoricus Monachus. Historia De Antiquitate Regum Norwagensium*. Tr. & Annot. By David and Ian Mcdougall, with an Introduction by Peter Foote (London 1998)], *Maal og Minne* 2000, 101–4.

— 2000c, 'Olav den Helliges mirakler i det 12. årh.: streng tekstkontrol eller fri fabuleren?', pp. 89–107 in I. Ekrem, L. B. Mortensen & K. Skovgaard-Petersen (eds.), *Olavslegenden*. København.

— 2000d, 'The Anchin Manuscript of *Passio Olaui* (Douai 295), William of Jumièges, and Theodoricus Monachus. New Evidence for Intellectual Relations between Norway and France in the 12th Century', *Symbolae Osloenses* 75, 165–89.

— 2000e, 'The Diffusion of Roman Histories in the Middle Ages. A List of Orosius, Eutropius, Paulus Diaconus, and Landolfus Sagax Manuscripts', *Filologia Mediolatina* VI–VII (1999–2000) 101–200.

Munch, Peter Andreas 1850 (ed. of *HN*), *Symbolæ ad historiam antiquiorem rerum Norvegicarum*. Kristiania.

Mundal, Else 1994: 'Íslendingabók vurdert som bispestolskrønike', *Alvíssmál. Forschungen zur mittelalterlichen Kultur Skandinaviens* 3, 63–72.

Munk Olsen, Birger 1982–89: *L'Étude des auteurs classiques latins aux XIe et XIIe siècles. Tome I: Catalogue des manuscrits classiques latins copiés du IXe au XIIe siècle. Apicius-Juvénal. Tome II: Livius-Vitruvius, florilèges, essais des plume. Tome III,1: Les classiques dans les bibliothèques médiévales. Tome III,2: Addenda et corrigenda, Tables*. Paris.

Nordal, Sigurður 1953, *Litteraturhistorie B. Norge og Island* (Nordisk kultur VIII:B). Stockholm, Oslo, København.

Nyberg, Tore 1984, 'Stad, skrift och stift. Några historiska inledningsfrågar', pp. 295–339 in *Adam av Bremen. Historien om Hamburgstiftet och dess biskopar* (trans. Emanuel Svenberg). Stockholm.

— 2000: *Monasticism in North-Western Europe, 800–1200*. Aldershot.

Østrem, Eyolf 2000, 'Om en nyoppdaget Olavslegende', pp. 186–224 in I. Ekrem, L. B. Mortensen & K. Skovgaard-Petersen (eds.), *Olavslegenden*. København.

Olavslegenden – see Ekrem, Mortensen, Skovgaard-Petersen (eds.).

Patrologia Latina, vols. 1–221 (ed. J.-P. Migne). Paris 1841–64. Ed. as database by Chadwick-Healy, *Patrologia Latina. The Full Text database* (*cf.* http://pld.chadwyck.com).

Paasche, Fredrik 1922, 'Tendens og syn i kongesagaen', *Edda. Nordisk tidsskrift for litteraturforskning* 17, 1–17.

— 1924, *Norges og Islands litteratur indtil utgangen av middelalderen* (Norsk litteratur historie, vol. I, eds. F. Bull and F. Paasche). Kristiania.

Phelpstead, Carl 2001 (ed.), *A History of Norway and The Passion and Miracles of the Blessed Óláfr*. Translated by Devra Kunin, edited with introduction and notes by Carl Phelpstead (Viking Society for Northern Research Text Series vol. XIII). London.

Robberstad, Knut 1949–51, 'Ordet patria i Historia Norvegiæ', *Historisk tidsskrift* 35, 187–91.

Salvesen, Astrid 1969 (trans.), *Norges historie. Theodricus Munk Historien om de gamle kongene. Historien om danenes ferd til Jerusalem*. Oslo.

San-Marte (*i.e.* Albert Schulz) 1853, *Die Sagen von Merlin*. Halle.

Sandaaker, Odd 1985, 'Historia Norvegiæ og Biskop Eirik av Stavanger', *Maal og Minne* 1985, 82–86.

Schreiner, Johan 1926, *Tradisjon og saga om Olav den hellige* (Skrifter utgitt av Det Norske Videnskaps-Akademi i Oslo. Hist.-Filos. Klasse 1926, 1). Oslo.

— 1927, *Saga og oldfunn. Studier til Norges eldste historie* (Skrifter utgitt av Det Norske Videnskaps-Akademi i Oslo II. Hist.-Filos. Klasse 1927, 4). Oslo.

Seegrün, Wolfgang 1967, *Das Papsttum und Skandinavien bis zur Vollendung der nordischen Kirchenorganisation (1164)* (Quellen und Forschungen zur Geschichte Schleswig-Holsteins vol. 51). Neumünster.

Simon, Gertrud 1958, 'Untersuchungen zur Topik der Widmungsbriefe mittelalterlicher Geschichtsschreiber bis zum Ende des 12. Jahrhunderts. Erster Teil', *Archiv für Diplomatik, Schriftgeschichte. Siegel- und Wappenkunde* 4, 52–119.

— 1959–60, 'Untersuchungen zur Topik der Widmungsbriefe mittelalterlicher Geschichtsschreiber bis zum Ende des 12. Jahrhunderts. Zweiter Teil', *Archiv für Diplomatik, Schriftgeschichte. Siegel- und Wappenkunde* 5–6, 73–153.

Skard, Eiliv 1930, *Målet i Historia Norwegiae* (Skrifter utgitt av Det Norske Videnskaps-Akademi i Oslo II. Hist.-Filos. Klasse 1930, 5). Oslo.

Skovgaard-Petersen, Karen 2001: *A Journey to the Promised Land. Crusading Theology in the Historia de profectione Danorum in Hierosolymam (c. 1200)*, Copenhagen.

— 2002, 'Et håndskriftfund i Lübeck ca. 1620 — om den spinkle overlevering af to norske nationalklenodier', *Fund og Forskning* 41, 107–27.

Steen, Sverre 1949–51, 'Tronfølgeloven av 1163', *Historisk tidsskrift* 35, 1–48.

Steinnes, Asgaut 1946–48, 'Ikring historia Norvegiæ', *Historisk tidsskrift* 34, 1–61.

— 1949-51, 'Meir om Historia Norvegiæ', *Historisk tidsskrift* 35, 173–87.

— 1965, 'Om kjeldene til eit arbeid av Anders Foss om kongsætt i Noreg og sumt om dei eldste Noregs-sogene', *Maal og minne* 1965, 1–44.

Storm, Gustav 1873a, *Snorre Sturlassöns historieskrivning. En kritisk undersøgelse*. København.

— 1873b, 'Yderligere Bemærkninger om den skotske "Historia Norvegiæ"', *Aarbøger for Nordisk Oldkyndighed og Historie* 1873, 361–85.

— 1876, *Nye Oplysninger om Peder Claussøn* (Forhandlinger i Videnskabs-Selskabet i Christiania 1876, 4). Kristiania.

— 1880 (ed.), *Monumenta historica Norvegiæ. Latinske kildeskrifter til Norges historie i middelalderen*. Kristiania (repr. Oslo 1973).

— 1888 (ed.), *Islandske Annaler indtil 1578*. Kristiania (repr. Oslo 1977).

— 1890, 'Ginnungagap i Mythologien og i Geografien', *Arkiv for nordisk filologi* 6 (N. F. 2), 340–50.

— 1895 (ed.), *Historisk-topografiske Skrifter om Norge og norske Landsdele, forfattede i Norge i det 16de Aarhundrede*. Kristiania.

Stotz, Peter 1996–2000: *Handbuch zur lateinischen Sprache des Mittelalters*, vols. II–IV (Handbuch der Altertumswissenschaft II.5.2–4). München.

Thomson, William P. L. 2001, *The New History of Orkney*. Edinburgh.

Tolley, Clive 1994, 'The Shamanic Séance in the *Historia Norvegiae*', *Shaman* 2, 135–56.

Ulset, Tor 1983, *Det genetiske forholdet mellom Ágrip, Historia Norwegiæ og Historia de antiquitate Regum Norwagiensium. En analyse med utgangspunkt i oversettelsesteknikk samt en diskusjon omkring begrepet "latinisme" i samband med norrøne tekster*. Oslo.

Vandvik, Eirik 1959 (ed.), *Latinske dokument til norsk historie fram til år 1204* [ed. V. Skånland]. Oslo.

— 1962 (ed.), *Magnus Erlingssons privilegiebrev og kongevigsle* (ed. V. Skånland, Skrifter utgitt av Det Norske Videnskaps-Akademi i Oslo II. Hist.-Filos. Klasse. Ny serie 1). Oslo.

Vries, Jan de 1967, *Altnordische Literaturgeschichte. Band II: Die Literatur von etwa 1150 bis 1300. Die Spätzeit nach 1300* (Grundriss der germanischen Philologie 16). Berlin (1st ed. 1942).

Walter, Hans 1963–67, *Proverbia Sententiaeque Latinitatis medii aevi. Lateinische Sprichwörter und Sentenzen des Mittelalters in alphabetischer Anordnung*, vols. 1–5. Göttingen.

Werner, Karl F. 1987, 'Gott, Herscher und Historiograph. Der Geschichtsschreiber als Interpret des Wirken Gottes in der Welt und Ratgeber der Könige (4.-12. Jahrhundert)' pp. 1–31 in E.-D. Hehl, H. Seibert & F. Staab (eds.), *Deus qui mutat tempora: Menschen und Institutionen im Wandel des Mittelalters. Festschrift für Alfons Becker zu seinem fünfundsechzigsten Geburtstag*. Sigmaringen.

Zimmermann, August 1915, *Etymologisches Wörterbuch der lateinischen Sprache*. Hannover.

Index nominum

The index comprises names (1) of persons living before *c.* 1750 including figures from Old Norse and Christian mythology, (2) of places (except 'Norway') and peoples, and (3) of anonymous works (except *HN* itself).

The lemma is mostly written in an English form when available, but sometimes a modern Scandinavian, an Old Norse or a Latin equivalent is given precedence. Cross-references are provided for all occuring forms, and equivalents are added in brackets after the lemma.

The index is alphabetized 'internationally', *i.e.* Æ, Á, Å, Ä, come before A, and Ø and Ö before O.

References are to paragraphs of the *HN* text (*i.e.* Roman plus Arabic numeral as 'VII 6') and to page numbers of all other indexed parts of the book (Introduction, Commentary, Essay).

Brief explanations are only given when more persons have the same name. The maps and the commentary usually offer more explanation.

Ægestav – see Vegestav
Ælfgifu (Elfigeua) XVIII 27, 152
Æthelred (Adelredus / Etelredus) XVIII 11, XVIII 18, 151
Æthelstan (Adalstanus) XII 3, 196
Ágrip 16, 18, 33, 138, 139, 142, 143, 145, 146, 148, 150, 152, 158, 160, 164, 182, 190, 191, 196, 197, 202, 206
Åker 200
Åle 220
Ålov Årbot 202
Ångermanland (Angaria) I 5, 114, 181, 182
Årstad – see Alrekstad
Åsta (Asta) XV 5, XV 6, XV 8, 200, 201
Abelard – see Petrus Abelardus
Adalstanus – see Æthelstan
Adam of Bremen 8, 17, 18, 20, 22, 25–28, 41, 108, 110–116, 118, 120–122, 124, 125, 128, 129, 131, 132, 133, 137, 142, 144, 145, 147–150, 153, 159, 160, 162, 168–177, 180, 183–186, 191–195, 197, 201–206, 208, 216, 217, 221, 223, 224
Adils IX 26, 136, 137
Africa (Affrica) I 11, 115, 116, 120, 126, 176, 183
Africans (Affricani) VI 7, 126
Agde 112
Agder 112, 117
Agnafit IX 16, 120, 135
Agne (Agni) IX 16, 135
Agnello da Pisa 158
Agnellus – see also Lambe, Orm, Omer
Agnellus 16, Prologus 7, 111, 157, 168, 173, 218, 222
Agnellus (Franciscan) 158
Agnellus (patriarch) 158
Agnellus of Wells (archdeacon) 159, 161
Agni – see Agne
Albia (Elbe, Götaelven, Storelven?) I 3, III 3, 113, 119
Alexander III 207
Alrecstathi – see Alrekstad
Alrek (Alricr, Alrikr) IX 14, 135
Alrekstad (Alrecstathi, Álreksstadir, Årstad) XIII 11, XIV 3, 140, 217
Alrikr – see Alrek
Alv (son of Agne) 136
Alvdalene – see Conualles Albie
Amazons 116, 118
Anastasius IV 224
Angaria – see Ångermanland
Angli (Englishmen) VI 9, VI 18, XI 5
Anglia – see England
Ansgar 172
Antenor 195
Argare 120
Ari Thorgilsson (froði) 16, 17, 41, 116, 125, 129, 130, 133, 135, 136, 138, 147, 160, 168, 175, 189, 191, 192, 195
Arnald 179, 193, 200
Asia 116, 134, 148
Asloia – see Oslo
Assur Lavskjegg (Tote) 139
Asta – see Åsta
Astrid (daughter of Olof of Sweden) 152
Astrid (Wendish princess) 208
Astrid (Astrida, mother of Olav Tryggvason) XV 9, XV 14, 142, 145, 198, 200, 207
Auchun – see Aukun
Augustinus 137
Aukun (Auchun) IX 21, 136
Aun – see Aukun

Aust-Agder 117
Baltic Sea (Balticum Mare) 25, I 5, IX 28, XVII 11, XVIII 4, 113, 115, 137
Bamble 117
Bavaria 20
Bayern – see Bavaria
Bede (Beda) 125, 129, 131, 132
Bera IX 19, 135
Bergen (Bergae, Bergonia) 22, 23, 24, XIV 3, 117, 120, 140, 163–167, 175, 197, 205, 217–219, 221, 225
Bergljot (Bergliota) XVI 2, 202
Bergonia – see Bergen
Bernard (Bernardus) XVIII 33, 153
Bernardus Silvestris 132
Berno – see Bjørn
Biarmonia (Bjarmeland) II 9, 115, 118, 157, 181, 182, 189
Biarmones (Bjarms) I 7, I 9, 115, 177, 182
Bjarmeland – see Biarmonia
Bjarms – see Biarmones
Bjørkedalsmyra 117
Bjørn (Berno) XI 5, XV 3, XV 4, 196, 197, 199
Black Sea 195
Blekinge 114
Børglum 159
Boeotia 131
Boethius 108, 109
Bohemus 113
Bohuslän 114
Boleslaw the Brave 148
Borgartingslag 117, 178
Bosau 18
Bothnic Gulf 115, 182
Braunschweig 20
Broutonund – see Braut-Ånund
Braut-Ånund (Broutonund) IX 29, 137
Bremen 17, 18, 162, 163, 204, 224
Bretons – see Britones
Britannia (Britain) 124, 126, 146
Britones (Bretons) XVIII 13
Brittany 151
Brutus (ancestor of the Britons) 113
Brutus, Marcus Junius 173
Caithness (Kathanasia) VI 9
Canones Nidrosienses 14, 198, 204, 210
Canutus – see Knud
Canutus Durus – see Harde-Knud
Carcus – see Kark
Caria 119
Caribdis – see Charybdis
Caspian Sea 114
Ceres 36, 41, IX 10, 134, 137
Charybdis (Caribdis) II 10, 118
Chaucer 30
Chrisa 120
Christian I (Danish king) 38
Christianus 109, 171, 174
Christus (Christ) XIII 10, XV 14, XVII 19, XVII 25, XVII 30, XVII 31, XVII 32, 207
Chronica Regum Maniæ 165
Chronicon Lethrense 121, 183
Cicero (Tullius) 27, Prologus 1, 108, 109, 173
Clement – see Klement
Compendium Saxonis 40, 140, 142
Conualles Albie (Alvdalene, Østerdalen) III 3, 119
Cornwall 146
Cosmas of Prague 113
Curi (Kurlanders) XVIII 77
Dacia – see Denmark
Dag (Dagr) 33, IX 13, 135
Dag (son of Harald Fairhair) 138
Dalarne 114
Dalsland 114
Damianus – see Petrus Damianus
Dan 113
Danes – see Dani
Dani (Danes) 20, IX 20, XVII 12, XVII 34, XVIII 12, XVIII 13, XVIII 21, 136, 139, 148, 194–198, 202–205, 207, 213, 214, 216, 219
Dania – see Denmark
De expulsione fratrum minorum 119
De rebus gestis in Majori monasterio 149
Decapolis II 1, 117, 180, 200
Denmark (Dania, Dacia) 18, 19, 23, 34, 44, I 5, I 2, IX 20, IX 25, XII 1, XVII 29, XVII 35, XVIII 9, XVIII 13, 114, 136, 139, 163, 164, 178, 195, 196, 197, 203, 205, 211, 216, 219, 221
Diana 41, IX 26, 137
Diflinnia – see Dublin
Diploma Orcadense – see *Orkney Genealogy*
Dis 137
Domalde (Domaldi) IX 10
Domar (Domarr) IX 11
Dovrefjell (Mons Doffrarum) III 4, 114
Dublin (Diflinnia) VI 9, 120
Dudo of St. Quentin 26, 195
Dyggve (Dyggui) IX 12
Edmund (Edmundus, Ironside) XVIII 18, XVIII 25, XVIII 26, XVIII 27, 151
Egil (foster-father of Astrid) 152
Egil Vendelkråke (Eigil Vendilcraco) IX 22, 136
Egil's saga 176, 182
Eigil – see Egil
Einar Skulason 220
Eirik (Erikr, son of Dag) IX 15
Eirik Bloodaxe (Blodøks, Blothex, Ericus Sanguinea Securis) XI 4, XII 1, XV 1, XV 10, 128, 138, 139, 143, 196–199, 202

Eirik Ivarsson (archbishop) 19, 22
Eirik jarl (Ericus filius Haconis comitis, son of Håkon jarl) XVII 29, XVII 40, XVII 48, 128, 203, 205, 207
Eirik Oddsson 22, 175
Eisisla – see Ösel
Eistria – see Estonia
Eistrii (people of Estonia) XVII 6, 145
Elbe (see also Albia) 119
Elfigeua – see Ælfgifu
Elgeseter 158
Emma 152
England (Anglia) 18, 23, VI 9, XII 3, XIII 2, XVII 13, XVIII 9, XVIII 15, 126, 142, 157 158, 161, 166, 168, 197, 199, 203–207, 214, 215, 221
Englishmen – see Angli
Ennius 122
Ericus – see Eirik
Ericus Olai
Erik of Pomerania (Danish-Norwegian king) 28, 38
Erikr – see Eirik
Erlend Haraldsson (earl of the Orkneys) 165
Erling (Erlingr, son of Eirik Bloodaxe) XII 2, XIII 8, 139
Erling the Old (Erlingus Senex) XIV 4, 141
Erling Skakke 164, 166
Estonia (Eistria) XVII 4, 144
Etelredus – see Æthelred
Etna (Ethna) VIII 6, 130, 193
Euboea 131
Eugenius III 165
Europe (Europa) 8, 11, 15, I 11, 115, 116, 126, 162, 166, 167, 169, 176, 177, 178, 201
Eustein – see Øystein
Eycisla / Eysisla – see Ösel
Eynorum Insula – see Öland
Eystein(n) – see Øystein
Faeroes (Insule Ouium, Fereyiar) 13, VII, VII 1, 129, 157, 159, 163, 164, 167, 184, 189–194, 217
Faeroese – see Fereyingenses
Fagrskinna 150
Fasta IX 25, 136
Fereyiar – see Faeroes
Fereyingenses (Faeroese) XVII 31, 147, 190
Finland 115, 120, 181, 200
Finni (Lapps, Sami) I 4, I 7, II 8, III 9, IV, IV 2, IV 11, IV 16, IV 17, IV 24, IV 26, 114, 118, 120–124, 148, 176, 177, 180–184, 192, 194, 196, 198, 217, 221
Finni Cornuti – see Horned Finns
Finnmarken 114, 120, 139, 181, 182
Finnskogene 120
Fiolni – see Fjolne
Fitjar (Fittium) XIII 7, 120
Fjolne (Fiolni) IX 5, 134
Fjordane 117
Flanders (Flandrea) XVII 13, 146, 203
Flandrea – see Flanders
Flateyjarbók 112, 225
Floke (Floko) 129, 191
Foss, Anders 197, 225
France 17, 18, 21, 23, 142
Frei (Frethi) XIII 6
Fresones VI 20
Frethi – see Frei
Friesland (Frisia) XVII 13, 145, 203
Friis, Peder Claussøn 195, 225
Frisia – see Friesland
Frisians – see Fresones
Frode 138
Frostatingslag 178
Frøy (Froyr) IX 3, IX 4, 134, 195
Gamal norsk homiliebok 213
Gamle (Gamli) XII 2, XIII 6, 139
Gamli – see Gamle
Gandvik 118
Gange-Rolv – see Rollo
Gardar (Gardarus) VIII 2, 129, 191
Gauldal (Gauladale) XVII 27, 117
Gauthier of Chatillon 18
Gautonia – see Götaland
Gautones (Götar) IX 27, XVII 12, 114, 203
Geisli 212, 220
Geoffrey of Monmouth 11, 18, 113, 128, 160, 191
Gerald of Wales 121, 183
Germany / German (see also Saxony) 17, 18, 20, 23, 25, VI 5, 121, 126, 163, 199, 204, 205
Gesta Cnutonis regis 122
Giraldus Cambrensis – see Gerald of Wales
Glaciales – see Icelanders
Glacialis Insula – see Iceland
Glomma 119
Götaelven (Gothelba, Albia?) 113, 181
Götaland (Gautonia) I 5, III 1, 114, 182
Götar – see Gautones
Gog 120
Gongurolfr – see Rollo
Gorm (Gormr, son of Eirik Bloodaxe) XII 2, XIII 8, 139
Gorm (Gormr Stultissimus, 'the Old', Danish king) 19, XII 1, 139, 197, 198
Gothia (see also Götaland) 113
Gothi (see also Gautones) 114
Goths 114, 195
Gotland (Gottorum Insula) XVIII 6, 114, 135
Gottorum Insula – see Gotland
Greenland (Terra Viridis) 13, 14, I 10, II 12, 115, 116, 118, 126, 157, 164, 167, 176, 178, 179, 183, 184, 188–190, 193, 194, 200

Greenlanders (Viridenses) I 9, I 12, 115
Grenland (Grenlandia) XV 4, 178
Grimkel (Grimkellus) XVIII 33, 153, 167, 208
Gualterus de Castellione – see Gauthier of Chatillon
Gudbrand Kula (Gudbrandus Cula) XV 5
Gudbrandsdalen (Valles Gudbrandi) III 3
Gudrød (king of the Hebrides and Man) 165
Gudrød (Gudrodus, son of Bjørn) XV 4
Gudrød (Guthrodus) XI 6, 138
Gudrød Veidekonge (Guthrodus Rex Venator) X 5, 138
Gulacenses (people from Gulatingslag) XVII 36
Gulacia – see Gulatingslag
Gulatingslag (Gulacia, – see also Gulacenses) II 3, V 1, XIII 7, XVII 34, 178–180, 204, 221
Gunnhild (daughter of Olav Haraldsson) 152
Gunnhild (Gunnilda, wife of Eirik Bloodaxe) 8, 19, XII 1, XII 2, XII 4, XIII 5, XIII 8, XIV 1, XVI 1, 139, 141, 197–199, 201, 219, 225
Gunnilda – see Gunnhild
Gunnrød (Gunrodus, son of Eirik Bloodaxe) XII 2, XIV 1, XIV 3, 139, 141, 143, 202
Gunnrød (Gunnrodus, son of Harald Fairhair) XI 6, 138
Gun(n)rodus – see Gunnrød
Guthrodus – see Gudrød
Guttorm (son of Harald Fairhair) 138, 139
Håkon (Hacon alumpnus Adelstani, 'the Good', Adalsteinsfostre) XI 5, XII 3, XIII 1, XIII 9, XV 1, 139, 140, 196, 199
Håkon jarl (Hacon Nequam, comes, 'the Wicked') 8, XVI 1, XVII 29, XVII 56, 128, 143, 144, 162, 201–203, 205, 207
Håkon Håkonsson 182
Håkonshella (Haconar hella, Haconis petra) XIII 11, 120
Hålogaland (Halogia) II 8, 118, 139, 177–182, 197, 202, 217
Hacon – see Håkon
Haconar hella / Haconis petra – see Håkonshella
Hadeland (Hatlandia) XI 7, XV 2, 138, 140, 182, 190
Hadrian IV – see Nicholas Breakspear
Halfdan(us) – see Halvdan
Hallfred Vandrædaskald 145, 160
Halland 114
Hallingdal (Vallis Haddingorum) III 5, 120, 179
Halogenses (people from Halogaland) XVI 2, 143
Halogia – see Hålogaland
Halvdan (son of Eirik Blodaxe) 139
Halvdan (Halfdanus, son of Sigurd the Giant (Rise)) XV 7
Halvdan the Black (Svarte, Halfdanus Niger) X 6, 137, 138, 196, 198, 200
Halvdan the Black (Svarte, son of Harald Hårfagre) 138
Halvdan Gold-Lavisher and Food-Niggard (Halfdan Auri Prodigus Cibique Tenacissimus, Gull-Harald) X 4, 137, 202
Halvdan Håføtt (Halfdanus Hafoeta) XI 6, XV 2, 138
Halvdan Hvitbein (Halfdanus Hwitbein) 31, 34, X 1, 137, 196, 200
Halvdan the White (Hvite, son of Harald Hårfagre) 138
Hamar 22, 41, 167, 179, 193, 200, 206, 211, 217, 219
Hamburg 17, 18, 20, 162, 163, 168, 169, 194, 204, 224
Harald (Haraldus, son of Eirik Bloodaxe) XIV 1
Harald (2, Danish king) 152
Harald Blåtand (Haraldus, Gormsson, Danish king) XII 6, 202
Harald Fairhair, (Hårfagre, Haraldus Comatus) 9, 16, 39, VI 8, VIII 1, XI 1, XV 1, XV 4, XV 7, XV 9, 125–127, 141, 189, 196–199, 202
Harald Gille (Gilchrist) 201
Harald Gråfell (Haraldus Grafeld, son of Eirik Bloodaxe) XII 2, 139, 140, 143, 202
Harald Grenske (Haroldus Grensci / Grenscensis) XV 4, XVIII 1, 199, 200
Harald Hardråde (Haroldus) XV 8, 142, 177, 201, 216, 217, 221
Harald Hårfagre – see Harald Fairhair
Harald Maddadsson (earl of Orkney) 12, 164, 165
Haraldus – see Harald
Harde-Knud (Canutus Durus, Danish king) XVIII 27, 152
Haroldus – see Harald
Hatlandia – see Hadeland
Hatlendenses (Shetlanders) XVII 31, 138, 147, 190
Hauk Erlendsson 115
Hebrides (Insule Merediane) 12, 13, V 3, 125, 164, 165, 167, 184–190, 192–194, 222
Hedmark (Heidmarchia) III 3, 138, 182
Heidmarchia – see Hedmark
Hekla (Mons Casule) 9, 11, VIII 6, 130, 193
Helmold of Bosau 18
Heming (archbishop) 32
Henry (son of King Henry II) 161
Henry I (English king) 11, VI 19, 128, 160–162, 190, 191

Henry II (English king) 11, 161, 162
Henry the Lion 20
Henry Sinclair – see Sinclair
Herod, 144, 207
Hetland – see Shetland
Hibernii (Irishmen) VI 9
Hildesheim 20
Himinheid (Himinheithy) IX 29, 120, 137
Hirnus 119
Hispania – see Spain
Hiorleifr (Hjorleiv) 34, VIII 2, 129, 191
Historia de profectione Danorum in Hierosolymam 42, 113, 122, 142
Hjaltland – see Shetland
Hjorleiv – see Hiorleifr
Høyer, Henrik 225
Holland (Hollandia) VI 20
Holmgard (Holmgardia, Novgorod) XVII 9, XVIII 2, 120, 145, 207
Holstein 18
Homiliebok – see *Gamal norsk homiliebok*
Honorius of Autun (Augustodunensis) 17–20, 25, 27, 108–114, 117, 118, 120–122, 126, 130, 132, 133, 134, 148, 159, 162, 168–175, 183, 186, 193, 224
Horace 140
Hordaland 117
Horned Finns (Finni Cornuti) I 7, 115, 177, 182
Hovedøya 165
Hugh of St Victor 108, 152
Huitfeldt, Arild 225
Hybernia – see Ireland
Iamtonia – see Jämtland
Iarmuthia – see Yarmouth
Ibernia – see Ireland
Iceland (Glacialis Insula, Tile) 13, 14, 23, 27, 41, I 9, VIII, VIII 1, 129–133, 157, 158, 167, 170, 175, 184, 189–194, 217
Icelanders (Telenses, Tilenses, Glaciales) I 11, XVII 24, XVII 32, 116, 147, 148, 157, 176, 190–193
Inge Haraldsson 'Krokrygg' 12, 22, 23, 163–166, 175, 183, 187, 196, 201, 217, 220, 221
Ingialdr – see Ingjald
Ingjald (Ingialdr, son of Braut-Ånund) IX 30
Ingjald (Ingialdr, son of Agne) IX 18, 135
Ingolv – see Ingulfr
Ingulfr (Ingolv) 129, 191
Ingui – see Yngvi
Ingwar VIII 2, 129
Innerøya 117
Insule Brumales (Shetland and Orkney) V 3
Insule Merediane – see Hebrides
Insule Ouium – see Faeroes
Insule Solunde – see Solund Islands
Iohannes – see Johannes
Iomne – see Jomsborg
Iorundr / Iorundus – see Jorund
Ireland (Ibernia / Hybernia) V 1, VI 9, XVII 14, 120, 124–126, 145, 185, 203
Irishmen – see Hibernii
Isidore 17
Isle of Man – see Man
Isle of Wight 151
Itali (Romans) VIII 1
Ivar Vidfadme (Iuarus Withfadm) IX 31, 137
Jämtland (Iamtonia) 13, I 5, 112, 114, 176, 181, 182, 188, 194
James IV (Scottish king) 30, 37
Jarislav (Iarezlafus) XVIII 30, 111, 152, 206, 214, 215
Jernestangen 117
Jerusalem 158, 164, 207
Johannes (Iohannes, John, English bishop) XVII 24, XVII 58, 205, 208
John – see also Johannes
John the Baptist 167
Jomsborg (Iomne) XVII 12, 120, 145
Jomsvikingesaga – see *Soga um Jomsvikingane*
Jordanes 195
Jorund (Iorundr, son of Ingjald) IX 20
Jorund (Iorundus, son of Harald Fairhair) XI 8
Judas 207
Julian 140
Karelia 182
Karelians – see Kyriali
Kark (Carcus) XVII 27
Karmøy 185
Kathanasia – see Caithness
Kaupang (in Sogn) 117
Kirjalers – see Kyriali
King's Mirror – see *Konungs Skuggsiá*
Kirkwall 38–39, 41, 225
Klement's Church (in Nidaros) 208
Knud (Canutus, 'the Great', Danish king) XVIII 9, XVIII 15, XVIII 22, XVIII 26, XVIII 27, 150–152, 205, 206, 213, 214
Knud Lavard 219
Kola 118
Konghelle 42, 117, 163
Konungs Skuggsiá (*King's Mirror*, *Kongespeilet*) 117–119, 131, 160, 183
Kongsberg 120
Kongsvinger 120
Kurland 150
Kurlanders – see Curi
Kvenland 112, 115
Kvens – see Kweni
Kweni (Kvens) I 7, 114–115, 177, 182

Kyriali (Kirjalers) I 7, 114–115, 177, 182
Lactantius 131
Lambe (Agnellus) 158
Lampert of Hersfeld 135
Land of Maidens – see Terra Virginum
Lapps – see Finni
Latvia 150
Legendary Saga of St Olav 160
Liber de legibus Angliae 152
Lilleelvedalen 119
Limafiorth – see Limfjorden
Limfjorden (Limafiorth) IX 20
Loarie – see Lom
Lofoten 185
Lom (Loarie) III 3
London (Londonia / Lundonia) XVIII 18, XVIII 25, 120, 151, 152
Long Serpent – see Serpens Longus
Lübeck 20
Lucanus 132, 137
Lund 18, 19, 22, 24, 41, 42, 44, 141, 163, 164, 192, 194, 198, 210
Lundonia – see London
Lyrskog hede (heath in Denmark)
Lyschander, Claus 225
Lyse 165
Mälaran 114
Macrobius 132
Magnus Berrføtt (Barefoot) 187, 201, 217
Magnus Eriksson (Swedish king) 31–32, 40
Magnus Erlingsson 13, 14, 166, 167, 176, 180, 201, 202, 209, 210, 221
Magnus the Good (den gode) 212, 216
Magnus Lagabøter 14
Magog 120, 195
Man (Isle of Man) 164, 167, 186, 187, 193, 194, 222
Margareta XVIII 29, XVIII 31, XVIII 32, 152
Mary 207
Massagetes (Massagetae) 118
Media – see Midøya
Menzies, David 38
Merlin (Merlinus) 11, 18, VI 19, 128, 160, 190, 191
Midøya (Media, Mien, Mia, Midja) II 3, 117
Miorsus – see Mjøsa
Mjøsa (Miorsus) III 6, 200
Mons Casule – see Hekla
Mons Doffrarum – see Dovrefjell
Møre (Mor) II 4, XVI 2, 127, 128, 140, 143, 161, 162, 183, 189, 190, 202
Mor – see Møre
Morenses (people from Møre) XVI 2, 143
Munkeliv 159, 217, 218
Närke (Næricia) 37, 114
Nadd-oddr (Oddus(?)) VIII 2, 129, 191
Neorth – see Njord
Neptune 134
Nicholas Breakspear 163, 165–168, 180, 188, 200, 204, 212, 213, 222, 224
Nidaros – see Trondheim
Nikolaus (Icelandic abbot) 176
Njord (Neorth) IX 2, 195
Noah 195
Nor I 1, 112, 113, 195
Nordland 118
Nordmøre (Northmore) XIII 6, 117, 140, 143
Norie, Robert 29–30
Normandia – see Normandy
Normandy (Normandia) 11, VI 15, VI 20, 124, 128, 157, 161, 189, 190
Northmore – see Nordmøre
North Sea (Solundicum Mare, Mare Occidentale) 8, 9, 13, 24, 42, V 1, VI 8, 118, 124, 125, 185, 189
Northimbri XII 5
Northimbria – see Northumbria
Northumbria (Northimbria) VI 9, XII 4, 127
Northumbrians – see Northimbri
Nortmannia (Norway) 124
Norwagenses (Norwegenses, Norwegians) VI 13, VIII 2, VIII 4, X 1, XVII 12, XVII 26, XVII 12, XVII 26, 112
Norwegenses – see Norwagenses
Norwegia (see also Nortmannia) I 1, I 2, I 7, I 15, II, II 9, IV 26, V 1, V 3, VI 21, VIII 21, IX 1, XII 3, XIII 1, XIV 2, XV 14, XVI 1, XVII 24, XVII 35, XVIII 33, 112, 124, 133
Norwegians – see Norwagenses
Novgorod – see Holmgard
Numedal 179
Østerdalen (Convalles Albie) 119
Øystein (Eustein, son of Adils) IX 27
Øystein (Eusteinus, son of Harald Fairhair) XI 8
Øystein Erlendsson (archbishop) 14, 16, 19, 20, 21, 22, 23, 198, 209, 210, 216, 220–222
Øystein Fart (Eustein Bumbus) X 3, 137
Øystein Haraldsson (king) 12, 13, 163–166, 183, 187, 196, 201, 220
Öland (Eynorum Insula) XVIII 6
Ösel (Eycisla / Eysisla / Eisisla) IX 28, XVII 5, XVIII 5, 137
Östergötland 114
Oceanus (Occeanus, The Great Ocean) I 5, 114, 115, 126, 131, 183
Odd – see Nadd-oddr
Oddr Munk (Odd(r) Snorreson) 18, 113, 142–145, 147, 149, 160, 167, 168, 177, 190, 195, 196, 208, 216
Oddesund (Oddasund) IX 20, 120
Odyssey 118

Olauus – see Olav, Olof
Olav (Olauus, companion of Olav Tryggvason) XVII 7, 145
Olav (son of Harald Fairhair) XI 5, XV 3, XV 9, 196, 197, 199
Olav Haraldsson (Olauus (filius Haraldi Grenscensis), St. Olav,) 8, 9, 14, 21, 24, 27, XV 3, XVIII 1, XVIII 10, XVIII 13, XVIII 22, XVIII 24, XVIII 29, XVIII 31, XVIII 33, 142, 148, 150–153, 157, 160, 164, 167, 168, 178, 192, 196, 199–201, 205–216, 221, 225
Olav Kyrre 201, 216
Olav Tretelgje (Olauus Tretelgia) IX 32, X 1, 133
Olav Tryggvason (Olauus (Turgonis filius)) 8, 9, 17, 18, 19, 27, 28, 44, XV 3, XV 14, XVII 6, XVII 16, XVII 23, XVII 24, XVII 26, XVII 30, XVII 33, XVII 34, XVII 41, XVII 49, XVII 58, 111, 112, 140, 143–145, 147–150, 153, 157, 160, 167, 190–192, 194, 196, 198–200, 203–217, 221, 224
Olof Skötkonung (Swedish king) XVII 40, XVII 46, XVIII 16, XVIII 29, 148, 151, 152, 205, 206
Omer (bishop of Ribe and Børglum) 159
Oppland 138
Orcadians – see Orchadenses
Orchadenses XV 2, XVII 31, 147, 190
Orchades – see Orkney
Orchanus (Orkan) V 2, 125, 128, 188, 189
Ordericus Vitalis 11, 112, 118, 127, 128, 141, 150, 191, 195
Orientales (people from Viken) XVII 35, 147, 148
Orkan – see Orchanus
Orkdal 117
Orkney ((Insule) Orchades, Insule Merediane) 12, 13, 19, 23, 29–31, 35, 37–44, V 2, V 3, VI, VI 3, VI 21, XV 14, XVII 1, 124–126, 128, 143, 157, 161, 164–167, 184–194, 197, 198, 203, 217, 222, 225
Orkney Genealogy 28, 29, 31, 37–41
Orm – see also Omer
Orm (abbot of Munkeliv) 159, 218, 219, 221
Orm (prior at Ringsted) 219
Orm (bishop of the Faeroese) 159, 163
Orm (bishop of Hamar) 219
Ormen den Lange – see Serpens Longus
Orosius 19, 28
Oslo (Asloia) 22, 23, 31, 41, 42, III 8, 117, 120, 138, 165, 167, 180, 200, 211,
Oslo Fjord – see Viken
Ottar (Ottarus, son of Egil Vendelkråke) IX 25, 136
Ottar (Ottarus, Váttr, Danish earl) IX 25, 128, 136
Ottar Birting 166
Ottar Svarte 160
Otto of Freising 109
Palestine 117
Pape 39, VI 1, VI 5, 125, 126, 129, 189
Papey VI 6, 126, 189
Paradise (Paradisus) XVII 32, 148
Passio Olaui 14, 18, 21, 22, 24, 42, 111, 117, 123, 127, 130, 143, 153, 178, 210, 212–216, 220, 225
Paulus Diaconus 118
Pentland Firth (Petlandicum Mare) VI 3, 118, 125, 189
Pentland (Terra Petorum) VI 3, 189
Pents – see Peti
Peti (Pents, Picts) 39, VI 1, VI 2, VI 3, 120, 125, 189
Petlandicum Mare – see Pentland Firth
Petrus Abelardus 173
Petrus Damianus 173
Philostratus, Flavius 172
Picts – see Peti
Pliny (the Elder) 119, 121
Priscian 122
Rabanus Maurus 173
Radulfus – see Rollo
Ragnar 138
Ragnfrød 139
Ragnvald (earl of the Orkneys) 164, 165, 225
Ragnvald Klerk (bishop of the Hebrides) 222, 225
Ragnvald Mørejarl (Rogwaldus) VI 8, 127, 143, 147
Ragnvald Rettilbeine (Rogualdus Recilbein) XI 7, XV 2, 125, 138, 141
Rainald of Dassel 109
Rand (Rond) X 7
Ranrike (prouincia Renorum) XV 10, XV 12, 142, 178, 199
Rastarkalv (Rastarcalf) XIII 6, 120
Regensburg 17, 20
Regnum Raumorum – see Romerike
Regnum Ringorum – see Ringerike
Reid, Robert (bishop) 29
Reidar 166, 168, 224
Reni – see Ranrike
Rheims 166
Ribe 159
Ricardus – see Richard
Richard I (Ricardus, duke of Normandy) VI 17
Richard II (Ricardus iunior, duke of Normandy) VI 18, 128
Richard III (duke of Normandy) 128
Richard of St. Victor 18
Ring (Ringr) XI 8
Ringerike (Regnum Ringorum) III 3, 142

Ringsted 219
Ringr – see Ring
Riphei montes 113
Rørek 138
Robert of Ely 219
Robert the Proud (duke of Normandy) 128
Robert of Torigni 128, 195
Roda – see Rouen
Rodolv (Rodulfus / Rudolfus, English bishop) XVIII 33, 153
Rodulfus – see Rollo, Rodolv
Rogaland 117
Rogualdus / Rogwaldus – see Ragnvald
Rolf – see Rollo
Rolf (Rolfr, son of Hårfagre) XI 8
Rollo (Rodulfus, Radulfus, Gongurolfr, Gange-Rolv) 24, VI 10, VI 16, VI 20, 127, 128, 189, 190
Romans – see Itali
Rome 184, 224, 225
Romerike (Regnum Raumorum) III 3, XV 9, 142
Romsdalen 117
Rond – see Rand
Roskilde 18, 159, 225
Roskilde Chronicle 18
Roslin 30
Rothomagus – see Rouen
Rouen (Rothomagus, Roda) 24, VI 10, 120, 127, 189, 214, 215
Ruscia – see Russia
Russia (Ruscia, Ruzzia) XVII 4, XVII 7, XVII 8, XVIII 1, XVIII 6, XVIII 30, 121, 144, 206, 207, 215
Rygjarbit I 2, 117, 120
Sæmund Sigfusson (froði) 16, 41, 147, 160, 174, 175, 216
Sakse (Saxa) XV12, 143
Sami – see Finni
Sallust 26
Sardinia 130
Sarpsborg 117, 119
Saxa – see Sakse
Saxo Grammaticus 16, 18, 20–22, 26, 27, 33, 40–42, 110, 113, 115, 116, 130, 131, 182, 183
Saxons (Saxones) III 7, 113, 180
Saxony (Saxonia) 20, 44, 130
Scandinavia 34, 114, 163, 169, 182, 224
Scilla – see Scylla
Sciotanuath – see Skjotansvad
Sclaui (Slavs, Wends) XVII 12, XVII 38, 203
Sclauia / Sclavonia – see Slavland
Scorre – see Skorre
Scoti (Scots) VI 9
Scotia – see Scotland
Scotland (Scotia) 28, 35, VI 3, VI 9, XVII 14, 125, 126, 164, 166, 189, 203
Scots – see Scoti
Screlingar – see Skrælings
Screyiu – see Skrøya
Scritefingi 121
Scylla (Scilla) II 10, 118
Scythia 114, 195
Selandia – see Sjælland
Septemtrionalis Sinus II 10, 118
Serpens Longus (The Long Serpent, Ormen den Lange) XVII 42, 203
Shetland (Insule Merediane) 12, V 3, 147, 157, 184, 186, 188, 190, 192, 194
Shetlanders – see Hatlendenses
Sicily (Sicilia) 118, 132
Sigfred (son of Harald Fairhair) 138
Sigfrid (Sigfridus / Sigafrid, English bishop) XVIII 33, 153
Sigtrygg (Sigtrygr) XI 8
Sigurd (English bishop), see Johannes
Sigurd (Siwardus, son of Eirik Bloodaxe) XIV 1, XIV 3, 139, 140, 202
Sigurd (bishop of Bergen) 163, 165
Sigurd (Siwardus, son of Yngvar) IX 29, 137
Sigurd Eiriksson Bjodaskalle
Sigurd the Giant (Rise, Siwardus Gigas) XI 6, XV 7, 138, 142, 196, 197, 201
Sigurd jarl (Siwardus) XVI 2, 202
Sigurd Jorsalfare 9, 164, 176
Sigurd Ljome (Siwardus Lioma) XII 2, 139
Sigurd Munn 163–166, 183, 196, 201
Sigurd Rise – see Sigurd the Giant
Sigurd Sow (Syr, Siwardus Scroffa) XV 6, 142, 199, 201
Sinclair, Henry 30, 37, 38
Sinclair, William 30–31, 38–39
Sinus Orientalis – see Viken
Sirmondus Jacobus
Siwardus – see Sigurd
Sjælland (Selandia, Zealand) XVII 34, XVII 39, 148, 203
Skåne 40, 41, 114, 141, 163, 195
Skaun 117
Skien 117
Skjotansvad (Sciotanuath) IX 13, 134, 135
Skorre (Scorra) XV 12, 143
Skrælings (Screlingar) I 12, 116, 157, 177
Skrøya (Screyiu) XV 12, 143
Slavland (Sclauia, Sclavonia, Wendland) XVII 12, 121, 145, 148
Slavs – see Sclaui
Småland 114
Snefrid 138
Snorri Sturluson 38, 133–136, 138, 139, 141, 143–145, 148–150, 152, 178, 200, 202, 214
Södermanland 114
Soga um Jomsvikingane 197
Sogn 117

Solinus 18, 19, VIII 13, 108, 116, 121, 131, 132, 159, 162, 168–172, 183, 184, 193, 224
Solør 120
Solundicum Mare – see North Sea
Solund Islands (Insule Solunde) V 1, 184, 185
Solund Sea – see North Sea
Sorø 18, 19, 159, 170
Spain (Hispania) XII 6, XVIII 13, 126
Sparbuen 117
St Andrews 38, 164, 185, 194
St Olav – see Olav Haraldsson
Stavanger 19, 22, 23, 117, 167, 180, 200, 211
Steinkjer 117
Stephen 11, 161
Stiklestad 150, 214, 215
Stjørdalen 117
Stockholm 135
Stord 185
Storelven – see Albia
Storelvedalen 119
Strinda 117
Sudrøyene – see Hebrides
Sunnmøre 117, 160
Sueones – see Sweones
Sueonia – see Sweden
Svealand (see also Sweden) 114
Svear – see Sweones
Sveigde (Swegthir) 36, IX 6
Svein jarl (Sweino, son of Håkon jarl) XVII 29, 128, 205
Sven Aggesen (Sueno Aggonis) 16, 26–27, 109, 110, 142, 145
Svend (son of Knud the Great) XVIII 27, 152
Svend Estridsen (Danish king) 204
Svend Tveskæg (Sweino / Sweyno Tiuguskegg, Danish king) XVII 29, XVII 33, XVII 34, XVII 40, XVII 41, XVII 45, XVII 56, XVIII 9, XVIII 11, 147, 148, 150, 152, 203, 205, 206
Sverre 12, 13, 19, 22, 176, 221
Sverris saga 18
Sviatoi Nos 118
Svjatoj-nos – see Sviatoi Nos
Svold(er) 27, 148, 203, 208
Swecia – see Sweden
Sweden / Svealand (Swethia, Swecia, Sueonia) 31, 32, 35, 40–44, I 5, IX 1, IX 11, IX 18, IX 32, X 1, XVII 2, XVII 4, 114, 121, 163, 177, 181, 182, 194, 195
Swedes – see Sweones
Swegthir – see Sveigde
Sweino – see Svein, Sven, Svend
Sweones (Swedes, Svear) IX 10, XVI 1, XVII 40, 114, 143
Swethia – see Sweden
Sweyno – see Svend Tveskæg
Syene 130
Tamisia – see Thames
Tanatos 126
Tangbrand (Tangbrandus) XVII 24, 192
Taprobane 117
Telemark (Thelamarchia) III 3, 182
Telenses – see Icelanders
Terra Petorum – see Pentland
Terra Virginum (Land of Maidens) I 9, 115, 157, 177, 184
Terra Viridis – see Greenland
Thames (Tamisia) XVIII 19
Thelamarchia – see Telemark
Theodoricus Monachus 8, 9, 16, 18, 20–22, 24, 27, 33, 42, 108–111, 114, 117, 118, 122, 126, 127, 130, 138, 140, 143, 152, 153, 158, 160, 171, 192, 199, 202, 206, 214, 216, 220, 225
Theutonicus – see Germany / German
Thierry of Chartres 132
Thore / Thorir – see Tore
Throndemia – see Trøndelag
Thule (Tile / Thile / Thyle, Glacialis Insula, Iceland) VIII 1, 116, 126, 129, 130
Thyri – see Tyra
Tilenses – see Icelanders
Tjodolv of Kvin 134, 160
Tønsberg 23, 41, 42, 117
Tonne – see Tunne
Toraren Lovtunge 210
Tore the Silent (Thor(e) Tacens) XVI 2, 143, 202
Torgeir Avrådskoll 160
Torgils 138
Torkell Klypp (Torkellus Clyppr) XIV 3
Torolv Luseskjegg (Thorolfus Lusaskeg) XVII 2, 144
Toten (Tothne) X 2
Tothne – see Toten
Trøndelag (Trondemia, Throndemia) II 6, III 2, IX 1, XVII 3, XVII 27, XVII 34, 112, 114, 117, 118, 133, 140, 160, 163, 179–182, 195, 196, 200, 204, 212, 217, 221
Troy 195
Troms 118
Trond 112
Trondemia – see Trøndelag
Trondheim (Nidaros) 13, 14, 16, 19, 20, 21, 22, 23, 24, 33, 38, 42, 44, 112, 117, 162, 164, 167, 169, 194, 200, 206, 210–212, 218, 220, 221, 223, 224
Trugguaroyr – see Tryggvarøyr
Truggui – see Tryggve
Tryggvarøyr (Trugguaroyr, Tumulus Turgonis) XV 10, 120
Tryggve (Truggui, son of H. Fairhair) XI 8

Tryggve (Turgo, son of Olav (son of Harald Fairhair)) XV 9, 142, 143, 150, 199
Tryggve (son of Olav Tryggvason) 212
Trysil 120
Tullius – see Cicero
Tulloch, Thomas (bishop, 15th cent.) 29, 38–40
Tulloch, Thomas (chamberlain, 16th cent.) 29
Tunne (Tonne) IX 23
Turgo – see Tryggve
Tyra (Thyri, Danish queen) XII 1, 139, 197, 198, 204
Tyra (Tyri, Svend Tveskæg's sister) XVII 33, 148
Ultima Thule – see Thule
Ulv Uspaksson 221
Ulvhild 152
Uplands (zona montana, the mountain region in Norway) 114, 119, 120, 142, 159, 160, 177–183, 194–197, 199, 200, 202, 210, 211, 217, 224
Uppland (region in Sweden) 14
Uppsala 32, 114, 195
Värmland 114
Västerbotten 112
Västergötland 114
Västmanland 114
Vättern 37
Váttr – see Ottar
Valdemar (I, Danish king) 23
Valdres (Waldresia) III 5, 120, 179
Valles Gudbrandi – see Gudbrandsdalen
Vallis Haddingorum – see Hallingdal
Vang 200
Vanlande (Wanlandi) IX 7
Vapnavad (Wapnawadh) 134, 135
Vegestav (Wegestaf) II 9, 118, 120, 181, 182
Vemund Volubrjot (Wemundus Volubriot) XIV 3
Vendel (Wendli, *i.e.* Vendsyssel) IX 25, 136
Vendsyssel – see Vendel
Veøy 117
Verdalen 117
Vergilius – see Virgil
Vestfold 178
Vetus Chronica Sialandie 126
Viken (Oslo Fjord, Wic, Sinus Orientalis – see also Orientales) 23, 24, 44, II 2, III 6, XV 10, 117, 118, 142, 178–180, 200
Vincent Kadlubek 26
Vingulmark 142, 178
Vinland 116
Virgil 118, 122, 127, 137, 138, 144
Viridenses – see Greenlanders
Visbur (Wisbur) IX 9, 134
Vita Gunneri episcopi Vibergensis 134
Vorma 119
Vorsi (people from Voss) XIV 3
Voss 141
Vulcan 134
Waldresia – see Valdres
Wales 146
Wallace, James 29
Wanlandi – see Vanlande
Wegestaf – see Vegestav
Wemundus – Vemund
Wendland – see Slavland
Wends – see Sclaui
White Sea 118, 182
Wilelmus Bastardus – see William the Conqueror
Willelmus Longosped – see William Longsword
Willelmus Rufus – see William Rufus
William the Conqueror (Wilelmus Bastardus) VI 18, 128, 161–162
William of Jumièges 127, 128, 150, 152, 195, 214
William Longsword (Willelmus Longosped) VI 17, 128, 189
William of Malmesbury 131
William the Old (bishop of the Orkneys) 164, 225
William Rufus (Willelmus Rufus) VI 19
William Sinclair – see Sinclair
Wisbur – see Visbur
Yarmouth (Iarmuthia) XVIII 17, 151
Ynglingatal 133–137
Yngvar the Hoary (Ynguar Canutus) IX 28, 137
Yngvar (son of Harald Fairhair) XI 8
Yngvi (Ingui, Yngve) IX 2, 133, 134, 135, 136, 195
York 164, 185, 194
Zealand – see Sjælland

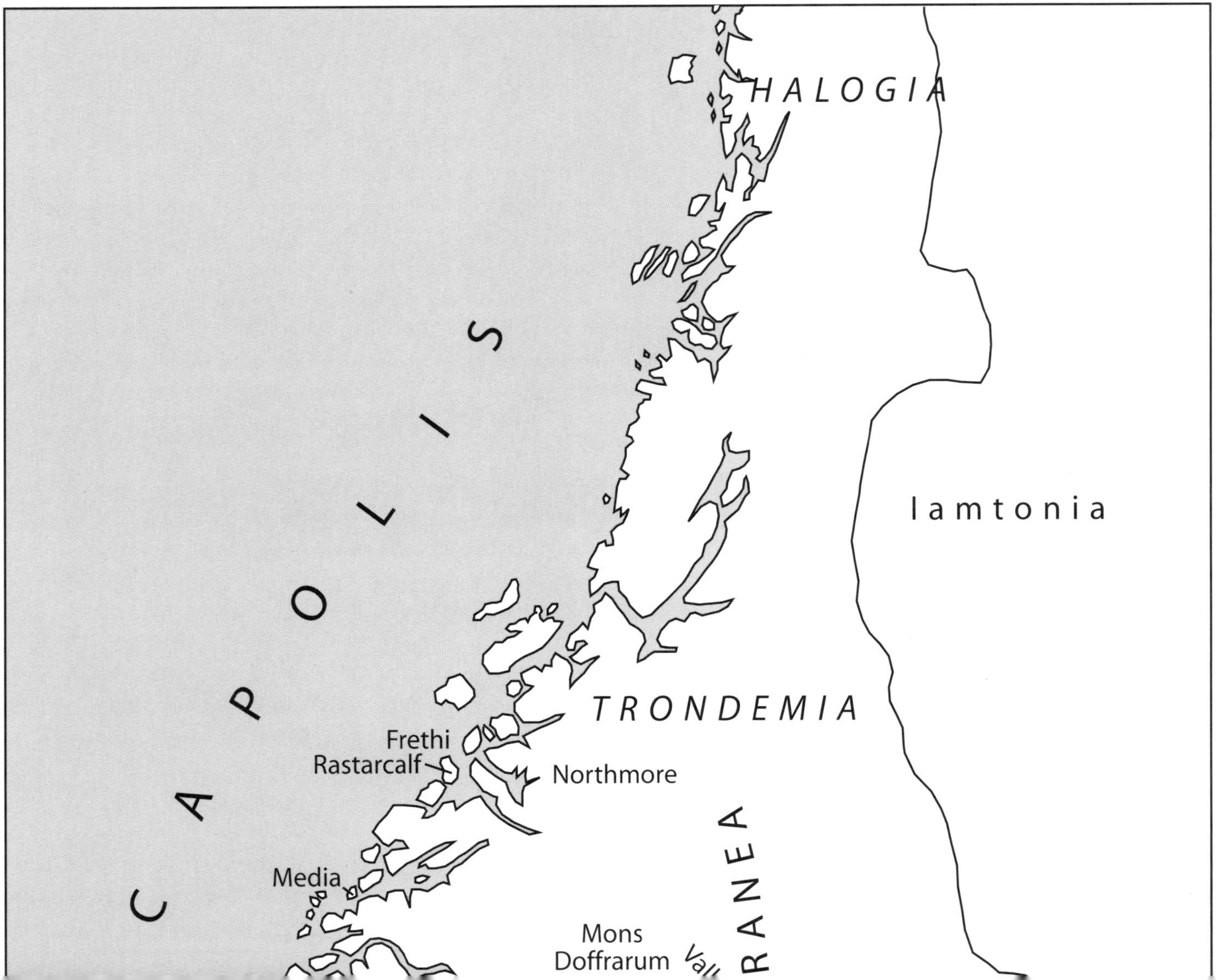
HALOGIA
Iamtonia
CAPOLIS
TRONDEMIA
Frethi
Rastarcalf
Northmore
Media
RANEA
Mons
Doffrarum